War and Peace
in International Rivalry

War and Peace
in International Rivalry

Paul F. Diehl and Gary Goertz

Ann Arbor

THE UNIVERSITY OF MICHIGAN PRESS

First paperback edition 2001
Copyright © by the University of Michigan 2000
All rights reserved
Published in the United States of America by
The University of Michigan Press
Manufactured in the United States of America
⊗ Printed on acid-free paper

2004   2003   2002   2001   5   4   3   2

A CIP catalog record for this book is available from the British Library.

Library of Congress Cataloging-in-Publication Data

Diehl, Paul F. (Paul Francis)
    War and peace in international rivalry / Paul F. Diehl and Gary Goertz.
        p.   cm.
    Includes bibliographical references and index.
    ISBN 0-472-11127-2 (alk. paper)
        1. International relations.   2. Balance of power.   3. War.   4. Peace.
    I. Goertz, Gary, 1953–   II. Title.

    JZ1313 .D54   2000
    327.1—dc21   99-462011

ISBN 0-472-08848-3 (pbk. : alk. paper)

Contents

Tables

Figures

Acknowledgments

We have received significant support from a number of programs and institutions in completing this manuscript. We would like to express our deep appreciation to all of them. The National Science Foundation (grant no. SES–9309840) provided much of the early support for our work on enduring rivalries. Essential research assistance was facilitated by grants from the University of Illinois Research Board. Release time for Paul Diehl to draft much of this book was graciously given by a sabbatical from the University of Illinois Board of Trustees and a fellowship from the University of Illinois Center for Advanced Study. Gary Goertz would like to thank the Department of Political Science at the University of Toronto for providing him time to work on this project by not inviting him to one committee meeting during his years there. He extends special thanks to the late Professor Paul Bairoch whose Institute for International Economic History at the University of Geneva provided a genial home and support during the beginning and end years of this research project.

Various individuals offered useful comments on the different chapters of this book, including preliminary versions that appeared as conference papers and journal articles. We are especially grateful to Paul Hensel, Scott Bennett, William Thompson, Nils Petter Gleditsch, and Manus Midlarsky in this regard. Some of the chapters here include material from collaborations with other scholars. Thus, we are thankful for the important roles that Paul Hensel played in the research in chapter 6 and that Jacob Bercovitch and Patrick Regan played in the analyses in chapter 10. Data for the analyses in this book were provided by the Correlates of War Project, with special thanks going to J. David Singer and Stuart Bremer, and by Jacob Bercovitch and his project on international mediation. Finally, we are grateful for Jaroslav Tir's assistance in editing and index preparation.

CHAPTER 1

Introduction

Since its origins, the study of international relations has centered on the analysis of war. This analysis has taken on various forms: Small and Singer (1982) and Bueno de Mesquita (1981) examined all wars since 1816, Jervis (1976) chose wars that related to his specific purposes, Van Evera (1984) examined the causes of World War I, and Lebow (1981) analyzed 13 crises, many of which ended in war. In spite of their ideological and methodological differences, war as the phenomenon to be explained unites these diverse scholars.

In contrast, we suggest in this volume that one can learn much about war by taking a step back and focusing attention on militarized relationships, what we refer to as rivalries. We argue that examining war only is like trying to understand a problem marriage by looking only at when a husband beats his wife. Understanding such a marriage requires understanding the kind of relationship in which violence is possible. Wars do not suddenly occur between two states, but rather almost always arise in situations in which the two countries have had serious conflicts and have been using the military instruments of foreign policy against one another. Only recently have students of war become conscious of what they already intuitively knew: a large portion of wars occur in long-term enduring rivalry relationships (see chapter 3).

Jervis, Singer and Small, Bueno de Mesquita, Lebow, Van Evera, and other scholars want to understand the causes of war. In contrast, we examine the causes and consequences of rivalry. For us, war is potentially both a cause and an effect of rivalry. War occurs within rivalry because both parties are managing their conflicts with military tools. Yet, at the same time, war can establish the relationship as militarized. For example, the Korean War initiated a militarized rivalry between the United States and China that lasted until a rapprochement between the states in the 1970s. This book explores some—certainly not all—of the implications that this fundamental shift in perspective from war to rivalry has for the study of international conflict.

1

Rivalries provide us with a way of thinking about many issues of war and peace—what we call the rivalry approach. The rivalry approach has theoretical, methodological, and empirical dimensions. The first part of the book delves into the many ramifications of the rivalry approach in terms of theory and methodology. There we examine how rivalries enter into standard theories of international conflict and how they provide new testing strategies for many classic hypotheses. The rivalry approach sheds new light on classic theories as well as classic phenomena such as power transitions. It also points out important phenomena for which there are no standard theories or explanations, because these phenomena appear only as a result of the rivalry framework. Here we see the multifaceted character of the rivalry approach. In chapter 6, for example, we use rivalries to test aspects of democracy that do not fit into standard methodologies, as we can look at regime changes *within* rivalries (interrupted time-series) as well as compare patterns of democracy and war *across* rivalries. The former escapes completely the cross-sectional methodologies that dominate the analysis of democratic peace, while the later uses a different unit of analysis, the rivalry.

The empirical dimension of the rivalry approach focuses on phenomena ignored by standard conflict theories. The second part of the book focuses on one such phenomenon—enduring rivalries. One characteristic of a useful theoretical framework is that it points out new phenomena that merit theoretical and empirical attention. The rivalry approach stresses the interconnectedness and the temporal duration of military rivalries. It brings into the limelight the existence of the phenomenon of enduring rivalries and at the same time calls out for a theoretical explanation. Scholars and policymakers are aware of long-term rivalries, but given the cross-sectional bias of most qualitative and quantitative conflict research, this knowledge rarely produces studies, models, and theories of enduring rivalries.

The existence of enduring rivalries cries out for theoretical and empirical treatment. Part 2 of this volume is our response. We argue that a central characteristic of enduring rivalries is their *stability*. Traditional balance-of-power or deterrence theories usually contrast stability (i.e., the absence of war) with instability, signified by crises and wars. Our model of enduring rivalry turns this standard view on its head. What we call the punctuated equilibrium model of enduring rivalries (see below) stresses the stability or continuity of these military conflicts. Instability in the form of political shocks (i.e., world wars, civil wars, regime shifts) is associated with the initiation and termination of rivalries. Hence, instead of instability being associated with war and crisis—essentially its negative connotation—we propose that it is also associated with peace and conflict termination. Wars and regime changes are shocks that upset the stability of enduring rivalries, setting the stage for a qualitative change in the relationship between would-be or actual rivals.

One side of the enduring rivalry coin is stability and duration, but the other is that they all have beginnings and ends. Hence a complete theory of the empirical phenomenon of enduring rivalries requires a consideration and analysis of conflict management and termination. Because rivalries exist over time, we can examine the impact of attempts at conflict mediation, shifts to democracy, and other factors potentially associated with conflict resolution and management. Because rivalries do end, the rivalry approach requires us to have not only a model of war, but also a model of peace. The literature on conflict resolution, mediation, and the like remains, as a rule, quite isolated from that on the causes of war. One would be hard pressed to find a book or theory that addresses the causes of war and the causes of peace within the same theoretical framework, but the rivalry approach outlined in the first part of the book all but demands this. Our punctuated equilibrium model of enduring rivalry deals with both military conflict and peace.

Part 1 of the book focuses on the theoretical and methodological implications of the rivalry approach for classic approaches, hypotheses, and theories of international conflict. We examine how rivalry factors appear in (mostly in the background of) classic theories, such as the power transition hypothesis and deterrence. We propose that the rivalry approach provides new ways (theoretically and methodologically) to test such classic hypotheses, and we provide an example ourselves using the democratic peace.

We view the second part of the book as a logical extension of the first part's emphasis on the rivalry approach to war and peace. Part 2 focuses on one crucial empirical phenomenon—enduring rivalries—that appears once one looks at international conflict through rivalry lenses. If scholars are directed to focus on rivalries, an unsurprising first step is to focus on the longest and most dangerous of them. Moreover, a focus on enduring rivalries permits a fuller explication of the rivalry approach, as many of its elements are used in our analyses. We propose a theoretical model of enduring rivalries, the punctuated equilibrium model, which we believe contributes to an understanding of the phenomena. This is not an inherent part of the rivalry approach, but the model is specified in terms of key rivalry components. We hope that even those who do not accept our rivalry approach or the punctuated equilibrium model (and there are several other scholars studying rivalries, some with different approaches) will find our empirical analyses and detection of key rivalry trends fruitful in their own theoretical pursuits.

Part 1: Rivalries and International Conflict

In the first part of this volume, we devote our attention to the general theoretical and methodological implications of the rivalry approach to international war and peace. We develop the implications of thinking about war in terms of militarized relationships. This turns out to recast our perceptions on virtually all aspects of conflict research, including data creation, testing, and theory.

Conceptualization and Data Creation

The first order of business is to define the fundamental concept of rivalry or militarized relationship. Just as the Correlates of War Project in its early stages concentrated much effort on conceptualizing and creating an operational definition of war, chapter 2 gives an analysis of the theoretical and operational dimensions of an international militarized rivalry. Conceptually, a rivalry is a relationship between two states in which both use, with some regularity, military threats and force as well as one in which both sides formulate foreign policy in military terms.[1] A classic example of this is deterrence policy. Deterrence involves military threats, hence by definition a military rivalry. Such, of course, was a large component of the U.S. policy toward the USSR after World War II, and vice versa. In contrast, U.S.-Canadian relations, while frequently conflictual, have not generally been conducted in military terms over the last century. Operationally, we shall use the existence of militarized disputes and wars to identify our universe of rivalries. Although it is theoretically possible for states to conduct militarized foreign policies without actual militarized exchanges, in practice this is just about impossible; crises, disputes, and war are the results of militarized foreign policies.

Given that most work has utilized the concept of enduring rivalry, we hasten to reemphasize that rivalries can be of any length: from very short to enduring. The enduring rivalry literature tends to confound two dimensions of a rivalry. The first is duration, indicated by the adjective enduring. The second, implicit, is the severity or seriousness of the rivalry. Just as Small and Singer (1982) described war on the dimensions of duration and fatalities, so too can we characterize rivalries. Until now attention has been explicitly focused on the extreme end of the duration dimension. Implicitly, scholars have assumed that long-term rivalries are also the most severe ones. Nevertheless, one can find short-term severe as well as long-term low-severity rivalries. Conceptually, we must allow this possibility. Empirically, we will find examples of this as well when we create a data set of over one thousand rivalries in the 1816–1992 period.

Rivalries and Hypothesis Testing

The intellectual history of the rivalry concept originates in its testing function. From the early 1980s until well into the 1990s, this remained its almost exclusive use. Rivalries proved useful in some theoretical contexts because they

---

[1]This definition reflects our focus on the violent aspects of rivalries. It is quite conceivable for rivalries to exist without violent interactions, for example between two economic competitors (see Hensel 1996 for a discussion of nonmilitarized rivalries). It is also possible to define rivalries without reliance on the militarized elements, as Thompson 1995 does. Yet it was our decision to focus on militarized rivalries because of their enormous impact on human life, representing a major cause of death in the twentieth century, and because of their impact on the conduct of international relations in general. Understanding and ultimately managing or solving these rivalries seemed to us to have the greatest priority.

provided a universe of cases with which to test a model or theory. The power transition hypothesis provides a good example of this phenomenon. According to Organski and Kugler (1980), for a power transition to cause a war, serious grievances must already exist between two countries. Power transitions between states at peace do not result in war, but such is not the case when there are underlying conflicts. The rivalry concept taps this distinction because the notion of a militarized rivalry implies some basic conflict. One can restate this hypothesis, then, to say that power transition results in war only if there is a rivalry relationship. Wayman (1982, 1996) did exactly that. He defined a rivalry as a minimum of two disputes in a 10-year period, and then proceeded to test the Organski and Kugler hypothesis on this universe of cases. Geller (1993) has conducted an analogous analysis on enduring rivalries.

In all of these testing applications, rivalries remain out of the limelight. They play a role in choosing cases but are then theoretically irrelevant. The focus of concern in such studies always stays with the conflict hypothesis, be it concerned with arms races, power transition, or deterrence. One result is that scholars develop different operational definitions of rivalry for their testing purposes. These range from Wayman's (1982) two-dispute, 10-year minimum to Jones's (1989) minimum of five disputes and 25 years (see chapter 2). Because few are thinking about rivalries per se, there is no debate about which universe of cases is most appropriate, because rivalries only serve to select specific cases for narrow purposes. By focusing on the rivalry part of the theory, we pose the question about what is the appropriate rivalry concept for testing theory. As we discuss below, by making clear the role of rivalry in hypotheses, we are forced to be more precise about the role of rivalry in testing. For many problems, rivalries provide a new—and perhaps better—way to test theory. Certainly, empirical tests of arms race hypotheses existed (Huntington 1958) before Diehl (1985a) used rivalries to analyze them. Yet there are other situations in which testing is difficult or almost impossible. There the rivalry approach can step in and make a valuable contribution.

For purposes of testing, deterrence constitutes perhaps the most controversial topic in world politics. Much of the debate revolves around the tendency to select cases in which deterrence fails and to ignore its successes. It is much easier to observe deterrence failure because it results in crisis or war, whereas deterrence success is easy to confound with cases in which deterrence is not attempted. As we mentioned above, deterrence policy implies a militarized relationship. Huth and Russett (1993) have turned this around to contend that if there is a rivalry relationship, then we can test deterrence. Thus, they can define deterrence success as those years in the rivalry without dispute or war. This application takes advantage of a fundamental characteristic of rivalries: they exist over time. Most statistical and case study approaches to deterrence select individual crises and wars. In such cases, it is not clear what the appropriate control or comparison group should be. With rivalries, one can compare years with disputes to years without disputes, as the rivalry approach itself provides a suitable control group. We address these and related concerns in detail in chapters 4 and 5, using deterrence studies as our central example.

Because rivalries consist of relationships over time, virtually every conflict hypothesis can be reanalyzed within this framework. To illustrate the potential of rivalries for theory development and testing, we examine the democratic peace in chapter 6. Using rivalries, we avoid many of the problems that have plagued cross-sectional approaches. We do not fret about the definition of "relevant dyads," nor do we need to worry about whether to focus on wars or war-years. We can compare periods when the dyad is nondemocratic to periods when it is a joint democracy: we know what the regime type is when the rivalry starts, and the relevant dyad is merely the rivalry. The standard causes-of-war approach has problems because it uses the dyad-year to organize its analysis. This chops relationships into tiny pieces and creates difficulties for multiyear wars. The rivalry approach divides the history of a relationship into militarized and peaceful periods, each of which can be very long or very short. Instead of the arbitrary "year" procedure, our approach uses more natural breakpoints, when the character of the relationship fundamentally changes.

Using the rivalry as a whole gives us a new way to look at the—already much looked at—question of democratic peace. It is largely accepted that relatively few disputes and virtually no wars have occurred between democracies (although there is some controversy over how much of this can be attributed to democratic factors; see Russett 1993 and Ray 1995 for an analysis of alleged democratic dyad wars). With the rivalry concept in hand we can go further and ask about the characteristic of militarized relationships between democracies. We can ask about the duration and severity of democratic (enduring) rivalries. For example, among the democracy versus democracy militarized disputes, it is possible to identify quite different patterns of rivalry. One extreme is enduring rivalries with many disputes. The other pole is isolated, brief, one-shot militarized rivalries. These two patterns have critically different implications for the democratic peace hypothesis: the former casts much more doubt on the peaceful character of relations between democracies, while the latter supports it. This kind of evidence concerning the democratic peace is not available until one considers the question in rivalry terms.

The issue of peace between democracies illustrates the hammerlock that traditional cross-sectional approaches to war hold on the discipline. Some studies do use rivalries in order to choose cases but still analyze the relationship in a cross-sectional fashion (or cross-sectional time-series). Huth and Russett's (1993) analyses of deterrence exemplify this practice. In investigating how well their model performs, they use techniques that treat each dispute as an isolated case. One could—and should—ask if their model works better for some rivalries than others. If almost all of the model's incorrect predictions are concentrated in a few rivalries, that outcome suggests what is wrong with the model, as well as hints at corrections (see chapter 5). In effect, this is what we propose to do for the democratic peace.

In brief, the rivalry approach creates new ways to test old hypotheses, ways that were difficult or impossible to achieve with traditional methods. This is a direct result of thinking about conflict within militarized relationships that can last for decades, rather than in isolation and devoid of context.

Hypothesis and Theory Generation

To think about war in terms of rivalry implies a certain theoretical orientation toward the phenomenon of international conflict. The tension between standard practice, which treats crisis and war as independent events,[2] and the common-sense expectation that wars between rivals are somehow related to each other motivated us to think about and develop the rivalry approach. We started from the simple observation that many wars have involved the same set of states, such as India and Pakistan, and Israel and its Arab neighbors. India and Pakistan have fought three wars in the last 50 years, with the outcome of each of the first two wars having a strong influence on the occurrence and timing of the war that followed. Similarly, Israel and various Arab states have clashed over the same pieces of territory four times since 1948. The Yom Kippur War in 1973 is the one that most obviously traces its roots to the circumstances and outcome of the previous war.

When we conceptualize rivalry, we make a nontrivial theoretical claim: disputes and wars occurring in the rivalry are not independent of each other because they belong to the same relationship. This can become a causal claim: some aspects of the war or crisis at time 1 are causes of war or crisis at time 2. Few theories of war explicitly link these events across time, war diffusion being the main exception, and even there the emphasis is more spatial than temporal. Underlying the rivalry approach lies an implicit theory connecting disputes over time.

As we have noted, rivalries have served as a case selection device to test well-known hypotheses and theories. If one thinks of rivalries as part of the theory instead of just the research design, then the appearance of these well-known models begins to change. To take up the power transition example again, as the label indicates, it is the power transition factor that receives all the attention. Yet if we examine its logical structure, the theory predicts that war is very likely if there is power transition *and* rivalry. Loosely, both are necessary for war to occur: "Only when a pair of states are relatively equal in capabilities can both sides in conflict realistically expect to win; only when the challenger is committed to change is there something over which to fight" (Lemke and Werner 1996,

---

[2] Statistical tests and fixes for error dependence (e.g., Beck, Katz, and Tucker 1998) may solve some methodological problems of dependence, but they do not reflect any *theoretical* analysis of interconflict linkages. See also Raknerud and Hegre 1997.

235). Lemke and Werner operationalize "commitment to change" through increasing military expenditures. In our terms, it is a commitment to a militarized foreign policy toward the rival. The two variables play a symmetrical role. War is very unlikely in the absence of either variable. Hence one needs to include rivalry variables explicitly in the theory, not bury them as case selection rules.

Almost all theories of learning refer to how events in the past influence current actions. "Learning" is an intervening variable that links the history of the rivalry to current decisions. Tetlock and Breslauer (1991) gathered together a large volume on learning involving relations between the United States and the Soviet Union, but did not recognize that it is one among many rivalries, or that one can use other rivalries to develop learning models. Particularly in enduring rivalries, leaders may rely on "lessons learned" from previous confrontations with the same enemy.

Once one is attentive to the rivalry relationship, it appears frequently in the conflict literature. For example, virtually all models of crisis include variables such as "background conflict." Lebow (1981, 337) starts his crisis model with "underlying hostility" (i.e., a rivalry relationship) with causal arrows leading to crisis and a feedback arrow leading back to underlying hostility. Brecher (1979) frequently describes "past experience" as a core input into various phases of the crises he analyzes. Rivalries provide one way to specify what background factors matter and how they influence crisis behavior. Within the comparative case study framework, it is hard to develop, and even harder to test, these aspects of crisis theories. For example, Lebow had as one of his three main interests the "relationship between crisis and underlying patterns of conflict" (1981, 5). He wanted to know: "In what ways do crises affect the long-term relations between protagonists? In what circumstances do they act to intensify or ameliorate the conflicts which they reflect?" (5). Given his cross-sectional case study approach, he was not able to examine this question in much detail (that part of his book has one chapter, in contrast with the three and four chapters each for the other two parts). To answer these sorts of question one needs longitudinal comparative case studies, just as quantitative researchers need time-series data.

Although these references to underlying hostility or background conflict appear in figures and tables, they remain undeveloped theoretically. We suggest that all these embryonic intuitions refer to rivalry relationships. Crises usually occur within a rivalry. Learning often refers to past events in the relationship. Once we have the conceptual tools of rivalry, we can think about how, when, and why crises arise within this situation, and what is learned from them. We can pose questions about the role of crises in prolonging or ending the relationship. Similar to Lebow, we can ask if rivalry participants have learned something from the crisis that influences their behavior in the next exchange. Theories of learning or crisis that link disputes between rivals imply a dynamic explanation. Learning is a theory of belief change. Once we see a rivalry as enduring, we naturally ask questions about its evolution: how and why does it change over its lifetime? (Hensel 1996; Maoz and Mor 1998; see also the other articles in Diehl 1998). A dynamic theory implies a longitudinal perspective, and conversely the longitudinal character of rivalries cries out for a dynamic explanation.

Not only does the rivalry approach change the way we perceive well-established research agendas, it generates hypotheses to be tested. These can be variations and refinements of existing agendas, as one reformulates power transition or crisis models, but there are also new hypotheses that relate to the phenomenon of rivalry itself—indeed the second half of this book is dedicated to exactly the latter. Once one replaces war as the core concept and phenomenon with rivalry, a new research program begins.

Chapter 4 develops these theoretical issues in a discussion of the rivalry approach to war and peace, detailing the ways it differs from the conventional "causes of war" approach as well as articulating the theoretical implications. Examples from different theoretical traditions and research programs, with deterrence studies being the primary example, illustrate the arguments. As a companion to its predecessor, chapter 5 focuses on the methodological implications of the rivalry approach for testing propositions about international conflict. The rivalry approach not only changes the way we think about old hypotheses, it has significant implications for the ways that research designs are constructed in testing old and new hypotheses alike.

Chapter 6 addresses perhaps the most interesting and important body of conflict research in the last decade, the notion of the "democratic peace"—the proposition that democracies rarely fight each other. In this chapter, we illustrate how the rivalry approach can lead to new insights on this phenomenon. The longitudinal character of the rivalry approach can help analyze changing conflict behavior and democratization over time. Thus, the question of why rivalries consisting of democratic dyads do not seem to evolve past a few disputes or escalate to war fits naturally into the rivalry framework of analysis. Furthermore, with a dynamic approach to conflict we can ask, for example, how changes in regime type influence the course of a rivalry. Does democratization of one or both rivals lead to the termination of the rivalry? Thus, we can hold most aspects of a given competition constant in order to see the impact of one factor (democracy) on conflict. Thus, chapter 6 serves as an illustration of the data, testing, and theory elements of the rivalry approach that are the centerpiece of the first half of this book.

Part 2: Enduring Rivalries

The first part of this volume develops a new way to think about war and peace, what we have termed the rivalry approach. We apply rivalry notions to diverse areas of international war and peace scholarship. The focus is on the application of rivalry concepts to existing theory and phenomena such as deterrence, power transition, and the like. Part 2 develops another dimension of the rivalry approach, which identifies important phenomena that require theoretical and empirical analysis: enduring rivalries.

In chapter 3, we indicate why enduring rivalries are an important empirical phenomenon, one worthy of extended study. A very large percentage of all disputes and wars is concentrated in this small number of dyads. As of 1992, there were approximately 17 thousand dyadic interstate relationships in the international system. As of that same year, there were only 37 ongoing enduring rivalries. Even if we limit our benchmark population to that of all rivalries, enduring rivalries still only constitute less than 6% of the total. Such a heavy concentration of military activity within a small number of enduring rivalries means that if we can understand them then we have made large steps in understanding war and other conflict in general.

As part of our focus in the second half of this book, we offer a general framework or model of enduring rivalries in order to understand their origins, dynamics, and termination. Accordingly, in chapter 7, we outline a punctuated equilibrium model of enduring rivalries.[3] The central elements of this model are stability and infrequent, abrupt change.

Punctuated equilibrium is a biological theory of great controversy, but it is now accepted by many natural scientists. Originally proposed by Eldredge and Gould (1972; for a general discussion see Eldredge 1985), it replaces the gradualistic evolution of standard Darwinism with one in which species are, for the most part, very stable. Yet periods of stability are occasionally disrupted by massive environmental shocks, which result in the death of many species and permit the rapid development of new species (Raup 1992). These environmental shocks consist of large-scale climate changes or the impact of large asteroids. Our punctuated equilibrium model of rivalry parallels quite faithfully in its general outlines the biological theory of punctuated equilibrium.

Many enduring rivalries last for decades, and this shows a remarkable stability in the relationship. Here we alter the common usage of the stability notion in international affairs. Traditional international relations theory (e.g., balance of power) often uses the physical metaphor of stability. This almost always means a condition of nonwar. One encounters the same language with regard to deterrence stability. In contrast, enduring rivalries are also a stable relationship in the sense that there is consistent recourse to force or the threat of force for decades on end. We also note a stability or consistency in the conflict levels of those violent interactions. We are faithful to the physical sense of stability, which refers to a situation of no change, and, more importantly, one resistant to change.

---

[3] There is inconsistency in the use of *equilibria* versus *equilibrium* with the modifier *punctuated*. Even with the field of evolutionary biology, the originators of the model, Gould and Eldredge, use the singular and plural version seemingly interchangeably. As we consider each rivalry to have its own and usually single pattern of stability, we adopt the singular form and therefore use the term *punctuated equilibrium* throughout the book

In a hypothesis-testing frame of mind, what would be the basic hypothesis for a punctuated equilibrium model of enduring rivalries? We suggest that the place to start—and perhaps to end—is with the "no change" pattern. It is not that the rivalry relationship experiences no ups and downs, but those ups and downs exhibit no secular trend. Visually, this is a horizontal line representing the basic rivalry relationship, with disputes, crises, and wars randomly distributed around it.

Related to the expectation of no evolution is what we call the "lock-in" hypothesis. States initially move into rivalry relationships, and the punctuated equilibrium model proposes that this occurs quite rapidly. Once locked in, the rivalry relationship does not fundamentally change. Of course, the word evolution does not in itself say anything about speed, but implicitly the notion is of gradual change. In contrast, the lock-in hypothesis implies a rapid evolution of rivalry in its initial phases. In terms of "evolution," there is rapid change initially as the militarized relationship gets established, but thereafter little or no fundamental change until that established relationship ends.

Thus, the first element of the punctuated equilibrium model is stability: rivalries and their patterns of conflict are stable over time. In chapter 9, we introduce the concept of the basic rivalry level, or BRL. At the heart of our approach lies the concept of militarized relationships: the BRL captures the level of hostility in this relationship. It is an unmeasured concept whose manifestations include war, disputes, crises, and the like. A high BRL corresponds roughly, in the conflict studies context, to a large number of battlefield casualties. The traditional international conflict literature is interested in why some disputes become wars. We are concerned with why some rivalries are more severe than others, in other words, why some have a higher basic rivalry level. We analyze different patterns in the evolution of rivalries and demonstrate that a constant BRL (a relatively flat distribution of conflict severity over time) represents the dominant pattern in our population of enduring rivalries.

One expectation in a punctuated equilibrium model of enduring rivalries is that the BRL will be largely unaffected in the short and medium term by most endogenous and exogenous events. Yet because enduring rivalries are the most dangerous forms of international conflict, there is special concern that such repeated confrontations be ameliorated, even if they can not be easily ended. Thus, we direct our attention to conflict management in enduring rivalries, looking not only to confirm the expectations of the punctuated equilibrium model, but also for insights on how such management might be understood and achieved.

Chapter 10 begins with a general discussion of how to conceptualize and operationalize conflict management within the context of enduring rivalries. The chapter then focuses specifically on how the evolution of enduring rivalries is affected by international attempts at conflict mediation and other forms of third-party intervention. Drawing on a new data set on international conflict management, we explore how often conflict management occurs in the context of enduring rivalries and try to understand when such efforts are made (if indeed they are made at all). Are conflict management efforts made only in the most severe rivalries, or are they attempted in rivalries before they become enduring? At what stage in the rivalry are mediation and other approaches attempted, and how do they compare to the prescriptions derived from the extensive literature on timing and mediation success? Beyond a description of conflict management in rivalries, we also wish to assess its impact on the medium-term dynamics of enduring rivalries. Do conflict management efforts in such a context help to postpone the onset of violence, abate conflict, or even end rivalries? This question will provide us with some insights on exogenous influences on the stability of rivalries. Consistent with the expectations of the punctuated equilibrium model, we discover that rivalry stability is largely resistant to international mediation attempts.

While chapters 9 and 10 emphasize the stability of enduring rivalries, they are indeed subject to alterations. The most notable of these modifications reflects the second element of the punctuated equilibrium model: abrupt change. In our formulation, abrupt change in rivalries comes as a result of a political shock, a massive change in the political environment: domestic, international, or both. It can be a world war, a dramatic shift in power distribution, a change in the type of government regime, or the creation of a new state. Shocks almost always involve both a power shift and a change in the character of some of the actors. These shocks set the stage for possible new enduring rivalries and at the same time disrupt the stability of existing ones, possibly allowing them to end.

Shocks can occur in two forms, dramatic changes either in the international system or in the character of the actor/state. Though realists focus on the former and ignore the latter, changes in the character of the state—and by extension almost always in leadership—have a key impact on foreign policy. We consider the possibility that system-level shocks, such as a change in the power distribution of the international system or a world war, set the stage for the beginning of new rivalries and the end of existing rivalries. In addition, we consider how state-level political shocks, such as civil wars and changes in regime, affect the onset and continuation of rivalries.

In terms of both the origin and the termination of enduring rivalries, we take the stability notion very seriously. It is easy to see how well entrenched hostile policies can become with the example of the Cold War still fresh in mind. One needs serious reasons to pay the costs of a long-lasting military conflict. Chapter 11 describes the stability hypotheses in more detail and presents our empirical analysis of them. We stress that political shocks are not sufficient for either creation or termination of rivalries, but they are quasi-necessary conditions. It is rare to find rivalry origination or termination without a political shock, but many shocks occur without starting or ending a rivalry. Stability means the ability to withstand shocks without losing equilibrium; hence we would expect enduring rivalries to weather some, but not all shocks.

Rivalries, similar to biological species, do not exist in isolation, and not all influences on their dynamics are of great magnitude. The rivalry approach privileges the dyad (it is not alone in this, e.g., Bremer 1992). Whether a rivalry makes it into the enduring category may very well depend on how the dyad interacts with other dyads. Big wars are almost always multilateral: a war's severity is largely a function of the number of participants. Alliances provide the classic means and reasons for additional parties to join a dispute or war. We introduce these considerations into the rivalry approach with the concept of *linked rivalries*. As with the war diffusion literature (for a survey see Most, Starr, and Siverson 1989), we see rivalries as connected by factors such as geography and alliances. We choose, however, the term *linked* to avoid the distracting and potentially misleading connotations of terms such as *diffusion* and *contagion*. The linkage concept represents a significant change in the view of war's expansion and diffusion. For example, because dyads (not states) are linked, the dependent variable in war diffusion studies becomes an independent variable for us: common participation in wars or disputes links rivalries (in addition to alliances and geography) and affects other conflict behavior. The causal arrow is also no longer completely determined by temporal order. For example, we argue that rivalries between two minor powers that are linked to a rivalry between major powers are influenced by that major-major rivalry, but the reverse causal influence does not necessarily hold. This is, of course, a hypothesis; many have argued that the tail sometimes wags the dog, (e.g., Israeli influence over the United States).

Beyond specific hypotheses, the key point in this introductory context is that one must consider the interactions between rivalries, as well as within them. The end of the Cold War rivalry between the United States and the USSR had major implications for many minor-minor power rivalries that were linked to it. Here we see shock and linkage variables working in tandem. The end of the Cold War was a political shock of the first magnitude, and at the same time it cut the links between a major-power rivalry and many smaller ones. Chapter 12 explores the different types of linkage between enduring rivalries and their impact on each other's conflict patterns.

Finally, as the conclusion to the book, chapter 13 presents a substantial research agenda for future work. There we return to the issues of data, testing, and theory construction in light of the rivalry approach. More substantially, we discuss promising avenues of research on the origins, dynamics, and termination of rivalries in light of the punctuated equilibrium model.

The rivalry approach attracts us because it generates new questions and provides new ways to examine traditional problems and theories. At every turn it has motivated us to rethink issues and practices, many of which we learned in graduate school and have not challenged since. As this volume shows, the rivalry approach requires new data, new concepts, and new theory. The life cycle of an (enduring) rivalry also demands explanation. Understanding international conflict requires more than theories about the causes of war: it necessitates putting war in the rivalry context. In this book, we sketch out many of the issues involved and propose some solutions.

Part I

The Rivalry Approach to War and Peace

CHAPTER 2

The Concept and Measurement of Rivalries

The concept of militarized rivalries lies at the core of our project. The existence of standard data sets of wars and disputes means that the concept and operational definition of war are now largely agreed upon, at least in practice. In contrast, the concept of a rivalry, particularly a nonenduring one, is new and cannot be taken for granted. We cannot understand enduring rivalries nor fully consider the utility of the rivalry approach until we have explicated the concept of a rivalry. We have spoken of the "rivalry approach" to war and peace, but this depends crucially on the concept of a militarized rivalry. Hence we devote this chapter to a theoretical and operational discussion of our core concept.

The historical origins of the idea of the *enduring* rivalry lie in its testing functions: enduring rivalry as a concept initially played a role only in case selection and was a minor theoretical concern at best. Our central focus is rivalries, and therefore the debate on "operational definitions" of enduring rivalries takes place in a very different light. One advantage of the rivalry approach is that it moves the focus of debate from enduring rivalries to rivalry relationships in general. Unlike recent work on enduring rivalries, we start with the concept of rivalry *tout court*. As we proposed in the previous chapter, rivalries can be brief or protracted. Although common usage does not refer to an isolated conflict as a rivalry, it is important to include such cases in the rivalry continuum.[1] This is largely because an isolated conflict is a potential rivalry, and one goal of research is to understand why some short-term conflicts do not become enduring rivalries. We will direct much of our attention to the more enduring rivalries, but it is crucial that the concept of rivalries not be limited to a particular

---

[1] In our conception, rivalries are placed along a continuum based on the duration of the competition and the time-density of major conflict events between the two rivals. Thus, the end points of the continuum would be very brief, single militarized encounters on one side and numerous, frequent clashes over many decades or centuries at the other extreme.

subset of enduring cases. We shall argue that the enduring subset is a very important one, but in order to understand its processes, we need a concept that encompasses rivalries that are very short as well as those that are very long.

The first half of this chapter thus focuses on the conceptual components of a militarized rivalry. The second half uses this conceptual framework to develop an operational definition of rivalry. With a clear view of what a rivalry is (and is not), we avoid potential confusion. For example, the "enduring" rivalry literature has tended to confound the duration of rivalry (i.e., "enduring") with its severity (e.g., frequency or magnitude of conflict). Empirically these two dimensions are modestly correlated, but conceptually we must keep them separate. This distinction should not be controversial because conflict studies usually concentrate on the severity of conflicts (e.g., disputes versus wars), not their duration. Historically, the concept of rivalry has not played a key role in conflict theories. Its use as a case selection device has meant that most users have skipped the conceptual step and moved directly to the operational definition of rivalries. Because the rivalry concept forms the core of our enterprise, we first consider the concept, after which we move to developing an operational definition of rivalry (with particular attention to enduring rivalries), generating the list of cases that will form the basis for analyses in the remainder of the book.

Conceptual Components of a Rivalry Relationship

The term *rivalry* has long been part of the lexicon of international relations scholars, used casually to characterize feelings of enmity between states. Rarely, however, has the concept of rivalry received close attention. Certainly it has not attracted the attention, for example, that power and interdependence have. Nevertheless, concepts similar to rivalry have appeared over the last twenty years, and recently several works have sought to define carefully the concept of rivalry, enduring rivalry in particular. We briefly review a number of those efforts (see also Hensel 1996 for a review), in preparation for the presentation of our own conceptual scheme.

Early work considered the idea of "international enemies" (Finlay, Holsti, and Fagan 1967; Feste 1982), which signified states that exhibited overt or latent hostility that might lead to war. The concept of enemies conveyed the militarized element characteristic of many rivalry schemes and definitions and indicated that war was recognized as a significant possibility; yet it provided little sense of temporal length. In contrast to the enemies concept, which tended to stress sovereignty, the concept of "protracted conflict" (Azar, Jureidini , and McLaurin 1978; Brecher 1984; see also Starr 1999) emphasized the temporal duration of conflicts. Protracted conflicts referred to a long series of hostile interactions. Although this concept included a temporal element not explicit in the idea of international enemies, it did not necessarily differentiate different degrees of hostility, potentially mixing trade disputes that are protracted but have little prospect of war with dangerous military competitions that may experience multiple wars over time. Ideas such as international enemies and protracted conflict were largely precursors to the recent attention given to enduring and other rivalries.

The first mentions of the term *enduring rivalry* in the scholarly literature (Wayman 1982; Diehl 1983; Gochman and Maoz 1984) did not explicitly discuss the concept. Rather, the term was used to describe an empirical set of cases characterized by states clashing repeatedly in militarized disputes (Gochman and Maoz 1984) over a period of time. This was a case of putting the cart before the horse, and rivalries did not receive extended conceptual attention until a small critical mass of studies had been conducted. It was then that scholars began to examine critically just what was meant by rivalry.

The literature on protracted conflicts, as well as the operational definitions of enduring rivalries, provides implicit criteria that define the rivalry concept. It contains three dimensions: (1) spatial consistency, (2) time or duration, and (3) militarized competitiveness or conflict. An adequate conceptualization of a militarized interstate rivalry must address satisfactorily these three issues. We discuss them in order of relative controversy in current debates about enduring rivalries.

Spatial Consistency

One dimension of rivalries is the character and number of actors. Actors in rivalries consist of *states,* and rivalries are *dyadic.* Rivalries consist of the same pair of states competing with one another, and the expectation of a future conflict relationship with the same specific opponent. These two aspects of spatial consistency have gone virtually unchallenged and hence are not discussed in the literature on enduring rivalries. For this reason, we discuss these two aspects of spatial consistency only briefly.

Because our project consists of the study of international conflict, the main actors are states. This is all the more so in that we focus on militarized relations. Although some colonial companies (e.g., the British East India Company) had their own armies, in international militarized relations states are the dominant group of actors. Heavily armed nonstate actors almost invariably are involved in civil, not international, wars (of course these civil wars may have international implications, and spill over into the international realm). Hence, we consider rivalries as consisting of a pair of states competing with each other repeatedly over time.

Given that most militarized conflict has thus far been dyadic (Gochman and Maoz 1984), one can anticipate that most rivalries will involve only two states. Nevertheless, it is possible that, by virtue of alliances, for example, more than two states might be involved in a rivalry; the hostility between some members of the North Atlantic Treaty Organization (NATO) and the Warsaw Pact (WTO) might qualify as such. It is also possible that a multistate rivalry might overlap with a dyadic rivalry. The Cold War competition between the United States and the Soviet Union included aspects related to the NATO–WTO competition. France and Britain were jointly involved in a series of conflicts with the declining Ottoman Empire during the nineteenth century. One could also envision a rivalry involving more than two states arrayed in opposition to one another in a multilateral fashion. Three major powers, for example, may compete among themselves over the same issues, no one power aligned with another and each with its own set of preferences that is incompatible with those of the other two states. An example might be the United States, the Soviet Union, and China in the postwar era (Goldstein and Freeman 1991). States in the Concert of Europe may also qualify.

Multilateral and linked dyadic rivalries are related to what Buzan (1983) refers to as a "security complex." A security complex is "a group of states whose primary security concerns link together sufficiently closely that their national securities cannot realistically be considered apart from one another. Security complexes tend to be durable, but they are neither permanent nor internally rigid" (106). Although security complexes are broader than rivalries, rivalries and related conflicts are often at the heart of the complex and define its parameters. Indeed, those who adopt security complexes as a framework for analysis are urged to focus attention on "sets of states whose security problems are closely interconnected" (1983, 113–14). Not surprisingly, Buzan uses the South Asian security complex as an example, with the India–Pakistan rivalry as its dominant feature.

As we note below in our operational definition, we see rivalries as dyadic relationships. In this way, we have emphasized the temporal component at the expense of the spatial one. It might be argued that such an emphasis is myopic. In part, our emphasis on the temporal aspects is a reaction against the dominant cross-sectional paradigm in conflict research. In addition, most multilateral disputes and wars (with rare exceptions) start as dyadic competitions, and decisions for intervention (or not) are individual ones for each state to make. We do not claim that rivalries are uninfluenced by outside parties or by other rivalries. Clearly rivalries with overlapping memberships influence each other; we explore this phenomenon in chapter 12. Yet one should not assume, as with China, the Soviet Union, and the United States, that each leg of the triadic linkage is symmetrical in duration, processes, or relative importance. By looking at rivalries as dyadic phenomena, we are able to assess the extent of the interrelationships present.

Another concern under spatial consistency is how many rivalries a state can maintain at one given time. We believe that many states are capable of carrying on several rivalries at the same time; it would seem likely that major powers, with global interests and capabilities, would be more likely to have multiple rivalries than weaker states. The possibility of multiple, concurrent rivalries permits us to see how the multiple rivalries a state is involved in influence one another, one of the several types of rivalry linkage that we consider in chapter 12. By considering multiple rivalries, scholars might also understand how the beginning or end of some rivalries is conditioned by the number and type of interactions with other rivalries; this would not be possible if one were to make a priori decisions to ignore lesser rivalries.

Time or Duration

Distinctive of the rivalry idea is its emphasis on the duration of rivalries. Hence the second component of rivalries is temporal. Although it is recognized that wars and disputes also have duration, this has never been a focal point of conflict studies (although a small literature on war duration exists; see, for example, Bennett and Stam 1996). With this background in mind, the emphasis on enduring rivalries is unsurprising. In some notable cases (e.g., United States–USSR), it is easy to think of the rivalry as one long, protracted conflict.

In the evolution of rivalry research, concern has revolved around the meaning of enduring. Operationally, the definition has increased over time, from 10–15 years in early research to current requirements that a rivalry last at least 20–25 years to qualify as enduring. Yet there is no reason to limit the general concept of rivalries to those that are enduring. Rivalries obviously vary in length, ranging from brief competitions to those that extend over many years, the latter of which we label enduring.

Enduring rivalries may be the most obvious candidates for study, but from a conceptual point of view they are not a good place to start. For example, if one wants to explain why some rivalries become enduring, one needs a control group of nonenduring rivalries. Empirically, we know that some militarized relationships are short-term. As an illustration, these will play a key role in our analysis of the democratic peace in chapter 6, because there is only one case of an enduring rivalry between two democratic states,[2] but several cases of short-term rivalries between democracies.

We might suggest that the duration of enduring rivalries be left to measurement rather than conceptual definition, generally requiring, however, that the militarized competition last long enough for the states involved to adjust their behavior and long-term strategy because of the competition. This allows for national security decisions that are not transitory and are conditioned by the competition; these include alliance formation, weapons acquisition, troop deployment, and the like. The duration of a rivalry in large part affects, at any given point in time, the relative influence of the past on current and future interactions in the rivalry relationship. It also helps determine the strength of the expectation of future hostile interactions.

---

[2]There is only one case of an enduring rivalry that involved states that were both democratic throughout the lifetime of the rivalry. There is another case in which two democratic states began an enduring rivalry, but during the course of the rivalry one of those states underwent a regime change and lost its democratic status. See chapter 6 for details.

Although we regard rivalry as a continuous concept, we can subdivide the rivalry continuum for some analytical purposes. For purposes of comparison and description, we divide it into several parts: (1) sporadic or isolated rivalries between a pair of states, (2) proto-rivalries, which consist of repeated conflict between the same states, but not to the extent that an enduring rivalry can be said to exist, and (3) enduring rivalries, which are severe and repeated conflicts between the same states over an extended period of time.

Isolated rivalries are those of brief duration. The conflict is sometimes very severe, but the bases of military conflict are resolved in a short period or wither away such that recurring conflict and war are no longer central concerns in the relationship.[3] Enduring rivalries are the longest of the rivalries and have the greatest expectations of an ongoing conflictual relationship. The impact of the past is also potentially greater because there is more history to affect the relationship. One might think of enduring rivalries as lasting elements in international affairs. Proto-rivalries represent something of a middle ground between the isolated and enduring kinds; they persist for moderate periods of time but last longer than isolated competitions. Indeed, proto-rivalries can be thought of as potential enduring rivalries that terminate in adolescence, whereas isolated rivalries undergo something akin to crib death. In the operational section, we develop specific criteria for classifying rivalries into these three categories. If for no other reasons we need proto- and isolated rivalries as control groups. For example, we cannot understand what makes an enduring rivalry persist or end, unless we compare them to potential enduring rivalries (i.e., proto-rivalries).

In summary, duration plays a central role in the conceptualization of a rivalry. The concept of war, as defined by the Correlates of War Project (Small and Singer 1982), involves only level-of-hostility criteria. Hence, the rivalry approach is much more symmetrical in that it understands duration to be as important as severity. In short, the second defining characteristic of rivalry is its temporal dimension, which can vary from short term to enduring.

Militarized Competitiveness

Rivalry relationships form a particular subset of international relations. As in traditional international relations scholarship, we focus on the relationships between states—as defined by Correlates of War (COW) Project criteria (Small and Singer 1982). Nevertheless, we do not focus on "relations" in general, but on those that are *militarized* and *conflictual*. A rivalry relationship means a conflict or competition in which one or both sides use the military tools of foreign policy: foreign policy is conceived of and conducted in military terms. This

---

[3]In our conception, rivalries could be as short as one day. Yet this still qualifies as a rivalry because it fits the conceptual criteria noted herein. Rather than merely an artifact of semantics, there are theoretical and empirical advantages to this kind of definition. For example, identifying very short competitions as rivalries and including them in the rivalry continuum allows scholars to ask (and potentially answer) why some competitions are so transitory and thus why they don't evolve in enduring rivalries.

dimension has, not surprisingly, provoked the most debate in discussions of enduring rivalries. On the dimensions of spatial consistency and duration, we currently have some consensus on dyadic, state relationships that last at least 20 years. On the competitiveness dimension, we find much more divergence in approaches.

When states are engaged in a rivalry, they have conflicting goals over the disposition of scarce goods. Conflicting goals do not necessarily mean that preferences of the competitors are irreconcilable or that the competition is entirely zero-sum (although this may be the case in some rivalries). These goods may be intangible, such as political influence (as in "power politics" conceptions) or ideological/religious dominance. States may also compete for more tangible goods such as natural resources or territory. In practice, individual rivalries reflect varying mixes of these sources of competition. As in conflict and war studies in general, we limit ourselves to competitions that take a military turn.

One alternative approach uses the idea of "issue" to conceptualize rivalry. In this approach, what characterizes a rivalry relationship is not military force, but conflict over one issue or set of issues. Issue constancy over time thus permits one to say that all the competition in the rivalry belongs to the "same" relationship. The advantage of issue conceptions is that they make one more certain that the various incidents in a rivalry belong together as part of same relationship. Because the issue or issues remain constant, one can link the various disputes of a rivalry. In addition, this approach makes it easier to code the beginning and end of rivalries. Once the issue or issues have been resolved, the rivalry is over. A looser variation of this approach is provided by Bennett (1993, 1996), who allows for the continuation of rivalries if there is a plausible connection across issues, such that the rivalry can be said to have continuity even if the original issue in dispute is no longer center stage or has been resolved.

All concepts of rivalry depend—implicitly or explicitly—on data about military conflict, either through diplomatic histories or data sets. Hence the military competitiveness dimension comes before the issue dimension. For example, Bennett (1996) begins with militarized relationships and *then* applies issue criteria to code rivalry termination. We can contrast this with an approach that looks at all conflicts over territory, for example, and then examines their beginning and end. Some of these conflicts become militarized, while others do not.

Although rivalries are competitions (often perceived to be zero-sum by the rivals), the source of the conflict is not necessarily consistent over the life of the rivalry. States may fight over essentially the same issues during a rivalry (e.g., the Egyptian-Israeli conflict since 1948), or there may be some variance in the issues (e.g., Britain and France in the eighteenth century). States may compete over a series of goods, and their confrontations may vary according to which goods are in dispute at the time. Rather than talk about issues in dispute, we use the concept of "the expectation of a continued militarized and conflictual relationship." This expectation can arise for different reasons, some of which fall under the idea of issues. Unresolved territorial claims are an issue that can produce such expectations, but so too can a history of mistrust and struggle between two states. It can be the case that different sources of competition lead to the same rivalry effect, much as different foreign policy choices can produce the same outcome (see the idea of "substitutability" in Most and Starr 1989). Hence for us the key factor is that the relationship between two states involves treating some issues with the military tools of foreign policy.

Thus, one must conceptualize rivalry as more than a continuing competition over one issue or set of issues (state competitions rarely address a single issue, and issues in a rivalry may shift over time). Nevertheless, there must be some connection between these "different" competitions. Too close a temporal connection might classify a single, integrated conflict event as a rivalry (e.g., long wars such as the Vietnam War). In contrast, too remote a connection leads one to question whether the competitions are indeed related. There seems to be a middle ground for tying rivalry competitions together. This connection may be provided by a temporal component (see below), but it is also established by the presence of a thread linking the competitions (e.g., regional hegemony), some intangible good (e.g., influence), or by the behavior of the states involved such that their actions are conditioned by previous interactions in the rivalry and by anticipation of future confrontations (the expectation of a continuing conflict relationship). The former is particularly conducive to rivalries, as intangible issues are more conflict-prone and less divisible, and therefore less likely to be resolved easily or quickly (Vasquez 1983).

The mere notion of competition or issue consistency is insufficient to constitute a rivalry (at least in the context of international conflict research). One could give any number of sports analogies that reveal that competitions can be friendly. Similarly, states and corporations compete for the same markets, but usually with little chance that such competition will result in war. In international conflict research, a rivalry connotes (and for us denotes) "militarization"—that the threat of, or actual use of, military force to resolve competing claims is an ever-present possibility. This requirement is similar to the notion of threat perception offered by Hensel (1996) and related to the necessity for hostile interactions stated by Bennett (1993). This is more than merely saying that one state is a potential threat to another; such claims are often made in the abstract. Here, rivalry means that the threat is immediate, serious, and may involve military force. Thus, competition in a rivalry (at least in this context) has a hostility dimension involving the significant likelihood of the use of military force (including, of course, full-scale war).

Some scholars argue that militarized competition, and therefore rivalries, must involve states that can realistically challenge one another's security; in effect, rivalries can exist only between states of approximately equal capabilities. There can be major-power or minor-power rivalries, but no mixed major-minor rivalries (Vasquez 1993). Thompson (1995) acknowledges the possibility of asymmetrical rivalries, but not among his critical "positional" types. Even among "spatial" rivalries, he expects the asymmetrical variety to be of lesser duration. Those who contend that rivalries are conducted between approximate equals believe that a preponderant state does not have to compete with a weaker foe because there is little chance that the weaker state will prevail in the competition. We think that this is an unnecessary limitation and argue that the question is an empirical one.

From the perspective of power politics, enduring conflict between unequals is implausible. Yet perhaps the power politics model is flawed in this respect. It is incorrect to assume that the distribution of power must remain constant throughout the rivalry. Furthermore, a rivalry does not begin or suddenly end merely because one side has dramatically increased its strength. Similarly, declaring a series of hostile interactions as a rivalry only after approximate parity is achieved may ignore the roots of the competition and the shift from preponderance to parity (e.g., the power transition model). Major-minor power rivalries may exhibit different characteristics than other types (as acknowledged by Vasquez and Thompson), but this is a theoretical and empirical question. We prefer not to exclude, a priori, any class of protracted hostile militarized interaction from consideration as a rivalry. If Vasquez and others are correct, then there should be few significant and enduring major-minor power rivalries identified when the operational criteria are applied. Recalling several historical instances of such rivalries and recognizing that even "big states lose little wars" (Maoz 1989), we do not expect this result.

Again, that foreign policies are conducted in a militarized fashion may mean that each state is a security threat to the other, but it could also show a preference for military force as opposed to other means of influence. The British used their naval forces, for example, to collect debts from Latin American states in the nineteenth century; although these states could hardly be called a security threat to Britain, such actions count as "militarized disputes" in conflict studies. Similar to our analysis of issues, we think these considerations are better left as hypotheses for analysis, not as components of the conceptualization of rivalry itself.

In short, rivalry for us means a militarized competition. One key dimension of a rivalry is how severe it is, with severity defined in terms of level of military force. This concept of rivalry severity replaces war as a dependent variable in many of our analyses. But unlike the "causes of war" approach, this is not the only defining characteristic of a rivalry. The rivalry approach emphasizes that these militarized relations can last for decades. At the more general level, all rivalry approaches implicitly or explicitly define the competition as militarized, since all these studies fall within the field of peace-and-war research. The debate is over how best to conceptualize military competition.

Other Conceptions of (Enduring) Rivalry

As we mentioned above, much of the debate in the rivalry literature revolves around the competitiveness dimension. The primary alternative approaches to enduring rivalries, Bennett's, Hensel's, and Thompson's and our own, agree on the dyadic, interstate character of rivalries. Many of us also agree that an enduring rivalry must last at least 20 years. Thompson focuses on the competitiveness dimension (see below). His "principal" rivalries, however, almost all qualify as protracted conflicts, and indeed he expects that principal rivalries will be on the whole longer than nonprincipal ones.[4] Given this general agreement on the first two dimensions of rivalry, we primarily concentrate our review on the third, disputed aspect of the rivalry concept.

Bennett (1993) has conceptualized enduring rivals as those states that have disagreed over the same issue for an extended period of time. Excluding minor disputes and those between allies, Bennett also stipulates that the rivals must have devoted significant resources (military, economic, and the like) to the rivalry, and his operational definition suggests that a willingness (and acting on that willingness) to use or threaten military force against one's rival is also an essential part of the rivalry relationship. Vasquez (1993) claims that states define rivals in terms of what gaining or losing stakes will mean for one's competitors; thus, the concern in rivalries is with relative, rather than exclusively absolute, gains and losses.

Hensel (1996) develops a general notion of rivalry that is not confined to a specific focus on enduring rivalries and is applicable beyond interstate relations. He argues that rivalries are composed of three elements: (1) competition, (2) threat perception, and (3) time. The first component, competition, is almost self-explanatory in that there must be some disagreement over the division of some good. Yet Hensel notes that his focus on militarized interstate rivalries requires the second component, namely that states believe that their rival threatens national security interests. Threat perception then distinguishes a wide variety of competitions (e.g., some trade disputes) from hostile disputes involving the potential use of military force. Hensel also introduces a temporal component, indicating that for a competition to be a rivalry, it must last long enough to focus each state/rival's attention on the other.

Hensel argues that multiple types of rivalry share these conceptual components. The foci of his study are militarized interstate rivalries, such as that between France and Germany between 1870 and 1945. Yet he also lists the possibility the rivalries can be nonmilitarized. In cases such as trade competitions

---

[4]The exception may be the principal rivalry of Britain versus Italy, which lasts only from 1934 to 1943. Yet, most of the other principal rivalries on his list last for several decades.

between the United States and Japan in the 1980s and after, states can perceive that national security is threatened, but no military threats or actions are contemplated or executed by the rivals. Furthermore, rivalries can also be nonenduring. This category of rivalries includes competitions in which the issues in dispute are resolved in a short period of time or in which rivals direct their attention away from the present competition to other threats to national security. Finally, Hensel indicates that rivalries do not have to involve nation-states. The components of rivalries might just as easily be applied to subnational or ethnic groups; the rivalries between the Serbs, Muslims, and Croats in Bosnia are an example.

The previous attempts at conceptualizing rivalry have been heavily influenced by a research focus on enduring rivalries and more subtly by the operational definitions of rivalry that rely on the occurrence of militarized disputes (see below). Thompson (1995) complains that the enduring aspect of enduring rivalry has been overemphasized at the expense of the competitiveness or importance of the rivalry. Accordingly, he sees most conceptual and operational definitions as overly broad. In his view, a state's rival is more than simply an external threat or continuing source of problems. In place of the typical notion of enduring rivalries, Thompson (1995) advocates the adoption of the term "principal rivalries." Principal rivals means that states have primary, some might say exclusive, opponents; thus, Thompson distinguishes competitions that represent the primary threat to security from those that are secondary (see also McGinnis and Williams 1989). Thompson, agreeing with Kuenne (1989), rejects the notion that rivalries are mere competitions. Unlike most market competitions, for example, rivalries exhibit nonanonymity in that the competition is focused directly on one competitor. Some level of duration is implicit in Thompson's idea of principal rivalry, but the importance of the rivalry seems to be a more major concern. So while much of the "enduring" rivalry literature places the first stress on duration and the second stress on importance, Thompson argues that the priorities should be reversed.

Thompson's more narrow focus on principal rivalries should not imply that he regards them as all the same. He classifies rivalries according to two dimensions: (1) the type of competition and (2) its locale or scope. With respect to competition type, he distinguishes spatial from positional rivalries. Spatial rivalries are fought over territorial control and tend to be less intense than their positional counterparts. Spatial rivalries are more likely to involve minor powers and can even involve states with asymmetrical capabilities, although such asymmetry is thought to make the rivalries end more quickly. In contrast, and more interesting from Thompson's theoretical perspective, positional rivalries are competitions over relative positions in a power hierarchy. These are essentially regional or global power struggles that inherently assume some capability symmetry (a competition over power and influence is unlikely if one state is dramatically stronger than another).

The second dimension, location, indicates where the rivalry is contested, and there are four possibilities: (1) dyadic, (2) regional, (3) global, and (4) regional-global. Dyadic rivalries are competitions confined to a narrow geographic area and are thought to be primarily of the spatial variety. Regional rivalries concentrate on slightly broader areas and are competitions over power in a more defined region, such as the rivalry between Spain and France in the sixteenth century. Global rivalries, such as between Venice and Portugal in the fifteenth century or the United States and the Soviet Union in the twentieth century, are international competitions for leadership, as with the framework of the long-cycles literature (Modelski 1987; Modelski and Thompson 1988). The final category combines the previous two and is illustrated by the Netherlands' rivalries with Spain and France in the sixteenth and seventeenth centuries respectively.

Summary

We end this section with a brief summary of our conceptualization of rivalries. On the spatial consistency dimension we adopt the standard limitation to *states* as the actors and the relationships as *dyadic*. In contrast with the literature that focuses exclusively on enduring rivalries, we insist that rivalries can be of any duration, from one day to decades. Rivalries are characterized by their duration, *but not by any particular duration*. We shall define categories of isolated, proto- and enduring rivalries, but each is a subcategory of the general rivalry concept. Finally, we conceive of rivalries as *militarized relationships:* rivalries are conflicts that governments conduct using the military means of foreign policy. The issue can vary from trade to finance, from territory to regime type; the common point is that states deal with the issue in military terms. Our approach focuses on the militarized behavior of states—actual militarized disputes and wars—and we make no requirement that issues remain constant.

There are clearly some limitations to our conceptual approach. Most obviously, we have confined our analysis to militarized relationships. Accordingly, we may miss significant competitions that involve some measures of threat or security risk for the participants, but never or rarely manifest themselves in direct militarized confrontations. This may lead us to miss competitions that share all the other characteristics of rivalry, but lack the militarized component. Thus, we will be limited in answering the questions of how, when, and why rivalries become militarized. Nevertheless, for largely normative reasons, we are most concerned with those rivalries that are militarized, while not diminishing the validity of considering the nonmilitarized variety. Our exclusive focus on states leads us to miss rivalries involving nonstate entities, a salient concern in the post–Cold War era. Nevertheless, we are not certain that nonstate rivalries necessarily follow the same patterns or exhibit the same causal processes as state rivalries and do not wish to mix apples and oranges in the same rivalry fruit basket. Thus, at this stage of the inquiry, we continue the traditional focus of international conflict scholars on state behavior.

FIGURE 2.1: Conceptualizing Rivalries

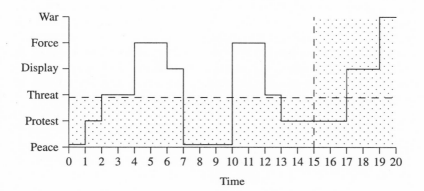

Operational Definitions of Rivalry

With a clear conceptual definition of rivalry, we move on to a discussion of how it should be operationalized. This must produce a comprehensive list of rivalries, and eventually enduring ones. Success in this enterprise will be evident not only by the face validity criterion—the list of rivalries appears plausible—but also by the convergence between the definition and criteria central to our theoretical purposes. We turn now to those criteria.

Criteria for Evaluating Rivalry Definitions

How are we to judge if a potential definition or operational measure of rivalries is adequate? In this section, we discuss what a good operational definition of rivalries must do, and in the following section we examine current definitions of rivalries.

In order to guide our discussion of criteria for a good definition, we use the hypothetical rivalry presented in figure 2.1. Two dimensions of the rivalry concept are represented by the x- and y-axis. On the x-axis we have time periods indicating the temporal component of rivalries, while on the y-axis we have the level of militarized competition.

Because many current operational definitions use the Correlates of War (COW) Project militarized dispute data set (Gochman and Maoz 1984; Jones, Bremer, and Singer 1996), we have constructed the hypothetical rivalry with that data set in mind, but it is clear that the same issues arise if other conflict data sets are used.[5] It is important to keep in mind that other options exist in distinguishing rivalries of differing severities. One can ask: what indicates a

---

[5] Rivalry lists or measures do not have to be generated with extant, quantitative data sets. Huth, Gelpi, and Bennett 1992 and Thompson 1995, 1998 developed their lists of rivalries through careful analysis of diplomatic histories.

militarized relationship? Clearly, the existence of militarized disputes and wars does, but other indicators can be found as well. For example, an arms race may signal a rivalry, but obviously we can have rivalries without arms races.[6] Hence we can examine foreign policy statements as well as arms acquisition and strategy for evidence of a rivalry. In a more behavioral mode, events data could be used to detect rivalries (see Hensel 1997). Because most of the work (including ours) on rivalries comes out of the COW tradition, we use the militarized disputes data set to illustrate our discussion, although no key conceptual points hang on doing so.

Rivalries do not endure forever—they have beginnings and endings. A good definition will pinpoint these two points in time. Many of the key aspects of a good definition of rivalries are interwoven with these two concerns. Rivalries are situations in which the risk of military confrontation is significant—the militarized competitiveness dimension. The rivalry can be considered to have begun when that risk reaches a certain level, when the relationship takes a militarized turn. Of course, there is a gray area between clearly nonmilitarized and clearly militarized relationships. A major theoretical and practical question is determining what this threshold should be.

The Correlates of War Project militarized dispute data set's (Gochman and Maoz 1984; Jones, Bremer, and Singer 1996) minimum threshold for inclusion is a "serious threat to use military force," symbolized by the dashed horizontal line in figure 2.1. In that figure, the rivalry begins at time 2, when the threshold is reached. Yet the possibility of military conflict has arisen at time 1, but was not severe enough to meet the definition of the COW dispute data set. Using events data, we might want to say that the rivalry began at time 1, or starting at that time the pair of states began to expect that the risk of war was significant. Depending on where the horizontal line representing the minimum threshold of militarized competitiveness is drawn, an operational definition may mistakenly designate the rivalry as starting too late or too early. A number of rivalries may be coded as beginning with a war, but we might suspect that for some period beforehand the threat of war was significant.

The symmetric problem occurs at the other end of the rivalry. In many respects, however, this problem is worse. If the beginnings of rivalries are often signaled by concrete events, rivalries often do not have clearly defined ends. Even peace treaties may not signal that a rivalry is over. In figure 2.1, the rivalry ends at time 7 when peaceful relations are reestablished and neither party sees a significant risk of war. The expectation now may be that future disagreements will be settled by diplomacy and not military force.

A new rivalry apparently begins at time 10, but is the rivalry indeed a new one, or is it a continuation of the previous rivalry (what might be called the interrupted rivalry problem)? An ideal definition should be capable of making such distinctions. Even if a new rivalry does not begin and no disputes occur

---

[6]For a discussion of how rivalries differ from arms races, see Goertz and Diehl 1993.

after time 7, a good definition must provide a basis for deciding when the rivalry is over. Thus, an ideal definition must have explicit termination criteria that determine accurately when the rivalry is over and distinguish between new and continuing rivalries. Of course, the exact precision needed for the ending date of an enduring rivalry will vary according to theoretical purpose. For example, a study may only posit that an effect will occur over a range of years rather than one year, making the specific end year of a rivalry less important than specifying an approximate range. Furthermore, we argue below that assigning an exact date of rivalry termination may be misleading.

The choice of criteria for rivalry termination has a significant effect on pinpointing the end of rivalry and influences the conclusions drawn from empirical analyses about rivalry termination. Bennett (1997b) compared the effect of detecting rivalry termination through (1) the absence of militarized conflict for a sustained period of time and (2) the timing of the resolution of the issues under contention. He reports that there can be a 25-year difference in determining when a rivalry is over. Furthermore, such divergent determinations may make a difference in empirical tests of models of rivalry termination.

A related concern is the interconnection of the conflict events in the rivalry. This not only affects the time frame of the rivalry, as noted above, but also the domain of events in the rivalry. For example, a certain conflict event may be unrelated to a rivalry. Wrongly classifying that event as part of the rivalry results in misleading conclusions about its dynamics. In addition to termination criteria, a good definition should also specify provisions to insure the interconnection of events within a rivalry.

Rivalry in our conception signifies a certain level of militarized competition; enduring means that the competition is not ephemeral. In figure 2.1, the first rivalry lasts for five periods (times 2–7), the second lasts for at least 11 (times 10–20). Depending on the time frames those periods represent, the second rivalry might be considered enduring, the first only a proto-rivalry. A good definition should provide convincing criteria and rationale for the choice of cutoff points between enduring and other rivalries. This will necessitate some attention to the temporal dimension of rivalries, as well as other considerations.

There are two approaches, which are not mutually exclusive, to the problems of defining the beginning, end, and persistence of rivalries, along with the subproblems of setting severity levels and the like. One is to base the definition on purely theoretical arguments. For example, it might be argued that actions below the militarized threat level do not indicate a significant probability of war. The second approach is empirical, that is, to make the judgments inductively after surveying the data. For example, there may be large numbers of state dyads at the "peace" level, few at the "low-intensity conflict" level, and a significant number at the militarized threat level, which is then a natural threshold for rivalries.

An ideal definition of rivalries, therefore, must in graphic terms draw three lines in figure 2.1: one horizontal representing the minimum level of severity (either at specific points or cumulatively) and two vertical denoting the beginning and end points of the rivalry. The definition must also specify the minimum time interval necessary to classify the rivalry as enduring and provide some basis for connecting important conflict events in the rivalry. In the next section, we describe some previous definitions of rivalry and evaluate each according to the considerations outlined here.

Previous Operational Rivalry Definitions

There have been no attempts to define rivalry operationally in a general way, but there have been a few systematic attempts to develop a population of enduring rivalries. This is not to say that scholars have not studied rivalries or conflict phenomena that can be labeled as rivalries. The dominant method in defining enduring rivalries has been to use historical judgment. In most of these efforts, a universe of cases is not the goal. These are historical case studies in which no attempt is made to generalize beyond the limited domain of the study. Some cases, such as the Anglo-German conflict at the beginning of the twentieth century or the U.S.-Soviet conflict after World War II (Nincic 1989), are consistent with conventional wisdom on what constitutes an enduring rivalry. For example, Lieberman (1995) is interested in the Arab-Israeli rivalry, which is relatively easy to delineate, with the independence of Israel as the event signaling the onset of the rivalry and several wars serving as signposts along the way. In other cases, the particular theoretical questions posed by the researcher inexorably lead to the identification of certain rivalries for study. For example, Kinsella (1995) sought to understand the effects of superpower competition and arms transfers on Third World conflict; obviously, he focuses on the U.S.-Soviet rivalry and on four other enduring rivalries (drawn from Huth and Russett 1993) that involve superpower client states. Yet these methods do not result in systematic criteria to develop a universe of cases.

Despite the absence of attempts to define rivalries in general, the range of definitions for enduring rivalries is such that we can use those efforts to develop an operational definition of rivalry. One consequence of the rivalry approach is to move away from dichotomous conceptions of rivalries (enduring and nonrivalries) to a continuous one. The rivalry perspective makes us view the definitional issue in a new light. Only after we define rivalry can we move on to the problem of enduring rivalries. In this section, we make reference to definitions of an enduring rivalry, as this is where existing work has concentrated, but this step is preliminary to the goal of defining rivalries of any variety.

There have been several data-based efforts (somewhat influenced by one another) to develop a list of enduring rivalries. Not surprisingly, most have relied on the COW list of militarized interstate disputes (see Gochman and Maoz

1984 for a discussion of the definition and operationalization of militarized disputes; and Jones, Bremer, and Singer 1996 for an update and presentation of the current version of the data set) to identify enduring rivalries. Each effort using militarized disputes has established some threshold for the frequency of such disputes involving the same pair of states over a given time to distinguish sporadic conflict from an enduring rivalry. The presence of militarized disputes is used to satisfy the militarized competitiveness component, whereas the temporal and spatial components are inferred from the time frames established and the same states' involvement.

Wayman (1982, 1996) designates a dyadic enduring rivalry as any instance in which two states oppose each other in two or more disputes within a 10-year period. He assumes that a militarized dispute has a decade-long impact on a dyadic relationship. If that hostile relationship is reinforced by another dispute, the two states have extended their hostility and are considered to be in an enduring rivalry. Thus, a rivalry lasts from the onset of the first dispute until 10 years after the last dispute.

Diehl (1985a, 1985b, 1985c; Diehl and Kingston 1987; Diehl 1994b) identifies an enduring rivalry as any situation in which two nations engage in at least three militarized disputes within a period of 15 years. Diehl argues that once established, enduring rivalries need a lesser frequency of disputes for their maintenance; the competition cannot be considered fully dissipated until the relationship experiences a significant period without military confrontation. Accordingly, the time frame for a given enduring rivalry is extended if a militarized dispute between the rivals occurs within 10 years of the last dispute in the original rivalry sequence. Therefore, a 10-year "dispute-free" interval must pass before a rivalry can be certified as ended. This definition specifically excludes disputes related to ongoing world wars, so as not to confuse their effects with those of the enduring rivalry. Diehl's criteria are more specific than Wayman's, and his definitions are more sensitive to the termination of rivalries.

Gochman and Maoz (1984) construct a list of enduring rivalry dyads that include major-power, minor-power, and mixed types. Their operational criteria, however, are somewhat vague. They include "the pairs . . . of states that most often have engaged in disputes with one another" (609). In practice, this turns out to be a minimum of seven militarized disputes over the 1816–1980 period. There appears to be no temporal criterion, as disputes may be years apart and involve unconnected issues. The only common factor is the participants.

The most developed set of criteria for enduring rivalries is that centered around the Correlates of War Project (Jones, 1989; Wayman and Jones 1991; Huth and Russett 1993; Goertz and Diehl 1992a, 1995b; Geller 1993; Bennett 1996; Hensel 1996; Maoz and Mor 1996). Each of these efforts shares a number of characteristics and produces similar lists of enduring rivalries. Despite the similarities in construction and output, there are minor differences in the definitions, and it is unlikely that there will be one uniform COW definition of enduring rivalries, as there is in the case of militarized disputes, for example. Nevertheless, we label this class of enduring rivalry definitions the COW definition, recognizing the common origins of that body or work, but not implying any official endorsement by the COW Project. The differences between the definitions are relatively minor, usually dealing with auxiliary conditions.

First, the COW definition specifies a severity condition. For an enduring rivalry to exist, there must be a minimum of five to seven militarized disputes involving the same two states. The second condition of the COW definition is durability. There must be at least 20 or 25 years between the outbreak of the first dispute and the termination of the last dispute.[7] The final condition is intensity. In order for any two disputes to be part of the same rivalry, there must be no more than 10 years between them, or in some conceptions the issues around which the disputes revolve must be the same and unresolved. This condition is designed to satisfy the notion that states must consistently be challenging one another either through frequency of conflict within a narrow time frame or over the same issue across a broader time frame.

In addition to these major requirements, certain minor conditions may be specified. In one variation, each dispute must last at least 30 days and include reciprocal threats, displays, or uses of military force (e.g., Jones 1989; Maoz and Mor 1996). The reciprocity requirement is designed to eliminate confrontations in which the use or threat of force did not prompt a reaction from the other party. This ensures that the disputes represent actual competition and hostility by both sides. The duration requirement (about the median for disputes involving the display of force) is apparently designed to prevent single incidents from being classified as rivalry-producing disputes; in effect, severity is inferred (in part) from prolonged confrontation. This adds a temporal requirement for the disputes as well as for the rivalry. In addition, several of the individual definitions in the COW group approach stipulate that the two rivals must be the primary initiator and primary target of the dispute, respectively, or that there needs to be direct and prolonged military confrontation between the rivals in a multiparty dispute in which they were not the primary parties. This requirement is designed to eliminate third-party interventions in which one rival does not directly confront the other.

The reader should keep in mind that each of these definitions was designed for a different purpose and that the criteria selected were related to this broader purpose. Wayman and Diehl looked only at major-power behavior and perhaps would not use the same definition of enduring rivalry if the focus included minor powers. Wayman used enduring rivalries to study power transitions. He sought to establish only that the two major powers had a significant hostile relationship (a prerequisite for a power transition war) in a given decade. Diehl's studies involved arms races. He wanted to define a context in which an arms

---

[7] Hensel 1996 is an exception, having no maximum elapsed time for a rivalry to qualify as enduring.

race was possible. In each case, the authors use enduring rivalries as a background condition to draw a sample for a different theoretical analysis. Gochman and Maoz described only the most dispute-prone dyads and used the label "enduring rivalries." Only the COW definition was developed for use in a wide variety of analyses. Whatever criticisms might be directed at each definition below, they are presented in the context of evaluating the general utility of the definition, not with respect to the authors' original purposes.

We should note that looking at militarized disputes is not the only mechanism to generate a list of rivalries, enduring or otherwise. The most notable alternative is to consult diplomatic and military histories for references to which states regard themselves as rivals. Such histories also reveal the defense resources and attention that are devoted by a given state toward other states. From these accounts, scholars can identify rivalries and approximate how long they last. Huth, Bennett, and Gelpi (1992) were the first to adopt this approach, identifying 18 great power rivalries over the period 1916–75. More systematically, Rasler and Thompson (1998a, 1998b) have developed a list of 25 major-power rivalries, using a similar, labor-intensive reading of historical documents.

A Comparison of Previous Operational Definitions

In order to evaluate the four data-based definitions of enduring rivalries, we consider their correspondence to the conceptual components and operational criteria noted above. What is clear is that these different definitions identify different levels of severity as the cutoff points for differentiating between enduring and nonenduring rivalries. There are several dimensions along which these definitions differ: (1) number of disputes, (2) minimum length, and (3) termination criteria. These will be crucial in defining rivalries in general as well as in classifying rivalries as isolated, proto, or enduring.

All four definitions use the same data set (a now outdated version of the Correlates of War Project militarized dispute data set—Gochman and Maoz 1984) and rely on the frequency of militarized disputes to identify enduring rivalries. On the one hand, each definition is open to the criticism that militarized disputes are only one manifestation of an enduring rivalry (Thompson 1995). Yet, militarized disputes are a better indicator than others such as arms races because they better meet the conceptual standard for militarized competitiveness, that the use of military force or resort to war is an ever-present danger.

Nevertheless, militarized disputes are not without their problems. Looking at figure 2.1, we can see that all the definitions will pick up on militarized dispute activity as it attains a certain threshold. According to all definitions, the enduring rivalry begins at $t = 2$, even though there was low-intensity conflict at $t = 1$. In statistical terms, the data are "truncated" from below (OLS regressions will accordingly give biased estimates), and the beginning of conflict in the rivalry may be missed. One effect of the minor requirements of some COW definitions is to raise the minimum level for rivalry in figure 2.1. Requirements about reciprocity, duration, and multilateral disputes mean that the truncation

TABLE 2.1: Data-Based Operational Definitions of Enduring Rivalries

Author	Minimum Years	Minimum Disputes	Maximum Interval	Multiple Disputes	End
Wayman	11	2	10	dyadic	10
Diehl	0	3	15	dyadic	10
Gochman and Maoz	0	7	0	dyadic	0
COW	25	5^a	10	primary parties only[b]	10

Source: Wayman 1982, Diehl 1985a, Gochman and Maoz 1984, COW (Jones 1989).
[a]Disputes must be reciprocated and last at least 30 days.
[b]Or, the dispute is over the same issue.

line is moved upward and this increases the risk of missing a rivalry or misdating one.

What is not apparent is the behavior of the rivals in the periods that do not include a high level of hostility. If interactions are still hostile (although not quite to the degree of a militarized dispute), this poses little problem; one can safely say that a rivalry is ongoing. Nevertheless, in figure 2.1, the "rivalry" becomes cooperative from $t = 7$ until a new dispute arises at $t = 10$. All rivalry definitions include this dispute as part of the old rivalry, when it might represent the beginning of a new one. If the interactions below the dispute threshold are cooperative, then there may be some question about the existence or continuation of a rivalry. Using only militarized disputes to identify rivalries is potentially vulnerable to this problem. It may also be the case that deterrence prevents the onset of militarized disputes, giving a false sense of how or when a rivalry is beginning, evolving, or ending.

Table 2.1 shows the variation of the four data-based definitions along various dimensions. For comparison purposes, we use the Jones (1989) definition from the COW group because it was the starting point for many of the later variations within the COW group definitions; as we note above, however, all the definitions in this group produce similar results. An important conceptual component of rivalries is the temporal one, and a good rivalry definition should be able to distinguish between different types of rivalries. A glance at the first column reveals that at least two of the definitions have serious problems meeting this standard. The Diehl definition requires only that three disputes occur within 15 years of each other. The Gochman and Maoz definition specifies no temporal component at all. In either case, a rivalry could be identified through the occurrence of the minimal number of disputes in a narrow time period, blurring the distinction between enduring and other kinds of rivalries (this is significant in that both definitions purport to identify only enduring rivalries). This might be very misleading in that such disputes may be over an isolated issue and the conflict may be quickly resolved. The Wayman definition is only slightly better in that it provides for a 10-year period following the last dispute for the rivalry to persist (but this causes difficulties in identifying its termination). Only the COW definition offers a broad time frame, requiring almost a generation of conflict before classifying hostilities as enduring. Because all definitions are focused only on identifying a population of enduring rivalries, they suffer from the tendency to classify rivalries dichotomously rather than treat rivalries as a continuous concept.

Another dilemma faced in operationalizing enduring rivalries is deciding how frequent conflict must be before it can be considered part of an enduring rivalry. Wayman requires only two disputes to establish a rivalry. The other definitions require a varying number of disputes, in part dependent on the time frame established for the rivalry. For example, Diehl sets three disputes for the minimum, an average of about one every five years (equivalent to the Wayman requirement for two disputes in a 10-year period and to some in the COW group who look for five disputes in a 25-year time frame), whereas the Gochman and Maoz requirement of seven disputes (the highest among definitions) translates to one every 23-years over the 1816–1980 period, and there may be little connection between those disputes. Although a serious military threat may be a potentially justifiable minimum level of militarized competitiveness, how long "enduring" should be is not clear. We know of no theoretical arguments for the minimum of 20–25 years, but as noted below, there is an empirical argument for it as a natural breakpoint in the distribution of rivalries.

Most of the definitions rely on temporal proximity to imply an interconnection between the disputes. Without specified theoretical underpinnings, three of the definitions use the somewhat arbitrary 10-year distance to define the termination period for an enduring rivalry. Only some of the COW group definitions specify an issue component, and even in that case, the temporal criterion (i.e., time between disputes) can override the requirement that the disputes concern the same issues.

There are also problems with ongoing rivalries when the data points end before the rivalry does (or begin in 1816). In figure 2.1, suppose that the data set ends at $t = 15$. There is no way to tell if the lack of disputes since $t = 13$ is the end of the rivalry or just a pause in dispute activity; indeed, figure 2.1 shows another dispute at $t = 17$. In statistical terms, the data are "censored," because we do not know the final outcome. The shaded areas of figure 2.1 are those that the enduring rivalry definitions that use dispute data will not detect: truncation, censoring, and peaceful interludes. As far as we can tell, most of the actual work on rivalries has not addressed this issue.

Another criterion of a good definition is the ability to detect the termination point of the rivalry. It is often easier to see a rivalry begin, because of a key set of events, than to understand when it is over. Almost none of the definitions provide termination criteria distinct from those related to the maximum time between disputes. The problem is that states might resolve their major differences through war and/or international agreement whereas all the definitions will not recognize the end of rivalry until at least 10 years after the last dispute. One cannot pinpoint the exact year of termination for the rivalry according to these approaches. If we refer again to figure 2.1, the definitions here will be unable to detect behavior below the threshold of militarized disputes. This means that the four approaches will only be able to pick up hostile actions and must await the passage of time to make an ex post facto judgment on termination. This is most evident in the recent demise of the Cold War, which according to the definitions here may not end until almost the turn of the century. The use of the COW dispute data set thus implies that all the definitions have problems accurately determining the beginning and end points of rivalries. All definitions (except ours, see below) consider that a rivalry continues 10 years after the last dispute, but similar consideration suggests that a rivalry could begin 10 years prior to the first dispute; none of the definitions appears to argue for this approach.

One important distinction is between (1) the criteria for deciding that rivalry is over and (2) the date the rivalry ended. The same applies to beginning dates. Because rivalries may begin and end gradually, there may be no clear-cut date to choose as the beginning or end. In figure 2.1 one could reasonably code the rivalry beginning at time 1 or time 2. A peace treaty might be considered the *effect* of the end of the rivalry, which occurred in fact earlier. The 10-year termination rules can thus be interpreted in two ways. One can take the end of the 10-year no-dispute period as the end of the rivalry (option 2) or use it as a diagnostic tool to say that the rivalry is considered over (option 1). We shall adopt the diagnostic view (see below). This is similar to a doctor who runs tests after chemical therapy and declares that the cancer is gone, without specifying when it was eradicated. The 10-year no-dispute period allows us to declare the rivalry dead, but we do not specify an exact time of death. Analogous arguments apply to beginning dates.

Bennett (1993, 1996) has estimated the actual time of death for enduring rivalries. Perhaps because he is interested in rivalry termination, he adopts additional and specific criteria, beyond no-dispute diagnostic tests. More than just a cessation of military hostilities, Bennett requires that the issues under dispute also be resolved. This is indicated by the signing of a formal agreement or a public renunciation of claims by the rivals. This method obviously better pinpoints the end of certain rivalries, but it does perhaps miss the conclusion of rivalries that "wither" away without final resolution.

Another concern in comparing different concepts of rivalries is interrupted rivalries. In a number of cases, such as Turkey and Greece, there are rivalries that end according to various criteria (e.g., 10 years without a dispute) and then start up again some time later. The behavioral definitions of Wayman and Diehl consider these as new rivalries. Some of the COW definition variations are more discriminating. They allow rivalries to have no significant behavioral signs (i.e., militarized disputes) for an extended period of time and still be considered enduring; the presence of unresolved issues is the means of connecting temporally disparate disputes. The extreme case is the Gochman and Maoz definition, which classifies all disputes between the states as part of the same rivalry; in this definition, there are no such things as interrupted rivalries. Yet this is hardly a satisfactory solution to the problem.

We also made a comparison between the dispute density definitions above and those based on historical and diplomatic documents. Necessarily there will be some differences, as the militarized component is an essential element of the former, whereas it is not a necessary condition for the latter. The comparisons also cannot be complete given that the historical approach has thus far only generated lists of major-power rivalries, whereas the dispute density lists include rivalries of all varieties. Nevertheless, we first find some convergence between the two historical lists of Huth, Bennett, and Gelpi (1992) and Rasler and Thompson (1998a, 1998b) respectively. They generally identify the same pairs of rivals. Nevertheless, there are significant differences. The beginning and ending dates for the rivalries identified on both lists are dramatically different. Rasler and Thompson also identify several rivalries that are absent from the Huth, Bennett, and Gelpi list, for example the United States–United Kingdom (1816–1904) and France–Russia (1816–90) rivalries.

The differences are more dramatic in comparing the dispute density and historically derived lists (see also Rasler and Thompson 1998a for a comparison). Virtually all the enduring rivalries identified in the COW lists appear on the Rasler and Thompson list, although they do not converge on the starting and ending dates. Yet the Rasler and Thompson list includes approximately 10 major power rivalries that are not found on the COW list. Rasler and Thompson might be criticized for including virtually all major-power combinations in which the two states have some opposing interests. Thus, to a great extent, their list of rivalries is related to one derived by simple dyadic combinations of all states with overlapping memberships in the major-power subsystem (Small and Singer 1982), with some concessions to political alignments. The reasons for the discrepancies are hard to determine and then assess, given that we do not yet have a full explication of coding procedures and criteria used for the historically derived lists.

A New Operational Definition of Rivalry

In devising our own operational definition of rivalry, we are influenced by both the strengths and the pitfalls of previous approaches. With this in mind, our general approach to measurement is characterized by several elements. First, we identify rivalries according to their propensity for military conflict. This is not to say that we do not recognize that rivalries cannot have other, less violent manifestations. Rather, our theoretical concern in this book with military conflict (its origins, repetition, escalation, and resolution) leads us to concentrate on militarized disputes and specify militarized competitiveness as an essential component of rivalries. Accordingly, we consider only militarized rivalries and are essentially concerned with those rivalries during the time of militarization, that is, from the onset of that militarization to the final acts involving military force. In this way, our approach is similar to that of Hensel (1996) and much of the rivalry literature for its focus on military force.

With a focus on militarized rivalries, we are therefore drawn, like many of our colleagues, to the Correlates of War Project data set on militarized interstate disputes (Gochman and Maoz 1984; Jones, Bremer, and Singer 1996). Our position is that militarized relationships signify overt and direct military conflict, not merely the hypothesized probability of it. In principle, but almost never in practice, deterrence policies utilized by both sides could result in no overt military conflict. We consider slight the risk (to researchers) that deterrence will completely suppress overt conflict. A more serious concern is that the MID data set the level of severity too high (i.e., we miss some military rivalries). This would be an argument for using events data collections that include data on less severe actions. Our impression is that this is also not a serious problem, at least in terms of identifying rivalries. It may become much more critical when it comes to deciding on beginning and end points of rivalries.

The COW data set now includes all disputes with at least one recognized nation-state (Small and Singer 1982) on each side of the dispute and meeting the threshold for militarization: "a set of interactions between or among states involving threats to use military force, displays of military force, or actual uses of military force . . . these acts must be explicit, overt, nonaccidental, and government sanctioned" (Gochman and Maoz 1984, 587). A total of 2,042 conflict incidents meet these criteria and form the basis for helping us identify when rivalries occur and how severe they become.[8]

Thus far, our approach is quite similar to those of our predecessors. Yet several other characteristics of our approach differ considerably from past efforts. The second characteristic of our measurement approach is the inductive method of identifying and classifying rivalries. Most previous approaches made some a priori designation of dispute frequency for the occurrence of an enduring rivalry (e.g., three or five militarized disputes). The logic behind these choices was often quite vague, with little sense of what theoretical principles

---

[8]The maintainers of the MID 2.1 data set have made minor modifications of that data set over time without changing the version number. This means that not all official MID 2.1 data sets are identical. Although most of these changes are minor, they do pose a problem for replication. The MID 2.1 data set we used is available on this book's web site—see appendix A for details—along with all the data used in the analyses in this book. We note, in passing, that even using exactly the same data in the "same" analysis will not guarantee exactly the same results reported here. Different statistical packages do things differently, and there are also bugs in hard- and software.

guided these choices, and there was certainly no suggestion that actual empirical patterns in conflict were used to distinguish enduring from other rivalries. We will consider those empirical patterns as a guide to understanding how conflict patterns are empirically manifested.

Although we adopt an inductive approach, our method of identifying rivalries is not "barefoot empiricism." As a guide, we rely heavily on the theoretical components that comprise rivalries. Thus, the third characteristic of our measurement approach is to rely on time-density of militarized disputes to identify rivalries and distinguish between them. This is consistent with our specification of time and militarized competitiveness as components of the rivalry concept. Militarized competition is signified not only by the presence of militarized disputes between states, but also by the frequency of those disputes. The time element is the basis under which competitive actions are connected to, or differentiated from, each other. That is, those conflict events closer in time are said to be connected (or may be part of the same rivalry), whereas those more distant in time are thought to be part of different competitions or rivalries. Put still another way, the time element is also a mechanism to help us construct termination criteria for rivalries; rivalries without the outward manifestations of a violent conflict behavior are said to be ended after a period of time has elapsed. The final characteristic of our approach is to focus on dyadic rivalries for the reasons discussed above in the section on spatial consistency (e.g., separable decision-making, desire to assess interconnections between rivalries, etc.) and because even among rivalries that overlap there is always some conflict behavior that is unique to the dyad (i.e., different rivalries never involve exactly the same set of disputes).

With these general principles in mind, we move to identifying a population of rivalries over the 1816–1992 period (the domain of the data). Following this, we can divide the rivalry continuum into several segments and in the next chapter begin an empirical description of rivalries. Disputes that occur within 10 to 15 years of each other are considered to be part of the same rivalry. A dispute is considered part of the same rivalry if it involves the same two states and occurs within 11 years of the first dispute of the sequence, 12 years after the second dispute, up to 15 years after the fifth dispute. This is consistent with extant data-based definitions of (enduring) rivalries and the notion that after a rivalry is well established, it needs fewer disputes to sustain itself (Diehl 1985a).

In order to identify rivalries, we took all possible combinations of states involved in a given dispute on the opposite sides of one another (for example, the Cuban Missile Crisis is a part of both the U.S.–Soviet Union rivalry and the U.S.–Cuba rivalry). The general assumption is that all states on one side of a multilateral dispute have a rivalry with all states on the other side. Nevertheless, this is not always the case. The most common occurrence of the problem is in multilateral wars in which states may formally declare war (e.g., Brazil in World War II) but never really join the fight against the enemy (e.g., Bulgaria).

Hence, we examined multilateral disputes in which there was more than one state on *each* side of the dispute. The coding rule is that there must have been direct interaction or intent for interaction between the two sides. This may have been facilitated by an ally—for example, the United States transporting Australian troops to Korea. We eliminated those dyads in which there was no clear contact between two states in a multilateral coalition (considerations of contiguity and the length of relative participation in the dispute, and consultation of historical narratives assisted in these decisions). We also eliminated pairs of states that were involved on opposite sides of the same dispute, but with no temporal overlap in participation (i.e., one disputant exits the dispute before the other enters). Generally, these cases involved World War I, World War II, the Korean War, and the Persian Gulf War. All total, we identified 1,166 rivalries, and these data are publicly available (see appendix A). These new data provide the empirical core of the rivalry approach. Instead of analyzing issues of war and peace with crises, disputes, or event data, we make use of rivalry data.

Defining Enduring Rivalries

Although many of our analyses utilize all rivalries, and indeed we are critical of an exclusive focus on enduring rivalries, it is necessary to differentiate rivalries for several reasons. First, we hope to contrast enduring rivalries with other types of rivalries in several analyses to show the distinguishing features of those phenomena, but it is also essential to test various propositions, including those related to the democratic peace in chapter 6. Second, the latter half of this book is devoted to enduring rivalries (although we again use other types of rivalries as control or comparison groups). Thus, we need some basis for differentiating enduring from other types of rivalries.

Above, we sought roughly to distinguish three types of rivalries—isolated, proto, and enduring—along the rivalry continuum. These three types of rivalries were primarily distinguished by their duration. But, more generally, we can distinguish rivalries on two dimensions: duration and dispute occurrence. These correspond to two facets of the rivalry concept: time and militarized competitiveness, respectively.

As we noted above, no definition of enduring rivalries provides a true theoretical rationale for its operationalization. In contrast, we have emphasized that rivalries lie on a continuum from short to enduring. Yet, like other researchers, we find enduring rivalries of particular interest. Hence, we need a method for identifying these rivalries, which form the focus of part 2 of this book. Although the rivalry continuum is smooth in a theoretical sense, empirically the distribution of rivalries along this continuum may be uneven. Our procedure, then, consists of examining the duration and dispute occurrence of our 1,166 rivalries and looking for empirical breakpoints to define isolated, proto-, and enduring rivalries. Tables 2.2 and 2.3 show rivalries by their dispute propensity and duration.

TABLE 2.2: Rivalries by Dispute Propensity, 1816–1992

Number of Disputes	Number of Rivalries	Mean Duration	Median Duration
1	678	0.63	0.16
2	202	3.43	2.46
3	101	5.86	4.39
4	54	9.96	8.34
5	33	14.89	11.44
6	25	17.80	17.81
7	10	17.70	15.19
8	11	22.90	22.57
9	8	29.06	32.74
10	6	26.21	29.97
11	5	26.21	19.05
12	3	39.87	45.01
13	3	23.53	24.44
14	4	31.77	32.31
15	2	30.39	30.39
16	2	22.44	22.44
17	4	48.83	52.26
18	3	53.38	45.97
20	2	41.31	41.31
21	1	64.12	64.12
22	1	36.55	36.55
24	1	22.89	22.89
34	1	84.90	84.90
36	1	41.05	41.05
40	1	43.95	43.95
43	1	89.58	89.58
45	1	38.23	38.23
50	1	124.08	124.08
53	1	39.91	39.91
Total	1,166	4.78	0.72

Most apparent is that over 75 percent of rivalries involve only one or two militarized disputes. Furthermore, most of these rivalries end within three years of onset. This type of rivalry allows virtually no "history" to have an impact, given that there are few confrontations that set the tone and pace of the rivalry, and given that the rivalry is over before firm expectations have a chance to set in. Whereas one- and two-dispute rivalries are relatively common, there is a significant drop in the number of rivalries that involve three disputes. There is also a jump in the average duration (whether calculated by mean or median) by almost 80 percent at that juncture as well (see table 2.2). The ability to distinguish rivalries by their duration at the lower end of the scale is less obvious. Most of the rivalries in the one-, two-, and three-dispute categories last less than eight years. Based on these patterns, we decided to rely on dispute frequency alone and designate any rivalry with one or two disputes as one of the "isolated" variety. These are conflicts of short duration and low dispute frequency, and not much pull of the past or push of the future is associated with them.

Having defined isolated rivalries, we now must distinguish between proto- and enduring rivalries among the remaining almost three hundred rivalries that involve three disputes or more. Turning again to the empirical patterns, there are several clear breakpoints in the data. First, the average duration jumps over 50 percent at the six-dispute threshold; the mean duration stabilizes there at around 18 years until the next dramatic jump at approximately eight-dispute rivalries. Second, the number of rivalries falls significantly through the five-, six-, and seven-dispute categories, with few rivalries ultimately having more than 17 militarized disputes between them (about 1 percent). Third, the mean number of disputes increases significantly with rivalries that have a duration of 22 years or greater (see table 2.3).

Extant definitions of enduring rivalries have tended to use a standard of five or six disputes as a cutoff point to distinguish enduring rivalries from other types of rivalries or conflict relationships. There is often some reference to a 15-, 20-, or 25-year time frame as well.[9] Our division of rivalries into proto and enduring categories must be based on concern for both the frequency and duration of disputes. An enduring rivalry is one with an established history and an expectation of future conflict. Those are achieved by a combination of dispute interactions and the passage of time in conflict. In light of our own empirical observations, it appears that the cutoff for enduring rivalries should fall between the five- and seven-dispute levels if one goes only by conflict frequency and between 20- and 25-year duration levels if one goes by the time element alone.

Keeping both past definitions (especially the COW set of definitions) and our own empirical observations in mind, we have decided to define as enduring rivalries any of those rivalries that involve six disputes or more *and* last for at least 20 years. The six-dispute minimum ensures that states have reached a significant level of military competition (the severity or seriousness part of enduring rivalry). The 20-year time ensures that the competition is indeed enduring, and therefore the conflicts are not bunched together in a narrow time frame. Indeed, most rivalries with six or more disputes last 20 or more years, and longer rivalries tend to have more than the minimum number of disputes. Only 16 rivalries meet the duration criteria but not the dispute threshold, and indeed many fall more than one dispute short of the six necessary to qualify as an enduring rivalry. Considerably more (35) meet the dispute threshold but not the duration one. Yet, several of these are competitions that had brief, but very intense, hostile interactions. Still others are cases "censored" by the data end

---

[9] Of course, prior definitions of enduring rivalries used an older version of the militarized dispute data set, which included significantly fewer disputes overall, and most definitions were not based on actual empirical patterns.

TABLE 2.3: Rivalries by Duration, 1816–1992

Duration in Years	Mean Number of Disputes	Median Number of Disputes	Number of Rivalries
1	1.06	1.00	609
2	1.80	2.00	87
3	1.80	2.00	86
4	2.28	2.00	72
5	2.42	2.00	43
6	2.66	2.00	38
7	2.73	3.00	22
8	3.59	3.00	17
9	3.36	2.50	14
10	3.44	3.00	18
11	4.24	4.00	17
12	4.63	4.00	19
13	5.50	5.00	4
14	3.50	3.50	6
15	4.64	4.00	11
16	6.50	6.50	2
17	4.75	5.00	4
18	7.00	6.00	9
19	8.50	8.50	4
20	8.00	5.00	5
21	4.80	5.00	5
22	5.17	5.00	6
23	10.75	7.00	4
24	6.60	7.00	5
25	7.93	6.00	14
30	11.79	9.00	24
40	20.69	17.00	13
50	16.75	17.00	4
78	42.33	43.00	3
80	18.00	18.00	1

in 1992, for which there has not been the opportunity for a full 20 years to pass; a good number of the 13 censored cases could eventually become enduring rivalries, although cases such as Zambia–South Africa are just as likely to end without reaching enduring status.

Thus, operationally, isolated rivalries are those that experience two or fewer disputes (by definition, these will be less than 11 years in duration, given how disputes are connected to one another in rivalries), and enduring rivalries are those that experience at least six disputes and do so in a time period lasting at least 20 years. Those rivalries not fitting in either category comprise the middle of the rivalry continuum and are therefore considered proto-rivalries.

The initiation date has not been the topic of much discussion in debates about the conceptualization of enduring rivalries. The standard procedure takes the first day of the first militarized dispute as the beginning. As we mentioned above, this takes as the initiation the first act that passes the minimum threshold (the dashed horizontal line in figure 2.1), which varies from one definition to another. Our position is that the beginning of the first dispute is the first "clinical sign" that the rivalry has started. It is quite possible that the relationship was militarized before this date, particularly if the first dispute is a war. Instead of coding a precise (day and month) date, we consider the rivalry to have potentially begun before this date. We continue to use the date of the first dispute for some purposes (for example, it was used to generate the data in tables 2.2 and 2.3) but for other purposes (see chapter 11) we consider that the rivalry may have begun before this date.

Analogous considerations determine our end dates. For descriptive purposes such as the tables above we use the last date of mutual participation in the last dispute.[10] We identify the last militarized dispute in the rivalry sequence, and the conclusion of that dispute signals the beginning of the period in which rivalry termination occurred. Generally, we consider rivalries ending somewhere between the date of the last dispute and approximately 10 years after that. As with the initiation, the end of the last dispute is the last clear signal that the relationship is militarized.

Determining exact dates of termination (and analogously of initiation) is akin to asking when someone was cured of cancer. One is reasonably certain about the cure only after a certain period of time with no symptoms, and a recurrence becomes less and less likely only after the passage of time. In such cases, one cannot say that the cancer was cured at any particular date. Similarly, the end dates of rivalries are important, but difficult to observe with exactitude. Formal agreements may apparently signal the end of a rivalry, but later events may prove otherwise. Sometimes the formal treaty symbolizes changes that have already taken place a few years before. Nevertheless, one should not misunderstand the problems with post hoc judgments. Viewing things post hoc does not mean that the coding decisions are wrong, but that we only really know post hoc. We may only know that cancer surgery succeeds some time after it is all over.

For our analyses of enduring rivalry initiation and termination we do not need precise dates because our key dependent variables—political shocks—also cannot be pinned down to a specific day or month. Hence we consider it more accurate to consider that initiation and termination occur over a period, and avoid the fallacy of misplaced accuracy in trying to fix a specific day or month to these events.

---

[10]If this happens to be a multilateral dispute, we take the earliest termination date of the two rivals, which may be before the end of the whole dispute. In other words, a given rival may continue in that multilateral dispute with other countries.

Caveats and Limitations

We do not have a monopoly on virtue when it comes to generating a list of rivalries. Indeed, we favor a modified pluralistic approach with respect to operational definitions. Certainly operational definitions of enduring and other rivalries must be systematic, be based on strong conceptual grounds, and have good face validity. Yet it is not inherently undesirable for scholars to begin with different definitions or lists. If there is a convergence of findings across multiple studies using somewhat different definitions, we have greater confidence in their robustness than in findings based on a single definition of enduring or other rivalries.

We recognize that our operational definition is open to a number of criticisms. Most simply, some of the enduring rivalries do not have face validity for what scholars would regard as the most serious international competitions; the United States–Haiti rivalry is cited as an example (Rasler and Thompson 1998a, 1998b). Although we acknowledge than any list of rivalries (and any other phenomenon for that matter) is likely to have an anomaly or two, one should not confound the severity dimension of rivalries with the duration dimension. Not all enduring rivalries are more serious than lesser rivalries. Some enduring rivalries may operate at lower levels or involve less than grand geopolitical issues, such as the United States–Haiti one. This should not eliminate them from a list of enduring rivalries, but rather should allow us to question why (assuming that empirical patterns bear this out) that such rivalries persist at lower levels of severity. And there are many potential answers—power asymmetry, lower salience issues—to such a question.

More serious are the critiques that center on our imprecision in designating beginning and ending dates for the rivalries (Rasler and Thompson 1998a, 1998b; Bennett 1997b). We readily admit that by focusing on the first and last dispute in the rivalry sequence, we run the risks of truncation and censoring in determining the origins and termination of rivalries. And indeed, different end dates for rivalries can have significant impact on empirical results, as Bennett (1997b) has demonstrated. Yet as our discussion above indicates, we have serious problems with assigning any one date to the beginning or end of a rivalry and assiduously avoid analyses in this book that require such a fixed point. Furthermore, it is not reassuring that the historical approaches of Huth, Bennett, and Gelpi (1992) and Rasler and Thompson (1998a, 1998b) are so divergent on their beginning and ending dates, even when they identify the same rivalries. Comparing their efforts to those of Bennett (1993, 1996, 1997b, 1998), who systematically codes end dates for enduring rivalries, does not produce any greater convergence. Although theoretically we have difficulty in identifying rivalry beginning and end dates, these comparisons suggest that no easy empirical solution is available, even if one does suspend those concerns.

Finally, Rasler and Thompson (1998a, 1998b) allege the problem of endogeneity, namely that rivalry data that are identified by the frequency of militarized disputes may then be used to explain the frequency of those same disputes. This, of course, ignores that there is a temporal dimension to rivalry identification and that it is not merely a matter of dispute frequency. Nevertheless, this is a serious charge that correctly points out the problems if scholars attempt to make circular arguments. Yet we are unaware of such efforts. Except for one analysis in chapter 3, in which we look at the frequency of disputes in different rivalry contexts (and even then we do an alternate analysis to control for endogeneity), we do not use rivalry context to explain dispute frequency. Indeed, we know of no previous research that does. More commonly, rivalry contexts are the objects of analysis, not independent variables. Although we may seek to explain certain characteristics of rivalry, the analyses contained herein are not contaminated by the definitional criteria.

Conclusion

In the introduction we stressed that the rivalry approach had significant implications for data, testing, and theory. This arises from changing the focus of conflict research from war and dispute to militarized rivalry. At the core of the rivalry approach lies the concept of a militarized rivalry. Actual hypothesis testing requires data on rivalries. This chapter thus lays the theoretical and empirical foundations for the rivalry approach. We have defined the rivalry concept along three dimensions: (1) spatial consistency, (2) duration, and (3) militarized competition. We created a data set of 1,166 rivalries of all sorts. Of course, enduring rivalries especially interest us and others. Instead of arbitrary criteria, we defined enduring rivalries based on natural breakpoints in the empirical distribution of rivalries. The rivalry concept and data developed here form the basis for all the chapters to come.

CHAPTER 3

The Empirical Importance of
the Rivalry Concept

We argue throughout this book that the rivalry approach provides a different, and novel, perspective on the issues of international war and peace. Enduring rivalries have drawn the attention of researchers because they represent dangerous dyads. Although it is easy to name prominent enduring rivalries—as one can do with prominent wars—we need to investigate systematically the population of rivalries. How dangerous are enduring rivalries? To what extent do wars and disputes occur within rivalries?

Naturally our descriptive analyses focus on the enduring rivalry category. Nevertheless, the isolated and proto-rivalry types are essential in the process of studying enduring rivalries. It is only by comparing *across* these three categories that we can distinguish key features of enduring rivalries. In chapter 5 we develop in detail the methodological aspect of a rivalry concept that runs from isolated to enduring. This chapter provides a foretaste of those arguments. For example, we discuss the debate about power symmetry in enduring rivalries (see the previous chapter for the conceptual issues). There was the suggestion that enduring rivalries occur primarily or exclusively in power symmetrical dyads. If we limited our analysis to enduring rivalries, however, we would conclude that this is incorrect because we identify some major-minor enduring rivalries. Yet, if we examine the trends from isolated to proto- to enduring rivalries, we find some support for the proposition.

In summary, if much war and dispute activity occurs within long-term rivalry contexts, then theories of conflict need to take rivalry characteristics into account. The rivalry concept has empirical importance if we find distinctive patterns of conflict activity within rivalries that cross-sectional approaches to war cannot see. We now turn to a descriptive analysis of the rivalry data set generated in the last chapter in order to discover what empirical facts about international conflict the rivalry approach reveals.

TABLE 3.1: Distribution of Cases Across Rivalry Types

Rivalry Type	N	(%)
Isolated	880	(76)
Proto	223	(19)
Enduring	63	(5)
6–13 disputes	36	(3)
>13 disputes	27	(2)
Total	1,166	(100)

Basic Patterns and Characteristics of Rivalries

Rivalries are a constant feature of international relations, evidenced by the large number of them over the past two hundred years. A closer inspection reveals a number of distinct patterns in rivalries across space and time. We use our categorization of rivalry—isolated, proto, and enduring—created in the last chapter, to give a new view of conflict phenomena. For analytical purposes, we also divide the enduring rivalry category in two, between more (greater than 13 militarized disputes) and less (6–12 disputes) intense variations of those rivalries.

Types

In the definitional chapter, we noted that most rivalries tended to be rather short (the median duration was less than a year, the mean less than five years) and involved very few disputes. Not surprisingly, the overwhelming majority of rivalries fall into the isolated category.

Over 75 percent of all rivalries are isolated ones, indicating that although conflict may be common across a wide range of dyads, it tends to end quickly and not reoccur in a narrow time frame (see table 3.1). An example of an isolated rivalry is United States–Grenada. Just under 20 percent of rivalries develop into proto-rivalries, but die out before reaching enduring status. An example is the United States–United Kingdom proto-rivalry centered in Latin America around 1900. Finally, barely more than 5 percent of all rivalries are of the enduring variety. These tend to be among the most famous of militarized competitions, including the Cold War rivalry between the United States and the Soviet Union after World War II, between Israel and its Arab neighbors, between India and Pakistan, and between Greece and Turkey (at two different junctures in history).

A second way to classify rivalries is by reference to the status of their participants. A conventional method has been to divide states into major or minor powers according to their capabilities and global importance. Classifying states into major and minor powers (for criteria and lists, see Small and Singer 1982)

TABLE 3.2: Distribution of Rivalry Cases by Relative Power Status of Rivals

Rivalry Type	Major-Major N (%)	Major-Minor N (%)	Minor-Minor N (%)
Isolated	31 (4)	443 (50)	406 (46)
Proto	27 (12)	95 (43)	101 (45)
Enduring	11 (18)	19 (30)	33 (52)
6–13 disputes	4 (11)	14 (39)	18 (50)
>13 disputes	7 (26)	5 (19)	15 (56)
Total	69 (6)	557 (48)	540 (46)

also allows us to see to what degree rivalries are conducted between states of approximately equal power. It has been the contention of some scholars (Vasquez 1993) that rivalries are best understood as competitions between states with symmetrical capabilities. Table 3.2 shows the breakdown of rivalries by the capability status of its participants.

Although major powers number only nine states maximum[1] at any given point in 1816–1992 period, and therefore a tiny fraction of all possible dyads, they are involved in over half (54 percent) of all rivalries. These are primarily with minor power (this is also reflected in an analysis of the states most active in rivalries, below in table 3.3). Thus, any claim that rivalries take place exclusively between equal powers is misguided.

We can ask more generally about the relationship between power, power asymmetry, and the duration of rivalries. This can be accomplished by noting patterns as one descends each column of table 3.2. It is of note that major powers rarely get involved in isolated conflicts with one another, just 4 percent of the isolated cases. As rivalries become more severe, however, a larger percentage of them involve major-major dyads. Twelve percent of the proto-rivalries occur between major-major pairs, while this figure reaches 18 percent for enduring rivalries. Among minor-minor rivalries—also cases of power symmetry—there is little change in the relative frequency as rivalries become more severe, from 46 percent in the isolated category to approximately 52 percent in the enduring category.

The patterns of major-major and minor-minor rivalry imply that the major-minor category must exhibit decline as rivalry severity increases. Indeed, the

[1] According to Small and Singer (1982), major powers are United States (1899–1992), United Kingdom (1816–1992), France (1816–1940 and 1945–92), Germany/Prussia (1816–1919 and 1925–45), Austria-Hungary (1816–1918), Italy/Sardinia (1860–1943), USSR/Russia (1816–1917 and 1922–92), China (1950–92), and Japan (1895–1945).

rate drops precipitously from about 50 percent in the isolated category to 30 percent in the enduring category. These trends support the general claim that enduring rivalries are much more likely to take place between countries of roughly equal power; that is, asymmetrical rivalries are more likely to die out or be resolved sooner than symmetrical ones. Nevertheless, major-minor rivalries are possible. Certainly, some of these lie embedded in major-major rivalries, such as the United States–Cuba rivalry, which is embedded in the United States–USSR rivalry, but in other cases the major-minor rivalry occurs relatively independently of others (e.g., United States–Haiti). Thus, it may be misguided to exclude a priori rivalries between states with asymmetrical capabilities, but there is some merit to the argument that major-minor power rivalries do become less likely as rivalries get more severe.

Rivalry Participants

With the prevalence of major powers in rivalries (as noted above), it is probably not surprising that a listing of the states most involved in rivalries includes a disproportionate number of major powers near the top of the list. Table 3.3 lists all the states with more than 20 rivalries over the period under study.

The six states most frequently involved in rivalries were major powers for some or all of the years under study. The United Kingdom is at the top of the list with over 123 separate rivalries; Germany/Prussia follows closely behind. The United Kingdom, France, Germany/Prussia, Italy, and USSR/Russia, as the leading European and colonial powers through the middle of the twentieth century, not surprisingly have a large number of rivalries, both between themselves and with many smaller states (both in Europe and abroad). A more recent member of the major-power club, the United States, is third on the list of states most involved in rivalries. Significantly, most of its rivalries occur in the twentieth century, *after* it attained major-power status. Not far behind the first group of six are two other major powers, Japan and China, which have been part of 58 and 48 rivalries respectively—both as major and as minor powers. Turkey/Ottoman Empire has also been frequently involved in rivalries, first as a declining former major power in the nineteenth century and more recently with other states in its region, most prominently against Greece.

The list of minor powers most involved in rivalries yields a few surprises. That Iran and Iraq occupy positions in the top 12 of states most involved in rivalries reveals that their recent propensity for conflict with neighbors and the United States is part of a longer pattern of violent involvement. Most notable is that both Iran and Iraq have been historically involved with other minor-power states (those in the region) and not major powers from outside that region.

Nine minor powers from the Western Hemisphere also are among those most involved in rivalries. At first glance, this may seem contrary to the idea of Latin America as a "zone of peace" and the relative lack of war in the Western

TABLE 3.3: Nations Most Frequently Involved in Rivalries

Nation	Total	Maj.-Maj.	Maj.-Min.	Min.-Min.	Total War	Mean Dur.	Isol.	Proto	E-R
UK	123	21	102		24	4.64	93	23	7
Germany	121	17	102	2	47	3.63	89	27	5
USA	103	14	76	13	18	6.00	70	24	9
USSR	92	19	73		29	9.20	61	23	8
France	87	20	67		25	4.61	63	20	4
Italy	84	15	61	8	35	3.79	69	11	4
Iraq	58		10	48	11	4.34	44	10	4
Japan	58	14	36	8	20	5.31	50	5	3
China	48	5	39	4	31	12.88	28	14	6
Turkey	47		22	25	25	9.93	28	12	7
Spain	44		18	26	6	2.90	35	7	2
Iran	44		10	34	2	5.02	29	13	2
Aus.-Hun.	39	12	27	0	21	3.64	33	6	0
Yugoslavia	35		12	23	11	4.39	28	5	2
Greece	31		19	12	12	7.38	20	8	3
Argentina	30		10	20	3	4.25	23	5	2
Brazil	27		13	14	3	2.73	23	3	1
Bulgaria	27		11	16	19	6.24	17	8	2
Romania	26		12	14	15	2.85	19	7	0
Chile	25		7	18	3	6.24	18	5	2
Portugal	25		9	16	3	2.66	19	6	0
Hungary	24		9	15	10	2.66	19	5	0
Egypt	24		8	16	9	5.06	16	7	1
Jordan	24		4	20	3	4.08	21	1	2
Cuba	23		8	15	1	2.85	21	1	1
Denmark	23		10	13	3	0.71	22	1	0
Nicaragua	22		9	13	2	3.34	16	5	1
Colombia	22		8	14	3	2.14	18	4	0
Israel	22		3	19	16	9.58	15	2	5
Peru	21		3	18	2	9.48	13	6	2
Haiti	20		10	10	0	1.88	18	2	0
Venezuela	20		11	9	0	2.96	17	3	0

Hemisphere cited by many analysts (e.g., Kacowicz 1998). Yet a closer inspection reveals that this familiar idea is not in contradiction to the large number of rivalries taking place in these regions. First, states in the Western Hemisphere have been independent for longer than states in almost all other regions, except for Europe, and many states have been independent since the early 1800s.

This means that there has been more opportunity for rivalries in the time period under study. If one were to control for the number of years that a state has been a full-fledged member of the international system, then Western Hemisphere states (except for the United States) would fall precipitously down the list. Second, although the number of rivalries for certain Western Hemisphere states is large, it is worthy to note that very few of these rivalries remain militarized over time, and indeed the average rivalry for those states is very short. Thus, although these states get involved in militarized conflict, they do so only briefly and are able to resolve their disputes without cycles of repeated confrontations. Thus, the relative infrequency of war in Latin America, for example, does not mean that competitions between states in the region do not exist, but rather that militarized conflict has been less likely to repeat.

With the exception of China and Japan, Asian states are generally absent from the list of states most frequently in rivalries. One has to go down to North Korea, at 17 rivalries, for the first Asian minor power on the list. Clearly, however, India has been involved in some of the most violent rivalries (with Pakistan and China), even if its aggregate number of rivalries has not been great. China has an unusual configuration of rivalries. Typically, most (overwhelmingly so) of the rivalries for any given state are of the isolated variety. For China, 42 percent of its rivalries are either proto- or enduring rivalries. Apparently, militarized competitions with the Chinese tend to be longer and more serious than with other states, in which rivalries tend to be more sporadic and die out quickly.

The African continent also has relatively few rivalries, with Uganda the most involved of sub-Saharan countries with 15 different rivalries. This is probably the product of the late independence of most of the states in that region. Yet it may also be the product of the agreement among states in the Organization of African Unity not to challenge existing border arrangements through the use of military force. As we suggest in the second part of the book, territorial disputes may be one of the primary mechanisms that generate recurring conflict and enduring rivalries.

Rivalries over Time

Just as rivalries are not evenly distributed across space, neither are they constant across time, although the patterns are considerably less distinct. Figure 3.1 plots the occurrence of rivalries in five-year blocks across the 1816–1992 time period. Just looking at the raw numbers, it is evident that the Concert of Europe did indeed provide a period of calm and stability, at least until it began to break down in the 1840s, when we see an increase in rivalries. There is another period of relative calm from about 1870 to the end of the century, when rivalries spiral upwards through two period of world wars.

FIGURE 3.1: Rivalries over Time, 1816–1992

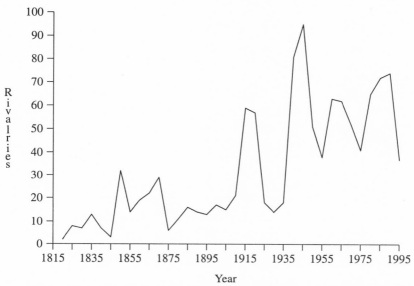

Rivalries have also become more frequent in the twentieth century. Is this a function of the greater number of states in the international system? Or does it reflect the greater conflict propensity of the system's members? It is conceivable that, because of improvements in technology, states have greater interactions (both positive and negative) with one another than in earlier times, and therefore more rivalries as a result. Technology may also permit the projection of military force more rapidly and over greater distances, thereby increasing the number of militarized confrontations that help define rivalries. To control the number of states in the system, and hence the "opportunity" for rivalry formation, we replotted rivalries over time, controlling for international system size (the number of independent states at any given time). Figure 3.2 shows that revised analysis.

Controlling for system size, the number of isolated and proto- rivalries does not increase over time, making the greater propensity for rivalries in the twentieth century a function of the increased number of states rather than some other, theoretically relevant factor. This analysis confirms that of Gochman and Maoz (1984), who find a relatively flat pattern of dispute initiation over the past two centuries, once they controlled for the number of states in the international system. This is not to say that rivalries are evenly distributed across time. There are obvious spikes in the number of rivalries around the times of the world wars.

FIGURE 3.2: Rivalries over Time, 1816–1992, Controlled for System Size

Yet this is largely what made them such global conflicts of epic proportions (Midlarsky 1988). Several rivalries converged around those wars, and those wars further diffused to create new rivalries (albeit some very short) as a result.

Patterns over time in enduring rivalries are less easy to discern. In large part, this is because enduring rivalries are relatively infrequent—they begin about only once every three years, whereas five isolated rivalries begin in the typical year. Thus, fluctuations in enduring rivalry formation are more apparent than real, reflecting that infrequency of occurrence rather than important patterns. The absence of enduring rivalries forming in the last decade or two is the result of data censoring rather than any positive trend toward less serious conflict or successful conflict resolution; all of the rivalries formed during this time have not had the requisite time (20 years) to qualify as enduring rivalries (although some of them surely will).

The Empirical Importance of Rivalries

The second part of this chapter explores the empirical significance of the rivalry concept for the study of international conflict. We examine whether conflict occurring in enduring rivalries was more frequent and severe than international conflict in other contexts, specifically conflict in isolation and in proto-rivalries.

The empirical or theoretical importance of the phenomena more or less intuitively guides the choice of research question. Studies of the major-power subsystem argue that this group of states generates the most conflict and war and has the greatest impact on international affairs as a whole. Statistical studies (e.g., Gochman and Maoz 1984) have demonstrated that the most powerful states are those most involved in international militarized disputes. The recent attention to democratic states' lack of war proneness (e.g., Russett 1993; Ray 1995) is motivated by the same impulse: as an empirical fact, democracies rarely go to war with one another. This has potentially great significance if the global trend toward democratization continues. In this chapter, we point to another phenomena of great empirical import: certain pairs of states—enduring rivalries—account for a large portion of international conflict and war. Enduring rivalries merit study for the same reasons as major powers and democracies. Their empirical significance imposes them on our attention. In part, this is the justification for our focus on the dynamics of enduring rivalries in the second half of this book. Nevertheless, we point out in the following chapter that consideration of other kinds of rivalries (as control groups and other functions) is essential even if the primary focus is on rivalries of the enduring variety.

Just as the peace-proneness of democratic states presents a theoretical and empirical puzzle, so too does the war-proneness of certain dyads. What theoretical perspective can best solve this puzzle? Some theoretical frameworks come immediately to mind because they emphasize repeated dyadic interaction. They pose questions such as the following. Do arms races always occur in rivalries? Can rivalries be modeled with sequential or repeated games? Is there a conflict learning process over time? Other frameworks, particularly those that emphasize system-level factors, pose other related questions. Are rivalries more common in bipolar systems? Does the rise and fall of a hegemon affect the formation or termination of rivalries? We discuss many of these questions elsewhere. Our goal in this chapter is not to solve the puzzles of enduring rivalries, but to demonstrate that they are puzzles worth solving.

We examine here the extent to which important phenomena, such as war and territorial changes, occur within the context of different kinds of rivalries. The dimensions along which we compare these types of conflict include the number of militarized disputes, severity of dispute hostility, frequency of war, and involvement in territorial changes.

Some Initial Expectations

If rivalry is an empirically important concept, we would anticipate that a large percentage of conflict-related phenomena occurs within the context of enduring rivalries. Specifically, we suggest the following:

1. *Dispute Proneness:* We expect that a large number of militarized international disputes will occur in the context of an enduring rivalry. This is contrary to a random conflict distribution model, which suggests that isolated conflict—sporadic conflict between all possible state dyads—would constitute the largest category. Because the number of enduring rivalry dyads is small relative to other conflictual dyads, we might also predict few disputes in the enduring rivalry category. There are good reasons to think that this is not the case, and we anticipate that enduring rivalries, despite their small numbers, will include many disputes. This is largely because disputes in the context of enduring rivalries will tend to generate future confrontations, albeit not necessarily in a mechanistic or linear fashion. Rivalry disputes prompt more rivalry disputes, unlike sporadic conflicts. As the proto-rivalry category is an intermediate one, we expect that its proportion of disputes lies between those of isolated conflicts and enduring rivalries. Thus, we suspect that a large percentage of disputes will fall within an advanced rivalry context, either proto or enduring.

2. *Dispute Severity:* We also hypothesize that the severity of disputes in an enduring rivalry will be greater on average than in other forms of conflict. Leng (1983) discovered that conflict became more severe with repeated disputes between two states; states adopted increasingly coercive bargaining strategies (and learned the lessons of realpolitik) in repeated interactions with the same enemy. Enduring rivalries may also include more salient disputes between the most bitter of enemies. Isolated conflict may actually occur between normally friendly states (e.g., a fishing dispute between Iceland and Great Britain). States involved in isolated conflict may not want to escalate tensions such that normally friendly, or at least less than completely hostile, relations are not jeopardized. There are no similar constraints in enduring rivalries, and there may be domestic political pressures to take hard lines against traditional enemies.

3. *War Proneness*: Beyond greater dispute frequency in enduring rivalries, we believe that wars will be more frequent in an advanced rivalry context (Brecher 1984). Not only is the hostility level higher for a given dispute, but the opportunity for escalating tensions, culminating in war, is always present. Disputes without a violent past are more likely to be resolved peacefully, or at least without resort to all-out military force.

4. *Increased Territorial Changes:* Beyond greater frequency and severity of military conflict, we also expect that enduring rivalries will be associated more with other significant international relations phenomena. In particular, we believe that enduring rivalries are the context for a large number of territorial changes, themselves a source of international conflict. According to some (Holsti 1991; Vasquez 1993), territory has been the primary source of interstate conflict over the past five centuries. Indeed, enduring rivalries may go hand in hand with territorial changes, as Weede (1973, 87) has noted: "the history of war and peace is largely coterminous with the history of territorial changes as results of war and causes of the next war." If territorial changes occur with more frequency in enduring rivalries than in proto-rivalries, then this is further evidence for the importance of enduring rivalries.

5. *Violent Territorial Changes:* A corollary is that those territorial changes that do occur in enduring rivalries are more likely to be achieved by military force than those that occur in other contexts. If a territorial change occurs between two historical enemies, it is more likely to be the result of military force than of peaceful diplomatic initiatives.

In summary, we suggest that a large percentage of important phenomena, such as disputes, wars, and territorial changes, occurs within the context of enduring rivalries.

Design and Measurement

In order to test these expectations, we look at patterns of conflict over the period 1816–1992, using the operational definitions of enduring, proto-, and isolated rivalries outlined in the previous chapter. With these three categories of rivalry defined, we compare them along several dimensions. Dispute severity is measured on a 0–200 scale. The indicator is constructed first with consideration for the level of hostility (Gochman and Maoz 1984; Jones, Bremer, and Singer 1996) exhibited by *each* rival in the dispute. Consideration is next given to the number of battle-related fatalities for the rivals in the dispute. Unlike other measures of dispute severity or hostility, wars are scaled together with nonwar disputes, and there can be significant differences in severity among wars. (See appendix B for a full explication.) Full-scale war is defined according to Small and Singer (1982) as one thousand or more battle-related fatalities. Territorial exchanges are the formal transfer of territorial sovereignty involving two recognized states of the international system (as identified by Goertz and Diehl 1992a and updated in Tir et al. 1998). Violence in those territorial changes is defined as armed conflict between organized forces of the gaining and losing sides of the territorial change within one year prior to the transfer.

TABLE 3.4: Rivalry Context and the Frequency of Disputes, 1816–1992

Rivalry Type	Number of Rivalries		Dispute Frequency	
	N	(%)	N	(%)
Isolated	880	(76)	525	(26)
Proto	223	(19)	705	(35)
Enduring	63	(5)	804	(40)
6–13 disputes	36	(3)	222	(11)
>13 disputes	27	(2)	582	(29)
Total	1,166	(100)	2,034	(100)

Empirical Results

The first concern is with the percentage of militarized, nonwar disputes that occurs within different rivalries. Table 3.4 provides the distribution of those disputes for each category of rivalry. There are some cases of multilateral disputes,
and therefore a dispute (or war) can be part of more than one rivalry. In this instance, the dispute is counted only once and placed in the most severe rivalry
category. This seems reasonable in that many of the multilateral disputes and
wars stem from large competitions such as World War II and result in a number of isolated rivalries between those on the Allied side and Germany or Japan,
for example. Furthermore, the original dyads prompting such multilateral wars
are almost always part of proto- and enduring rivalries, whereas those pairs that
join the conflict later are more likely to be part of isolated rivalries. To include
all the dyads from multilateral wars in this analysis would have the latter drive
the results and do so in a misleading fashion.

We first note that just 26 percent of militarized disputes occur within isolated rivalries. This suggests that assumptions of independence between conflict events in traditional war studies may be badly misplaced. Forty percent of
militarized disputes occur within the context of enduring rivalries. Thus, only
a small percentage of all conflictual dyads (5 percent), and an even smaller percentage of all possible dyads, accounts for a disproportionate amount of international conflict. The results are even more dramatic with respect to the most
severe of enduring rivalries. Almost 30 percent of all disputes are generated by
2.5 percent of the rivalries, or 27 dyads.

Militarized disputes are used to define rivalries, and therefore one might
expect greater dispute propensity in that context. Yet, even controlling for this
effect, it is still stunning that more than twice as many disputes as expected occur in enduring rivalries than in isolation.[2] The effect is even more dramatic

---

[2]The expected percentage of disputes for each rivalry category is calculated by reference to the
minimum number of disputes necessary for each rivalry category and the actual number of rivalries
in each category.

TABLE 3.5: Rivalry Context and the Severity of Disputes, 1816–1992

Rivalry Type	Mean Severity	N
Isolated	81.23	1,082
Proto	79.34	938
Enduring	81.37	964
6–13 disputes	78.77	316
>13 disputes	82.64	648
Total	80.68	2,984

Note: Unit of analysis is dyadic dispute.

for those in the most severe category of enduring rivalries. The vast majority of disputes (almost three-fourths) take place in some advanced rivalry context, be it proto or enduring.

In contrast, the results in table 3.5 on the severity of those disputes are less dramatic.[3] The relative severity of disputes does not increase as we move along the rivalry continuum.[4] There is a greater propensity for the most severe events, full-scale war, in enduring rivalries. But every dispute in enduring rivalries is not more severe than every dispute in other rivalry contexts. Rather, enduring rivalries usually include disputes of a variety of severities. Indeed, the average severity of a dispute may be misleading for enduring rivalries, because it is un-likely that war erupts frequently in repeated disputes within the same rivalry. In rivalries with greater than thirteen disputes, three or four wars is a large num-ber, but with so many disputes the average level of severity is reduced by the other, lower level disputes. A more useful comparison of the relative severity level is the occurrence of war in the rivalry; this can indicate how frequently the most severe level of conflict is reached in a rivalry.

Tables 3.6 and 3.7 provide clear evidence that enduring rivalries have a greater propensity for war than other categories of international conflict. Ta-ble 3.6 uses war as the unit of analysis, and thus each war is counted only once. Table 3.7 uses rivalry as the unit of analysis, and hence multilateral wars may be counted more than once. Only 18 percent of wars occur in isolation, whereas almost half (49 percent) take place in enduring rivalries. In addition, a dispute in an enduring rivalry is almost twice as likely to end in war as one in isolation (this can be calculated from the data in tables 3.4 and 3.6).

Another test is to treat the rivalry as a unit of analysis in order to see if at least one war occurs at some point in the rivalry. As table 3.7 reveals, the

[3]This analysis includes all disputes, including all combinations from multilateral wars. Unlike the analysis of wars above, there is a different severity score of each dyad, and the inclusion of multilateral wars does not necessarily distort or drive the results.

[4]The results reported in table 3.5, which uses disputes as the unit of analysis, are quite similar to those that use whole rivalries as the unit of analysis.

TABLE 3.6: Rivalry Context and the Frequency of War, 1816–1992

Rivalry Type	Number of Rivalries (percent)	War Frequency (percent)
Isolated	880 (76)	14 (18)
Proto	223 (19)	26 (33)
Enduring	63 (5)	39 (49)
6–13 disputes	36 (3)	10 (13)
>13 disputes	27 (2)	29 (37)
Total	1,166 (100)	79 (100)

Note: Unit of analysis is war.

propensity for war grows dramatically as one moves from isolated conflict to the most severe enduring rivalries (almost four times as great in enduring rivalries as in the lowest rivalry category). In enduring rivalries, the chances are 59 percent that the two states will go to war at some point in their competition. These findings show that not only is the propensity of a single dispute ending in war greater, but so is the chance of war sometime in the relationship as the rivalry becomes longer and more serious.

Moving from a consideration of disputes and wars, we turn now to the intersection of rivalries and territorial changes.[5] We first note that most territorial changes take place outside of the context of rivalries. Indeed, about three-fourths of all territorial changes involve no interstate rivalry, with the territorial transfer taking place between states at peace or between a state and a nonstate political entity. Nevertheless, 210 territorial changes take place in the context of rivalries.[6] Table 3.8 presents the distribution of those changes across the rivalry types.

The first notable pattern is that when a territorial change takes place in a rivalry context, the chances are almost half that it will occur in an enduring rivalry (96 out of 210). As we noted with respect to militarized disputes, the small number of enduring rivalry dyads accounts for a disproportionately large percentage of international relations phenomena. For every 10 isolated rivalries, there is typically less than one territorial change among them. In contrast, the average enduring rivalry includes 1.5 territorial changes, more than eight

---

[5]The results reported below, and directly above, may be somewhat different than those originally given in Goertz and Diehl 1992a. This is largely because of the more restrictive definition of enduring rivalry used here, and the application of revised and updated data on militarized disputes and territorial changes.

[6]If a territorial change occurred within 10 years of the beginning or 10 years of the end of a rivalry, we considered it to fall into the context of the rivalry.

TABLE 3.7: Rivalry Context and the Probability of at Least One War

Rivalry Type	Number with War	Probability of War
Isolated	139	0.16
Proto	71	0.32
Enduring	37	0.59
6–13 disputes	20	0.56
>13 disputes	17	0.63
Total	247	0.21

Note: Unit of analysis is rivalry.

TABLE 3.8: Rivalry Context and Territorial Changes, 1816–1992

Rivalry Type	Number of Territorial Changes (%)	Changes per Rivalry
Isolated	69 (33)	.08
Proto	45 (21)	.20
Enduring	96 (46)	1.52
6–13 disputes	50 (28)	1.39
>13 disputes	46 (22)	1.70
Total	210 (100)	.18

times the overall norm and more than seven times what is typical even of proto-rivalries. Thus, our expectation that territorial changes would be more common in enduring rivalries than other rivalry contexts is confirmed.

The findings with respect to violence in territorial changes are less clear, as shown in table 3.9. It is important to note that most territorial changes are completed peacefully (Goertz and Diehl 1992a; Tir et al. 1998). Yet territorial changes occurring in any rivalry context are significantly more likely (a 40 percent probability) to involve violence than territorial changes outside of any rivalry context (22 percent). Thus, there is again something about the rivalry context (hostility, suspicion, etc.) that makes peaceful interactions of all varieties more difficult, although not impossible. Nevertheless, one finding inconsistent with our expectations is that the probability that a given territorial change will involve violence is not substantially greater in an enduring rivalry than in an isolated one. Indeed, for reasons we cannot explain, it is the category of proto-rivalries that have the highest probability of conflict, almost 60 percent.

TABLE 3.9: Rivalry Context and Violent Territorial Changes, 1816–1992

Rivalry Type	Probability of Violent Territorial Change	Probability of One or More Violent Changes
Isolated	.32	.36
Proto	.58	.58
Enduring	.38	.71
6–13 disputes	.26	.50
>13 disputes	.50	1.00
Total	.40	.51

More consistent with our expectations are the findings from using the rivalry as the unit of analysis. Consistent with the findings on war, the probability of at least one violent territorial change increases with the severity of the rivalry context. Almost three-quarters of enduring rivalries experience at least one militarized transfer of territory, with the most severe enduring rivalries certain (probability = 1.00) to clash over territory during the course of the rivalry.

Conclusion

In this brief empirical analysis, we set out to examine whether conflict occurring in enduring rivalries was more frequent and severe than international conflict in isolation or in proto-rivalries. Our empirical results indicate that a large portion of nonwar militarized disputes takes place in the context of rivalries, especially enduring rivalries. Enduring rivalries are also the setting for almost half of the interstate wars since 1816; enduring rivalries at the extreme are almost four times as likely to experience a war as a pair of states in an isolated conflict. Enduring rivalries are also involved in a disproportionate number of territorial changes.

We set out to pose more questions than we answer, but in one respect the concept of enduring rivalries may have provided an answer to at least one question. The literature on war diffusion (e.g., Siverson and Starr 1991) has produced evidence for the clustering of conflicts across space, but has found little in the way of the spread of conflict across time (temporal diffusion), whether at the system (e.g., Levy 1983) or nation-state (e.g., Stoll 1984) level of analysis. Just as conflicts are concentrated over space (as the spatial diffusion hypothesis argues), so too we have seen that they are related over time in certain dyads.

The results in this chapter, and implicit in others' use of enduring rivalries, confirm that the basic intuition behind the temporal diffusion concept is correct. What has been lacking is the proper framework within which to investigate the problem. Instead of focusing on the system or individual nation, the rivalry concept emphasizes the dyad. Conflict addiction studies have focused on correlating conflicts that occur within a short period of time, typically within one to five years of one another. Conflicts that occur in enduring rivalries do not necessarily occur on a regular basis, nor do the conflicts necessarily succeed each other in a rapid fashion, as most previous diffusion work has implicitly assumed. The rivalry framework is thus better able to reflect actual conflict patterns and to allow scholars to understand irregular, but interconnected, conflict over long periods of time.

We proposed that the rivalry approach generates a new perspective on international conflict. Our empirical analyses quite consistently showed that wars, disputes, and territorial changes occur disproportionately within medium- to long-term rivalry contexts. This provides prima facie evidence that we need to consider conflicts, not atomistically, but as part of a wider rivalry relationship. The next two chapters explore some of the theoretical and methodological implications of thinking about international conflict in terms of militarized rivalries. As we shall demonstrate, this involves significant theoretical and methodological challenges to standard ways of thinking about the causes of war.

CHAPTER 4

The Rivalry Approach to War and Peace

Rivalries are not merely a new topic of research—an extension of the logic behind studying "dangerous dyads" (Bremer 1992)—nor are they simply a useful research tool and case selection device. Part of what has hindered a clear understanding of the wide-ranging ramifications of the rivalry concept comes from an exclusive focus on enduring rivalries. This entire book, and this chapter in particular, argues that one must move beyond enduring rivalries as acute conflict phenomena and start thinking about war and peace in terms of rivalry.

The concept of a militarized relationship that begins with peace, ends with peace, and that exists over time has wide-ranging ramifications for the study of international conflict. This chapter examines some of the general theoretical and conceptual implications of the rivalry approach. We discuss why it constitutes a general framework for examining many issues and hypotheses in the international conflict literature. It is not just another hypothesis to be added to an already long list, but rather is more like Most and Starr's (1989) "opportunity and willingness" framework for the study of international conflict. We are able to demonstrate that the rivalry approach raises new questions, including new twists on old hypotheses, particularly about the relationship of war to peace. The rivalry approach also suggests some alterations in the typical methodologies used to test hypotheses about international conflict. The next chapter continues this theoretical discussion with an analysis of the implications of the rivalry approach for testing. We then apply the framework outlined here and the testing guidelines to the question of the democratic peace in chapter 6 as an illustration of our framework.

The "Causes of War" Approach

In proposing a rivalry approach to war and peace, we are explicitly presenting an alternative to standard practice in the study of international conflict. For comparison purposes, we have grouped standard quantitative and comparative case study research in this field under the label, "causes-of-war approach." Let us briefly introduce here what we mean by this phrase. The contrast between this approach to the study of war and the rivalry approach will be a consistent theme in the chapters to follow (as it already implicitly has been in preceding chapters).

In some sense, there is no one approach to the study of international conflict that all scholars adopt, and indeed most scholars do not explicitly accept or reject, much less discuss, many assumptions and procedures that they adopt in their analyses. Yet one can identify a core of purposes, assumptions, and ideas that a large portion of international conflict scholarship shares. Because they have been embedded so deeply in many research programs, they are accepted without reflection or adequate consideration for their implications. Every causes-of-war study does not exhibit the characteristics noted below (and even those that do may not manifest them fully), and therefore they are not all equally subject to the same criticisms. What we describe below are better understood as central tendencies, more applicable to the international conflict field as a whole than to its individual components. The literature surveys of Midlarsky (1989) and Geller and Singer (1998) illustrate the causes-of-war approach, at least with respect to behavioral studies. We propose that the characteristics of the approach we identify below are core ones and that they commonly fit the scholarship represented in these two works.

The first central feature of the causes-of-war approach is, as the name implies, its focus on the phenomenon to be explained: war. That is, standard approaches seek to understand why states go to war with one another. One can generally distinguish three "situations" within which a dyad or pair of states can find itself: (1) nonmilitarized conflict or nonconflict, (2) a militarized dispute or crisis, and (3) war. The situation of war or dispute usually forms the phenomenon to be explained, while the other level or levels below it become the control group. When focusing on war, many of these studies, especially studies from the Correlates of War Project in the last two decades, take militarized conflict as a given, and the focus is whether such conflict escalates to war or ends short of it. Thus, typically the object of study for these studies is a militarized dispute (Jones, Bremer, and Singer 1996) or an international crisis (Brecher 1993). Significant is what these studies are not interested in as a result of this focus. Most standard approaches are not particularly concerned with the origins of conflict—the conditions that gave rise to a dispute in the first place.

The second core characteristic of the causes-of-war approach is that all cases (control or not) are treated in a cross-sectional fashion. There is little concern for the potential interdependence of conflicts involving a given dyad (or across dyads). Concern for interdependence can take two general forms: (1) theoretical preoccupations that lead to the inclusion of explanatory variables in the model that reflect conflict interrelationships and (2) worries about statistical assumptions, for example, error term correlation. We address methodological issues in chapter 5, but we note here that virtually no study takes into account the possible, and probable, violation of statistical assumptions for disputes occurring within a given rivalry.

More important for our purposes in the chapter, as well as in general, are the theoretical concerns. At the heart of our project and the rivalry approach lies the claim that one cannot understand disputes, crises, and war without considering the rivalry context. The causes-of-war approach consistently looks at factors occurring at time $t - 1$ for disputes and wars occurring at time t: to predict the onset of war, these studies look at contemporaneous conditions (those at the time of the crisis or dispute, or immediately before those events). Quantitative studies have often been accused of being ahistorical. It is not exactly clear what that means (see Goertz 1994 for an extensive discussion), but it is certainly rare to find studies that include variables representing the history of the dyad (a notable exception is Huth's 1988 work on deterrence). There is no concern for path dependency or the process of international conflict. Previous disputes or interactions between the same states are not generally considered relevant to the behavior of states in the current crisis or dispute. The cross-sectional design also generally indicates that what occurs after the war (or the absence of escalation) is not of concern. All elements of "no war" are treated synonymously, and scholars generally do not investigate which mechanisms or conditions were responsible for successful conflict management, for example, versus continued high levels of hostility (albeit short of war). Furthermore, there is little concern with the relationship between the crisis or dispute participants after the war until the next crisis or dispute occurs.

In summary, the causes-of-war approach is typified by its focus on war or dispute as the phenomenon to be explained and by its cross-sectional methodological and ahistorical theoretical claims. Several theoretical and methodological consequences flow from these two core characteristics, many of which we explore in the chapters to come (most notably in this chapter and its successor). The rivalry approach takes a different route with regard to these two defining features of much of the conflict literature.

There are three general ways in which the rivalry approach focuses attention on issues normally beyond the horizon of the traditional international conflict literature, or what we have labeled the causes-of-war approach. The first of these is perhaps the most fundamental because it removes war from center stage. In virtually all analyses of conflict, war or dispute/crisis is the basic focus of the analysis. In the rivalry approach, the rivalry relationship takes over as the fundamental object of study. A rivalry relationship is a militarized competition between the same pair of states over a given period of time. With the rivalry approach, instead of trying to explain the causes of war, one tries to explain the causes of rivalry. Because the rivalry process does not end in war—although it may contain war—but finally ends in peace, the rivalry approach forces the researcher to consider issues of peace and conflict resolution as well. This shift in the basic phenomenon under analysis presents a whole new range of propositions and some variations on old ones, a few of which we present as illustrations in the next section.

The second important way that the rivalry approach shifts the focus of international conflict research is in its emphasis on the longitudinal and dynamic aspects of the rivalry relationship. The literature on international conflict is primarily static and cross-sectional, as exemplified by the work of the Correlates of War Project (two exceptions are Leng 1983 and Goldstein and Freeman 1991). Such work analyzes conflicts as if they were independent of one another, and generally without regard to the history or future prospects of the rivalry. Even dynamic, process-oriented hypotheses, such as those concerning power transitions and arms races, are empirically studied in a cross-sectional manner. Implicit in the longitudinal study of the United States and the USSR during the Cold War, for example, is a long-term conflictual relationship. The rivalry approach extends this understanding generally and considers all conflict as a part of some short- or long-term relationship. Instead of studying only long-term conflict relationships, such as enduring rivalries, the rivalry approach asks why some relationships become long term (or not) and why some include war (or not). With a longitudinal approach to conflict, for example, we can ask how changes in regime type influence the course of a rivalry. Does democratization of one or both rivals lead to the termination of the rivalry? (see chapter 6).

The third way that the rivalry approach reorients hypotheses about war is by altering the traditional approach of assuming rivalries as prerequisites in some hypotheses about war. Many models of international conflict, such as the power transition model or those related to deterrence, assume a context of hostility between two or more states. That assumption is traditionally translated into case selection rules. For example, one does not look at deterrence between all possible, or even all contiguous, dyads, but only those involved in conflictual relationships (and often just enduring rivalries; see the discussion in chapter 5). The rivalry approach suggests that characteristics of the conflictual relationship—the background context—should be directly incorporated into the theory. The rivalry approach moves rivalries out of the research design background and places them in the theoretical explanation.

In the next sections, we explore these three aspects of the rivalry approach, illustrating our points primarily by reference to the scholarly work on deterrence. We choose deterrence as our illustrative case not only because it has occupied center stage in international relations research over the past five decades, but also because some recent studies (e.g., Huth and Russett 1993; Lieberman 1995) have adopted enduring rivalries as a case selection device. Yet, they have not benefited from insights gained through the rivalry approach. Beyond considering deterrence studies, however, we use other examples drawn from neorealism, expected utility, liberalism, arms races, power transitions, diffusion, and long-cycles research in order to illustrate the broad applicability of the framework.

Changing the Object of Study: From War to Rivalry

As we noted above, perhaps the most fundamental shift that the rivalry approach imposes is the move from war to rivalry as the phenomenon under analysis. The resulting focus on rivalries has important consequences for what we study in international conflict.

Research using the traditional causes-of-war framework tries to explain war as the result of certain hypothesized causes such as military expenditure patterns or political regime types. Scholars in this tradition search for the presence of the hypothesized causes shortly before or coterminous with the outbreak of war in a set of war cases as well as in control groups in which no war occurs. Transferring these sorts of explanatory models into the rivalry framework leads us to look for the presence or occurrence of hypothesized events or conditions before the rivalry starts and just before it ends. The former could be called the "causes of rivalry" hypotheses and the latter could be called the "causes of peace" hypotheses. Although the causes-of-war literature provides many useful ideas for understanding the causes of rivalry, the causes of peace prove more problematic. The problem with peace is that it has been conceptualized as "not war" (this also led to Galtung's 1969 critique of standard approaches): how does one explain a nonevent? With rivalry as the unit of analysis, we have a potential event to analyze: the death of the rivalry. Although determining the termination date of a rivalry is not a trivial problem (see chapter 2), it is certainly not insoluble (see also Bennett 1993, 1996, 1997b, who codes end dates for enduring rivalries). Because of the temporal duration of a rivalry, we have two equally important questions: why rivalry starts and why it ends.

Explaining Rivalry

Many of the hypotheses about the causes of war are relevant to explaining the occurrence and severity of rivalries. For example, there has been a somewhat sterile debate in the literature over the past several decades about the relative war-proneness of bipolar and multipolar systems (beginning with Waltz 1964; and Deutsch and Singer 1964), which has produced few new insights about international conflict. By turning our attention away from war to rivalries, fresh questions can be addressed and some old controversies potentially settled. Do certain system structures produce more rivalries that are of greater severity (even short of war) and of longer duration? Multipolar systems and their alleged greater fluidity should produce shorter and more numerous rivalries, whereas bipolar systems should produce fewer and more enduring rivalries, according to the prevailing logics of each argument. If major-power war is generally avoided in a given system, does this beneficial effect also extend to conflict resolution between the major actors? How does system change affect the conduct of ongoing rivalries? Each of these questions has the potential to provide new insights into old debates as well as to offer some new bases for understanding the impact of system structure on state behavior. The research question shifts from using system structure to account for the "long peace" as a "no-war" situation to accounting for the number, duration, and severity of rivalries in different systems. War plays an important role in defining the severity of a rivalry and may well play a role in explaining its duration. Yet we have much more nuanced hypotheses as a result of using rivalry as the framework of analysis.

In the study of deterrence, the standard focus is on explaining its success or failure (i.e., was there war or not) in a single instance. More creatively, we can look at the impact that deterrence has on the conduct of rivalries, including the propensity for deterrence failure over time. By focusing on rivalries, we might also consider the relative mix of compellence and deterrence in rivalries. Deterrence analysts generally ignore compellence attempts, and it may be the case that such compellence actions may influence deterrence success and the dynamics of rivalry behavior. Another concern is how deterrence influences the development of rivalries. Does successful (or failed) deterrence keep a nascent rivalry from becoming enduring? Do certain patterns of deterrence promote the development of enduring competitions (as opposed to shorter and less severe rivalries, what we have termed isolated and proto-rivalries). These questions are strongly suggested by the rivalry framework and cannot be examined in the standard deterrence analysis that uses enduring rivalries only as a case selection device.

Some of the classic hypotheses about war also seem to be good candidates for the job of explaining rivalry. For example, the long-cycle and power transition theories suggest places to look for rivalries to arise. The long-cycle approach (Modelski 1987; Thompson 1988) suggests that conflict is virtually inevitable between nations at the top of the international hierarchy during periods of hegemonic decline and/or rise of challengers. The power transition hypothesis as originally proposed by Organski and Kugler (Organski 1958; Kugler and Organski 1989) required preexisting conflict (i.e., a rivalry) in order to predict a war outcome. The rivalry approach may help to sort out which power transitions will lead to war (e.g., France–Germany prior to 1870) and which will be completed peacefully (e.g., United States–Britain in the early twentieth century), by reference to certain processes or characteristics of those rivalries. As discussed below, this makes the theoretical components of the background rivalry condition an explicit part of the explanation. Also, we shall suggest below that many hypotheses fit better into the dynamics of an already existing rivalry. The power transition hypothesis of Organski and Kugler illustrates this with its requirement of preexisting conflict. With the rivalry approach, however, we can reformulate the question as one explicitly involving rivalries and in particular differentiate power transitions that take place within a rivalry from those that do not.

Explaining Peace

Changing the object of analysis expands the horizon of international conflict scholars. They become concerned with the outbreak of peace as well as war, with peace defined as the end of the rivalry relationship rather than simply the end or absence of war. Thus, those who adopt the rivalry approach are able to explore conflict management and resolution, and they do not lump all aspects of the absence of a shooting war together. International conflict scholars have long been criticized for their exclusive focus on war, with the accompanying ignorance of cooperative and lower-level conflictual relationships. The rivalry approach addresses this critique, in part, by putting conflict resolution (not just war termination) on the research agenda and by providing some concern for the stability of peace achievements (as the rivalry approach is also concerned with how rivalries begin). The traditional causes-of-war approach has difficulty dealing with the relationships of states between wars. The rivalry approach is better able to chart the ebbs and flows of the conflictual and cooperative relationships between states over time, rather than simply pinpointing occurrence of an extreme, but comparatively rare, event—war.

By considering peace as part of the research agenda, deterrence scholars can understand the role of deterrence in promoting conflict resolution instead of seeing only how war is avoided. Looking at rivalries as the objects of analysis allows scholars to consider the possibility that successful deterrence may actually prolong rivalries (George and Smoke 1989) and thereby inhibit conflict resolution. Understanding rivalry necessarily means understanding the origins and termination of those competitions, something deterrence studies ignore, as they take militarized conflict as a given in the study of two states. Yet one might think that if general deterrence is successful, then a given rivalry may never begin, or suddenly the need for immediate deterrence is past and the most dangerous part of a rivalry is effectively over. Looking only at militarized disputes in one kind of rivalry (enduring) leads scholars to ignore considerations such as these, which have important implications for understanding rivalries and deterrence alike.

The issue of the democratic peace revolves around the ability of democratic countries to manage their conflicts with each other. The causes-of-war approach has generally been concerned only with regime type and the occurrence of war or militarized disputes at specific points in time. Yet the beginning and particularly the end of rivalries do not necessarily coincide with a dispute or a war. This, combined with the empirical fact that regime type can change during the course of a rivalry, opens up a whole series of hypotheses regarding the democratic peace that can be studied by changing the basic theoretical orientation. One possibility is that the conflict patterns in a rivalry might not be disrupted when both rivals become democratic in the middle of the rivalry, suggesting a limitation on the democratic peace thesis. We address this possibility in our empirical analyses in chapter 6.

Although the use of rivalry as the basic conceptual framework cannot explain peace per se, it can be used to explain why peace breaks out between countries that might go to war. It can help explain an important class of situations of particular interest to peace researchers: the transition from a war-probable dyad to a war-improbable one. We find this integrative aspect of the rivalry approach attractive, in part because the literature on conflict management is diverse and lacks strong theoretical coherence. To be able to understand war and peace within one framework (if this is indeed possible) would be a major achievement.

From War Diffusion to Linking Rivalries

Another set of consequences resulting from the new object of analysis is a better understanding of the linkage between conflicts. Diffusion research has focused on how war begets war (Siverson and Starr 1991; Most, Starr, and Siverson 1989). Within the rivalry approach, this becomes much broader—we are concerned with how rivalries influence each other. The rivalry approach incorporates not only temporal dynamics, but spatial ones as well. For example, alliances are usually thought of as linking states, but for us alliances are just one of the elements that connect dyadic rivalries. An alliance can be a cause of a new rivalry or a consequence of the tighter linking of two existing rivalries. Thus, the rivalry approach can provide a more complex and, we believe, more accurate understanding of the effect of alliances on the spread of conflict (and vice versa). Results in chapter 12 indicate that rivalry linkage is an essential element in understanding the severity of conflict between rivals.

The rivalry approach further changes the orientation of traditional diffusion studies. One consequence of replacing war with rivalry in the diffusion framework is that war can arise without a previous war occurring as the initial cause. This is possible because we assume that the rivalry continues during times without active hostilities. Thus, there may be no war at time $t - 1$, but there still may be conflict diffusion at time t as long as there was a rivalry at $t - 1$. The rivalry approach is broader in that (1) it accounts for diffusion in the absence of war, and (2) it identifies diffusion involving lower levels of conflict than full-scale war.

Another consequence of the rivalry approach is to propose an explanation for the absence of war diffusion (or so-called negative diffusion). The attention and resources that must be devoted to an ongoing rivalry relationship may reduce the ability of individual rivals to engage in conflict with other adversaries. Rivalries (particularly enduring ones) may generate conflict locally (as suggested by the diffusion literature), but at the same time other disputes involving the same protagonists become less likely. Thus, the rivalry approach is more nuanced in that it offers an explanation for why some conflicts expand and why others are less likely to occur.

We suspect that one factor helping to create enduring rivalries is the linking together of dyadic rivalries, each reinforcing the other. One way to view the changes in alliance structure prior to World War I is as a progressive linking of rivalries into two blocks (Sabrosky 1975; Vasquez 1993). A large number of rivalries in the Cold War era appear related to each other; such patterns are evident in the Middle East, Southeast Asia, and South Asia.

Most standard studies of deterrence focus on dyadic relationships and have little concern with how success or failure of deterrence in one context influences deterrence in other relationships. The closest such studies come is with respect to a concern with reputation (see below), but deterrence theory generally lacks a framework to understand how deterrence relationships are interconnected, and the diffusion literature is largely inapplicable here. Looking at linked rivalries provides an explicit mechanism for understanding how the relationships are related as well as for assessing how the failure of deterrence in one instance may have a short-term or immediate effect on the viability of deterrence in a related context. There has been much written about extended deterrence, and the rivalry focus provides a framework for how the conduct of the United States–USSR superpower rivalry, for example, affected deterrence and the propensity for war in Europe and other proxy conflicts.

Linkage analysis may also be important for long-cycles research (Modelski 1987; Thompson 1988). For example, how does the involvement of a major power in a spatial or global structural rivalry affect the patterns of interaction in a simultaneous regional structural rivalry (Thompson 1995)? There may also be linkages between spatial rivalries involving small states and structural rivalries between the major powers. In order to understand minor-power rivalries, it may be necessary to consider structural rivalries, in which each major power provides arms and other assistance to a patron state in the spatial rivalries (Kinsella 1994b, 1995). It may also be that involvement in these minor-power rivalries overextends the system leader's capabilities and hastens its decline (Kennedy 1987). A focus on the interaction of rivalries at various levels would not only help us understand rivalries, but could also enrich long-cycles work and help to specify the processes of conflict interaction in each of the leadership phases postulated by that model.

If rivalries can be linked, they can also be "delinked." Delinkage is the process by which these rivalries become detached from each other. One way to view the history of Arab-Israeli relations is as an evolution of rivalries that progressively link or delink, and to varying degrees. Jordan was probably the first Arab country to delink (although not fully) after the 1967 war; Egypt delinked in 1979; and the Palestinians started the process in 1993, although events at the time of this writing suggest the process is far from complete and may be even stagnated. The United States–USSR rivalry starts to decline in severity in the mid-1960s, leading to detente in the 1970s (and this is consistent with most common perceptions). A common explanation gives pride of place to the conflict management lessons of the Cuban missile crisis, but we also note that at the same time the linkage between the United States–China and United States– USSR rivalries was dramatically loosening. As with all questions of rivalry and conflict management, these particular implications of the rivalry approach remain the least explored.

The dangerous dyad perspective on enduring rivalry privileges the temporal aspect of conflict relationships. While rivalry connects conflict over time, linkage connects rivalries over space. Just as rivalries ebb and flow as well as begin and end, so too can the degree of linkage vary from completely linked to completely unlinked. With the concept of rivalry linkage, the rivalry approach brings the spatial dimension of conflict into a unified framework of analysis.

Longitudinal and Dynamic Implications of the Rivalry Approach

Treating rivalry as the unit of analysis generates many new hypotheses and is particularly appropriate when trying to understand the initiation and termination of rivalries. Yet, the core of the rivalry approach also stresses the longitudinal and dynamic character of the rivalry relationship; it is an interaction that exists over time. Another whole series of questions thus arises about the dynamics of rivalries.

In many ways, developments in game theory over the last 10 to 15 years have pointed in the same direction. Much of the new research has involved repeated game play. Repeated or iterated games, sequential games, and the theory of moves (Brams 1993) all reflect that most interactions are not one-shot affairs. For example, when Powell (1989) examines the temporal sequence of equilibria in nuclear deterrence strategy, he is assuming some rivalry-like setting. How these new game theoretic techniques can inform the study of rivalry remains an open question. Maoz and Mor (1998) have used Brams's (1993) theory of moves to model the evolution of the Israel–Egypt and other rivalries.

Rivalry as the Expectation of Future Conflict

Many rational choice models focus on the impact of expectations about the future on choice. The relative importance of the shadow of the future is a key parameter in Axelrod's (1984) Prisoners' Dilemma analysis. We see certain kinds of expectations as central to understanding rivalries. An enduring rivalry is a hostile and competitive relationship in which each side views the other as posing a significant threat to its own interests. In such a relationship, rivals expect that disputes, crises, and even war will continue into the future. These expectations condition current foreign policy choices, which may then feed back to help cause future war (the positive feedback of an arms race model), or prevent it (the negative feedback of deterrence models). Static models based on national attributes or current conditions will not capture this long-range outlook. We argue later in the book that enduring rivalries have a peculiar stability, which is reinforced by the expectation of future conflict.

The study of immediate deterrence is inherently concerned with the present, but a concern with general deterrence implicitly indicates that future conflict is expected. The acquisition of alliances or enhancement of weapons capacity is generally done in order to meet future challenges, as such actions are generally not possible in the midst of a crisis, when immediate deterrence is the goal. By focusing on the expectation of future conflict in the rivalry approach, deterrence analysts could ascertain how that expectation conditions behavior as states seek both to prepare for future challenges and to establish or reinforce "reputation." Without consideration of the future, a state may appear to overreact to a contemporary crisis, unless one considers that the state is attempting to deter and gain an advantage in the long run. Short-term analyses of deterrence will misinterpret such actions.

A longitudinal analysis of power transitions might lead to the discovery of "preventive wars" (Levy 1987) launched by the status quo state in anticipation of the future loss of power. Thus, the rivalry approach has the potential to integrate both power transitions and preventive wars in the same process. Furthermore, the concern with the future may lead the status quo state to pursue a range of different options (beyond preventive war) to stave off the challenger (alliances, military buildup, arms control agreement) and preserve its advantage. If effective, these may be important reasons why no power transition occurs or why it occurs peacefully. In each case, such actions can be understood only by consideration of the future expectations of the parties.

The Push of the Past on Rivalries

If future expectations are significant in rivalries, one might ask where they come from. One obvious response is past interactions. Rivalries have a joint history in addition to a joint future. Rivalries can be both pulled by future expectations and pushed by the not-so-dead hand of the past. The United States has often referred to its "commitments" as a justification for its behavior. An alliance treaty is one type of commitment that may "constrain" states. Tit-for-tat and arms race models provide two examples in which current behavior is a function of past acts. Leng (1983) found a tendency toward escalatory tactics from one crisis to the next, but scholars have yet to explore whether the reverse de-escalatory process helps explain the end of rivalries.

The concept of "learning" has received a great deal of attention in recent years (see Levy 1994 for a review of this literature). Levy (1994) recommends that one examine learning in the context of one crisis. We suggest that learning models can neither be conceptualized nor studied except in a dynamic, longitudinal fashion. If a state has learned something, that learning will be evident on many future occasions. If such evidence is not forthcoming, doubt is cast on whether any learning took place. If it is a trial-and-error or search process, then we can only see that process over multiple trials. If one examines models of learning, all involve a process that takes place over time. Bayesian updating as a model of learning makes little sense in a one-shot situation. Bayesian techniques permit updating of current information based on past experience (Wagner 1989); the past plays a role because of imperfect information. For us, learning is an intervening variable mediating the impact of the past on the present. The rivalry approach provides a framework for examining different models of state learning. Particularly in enduring rivalries, governments make immense efforts to understand their rivals and expend great effort analyzing previous crises and wars.

The push of the past in rivalries is often not adequately considered in cross-sectional studies of deterrence. The most obvious way that the historical experience of the rivals comes into deterrence models is through the concept of reputation and credibility. The credibility of current deterrence threats depends (at least in part) on past behavior in the rivalry, which appears prima facie to be relevant, as well as on linked rivalry behavior. Although this has been the subject of some conceptual assessment, reputation has received relatively little attention in the quantitative literature on deterrence (Levy 1988). Even studies that do explicitly consider reputation "pay far less attention to the impact of the past on the way participants define their roles, the legitimacy of their purposes, and their strategies" (Lebow and Stein 1990, 356).

Part of the reason that deterrence studies downplayed the impact of the past is that they heretofore lacked a framework for addressing such concerns. The rivalry approach provides such a framework and permits empirical analysis. For example, Lebow (1981, 5) had as one of his three main interests "the relationship between crisis and underlying patterns of conflict," what we might term as prior interactions in the rivalry. He specifically asks, "In what ways do crises affect the long-term relations between protagonists? In what circumstances do they act to intensify or ameliorate the conflicts which they reflect?" (1981, 5). To answer such questions, one needs the longitudinal comparative case studies that are facilitated under the rivalry approach.

Preferences are part of all rational actor models. Normally, the origin of these preferences is not an issue (they are assumed to be exogenous to the model), and they are assumed to be constant. Yet one may legitimately ask why a state has the preferences it does, and one may reject the assumption that preferences are constant. Preferences are formed, in part, by the past interactions with a given state. It is likely that current preferences are partially affected by prior wars and hostile interactions (see Elster 1983 for a survey of theories of endogenous preference change). Loss of territory may create new preferences—to maintain the new status quo for the gaining side or to prompt the losing side to seek revenge. One notable outcome of World War II was to change Japan and Germany from enemies of the United States, Britain, and

France to close allies. If this is the case, it implies that preferences are not constant, as "previous experience" is constantly changing. Indeed, Maoz and Mor (1998) have found some preference change in their analysis of Middle East rivalries.

The relative weights of future expectations and past experience might vary over the course of the rivalry, although it may be hard to distinguish between the two because the strength of future expectations could depend, in large part, on the length of previous experience: the more entrenched the rivalry, the more firmly entrenched the expectations. One consequence of the rivalry approach is to inquire about the stability of preferences and the origin of expectations. We suggest that answering these questions will put international conflict in the context of a past and a future. Part of the key to understanding rivalry will be making the links between the two.

After War or Crisis, What?

As we have already discussed, the causes-of-war approach postulates a series of events or states of affairs occurring just before war as potential explanations of war. In the rivalry approach, war most often occurs somewhere in the middle of the rivalry. Hence, we are naturally concerned with what happened before the war in the rivalry, but just as often we are concerned with what happens after wars. In a symmetrical fashion, many of the phenomena that occur before a war can take place following it; that is, many of the causes of war can also be the effects of war. For example, does war result in a power transition? in an arms race? in a regime change?

One of key aspects of putting deterrence into the context of rivalries is that it permits us to ask what happens after deterrence. The standard approach is concerned with only the success or failure of deterrence at a given point in time. There is no real afterlife. Yet in most instances the *after* is also a *before,* thus opening up the question of how long a general deterrence strategy is successful. "The focus on immediate deterrence . . . is troublesome . . . because it can lead us to miss perhaps the most important feature of the last quarter century: the paucity of superpower crises" (Jervis 1989, 195), especially in that the Cuban missile crisis was the last such confrontation. The traditional approach stops with war and crisis, but rivalries end with peace and begin similarly, allowing the analyst to trace the end of competition and assess deterrence behavior well after the last crisis has occurred in the rivalry (which does not necessarily represent the last serious threat to peace). Huth (1988) has been criticized for exactly this point. Sagan (1991) argues that deterrence in one crisis might lead a potential aggressor never again to challenge the status quo. Quantitative analysis, he argues, therefore must look forward from the cases rather than just backward in understanding deterrence. The rivalry approach not only facilitates such an analysis, it all but demands that scholars not stop with the end of a particular discrete event of interest, be it war or crisis.

The Dynamics of Rivalry

A central focus of the rivalry approach is the dynamics of rivalries' evolution. Here we move away from juxtaposing the rivalry approach with important hypotheses in the war literature. Although the causes-of-war literature can provide us with many suggestive ideas, it cannot address the evolution of conflictual relationships. The dynamics of rivalry are certainly related to the dynamics of other phenomena. Most of the dynamic hypotheses in the war literature involve escalatory processes, but rivalries escalate and de-escalate; periods of calm are punctuated by the storms that occasionally shake the relationship. We need theories that relate periods of calm to periods of crisis. We need to know if and when crises, disputes, and wars affect the basic parameters of the relationship and when they do not. These questions make sense only within the rivalry approach. For example, if in rivalries we find that periods of calm are associated with democratic regimes (or democratization) and periods of greater conflict with nondemocratic regimes, then we have direct evidence for the democratic peace hypothesis.

One general way to pose the process question is to ask about patterns of rivalry development. Leng's (1993) conclusions about learning imply a certain pattern to crisis behavior over time. Does one often find that kind of escalatory pattern with enduring rivalries? Does one often find a similar de-escalatory pattern? Can one detect a secular trend in the severity of the rivalry relationship? (We address these questions in chapter 9.) Leng (1993) classified bargaining strategies into four types based on the analysis of crisis behavior. Could one do the same on the larger scale of enduring rivalries?

Most of the process theories in international relations tend to describe such processes before war, but few connect wars and disputes with each other. The rivalry approach poses a new set of problems and provides ground for new theorizing about international conflict. One test of a theoretical framework is how many answers it can provide. But another test is how many interesting new questions it raises. Above, we argued that the new question "Why rivalry?" can replace "Why war?" In this section, we face the fundamental question of explaining how crises, disputes, and wars interact in the dynamics of the rivalry relationship.

Rivalry as a Contextual Factor

Until recently, the primary use of enduring rivalry has been as a case selection device. Most of the studies that have used enduring rivalries in such a fashion have in effect argued that a given relationship (e.g., between arms races and war—Diehl 1985a) or process (e.g., between power transition and war—Wayman 1982) occurs only when there is some preexisting conflict relationship. Huth, Bennett, and Gelpi illustrate this case selection usage: "the concept of a Great Power rivalry is critical because it identifies the population of cases to be used for testing the model's propositions" (1992, 483). (This point is discussed in more detail in the next chapter.) We suggest that this is a crude way of linking rivalries to phenomena such as deterrence. What these authors are doing is making a theoretical claim about situations in which deterrent threats, for example, are likely to be made; the variables in their models then try to explain why such threats work or not. We suggest that these are related concerns and should be addressed together in the theory, and not relegated to simple research design questions.

As we saw above, some important hypotheses in the causes-of-war framework suggest parallel hypotheses for explaining the origins of rivalries, and in particular enduring rivalries. Neorealist structural theories and long-cycles hypotheses are prime candidates for understanding how rivalries between major powers occur and how they affect minor-power rivalries. Other hypotheses, in contrast, seem to fit better within the dynamics of an already existing rivalry. For example, the idea of an arms race presupposes some conflictual relationships, as Richardson (1960) argues. Deterrence is another example of a concept that seems to presuppose a rivalry relationship. Deterrent threats are not usually made against a generic foe, but rather against a clearly defined adversary. Some hypotheses seem to function in both roles, as explanations of rivalries but at the same time important in the internal dynamics of rivalry. The power transition model fits these criteria. One can see power transitions as giving rise to rivalries, as suggested here, or one can assume a rivalry background, as do Kugler and Organski (1989).

In the arms race literature, formal models of arms race processes assume an underlying potential conflict. The positive feedback model, whereby one side's arms expenditures influence those of the other, does not make sense outside of a context marked by basic hostility. This becomes more clear in the empirical literature on arms races. In particular, how does one decide who is racing against whom? A given country's arms acquisitions could be driven by the behavior of a large number of potential adversaries. Such issues these are often ignored or sidestepped with the assumption that arms increases are primarily directed against one opponent (with the other enemies ignored) (Smith 1980). These rather ad hoc methods can be replaced by the rivalry concept.

The logical next step is to include rivalry characteristics in the theoretical framework itself. First of all, this means abandoning the notion that there is necessarily a radical break between enduring and lower-level rivalries. It also means that the characteristics of the rivalry relationship are thought to influence the process under scrutiny, whether it be deterrence or the escalation of arms races to war. This prompts the scholar to identify those characteristics rather than to leave them broadly subsumed under the surrogate rivalry relationship variable.

Perhaps an appropriate way to theorize about how the rivalry context may affect deterrent threats is to see the effectiveness of the deterrence variables, for example, as changing according to the underlying rivalry relationship. As we have seen, however, rivalry is really a continuous variable, and we may wish to include multiple rivalry characteristics in the model. For example, credibility may be less effective in a short-term rivalry or an early stage of an enduring rivalry, as rivals have had little opportunity to build reputation. These types of models are called "contextual" (there is a large literature on contextual models in American politics; for applications to international relations, see Goertz 1994).

A third alternative is to see the rivalry context as the cause of the phenomenon, such as an arms race. Here the arms race "intervenes" between the rivalry relationship and war (Diehl and Crescenzi 1998). In Richardson's (1960) model, each nation's arms expenditures are driven by two causal variables: the other side's expenditures and the "grievance" held by each side. This grievance term influences arms expenditures, which then may cause a war. Thus, the rivalry as a background factor can enter many ways (our list is certainly not complete) into a better understanding of how certain phenomena like arms races are linked to war.

Several contextual variables might be incorporated in analyses of deterrence, arms races, and power transitions. A critical assumption of all those analyses is that the states in question view each other as the primary (in some cases the exclusive) security threat. This can be tested by incorporating the degree of concentration or interaction (vis-à-vis all other states) between the rivals. This, in turn, could affect the arms race levels, as Goldstein and Freeman (1991) have demonstrated in the triangular relations among the United States, the Soviet Union, and China. The salience of competing claims between the two sides may also influence the propensity for deterrent attempts to be successful or for power transitions to spawn conflict. This can be incorporated into the model explicitly rather than assuming that all cases are equally salient or picking only cases that seem to meet some unspecified threshold.

Specifically, one might want to model previous outcomes of disputes or deterrent attempts in analyses of deterrence. The availability of substitutes (e.g., alliances) for arms races might be essential in tests of that phenomenon's relationship to war. The degree of hostility or common interests between two states has already been intimated as a key concern in determining which rivals in a power transition will go to war and which will experience a transition peacefully. Merely using enduring rivalries as a case selection method sweeps these theoretical concerns under the rug and may ignore the variations that exist even among enduring rivalries. The rivalry approach forces the scholar to deal with these concerns theoretically and subjects many of the assumptions to empirical tests.

Conclusion

Rivalries are crucial contexts for the understanding of crisis behavior. In addition, crises and wars define a rivalry and in an important sense keep it alive. The rivalry approach suggests that understanding crisis and war requires that these events be put into some larger context. This aspect of rivalry is perhaps more fundamental than issues of power transition, arms races, and deterrence. Rivalries can exist without an arms race, or a power transition, but they cannot exist without crises or disputes. If we exclude the possibly dubious category of long-term latent conflict, our conceptualization of a rivalry centers around the occurrence of crises and disputes that involve militarized moves, and the eventual possibility of war.

Over the past decade we have seen studies of enduring rivalries and such topics as power transition, deterrence, and the democratic peace (e.g., Geller 1993; Lieberman 1995). One might suspect that enduring rivalries are a new way to prolong the life of a few old warhorse hypotheses. We have argued that far from being a new test for old hypotheses, rivalries provide new ways to think about issues of war and peace: it is because the rivalry approach is so valuable that it is natural to use it to examine deterrence, arms races, and the like.

Most of the studies that use rivalries to test a hypothesis use *enduring* rivalries. But if one examines the theory involved, for example, deterrence, nothing in the theory restricts its application to the enduring rivalries subset of all rivalries. Using that subset of rivalries is not required by the theory, but also produces unnecessary sampling bias. There are perhaps good reasons why deterrence may work differently in enduring rivalries, but of course one cannot know this without a comparison group.

We have argued that the first step in putting rivalry at the core of theoretical concerns lies in using it as the object of study. We can then ask new questions, for example, why some rivalries have more deterrence failures than others. If one takes the usual war/dispute/crisis as the object of analysis, this question never gets posed (e.g., Huth and Russett 1993). Because all rivalries eventually end, we can ask about the impact of deterrence strategies, success, and failure on the duration and termination of rivalries. Does successful deterrence prolong the rivalry relationship, as some have suggested (George and Smoke 1989)? As most research stops its analysis with crisis or war, it never poses the question about deterrence and conflict termination.

Key to the whole rivalry approach is that rivalries exist over time. The concept of a rivalry emphasizes the longitudinal aspect of conflict relations, in contrast with the cross-sectional character of most comparative case study and quantitative work. The rivalry approach provides a natural framework for investigating theories with longitudinal or dynamic components. For example, the concept of reputation plays a key role in the deterrence debate. To say that reputation matters means that behavior in the current conflict is influenced by behavior in the previous one. Lieberman (1995) argues that the actual carrying out of deterrence threats (i.e., war) is crucial for the deterrent threat to be credible in the next round. Rivalries provide him with framework within which to examine that hypothesis.

Rivalries can also fill in key gaps in theory construction. For example, Lebow (1981, 337) begins his model of crisis behavior with a concept labeled "underlying hostility," which has an arrow leading to crisis and eventually war. There is also a feedback arrow from crisis back to "underlying hostility." "Underlying hostility" is, of course, a rivalry. The feedback arrow gives a model of how a rivalry is maintained. With the rivalry approach, we can complete his model by including the beginnings and endings of rivalries. Lebow suggests that crises are embedded in the context of a rivalry relationship. This is true of many phenomena that interest scholars of international conflict, such as arms races, deterrence, and regime type. We have argued that explicitly including rivalry in the model can have important theoretical payoffs.

In this chapter, we have discussed the conceptual and theoretical implications of adopting the rivalry approach to war and peace. We believe that adoption of this orientation provides new insights into the way that we think about international conflict and offers some new ways to address long-standing controversies in the field. Yet along with the theoretical alterations that accompany the rivalry approach, there are also methodological ones. In the next chapter, we look at the implications for testing hypotheses that follow from many of the theoretical concerns noted here.

CHAPTER 5

Rivalries as a Testing Methodology

The previous chapter showed that the rivalry approach gives us a new perspective on war and conflict. Yet the rivalry approach does not merely require new ways of theorizing about the traditional foci of studies of international conflict. Such changes must be accompanied by new ways of testing hypotheses. This means alterations in the research design and methodologies employed in the traditional causes-of-war literature. These new tests often have significant advantages vis-à-vis previous methodologies. In this chapter, we illustrate how the rivalry approach transforms standard testing procedures. The rivalry approach provides new means to investigate classic hypotheses, often addressing weaknesses in standard methodologies.

Our critique and reformulation of existing methodologies addresses itself not only to large-N statistical studies, but encompasses comparative case study techniques as well. Though much separates the large-N from the small-N researcher, from our perspective, the commonalties dominate: both are cross-sectional and use the dispute, crisis, or war as the object of study. These two elements characterize most of the causes-of-war literature. The rivalry approach alters these two traditional testing features, as well as transforming the previous, limited attempts to incorporate rivalries in the research design. The rivalry approach does utilize cross-sectional analyses, but it is the rivalry, not the dispute, that is the cross-sectional unit. Furthermore, we shall see that other cross-sectional units can be created. We argue that testing techniques based on rivalries serve to replace or supplement the dispute or dyad-year as the unit of analysis.

Rivalries also fundamentally involve time. In the temporal dimension of a rivalry lies fertile new ground for hypothesis testing. This proves crucial in defining new—and often better—control groups. The causes-of-war literature looks at wars compared to nonwar disputes. Using rivalries, we can compare war with nonwar periods *within* a rivalry; hence by definition we control for many possibly confounding variables. These and related concerns are addressed in the section below that emphasizes testing implications that flow from longitudinal aspects of rivalries.

Creating new tests also means creating new dependent variables that the theory or model in question implies. For example, the democratic peace literature revolves around the proposition that democracies do not fight wars, but it implies other propositions as well. If a rivalry changes from a nondemocratic to democratic dyad, then the democratic peace hypothesis suggests that the rivalry will end. In short, the rivalry approach increases significantly the means for testing empirically a theory or model.

As we noted in the last chapter, changing the focus of analysis to rivalry results in some fundamental shifts in the way we think about traditional questions about war and peace. Yet it also means that we conduct research differently than in the past. These changes go beyond using rivalries only as a case selection device, replacing disputes or crises as the objects of study. As we discuss in the next section, some of the early work on rivalries has moved beyond the traditional causes-of-war framework, but has not truly adopted the rivalry approach in all its manifestations. Thus, beyond reviewing those efforts, we also address here the testing implications of moving beyond rivalries as a simple device to select a population of cases for study.

We begin by reviewing the history of rivalry use in international conflict research as a prelude to our discussion of how the rivalry approach extends, and we believe improves, these limited efforts. We then consider the changes brought by the rivalry approach to testing methodology, organized under three of the concerns previously mentioned: case selection, cross-sectional analysis, and longitudinal analysis. We again use deterrence analyses as our primary example (although we also occasionally make reference to the democratic peace, the subject of our empirical application in the next chapter), as deterrence hypotheses have proven difficult to test using standard research designs (see Harvey 1998).

The History of Rivalries and Testing

In the early 1980s, the concept of rivalry, specifically enduring rivalry, was introduced as a part of the testing of some hypotheses about international conflict (the first to do this, to the best of our knowledge was Wayman 1982).[1] As we noted in the previous chapter, rivalries were not necessarily an explicit part of the theorizing in those tests; they served as background conditions to select cases for testing. The studies using rivalries shared a number of characteristics in the early period.

---

[1] Rivalries appear relatively early in the international conflict literature, but much of that early work is not interested in rivalries in general, but rather one specific rivalry, for example the U.S.-Soviet or Arab-Israeli rivalries. That is, the concept of rivalry did not play any role in the research design or testing elements of the research of what were essentially descriptive case studies.

First, the focus was almost entirely on *enduring* rivalries, not the broader continuum of rivalries.[2] Second, despite the use of rivalries to select cases, virtually all these studies employed cross-sectional designs and thereby largely ignored the longitudinal elements of conflict relations that are the centerpieces of the rivalry concept. Typically after choosing a set of rivalry cases, scholars still employed disputes, wars, dyad-years, and other traditional units of analysis in conducting their analyses. Third, most of these studies made the implicit assumption that state behavior in enduring rivalries is different from that in other contexts. We have shown in chapter 3 that this is largely true, but our conclusions are limited to certain specific characteristics and are empirically derived. Studies that used enduring rivalries as a case selection device made this assumption with respect to their phenomenon of interest (e.g., arms races, deterrence) and did so without apparent empirical support (although there may have been some theoretical reasons to suspect so). Fourth, all of the studies saw some things in enduring rivalries and their characteristics that were essential for the phenomenon under study to occur. These characteristics were assumed to be constant and unique to enduring rivalries. They served only as justification in case selection and thereby the focus on enduring rivalries. Finally, these sets of studies were not generally concerned with rivalries per se, be it their origins, dynamics, or termination (subjects that are addressed in the second part of this book). Neither were these studies influenced by new questions or insights of the rivalry approach, as illustrated in the last chapter. Rather, they distinctly were testing classic hypotheses within the causes-of-war framework, but applied to a new set of cases.

Enduring rivalries as a background condition have appeared in a number of theoretical contexts. The most obvious use of enduring rivalries as a background condition is in the study of power transitions (Wayman 1982; Geller 1993; Wayman 1996). Power transition theory (Organski 1958; Organski and Kugler 1980; Kugler and Lemke 1996) posits that war will occur when a challenging state approaches and then surpasses a formerly dominant state. This implies that some kind of competition exists between the states, and, unlike many other international conflict models, there is a dynamic element to this approach. The focus on enduring rivalries performs several functions. First, the existence of an enduring rivalry indicates some long-standing competition between two states and establishes that war is an ongoing threat (rather than a hypothetical, perhaps low, possibility). Studying dyads other than enduring rivals might be open to the criticism that the states involved were not directly attuned to the actions of the other state or that the other state was not its primary rival. Enduring rivalries also present the dynamic and longitudinal feature that is implicit in the power transition model, although in practice, many analyses

---

[2]Yet using today's standards of operational measures, what many of these studies were actually studying was lesser as well as longer and more severe rivalries; they often used two- or three-dispute minima to signify the existence of enduring rivalries. In effect, many of these studies were considering, in our language, proto- *and* enduring rivalries.

of power transition still ignore this element and adopt a static cross-sectional design.

A second, and similar, use of enduring rivalries selects cases in the study of arms races and war (Diehl 1985a; Diehl 1985b; Diehl and Kingston 1987; Diehl and Crescenzi 1998). Arms races are a highly probable manifestation of rivalries because the building up of weapons and military capability is likely to be part of the rivalry competition, as are war and other phenomena (see Goertz and Diehl 1993 for a comparison of the rivalry and arms race concepts). Implicitly then, enduring rivalries indicate the proper context for an arms race to occur, and indeed it may not be possible for a true arms race to occur outside of one; by definition, an arms race is a militarized relationship. As a case selection device, looking at enduring rivalries provides some assurance that new weapons acquisition is directed at a specific opponent and that such increases are viewed as threatening. We know that enduring rivalries indicate the ongoing threat of war between two states, and arming decisions might be a result of that expectation of future conflict. Looking at cases other than enduring rivalries might not reveal true arms races, but mutual military buildups by two states that are not directed exclusively or primarily at each other, but rather against third parties. In those instances, inferences about the alleged effects of those buildups on conflict behavior would be misguided.

Similar to the studies of arms races and war, analyses of the substitutability of alliances and arms races also rely on enduring rivalries to identify the context under which such a phenomenon is likely (Sorokin 1994; Diehl 1994b). The substitution effect requires first an ongoing security threat that presents states with choices on how to respond, of which arming and forming alliances are prominent options. Again, the pull of the future (future threats) is a significant part of the calculation. States are not capable of arming rapidly in order to meet immediate threats, and many alliances cannot be negotiated and executed that quickly. Enduring rivalries present the ongoing security threat and future conflict expectations in which state security choices can be observed. Enduring rivalries have long lives, and thus scholars can observe trade-offs between arms races and alliances over time, especially as the formation of the latter is not common on a year-to-year basis. Enduring rivalries have also been used to study the impact of system-level variables on conflict behavior (Huth, Gelpi, and Bennett 1992) and to test the robustness of the democratic peace (Maoz 1997), the latter of which we ourselves address in the next chapter.

As we illustrate in more detail in the following sections, deterrence studies are also a popular venue for the use of enduring rivalries in case selection. Scholars must identify instances in which deterrence is even being attempted and therefore they must demonstrate that the relevant parties regard each other as serious security threats and that there is some significant probability that one or both sides will use military force against the other. Enduring rivalries are the context under which these conditions are fulfilled (Huth and Russett 1993;

Lieberman 1994, 1995); in another population of cases, one might be unsure of whether any deterrent threats are conceivable or likely. Thus, the past of a rivalry establishes the bases under which threats and reputational elements are developed. The expectation of the future conflict, provided by rivalries, is the central part of deterrence; deterrence, at least of a general variety, is inherently future oriented. We develop more of these applications below.

Table 5.1 summarizes the different foci for which rivalries have been used in the research design. The common ground lies in that they assume some conflict context that is represented by enduring rivalries. The use of rivalries as a background condition and a case selection device is an improvement in many instances over the past testing designs that considered all possible or all contiguous dyads. Indeed, most models or theories that assume preexisting conflict could be tested using rivalries. In that sense, the use of the rivalry concept has improved the validity of the findings on important subjects such as alliances and arms races as well as deterrence and power transition. One need but compare Russett 1963, Huth and Russett 1984, and Huth and Russett 1993 to see the evolution in case selection. We see this as a positive trend. Nevertheless, we regard such efforts as incomplete and not fully reflective of the insights that can be gained from the rivalry approach. In the following sections, we demonstrate how rivalries can be incorporated into research designs beyond their use in case selection. Yet we begin with an analysis of case selection and show that the rivalry approach involves more than a specification of a population of cases.

Case Selection

In moving from theory to empirical testing, one inevitably confronts the problem: what cases are appropriate for an empirical test? On the one hand, the theory or the hypothesis itself should define the limits and the universe to which it applies. In practice, a large region of indeterminacy surrounds most case selection. The deterrence literature illustrates the controversy that case selection can provoke, notably when cases are "selected on the dependent variable." Many studies only look at deterrence failures, much as many other studies of international conflict select cases based on the occurrence of wars, crises, or militarized disputes. This relates fundamentally to the general problem of what should be the control group in the analysis. The generic situation may be termed the "dog that doesn't bark" problem, and it occurs frequently in conflict research. The temptation is to select the cases where the dog barks (Achen and Snidal 1989; Most and Starr 1989). As with the democratic peace, we need a control group of nonconflict dyads. Yet it is not obvious which "nonbarking dogs" we should use. In the worst-case scenario, selecting only on the occurrence of the dependent variable, there is no control group at all. We shall return to this general problem of defining the comparison group at various points because it lies at the heart of testing problems, and it shows the value of the rivalry approach in helping resolve those problems.

TABLE 5.1: The History of Rivalry Testing

Author	Question	Population
Wayman 1982	Does a shift in relative power produce war?	Major power rivalries, 1816–1976
Diehl 1985a	Do arms races increase chances for war?	Twenty-two major-power enduring rivalries, 1816–1980
Huth, Bennett, and Gelpi 1992	How does interaction between system structure and leaders' risk propensity affect initiation of militarized interstate disputes?	Eighteen great power rivalries, 1816–1975
Geller 1993	What is the effect of static and dynamic power differentials on the conflict patterns of dispute-prone dyads?	Thirty-two enduring rivalries, 1816–1986
Huth and Russett 1993	Under which circumstances are challengers likely to initiate militarized disputes?	Fourteen enduring rivalries, 1948–82
Diehl 1994b	Under what conditions and to what extent do alliances substitute for or complement military buildups?	Twenty-two major-power enduring rivalries, 1816–1976
Kinsella 1994a	What is the impact of superpower arms transfers on enduring Third World rivalries?	U.S. and Soviet arms transfers into Middle Eastern and Persian Gulf enduring rivalries, 1949–88
Lieberman 1994	Do deterrence successes rarely occur and do leaders challenge deterrence, despite credible threats, due to political vulnerabilities?	Israel–Egypt enduring rivalry, 1948–77
Sorokin 1994	What mix of arms and alliances does a state choose to maximize its security?	Austria-Hungary (1880–1913), France (1880–1913), Israel (1963–88), Syria (1963–88), and their allies and enduring rivals
Kinsella 1995	What is the impact of an arms transfer link between superpower and regional rivalries?	U.S. and Soviet arms transfers into Middle Eastern, Persian Gulf, South Asian, and the Horn of Africa rivalries, 1950–90
Lieberman 1995	Does deterrence work and, if so, what makes it work?	Egypt–Israel enduring rivalry, 1948–73
Maoz 1997	Do realist and cultural critiques undermine the empirical validity of the democratic peace proposition?	Different samples, one of which is 15,805 enduring dyad-years, 1816–1986
Diehl and Crescenzi 1998	Is the arms race–war connection meaningful or spurious?	Sixty-three enduring rivalries, 1816–1992

Achen and Snidal (1989) critique a number of scholars for selecting on the dependent variable, that is, not providing a control group of deterrence success. We propose that the rivalry approach provides a solution for which Achen and Snidal were looking. Given the amount of scholarly attention that has been devoted to this issue, we regard this as a nontrivial claim. Huth and Russett's (1993) use of enduring rivalry is on the right track, but remains rooted in the basic cross-sectional causes-of-war methodological framework.

Disputes and crises provide the immediate context for most discussions of deterrence success.[3] Although the distinction between general and immediate deterrence seems widely accepted, most studies choose deterrence in crisis situations as their focus, and thereby focus on the latter form of deterrence. For Huth and Russett (1984), as well as others, immediate deterrence arises *once a crisis or dispute is under way.* Scholars disagree about which crises should be included as deterrence cases (see Lebow and Stein 1990 and the Huth and Russett 1990 response), but they agree that immediate deterrence, by definition, takes place in a crisis context. All sample from the universe of crises and disputes; for example, Huth and Russett depend heavily on Correlates of War Project data sets. Similar problems arise in the much of the arms race–war literature (Wallace 1979; Diehl 1985a; Sample 1997) in which scholars study only the impact of arms on dispute escalation; that is, they study only cases in which militarized conflict has already occurred. Thus, circumstances in which arms races inhibit or deter conflict are ignored, and therefore scholars begin with biased sample of cases (Diehl and Crescenzi 1998).

Because Achen and Snidal have been at the center of this debate, we may ask how they conceive of the universe of deterrence cases. A consistent theme in their discussion is that one tests deterrence in situations in which there already exists a hostile relationship: "Suppose that there are 100 countries in the world, each of them in a deterrence relationship [!] with an average of 5 of the others. Thus, each year there are 250 war-prone dyads ... Presumably the relevant population [for studying deterrence] for any time period consists of those states that have a 'serious' dispute with another state, where 'serious' is defined by the potential for war ... pacific intentions are easily confused with successful deterrence, and vice versa. Rational deterrence theory does contain some minimal psychological content: for example the initiator must realize that the defender exists and threatens to defend" (1989, 161–64). In rivalry terms, general deterrence becomes relevant most clearly *after* the hostile relationship is under-way; deterrence theory not does relate to the birth of rivalries, but is more concerned with their maturity, that is, with youth through old age. Within rivalries, "pacific intentions" are usually assumed by both sides not to exist. Achen and Snidal's hypothetical cases do not include the U.S.-Canadian or the Dutch-Belgian ones, as they include cases in which there was already a hostile

---

[3] We use deterrence success and nonfailure as synonyms. From the absence of a challenge, one cannot necessarily conclude that the deterrent threat is the explanation.

relationship. Within the rivalry literature, the existence of militarized disputes has been taken as the behavioral indication that such hostile relationships exist. The concept of rivalry based on dispute incidence assumes that hostile relations continue between dispute outbreaks (something that may not always be true) and hence justifies considering all these disputes as part of the same rivalry.

Scholars can use the temporal duration of rivalries in addition to this pre-existing conflict requirement of deterrence to choose cases for testing general deterrence. The beginning of a rivalry becomes the case selection device: in concrete terms this could be, perhaps, the first one or two militarized disputes.[4] The first dispute or two serves to ascertain the existence of "underlying hostility" (to use Lebow's 1981 expression), the existence of general deterrence relationship. We take this as an indication that states have entered into a potential deterrence relationship. Indeed this is consistent with our notion of a quick "lock-in" to the rivalry relationship, discussed in the second half of the book. States realize that they are in it for the long haul only after a couple of crises or wars. The U.S. developed its deterrence strategy vis-à-vis the USSR after the crises of the mid-1940s. In deterrence terms, general deterrence strategies are put into place after some immediate deterrence failures (or successes). The population for testing is the rest of the rivalry life-cycle until the underlying hostility is gone (i.e., peace). We thus have a set of rivalries and dyad-years in which to study deterrence. Some of these rivalries will have no further disputes, whereas others will go on to become enduring rivalries with multiple crises and wars. We do not claim that such a population covers all deterrence relationships, but it does include hundreds of rivalries and thousands of years.

One can see this proposal as a continuation of the research direction taken by Huth and Russett (1993). They argued that enduring rivalries provide a suitable framework within which one can study general deterrence and solve the control group problem. Failure of immediate deterrence in a crisis results in serious military conflict or war. Failure of general deterrence thus becomes dispute or crisis initiation. The standard problem with studying general deterrence lies in determining the control group of deterrence success. The use of enduring rivalries permits this to be defined as nondispute years in the rivalry. The rivalry is assumed to continue in the interdispute periods, providing a control group of general deterrence nonfailures. Huth and Russett do not move beyond this case selection use of rivalries. Yet it is useful to step back and ask: on which populations should one test general deterrence? The main differences between the approach of Huth and Russett and ours are in that according to the latter (1) one excludes the rivalry formation disputes/years from the analysis, that is, those years during which the deterrence relationship is being set up, and (2) one uses not just enduring rivalries, but all "deterrence relationships" (which would

---

[4]There are other possible indicators that could indicate a rivalry has begun: alliance treaties, lower-level hostility, military planning data, et cetera. Unfortunately, the rivalry literature has relied on disputes, and thus we continue with this particular approach.

include some rivalries that do not become enduring because deterrence is successful in eliminating or minimizing militarized conflict in the relationship).

Standard methodology only looks backward at events before war, but studying deterrence involves looking at events after crises as well. This is crucial in testing deterrence theory. "He [Huth 1988] does not consider the possibility that a policy of unyielding firmness in one crisis might also lead a potential aggressor never again to challenge the status quo.... Statistical work would have to look *forward* from the cases, that is, analyzing future behavior, rather than just *backward,* that is assessing past behavior. Do states that practice conciliatory or bullying behavior get involved in fewer cases with the same adversaries in the future?" (Sagan 1991, 84). Huth and Russett respond to this criticism by including dyad-years until the end of the rivalry: "We begin a rivalry with the first publicly expressed claim of one government to the territory of the other and end it only when a formal agreement resolving competing claims is implemented[,] that is, when both parties accept it" (1993, 63). Rivalries end when they move out of the "war-prone" category, into what we have called "peace." This usually happens sometime after the last dispute/war. Excluding these postcrisis, prepeace periods constitutes a serious selection bias.

Using rivalries to select cases in the manner outlined above identifies dyads that fit the "war-proneness" criteria that Achen and Snidal (1989) require much better other procedures that they (briefly) suggested. Other typical procedures, such as territorial contiguity (used to define "politically relevant" dyads), have a majority of unsuitable cases (as Lebow and Stein 1990 are quick to point out), because most contiguous dyads have peaceful relations. Selection bias most obviously may enter in through the initial disputes and wars that are used to select rivalries (when the deterrence relationship is being established), but which are then eliminated from actual testing.[5]

To see the grasp that the cross-sectional approach has on the comparative case study methodology, we look to studies that explicitly compare the same dyad over time. Lieberman's (1994) study of the Arab-Israeli rivalry points in the right direction from a rivalry perspective: one needs longitudinal comparative case studies (Hybel 1990 and Hopf 1994 provide two examples of a comparative, longitudinal case study). The parallel with quantitative studies is striking—in both cases the cross-sectional approach is hegemonic. The point to recall here, underappreciated in the deterrence literature, is the assumption that states are already in a hostile relationship. Deterrence theory does not address why state A and state B get into a situation in which each needs to deter the other. This is not something specific to rational deterrence theory. If one

---

[5] In our analysis of enduring rivalries, we argue that the beginning of an enduring rivalry is when states lock-in to the rivalry. Testing deterrence during this period thus may lead to misleading conclusions about deterrence in an ongoing rivalry.

examines Lebow's model of crisis (1981, 337), one sees that it starts with "underlying hostility." The concept of a rivalry provides a natural way of testing hypotheses that make preexisting conflict assumptions.

Achen and Snidal (1989) criticize much of the deterrence literature for its failure to choose an appropriate control group—or any control group at all. They focused their attacks on comparative case studies of deterrence. But they do not provide a viable proposal about how to solve the problem, as their solutions focus more on large-N studies. The rivalry approach steps in to give some concrete suggestions. Huth and Russett (1993) illustrate how this works; we have just extended and developed the logic inherent in their research design. Central to Lieberman's (1995) argument is that deterrence was successful in some of the interwar years in the Egyptian-Israeli rivalry. Fundamentally his project involves comparing deterrence failures (i.e., wars) with deterrence success (i.e., nonwar periods). Thus, even within single-case studies, the rivalry approach can provide a control group without adding additional cases for comparison.

As we noted in the previous chapter, using rivalries as a case selection device should not be a substitute for theorizing; rivalry characteristics should be incorporated into the model rather than buried under case selection. We have made this case theoretically; now let us illustrate the methodological implications. These considerations go beyond selecting a suitable population or ensuring a proper control group, worthy goals in and of themselves. Implicitly, the case selection mechanism implies a necessary condition relationship: the rivalry is a necessary condition for the relationship or process. For example, some underlying conflict is necessary for an arms race to lead to war. There are many ways to model necessary conditions, one of which is through interaction terms (Goertz 1994). Crudely, this can be expressed as, for example, ATTACK = β_i(DETERRENCE EFFECTIVENESS VARIABLES × RIVALRY), where a score of zero on the rivalry variable eliminates the possibility of the process leading to war. For Huth and Russett (1993), this means that cases in which RIVALRY is 0 are excluded from analysis, and when RIVALRY equals 1 they are included. But a more reasonable interpretation of their theoretical framework would suggest that (1) there is no radical break between enduring and lower-level rivalries and (2) characteristics of the rivalry relationship influence the effectiveness of the deterrent threat. Point 1 means that one need not code rivalry dichotomously and that it might be reasonably treated as a continuous variable. Many of the "deterrence effectiveness variables" are in fact characteristics of the rivalry in question (point 2). But this is just our contention: rivalry is really part of the theoretical framework, and its theoretical role should not be obscured by its use as a case selection device. Thus, one may want to model the relationship as $\beta_i = f$(RIVALRY CHARACTERISTICS). This states that the effectiveness of a factor in deterrence (i.e., β_i) depends upon the rivalry in which that deterrent factor is embedded. Although we regard case selection as important, the rivalry approach also encourages greater theoretical attention to the underlying bases of case selection and therefore better specification of the model underlying the relationship under scrutiny.

Although the rivalry approach makes a significant contribution to case selection, its utility is not confined to this aspect of research design. Rivalries also have an impact on other testing aspects, and we turn to the longitudinal implications of the rivalry approach for testing in the next section.

Testing Hypotheses over Time in Rivalries

Rivalries exist over time, and this quality has some methodological implications for how to design research. In this section, we look at the longitudinal implications of the rivalry approach with particular reference to the use of interrupted time-series and multiple data points for analysis.

The temporal duration of an enduring rivalry proved crucial in Huth and Russett's (1993) testing of general deterrence. The continued existence of a rivalry in between militarized disputes and wars simultaneously provided a control group and defined deterrence success. But the methodological implications of the temporal duration of rivalries extend beyond this provision of a valid control group. In deterrence studies, the focus of analysis remained the dispute and war, more specifically dyad-years with or without disputes. We have taken a modest step away from the causes-of-war methodology, but once the case is chosen, the individual character of rivalries tends to disappear. Nevertheless, another application of the time-series component uses that element more directly. It takes advantage of the fact that we can compare rivalries before and after some critical event. We call this the interrupted time-series aspect of rivalry methodology. The democratic peace suggests just such an analysis. It implies that if a rivalry moves from a nondemocratic to a democratic dyad, it should end shortly thereafter or at very least exhibit considerably less conflict. The democratization of the dyad should fundamentally change the character of the rivalry relationship.

Similar to deterrence, the democratic peace literature has been plagued by the problem of defining an appropriate control group. Instead of using the interdispute periods as control groups (as in deterrence testing), the control period is the rivalry before democratization. Compare this simple solution to the problems encountered with cross-sectional causes-of-war methodology. Much of the debate revolves around the definition of "relevant dyads," pairs of states that could have a dispute (i.e., "dogs that could bark"). The usual solution is to take some combination of contiguity and (major) power status to define a control group (see also Lemke 1995; Reed 1998). Inevitably, this misses some cases and includes other improbable ones. With the interrupted time-series design for rivalries, the relevant dyad problem evaporates because one is using the same dyad in the test and control groups.

The interrupted time-series methodology shows the limitations of using just enduring rivalries for case selection. The democratic peace dramatically illustrates this because we would have only one true case to analyze if we restricted ourselves to enduring rivalries (see chapter 6). Furthermore, there is no reason to assume that the critical event will occur after the 20 years required for a rivalry to become enduring. War hypotheses rarely refer specifically to enduring rivalries. Hence, in terms of case selection, we need not limit ourselves to a particular subset of rivalries. We have seen this already in the deterrence case. None of the Huth and Russett hypotheses is necessarily specific to *enduring* rivalries; isolated and proto-rivalries fit, to varying degrees, within their theoretical framework.

The above point becomes critical in examining conflict management and termination hypotheses. Early democratization of a rivalry may prevent it from becoming an enduring one. Hence proto- and isolated rivalries are just as important, if not more so, than enduring rivalries in the research design. In terms of control group language, the isolated and proto-rivalries are "successes" compared to the enduring rivalries, which represent conflict-ridden failures. Because proto- and isolated rivalries do not become enduring ones (i.e., the cycle of militarized conflict is broken), they might be taken as evidence that general deterrence or conflict management was effective. Even within enduring rivalries, the interrupted time-series design can be useful. For example, Gibler (1997) investigated the impact of alliances that were also territorial settlement treaties on rivalry behavior. He noted that rivals have significantly fewer disputes and less chance for war after such a settlement than in its absence. The comparison of the same rivalry prior to the key event (and which establishes a baseline of behavior) can be compared with rival behavior after the key event, here the removal of territorial dispute issues from the relationship.

Implicitly or explicitly, the interrupted time-series characteristic lies at the heart of tests of conflict termination hypotheses. Sometimes this remains implicit, as with event history analysis (Allison 1984; Yamaguchi 1991). For example, Bennett (1996) defines his dependent variable as the end of the enduring rivalry. Implicit is a comparison of that end, hence future peaceful relations, with the rivalry period. If one were to use event data (Hensel 1997), one might expect to see a standard interrupted time-series effect of reduced conflict after the critical event. Of course, other hypotheses naturally lend themselves to interrupted time-series tests. For example, this methodology provides a natural test of the power transition hypothesis. One would compare the power transition periods to the nonpower transition phases of the rivalry in order to evaluate whether the behavior of the two states differs substantially.

The temporal component of rivalry also can enter more directly into the testing of theory. We have seen that the Huth and Russett research design uses the interdispute period to define a control group of general deterrence success. Focusing on the temporal aspect of a rivalry suggests other dependent variables.

One aspect of general deterrence success is how long it works until it fails the next time (or the rivalry ends).

One of the key aspects of putting deterrence into the context of rivalries is that it permits us to ask what happens following instances of deterrence. The standard approach examines states of affairs before the deterrence success or failure. There is no real afterlife. Except for the endgame of rivalries, there is always an "after." This "after" period can provide new ways to evaluate hypotheses. In most instances, the "after" is also a "before." Thus, one measure of the effectiveness of general deterrence strategies is how long they are successful. Huth and Russett (1993) use disputes/war occurrence as the definition of general deterrence failure. One aspect of general deterrence is when it breaks down, but another is explaining how long it succeeds. Here we have a new dependent variable: "the waiting" time until the next deterrence breakdown.

The same definition of success can be used for conflict management analyses. Bercovitch and Diehl (1997) look at the impact of international mediation attempts on conflict within enduring rivalries. They are not so much concerned with the immediate success of such efforts, but rather with a longer-term impact on rivalry conflict patterns. Thus, they choose as dependent variables the occurrence of future disputes, the severity of those disputes, and the waiting times until those next disputes. We perform similar analyses in chapter 10. The focus on rivalries, and their longitudinal character, permits this kind of analysis, whereas more static approaches would limit the choice of dependent variables to those immediately surrounding the mediation attempt or crisis that precipitated the intervention.

Finally, we note that dynamic hypotheses, almost by definition, require time-series data. Much in deterrence theory refers to credibility and reputation, which are created and modified as states interact. The most obvious way that the historical experience of the rivals comes into deterrence models is through the concept of reputation and threat credibility. Reputation itself makes explicit reference to past behavior. One can say that the credibility of a current deterrent threat depends, in part, on the behavior of the state in previous (deterrence) situations.

In these generic formulations, rivalries do not necessarily play a role. One can search all previous or recent deterrence situations to help evaluate the credibility of the current threat. Rivalries can enter into the evaluation by suggesting that all this information is not equally valuable. In particular, the experience within the rival dyad will outweigh evidence from other interactions. Both Lieberman (1994) and Huth (1988) take this approach. It is previous interactions within the same dyad (i.e., with the same rival) that influence beliefs. This is all the more convincing in enduring rivalries. In many of these cases, the attention of decision makers and bureaucracies is focused primarily on the behavior of the other rival. The emphasis of rivalries on dyadic history parallels the psychology and organizational behavior of states and decision makers. Investing in a reputation only makes sense—in a cost-benefit sense—if the likelihood of future interactions is high: one invests (pays costs) in a reputation in order to reap future gains. If there are no future gains, then the initial investment is a loss. One desirable conceptual definition of an enduring rivalry states that it exists when decision makers see themselves in a state of militarized conflict for the indefinite future, and make plans assuming that future crises are likely. These rivalry dyads then constitute exactly the sort of situation in which leaders find it worthwhile to invest in reputation.

In our reading, the principal way that the history and context of rivalries enter into rational deterrence theories is through credibility and reputation effects. Part of the theoretical implications of the rivalry approach for deterrence lies in the implication that there are perhaps other ways in which current crisis behavior depends on the rivalry context. For example, Huth (1988) includes two rivalry variables, what he calls "past behavior" of defender and attacker. Given the natural emphasis on deterrence strategy, he investigated if previous strategies influenced outcomes in current cases. Hence, he differentiated between "conciliatory" and "intransigent" strategies. He found no difference between strategies; both decreased the likelihood of extended deterrence success. From the rivalry perspective, the first question we would ask is about the mere existence of previous conflict. Huth's results support the hypothesis that the more well entrenched the rivalry, the harder it is to deter the other side. This becomes clear when one understands that Huth coded cases with no history as 0 and cases with some history as 1. Combining the past behavior variables permits the quite legitimate interpretation of his analysis as a test of "rivalry effects."[6] Yet a broader rivalry perspective would suggest a more refined measure of those effects, including perhaps multiple variables (based on a given theoretical framework) and accompanying interval level measures. Some of those variables might include the outcomes of previous confrontations (e.g., compromise, capitulation, stalemates) or the relative success of the bargaining strategies employed (e.g., coercive, accommodative), to offer a few possibilities.

Rational deterrence theory tells us that deterrence success depends on the cost-benefit analysis for each crisis. Threats become more credible and the level required for an effective threat increases as the rivalry continues and becomes even better entrenched. This suggests that there are other aspects between crises than just credibility and reputation. How does one get at the motivational aspects of deterrence, the costs one side is willing to bear, and hence the magnitude required for a successful deterrent threat? In the "contextless" world of many rational choice models, these are exogenously determined. Yet in the real world of state relations, they are determined, in part, by the past relations of

---

[6]Fearon (1994b) explicitly confirmed this in his reanalysis of Huth's 1988 data. In recent work on territorial enduring rivalries, Huth (1996a) also found that a history of militarized disputes was strongly associated with conflict escalation.

the rivals. To say that current credibility and reputation depend on past behavior is to put forth some sort of learning or cognitive theory. Lieberman (1994) proposes that it is through deterrence failure (i.e., actually having to carry out deterrent threats) that a rival learns that a threat is credible. He argues that we should not be surprised to see deterrence failure early in the rivalry followed by deterrence success.

In summary, much in deterrence as well as crisis theory links crises to each other (reputation and credibility). This, according to some, has been overemphasized: "because the second wave [of deterrence theory] overestimates the importance of commitment and the extent to which outcomes are interdependent, it exaggerates the costs of retreats and the advantages of victories" (Jervis 1979, 319). On the other hand, these links have not been much studied in the quantitative literature: "another aspect of deterrence theory requiring further research is the role of reputation, or the impact of past behavior of the adversaries. This variable has received little attention in the quantitative empirical literature on deterrence, not only because of the difficulty of constructing an operational indicator for a large-N study but also because of the limited development of this variable in the theoretical literature" (Levy 1988, 511).

It is only through looking at behavior over time, and ideally in rivalries, that we are able to pick up this behavior. And this requires different methodological approaches, most notably the adoption of dynamic analyses and models. Most suitable would be a model similar to that of Muncaster and Zinnes (1993), which permits an updating of behavior over time as past interactions and their outcomes serve to redefine the current relationships of pairs of states in a given system. In their model, the outcome of a dispute between two states, A and B, influences the relative hostility level in their future relationship. Furthermore, the dispute between A and B may also serve to alter the relationships between other pairs of states in the system. This type of model, with some modification, provides the framework under which the past, and issues of credibility and reputation, can be analyzed.

We can contrast this with the interrupted time-series application of rivalries. In that situation, we divide the rivalry by the occurrence of some critical event. Or, we can break rivalries into beginning, middle, and end, suggesting that these contexts matter in terms of the impact of important variables. In a related theoretical literature, almost all theories of crisis include "context," "background," or "past experience" variables.[7] For example, Brecher (1979) frequently described "past experience" as a core input into various phases of the crises he analyzed. Rivalries provide one way to begin to specify *what* background factors matter and *how* they influence crisis behavior. Vaguely, these authors suggest that it matters exactly when within the rivalry the crisis takes

---

[7]Not all studies, however, do this. For example, George and Smoke (1974) include no past behavior variables in their list of questions.

place. The hypotheses remain almost always very fuzzy and not explicitly formulated. With the rivalry concept in hand, the possibility of investigating these kinds of relationships now exists. The rivalry approach provides not only new tests for hypotheses that have already been exposed to intensive quantitative testing, but suggests means for quantitative or qualitative testing of hypotheses that have been around for a while with no tests. Here, we can include as another example the frustration-aggression hypothesis in the deterrence literature, which remains untested, to our knowledge.

Instead of using the interdispute period as part of the dependent variable, it appears as the independent variable in the "frustration-aggression" deterrence hypothesis: can early deterrence success lead to failure in later crises? This pattern fits easily into the frustration-aggression framework. Deterrence success means that the rival, "frustrated" by the successful threat, becomes more aggressive in the next dispute. "Deterrence can severely frustrate an adversary who is strongly motivated to change a status quo that he regards as invidious, especially when he feels it legitimate to do so. The consequences of continued frustration are not easily predictable and are not always favorable to the deterring power. Deterrence success in the short run is not always beneficial in the longer run; the adversary may become more desperate to mount a challenge and may proceed to acquire greater resources for doing so" (George and Smoke 1989, 182). "The success of immediate deterrence can weaken general deterrence in the future by increasing the loser's grievances, convincing it that the state is a grave menace, increasing its incentives to stand firm in the next confrontation or even leading it to fight in order to change a situation which has become intolerable or is expected to deteriorate" (Jervis 1989, 199). This contrasts with the standard hypothesis that deterrence success leads to more success in the future.[8] By looking at rivalries over time and adopting a dynamic approach, perhaps we can understand why some patterns appear in certain rivalries.

These issues imply another general class of time-series analyses: the tests of the beginning of rivalries versus the middle versus the end of rivalries. All cross-sectional time-series analyses ignore when the dispute takes place within the lifetime of the rivalry. But implicit in many deterrence hypotheses lies the idea that deterrence operates differently in a mature period of an enduring rivalry than in its beginning. One would like to see an evaluation of Huth and Russett's (1993) model in terms of different rivalry periods: does it work equally well in all of them?

The longitudinal research design may also be essential for detecting empirical patterns and drawing proper conclusions about a given phenomenon. For example, consider a study of deterrence that analyzes 10 deterrence attempts in 10 rivalries, with those deterrence attempts successful 90 percent of the time.

---

[8]Other explanations can be given for the success-then-failure pattern, such as "designing around deterrence," complacency, and the like.

TABLE 5.2: Patterns of Deterrence Failure in Rivalries: Pattern 1

Rivalry	Dispute									
	1	2	3	4	5	6	7	8	9	10
1	X	O	O	O	O	O	O	O	O	O
2	O	X	O	O	O	O	O	O	O	O
3	X	O	O	O	O	O	O	O	O	O
4	O	X	O	O	O	O	O	O	O	O
5	X	O	O	O	O	O	O	O	O	O
6	X	O	O	O	O	O	O	O	O	O
7	X	O	O	O	O	O	O	O	O	O
8	O	X	O	O	O	O	O	O	O	O
9	X	O	O	O	O	O	O	O	O	O
10	X	O	O	O	O	O	O	O	O	O

Note: O = success, X = failure.

A typical static and cross-sectional analysis would consider only circumstances surrounding the different deterrence attempts and ignore any interconnection between events. Yet what if the pattern of deterrence failure was evenly spread out among the 10 rivalries, but all the failures occurred near the outset of those rivalries, as illustrated in table 5.2. The longitudinal design would permit a scholar to identify this pattern and likely draw a different set of conclusions than a cross-sectional design would. Several possibilities include that deterrence failure is very likely in the early stages of any relationship (as suggested by Lieberman 1994). More sophisticated would be a model of deterrence based on learning or signaling in which several interactions and at least one failure are needed in order to establish a stable relationship.

Another possible pattern in deterrence failure is that those failures are concentrated in a small number of rivalries, two according to the example given in table 5.3. From this design, one might conduct queries that investigate differences across rivalries as opposed to differences across disputes, the latter of which is suggested by a cross-sectional design. More than just using the interrupted time-series design, the longitudinal design of the rivalry approach in general will assist the analyst in detecting patterns and interpreting results that are not possible, even discouraged, by the traditional causes-of-war approach.

We view the testing possibilities offered by the time-series aspect of rivalry as a framework for addressing the various critiques made about the deterrence literature, but also for a wider range of other conflict concerns. The rivalry approach gives a methodological framework for testing numerous conflict, conflict management, and conflict termination hypotheses. This becomes possible because of two fundamental characteristics of rivalries: they exist over time

TABLE 5.3: Patterns of Deterrence Failure in Rivalries: Pattern 2

Rivalry	Dispute									
	1	2	3	4	5	6	7	8	9	10
1	O	O	O	O	O	O	O	O	O	O
2	O	O	O	O	O	O	O	O	O	O
3	O	O	O	O	O	O	O	O	O	O
4	O	O	O	O	O	O	O	O	O	O
5	X	X	O	O	X	O	O	X	O	X
6	X	O	X	O	X	O	O	X	X	O
7	O	O	O	O	O	O	O	O	O	O
8	O	O	O	O	O	O	O	O	O	O
9	O	O	O	O	O	O	O	O	O	O
10	O	O	O	O	O	O	O	O	O	O

Note: O = success, X = failure.

and they eventually move into nonrivalry phases. These characteristics allow one to define new tests that avoid many of the problems that plague traditional cross-sectional analyses, particularly those that need to define control groups composed of nonconflict dyads.

Cross-Sectional Aspects of Rivalry Methodology

In addition to its time-series components, the rivalry approach provides new cross-sectional analyses. By now the reason for this should be clear. We started our volume with an analysis of our grounding concept: militarized rivalries. We suggested that they could serve as a fundamental object of study, analogous to militarized international disputes or crises. The natural tendency of the causes-of-war methodology is to use rivalries in cross-sectional time-series, with the dyad-year as the unit of analysis. To emphasize the additional testing possibilities that the rivalry approach gives, we generally rely on neither the dispute nor the dyad-year as the statistical or theoretical focus of analysis in the our study of the democratic peace in the next chapter. Our purpose is not to argue that standard methodologies are wrong, but rather that other testing possibilities exist. We see this as an exercise in enlarging the methodological tool-kit of students of international peace and conflict.

The democratic peace is usually defined in terms of the absence of war between two democratic states, but one can reformulate the question in terms of rivalries: what flows from the democratic peace framework and applies to rivalries? The answer to this question can influence our view of democratic peace phenomena. For example, if we have 20 different of disputes between democratic states, they can form rivalries in numerous ways. These range from 20 isolated, one-dispute rivalries to one 20-dispute enduring rivalry. Clearly, the former supports the democratic peace proposition more than the latter does. We explore some of these possibilities and provide actual numbers to these formulations in the next chapter.

The cross-sectional possibilities of the rivalry approach remain tremendously underexploited in the rivalry literature. Being generous, one can find only a handful of studies that test hypotheses with explicit use of the rivalry as the primary focus of analysis. For example, Gibler (1997) looked at the effect of territorial settlement treaties on the termination of rivalries. In those cases, however, the primary subject of those analyses was rivalries. That is, he was attempting to draw generalizations about rivalries and their dynamics and thus the choice of rivalries as the focus of analysis was obvious.

We think it makes sense to start with the rivalry as the phenomenon to be explained before moving to cross-sectional time-series. In chapter 11, we argue that political shocks are almost a necessary condition for enduring rivalry development and termination. A first step is to ascertain the percentage of rivalries that terminated at the time of a political shock. The N here is obviously the number of enduring rivalries. But it also illustrates the conceptual hold of traditional methodologies. We know of very few analyses that report statistics using rivalry as the unit of comparison, even simple ones like the proportions reported by us in that chapter. For example, Bennett in his studies (e.g., 1997a) never provides simple statistics with rivalry as the unit of analysis, it is always event history analysis with dyad-years.

Rivalry as the unit of analysis is an essential tool for the evaluation of cross-sectional time-series results. For example, Huth and Russett examined the predictive power of their model across disputes, but not across rivalries (1993, 69). From the rivalry viewpoint, the cross-sectional question can be stated: "Does their model work better for some rivalries than others?" Knowing which rivalries fit and which do not fit their model provides us with crucial information, both in order to evaluate the theory as well as to suggest improvements, as we have seen above.

All cross-sectional time-series analyses need to be complemented by an examination at the level of the rivalry. This principle is important for theoretical and statistical reasons. Most researchers know about autocorrelation problems and their solutions, but the same potential problem exists over space. If the residuals for one rivalry are all positive, then independence of error term assumptions are violated and parameter estimates are biased (see Raknerud and Hegre 1997). Theoretically, knowing that the model works poorly for some rivalries likely implies that improvements to the model are necessary.

Between the extremes of the rivalry-as-a-whole and the dyad-year lie other cross-sectional possibilities. We have mentioned that the democratic peace has been plagued with problems of defining "relevant dyads" and how to code multiple-year wars. The rivalry approach suggests that rivalry equivalent of the dyad-year can be peaceful and militarized periods. Instead of dividing a relationship into years and coding them as war and peace, we break relations into rivalry and nonrivalry periods. Each period counts as one observation. Although we still have to define relevant dyads, the dubious ones (e.g., France vs. Bolivia) count only as one case (assuming there are no disputes between the two) instead of the x number of dyad-years under usual procedures. Instead of the huge Ns, with which statistical significance is all but assured, as one encounters in studies of the democratic peace (e.g., $N = 185,000+$ for Farber and Gowa 1995), we get a more reasonable universe of cases.

In summary, the cross-sectional unit can take various forms. We have seen four ways that this can work. First, we take the rivalry as the unit of analysis. Second, we divide relationships into rivalry and nonrivalry periods. Third, we divide the rivalry into beginning, middle, and end periods. Finally, of course, we can split rivalries into dyad-years. We have focused our attention on the first three because they are radically underrepresented in the current empirical literature.

We emphasize again that cross-sectional analyses frequently should include all rivalries, not just enduring ones. Otherwise, the hypothesis may not be fully tested. In particular, conflict termination propositions need to consider proto- and isolated rivalries in order to get a clear evaluation of the hypothesis. This relates to the yet unexplored question of why some rivalries become enduring while others do not. Here the proto- and isolated rivalries become the control group. The survival analysis of Cioffi-Revilla (1998) shows that using only enduring rivalries can significantly bias the results. He found that if one looked only at enduring rivalries, one would claim that, counterintuitively, they weaken over time. Once all rivalries are included in the analysis, however, it becomes clear that this is what happens at the end of enduring rivalries, not necessarily what happens before rivalries reach maturity (i.e., approximately 20 years).

Conclusion

The rivalry approach addresses methodology, research design, and testing procedures, with implications that apply to virtually all standard (and probably nonstandard) hypotheses in the international conflict literature. We have just focused primarily on deterrence studies to make our point. A number of studies have utilized rivalries in case selection and testing, but only a small proportion of the possibilities have been exploited in the process. Although rivalries have been used for testing for over a decade, it is rare to find studies that include both time-series and cross-sectional analyses (an exception is Gibler 1997).

International conflict phenomena are multifaceted; by definition, different dependent variables explore different facets. Our argument is that the rivalry approach illuminates aspects of deterrence, the democratic peace, and other classic hypotheses hidden from traditional methodologies. Many of these new testing procedures investigate the implications of some general proposition. The general democratic peace idea has many wide-ranging ramifications. As scholars investigate them, we understand better what the democratic peace is. In terms of deterrence, using rivalries can help to understand how deterrence success and failure relate to one another. Because of the multidimensional character of these phenomena, there is no single "rivalry test," as multiple possibilities exist in every circumstance. Given the character of our data, indicators, and theory, this proves to be a real plus. If results of these multiple tests—time-series to cross-sectional and combinations of the two—converge, then our confidence in the results should be strongly reinforced.

We have argued that beyond providing additional tests, the rivalry approach solves some serious testing problems. For example, it provides a framework for case selection in the controversial deterrence literature, with much more validity than current approaches. Similarly, using rivalries to examine the democratic peace helps avoid many problematic features of standard methodologies. We conclude by stressing that many of these techniques have hardly begun to be exploited, not to mention the research design possibilities that remain unknown to us. We see the next chapter as an extended, but preliminary, exploration of some of the proposals we have put forth here. Again, they do not exhaust the methodological vein that constitutes part of the rivalry approach. One must evaluate theoretical approaches on multiple dimensions. On the methodological, research design dimension the rivalry approach gives us new—and often better—means for getting an empirical grasp on many significant hypotheses in the war-and-peace literature. For this reason alone, it merits attention and respect.

CHAPTER 6

The Rivalry Approach to the Democratic Peace

We have emphasized that the rivalry approach applies to issues of both war and peace. In the last two chapters, we have focused on the conflictual side in our use of deterrence theory as a continuing example. Here we redress the balance by addressing the issue of the democratic peace through the rivalry lens. More specifically, we consider how the rivalry approach poses new questions in a heavily researched area, but also how it helps address key questions that have proven problematic with traditional cross-sectional methodologies.

We chose the democratic peace because it is perhaps the most interesting and important body of international conflict research in the last decade. The democratic peace centers on the proposition that democracies rarely fight each other. Although democracies may be no more or less conflict-prone overall than authoritarian regimes (for different levels of analysis in the democratic peace, see Gleditsch and Hegre 1997), two democracies have almost never fought against each other in the modern era (Small and Singer 1976; Russett 1993; Ray 1995).

Although there has been an abundance of work on this subject over the past several years and a seeming exhaustion of interesting lines of research, we propose that new insights can be gained into the democratic peace by looking at the phenomena through the lenses of the rivalry framework. Chan (1993) has noted that the analyses of the democratic peace (and indeed international conflict in general) have been static and cross-sectional comparisons of democratic and nondemocratic dyads, with little concern for the processes that generate interstate conflict or peace. We believe that the rivalry approach addresses that concern and provides new ways of looking at the democratic peace. In this way, studying the democratic peace offers an illustrative example of many of the themes, characteristics, principles, and methodologies outlined in the last two chapters.

This study reformulates the democratic peace debate using the rivalry framework. First, it allows us to extend the democratic peace argument to phenomena beyond war. According to Doyle (1996), this is essential to test both the validity and elasticity of the democratic peace argument. Instead of asking whether or how often democratic states fight wars, the rivalry framework allows us to focus on how often and in what kinds of rivalries democratic states become involved. This permits us to test whether the democratic peace applies to repeated conflict; that is, whether joint democracy not only inhibits war or initial militarized conflict, but whether given conflict it stifles repeated confrontations between the same pair of states.

Second, the rivalry framework provides for a more dynamic, longitudinal research design that permits scholars to study the conflict behavior of each dyad over its entire history, including both democratic and nondemocratic periods. Most existing research on the democratic peace has compared the conflict behavior of democratic dyads with that of nondemocratic dyads at some arbitrary point in time. The rivalry approach is consistent with Spiro's (1994) call to explore a dyad over its history in evaluating the democratic peace rather than just at one point in time. If dyads avoided militarized conflict while democratic and were also peaceful while one or both states were nondemocratic, questions could be raised about the importance of joint democracy in maintaining the observed peace. Yet if many democratic dyads engaged in frequent militarized confrontations in nondemocratic periods, but stopped doing so once both states in the dyad became democratic, our confidence in the democratic peace as a pacifying influence would be strengthened. A longitudinal analysis meets the concerns of Russett (1995), who suggests that studying conflict over the lifetime of each dyad can greatly extend our understanding of the democratic peace beyond the year-to-year cross-sectional comparisons that have dominated previous research.

Specifically, the longitudinal character of the rivalry approach can also help uncover changing conflict behavior over time in response to democratization. With the rivalry approach, we can hold most aspects of a given competition constant by looking at changes within individual rivalries, which allows us to study the impact of changes in one factor—democracy—on conflict. Most other analyses of the democratic peace are unable to "equalize" the comparison of disparate dyads, being at best forced to institute as many controls as possible (e.g., Maoz and Russett 1992) in order to account for national differences that might be responsible for the observed relationships. In our analyses, different phases of the rivalry itself effectively offer us a control group for comparison with each other, allowing us to study the effect of changing democracy levels on the occurrence and severity of militarized conflicts. A similar approach was taken by Chan (1984), who supplemented an aggregated analysis of all "relatively free" and "relatively unfree" states with a more fine-grained analysis of individual states that experienced periods of both free and unfree rule. Thus, the second contribution of the rivalry approach is to provide an analysis of rivalries in which the states underwent a regime change such that a democratic dyad resulted (or vice versa). We then assess whether joint democracy had any impact on rivalry dynamics.

A third contribution of the rivalry approach to the study of the democratic peace is an extension of the previous one. How strong is the impact of democracy on rivalry dynamics? Above, we considered whether new joint democracy affected a rivalry. We can also assess whether democracy can completely arrest a rivalry, thereby precipitating its end. Thus, the rivalry approach can extend the democratic peace argument to new venues, help assess its impact by studying the impact of regime change on rivalry competition, and determine whether democracy has a strong enough effect to end ongoing militarized competitions. Rasler and Thompson's (1998b) findings suggest that effects from ongoing rivalries may outweigh any pacifying impact from democracy.

Finally, the rivalry framework facilitates the use of democracy as a dependent variable as well as an independent one. Previous analyses of the democratic peace looked only at how democracy inhibited conflict. In our analysis, we also explore how rivalries (specifically their onset and their termination) affect democratization within the rival states. In this way, we explore whether democracy is a consequence, as well as a facilitator, of peace. Thus, the rivalry approach permits us to examine the possibility of reverse or recursive causality cited by Thompson (1996), Gates, Knutsen, and Moses (1996), and others.

We begin with the simplest application of the rivalry approach, changing the focus of analysis from war to rivalry. This is an incremental step away from traditional studies of the democratic, but one that still yields new insights. We then exploit the potential of the rivalry approach more fully by looking at rivalries over time, with special attention to changes in regimes of the rivals over time. Because the democratic peace debate is so well known, we dispense with the usual literature review (see Russett 1993; Ray 1995; Brown, Lynn-Jones, and Miller 1996) and discuss only those elements directly relevant to our argument. The final part of our analysis explores the causal direction of the rivalry-democracy relationship. As this has not been explored extensively, we devote significantly more attention to previous studies on related topics that offer us some guidance in formulating our expectations.

Rivalry as the Focus of Analysis

Our hypotheses begin with the first concern, testing the democratic peace argument on new phenomena. Our expectation is that democratic dyads will become involved in militarized rivalries of any form less frequently than other dyad types. This expectation is a logical extension of previous research on democracy and conflict, which has repeatedly found that democracies less frequently engage in militarized conflict and only rarely, if ever, in full-scale interstate wars. Because militarized rivalry involves protracted adversarial relationships with multiple confrontations between the rivals, the previously observed rarity of militarized conflict between democracies suggests that democracies should also become involved in very few rivalries. Yet, we also expect that this relationship will be even stronger for more severe forms of rivalry. That is, joint democratic dyads should be somewhat less likely than other types of dyads to engage in isolated conflict, which is a type of adversarial relationship involving one or two militarized confrontations. But democracies should be even less likely than other pairs of states to engage in proto-rivalries or enduring rivalries.

Democracy and Peace Within Rivalries

The next two expectations concern a specific subset of all interstate rivalries: those rivalries that experience at least one change in dyadic democracy status during the course of the rivalry. Such regime-change rivalries offer a useful opportunity to reconsider the relationship between democracy and peace, because they allow us to study the effects of changing democracy levels within the same dyads while holding almost all other factors constant. Maoz (1997) looks at a series of dyads and compares their militarized dispute proclivity during periods of joint democracy and other regime configurations; he finds that joint democratic periods are much less dispute prone than others. Nevertheless, his comparisons are made across a broad sweep of dyad-years over two centuries, and it is not clear how comparable the two time frames really are. For example, are the historical contexts and all other relevant variables comparable in dyad relations in the early nineteenth and later twentieth centuries? The focus on rivalries, which range from a few years to an average of 30 to 40 years for enduring rivalries, is less subject to this limitation and provides a better basis for comparison (as we are comparing periods in close proximity to one another in the same ongoing competition).

When a regime transition during an ongoing rivalry leads to the creation of a joint-democratic dyad (or to the reversal of joint-democratic status), we expect the transition to have an important impact on rivalry behavior. If the pacifying effect of democracy is to be considered meaningful, then we should expect to observe a rapid reduction in the frequency or severity of militarized conflict within rivalries that undergo a transition to joint-democratic status. Similarly, we should expect a noticeable increase in the frequency or severity of conflict in rivalries following a transition away from joint democracy.

We recognize that the pacifying effect of joint democracy may not be immediate and may vary depending on the history of conflict between the adversaries during their rivalry before the regime transition (Hensel 1995). Similarly, Mansfield and Snyder (1995b) suggest that the process of democratization may actually increase the short-term likelihood of militarized conflict, due to the risks of a volatile rise in mass politics in a setting with relatively new and unstable democratic political institutions. It should be noted, however, that Enterline (1996) identifies numerous problems in Mansfield and Snyder's research design and evidence, and that his reanalyses find an immediate pacifying effect of democratization. We will test for the possibility of a lagged effect.

A final dimension of the democracy-rivalry linkage that bears consideration is the impact of democracy on the termination of rivalry. Bennett (1997a) finds a significant relationship between polity change and rivalry termination, especially when that change leads to joint democracy among the rivals. The effect of introducing democratic changes into a rivalry may be the equivalent of an endogenous shock (see chapter 11) that disrupts rivalry patterns and provides the conditions under which that rivalry can end. Thus, consistent with the logic of the democratic peace, we expect joint democracy to have a powerful effect on rivalry behavior, strong enough to end an ongoing rivalry.

Rivalry and Democracy

We now consider the impact that rivalry can have on democracy levels. In previous empirical research on the democratic peace, democracy has functioned as the independent variable, which has been hypothesized to affect conflict propensity or conflict escalation. Looking at the democratic peace through the lenses of the rivalry approach, however, we have reason to expect that the causal direction might also run in the opposite direction. Our final two hypotheses consider the impact of rivalry on democracy, focusing on whether involvement in a militarized rivalry leads to decreases in democracy levels and on whether the end of militarized competition in turn promotes greater democratization.

If these final two hypotheses receive empirical support, then at the very least we could conclude that the relationship between democracy and peace is recursive. It may even be the case that the democratic peace literature has the wrong causal direction, namely that periods of conflict and rivalry typically reduce democracy levels and that the end of serious military conflict may be a prerequisite for the establishment of stable democratic processes. Gates, Knutsen, and Moses (1996), for example, suggest that greater levels of international peace and stability may contribute to the growth of democracy, while less peace internationally may lead to restrictions on democracy.

Our first expectation on the rivalry-democracy linkage concerns the effects of an ongoing rivalry on political democracy. The extant empirical evidence for this proposition is thus far mixed. Modern warfare, with its reliance on mass-mobilized armies, requires the support—or at least acquiescence—of the masses both in the military and on the home front. As a result, states may extend citizenship rights during wartime, in order to mobilize the population and to ensure their support in the war effort (Therborn 1977). Rueschemeyer, Stephens, and Stephens (1992) and Howard (1991) note that working-class organizations must often be included in the ruling coalition to a much greater extent than in peacetime, and that war can generate mounting pressures to extend the vote to women and excluded racial groups. More generally, Tilly (1985) and Howard (1983, 1991) argue that war making and state making were closely related in the development of European states. Such states developed out of leaders' quest for power within a secure or expanding territory, which involved conflict with internal and external enemies. To succeed in this conflict, the state needed to build up a strong military, which required the extraction of substantial resources and the formation of alliances with selected social classes within the state. In return for their participation, the state rewarded these classes with "protection" from their enemies in ways that often constrained the state's rulers themselves, such as courts, assemblies, or reliance on credit and technical expertise. Thompson (1996) argues similarly that in many cases, the scope of franchise extensions expanded with the increasing number of people regarded as important to war-making efforts as soldiers, workers, and taxpayers.

The evidence from individual cases, however, seems to suggest quite the opposite relationship more recently, which is consistent with our expectation. For example, Thompson (1996) notes that participation in warfare—particularly frequent or intensive warfare—typically encourages and rewards more authoritarian approaches to decision making and resource mobilization. Gates, Knutsen, and Moses (1996) note that governments in wartime have often restricted their citizens' rights and freedoms, and that even democratic governments in wartime have declared martial laws or postponed elections in the name of security. Similarly, Tilly (1985) notes that the European model does not apply very well to many states that have developed recently. Many newly independent states have been able to meet their military needs through external sources of equipment and expertise in return for commodities or military alliance. As a result, they have not needed to build the same domestic alliances in the course of war making and state making, and therefore have not been subjected to the same constraints as their European predecessors. In such cases, Tilly (1985, 186) notes, the new states often develop "powerful, unconstrained organizations that easily overshadow all other organizations within their territories," with little incentive to grant civil liberties or broad political participation.

Most of the literature cited above deals with periods of active warfare, rather than the typically less severe concept of rivalry (although many rivalries are characterized by periods of warfare at least once in their duration). Yet similar arguments can be made for the effects of a situation of protracted external security threat. As Thompson (1996, 144) notes, "even the threat of impending war" can make more democratic power-sharing arrangements relatively inefficient or undesirable, and "political systems are quite likely to become more authoritarian as they become engaged in crises of national security." Layne (1994, 45) also argues that "The greater the external threat a state faces (or believes it does), the more 'autocratic' its foreign policymaking process will be, and the more centralized its political structures will be." That is, states in high-threat international environments tend to adopt more autocratic governmental structures to enhance their strategic posture and allow them to deal with the threatening situation more efficiently.

Regarding the positive effects of external conflict on political mobilization, Howard (1991) and Kaufman (1993) note that Israel's environment of continual external threat has been an important integrative force for social mobilization, consensus, and conciliation in Israeli society, "shaping Israel's civil society in to a highly participatory community" (Kaufman 1993, 115). Nonetheless, Howard (1991, 47) suggests, it has also created a beleaguered garrison state "where the distinction between the armed forces and the civilian population is one simply of function." Along these lines, Pinkas (1993, 62) suggests that the Israeli occupation of Arab territories captured in the 1967 war "has exacted a heavy price from Israeli democracy, impairing its development." According to Pinkas (1993, 62), the occupation has negatively influenced public perceptions of democracy ("corrupting the soul of Israeli society"), as well as negatively influencing the institutions of democracy itself by blurring the line between democracy and nondemocratic military government. He further argues that the Israeli public is willing to accept the suspension of certain democratic rights or infringement of certain civil rights in the name of security. Examples cited by Pinkas include censorship of the press, reliance on emergency security legislation passed and enforced with little parliamentary supervision, and restrictions on the rule of law in the occupied territories. Kaufman (1993) further notes that while Israelis overwhelmingly support abstract democratic principles, they also prefer strong leadership, restrictions on minority rights, and the general subordination of political rights to security considerations.

Beyond the case of Israel, Nincic (1989, 3–4; see also Vasquez 1993) argues that the Cold War had "permanent and pernicious"—although rarely recognized—domestic consequences in both the United States and the Soviet Union. Defense and intelligence agencies achieved privileged positions of power within the U.S. government, giving them a preeminent role in shaping national priorities (particularly regarding U.S.-Soviet relations) with less possibility of oversight by nonmilitaristic elements of government or society. Society itself was also influenced by the rivalry, with opposition to the government's policies being seen as reflecting a communist or left-wing (and certainly unpatriotic) position. Nincic identified similar trends in the Soviet Union, with the dominance of the national security bureaucracy and the narrowing of permitted political discourse. The protracted rivalry thus corrupted the practice of democratic principles in the United States (even if the actual institutions were not altered substantially) and solidified or exacerbated the repressive tendencies of the Soviet leadership.

Scholars have argued, then, that the impact of war or rivalry on democracy can take several forms, ranging from increased political inclusion to reduced civil and political liberties. We suggest that a similar relationship should hold with respect to interstate rivalries—which typically last much longer than wars, and thus present greater opportunities for the external security threat to lead to restrictions or limitations on political democracy. Thus, we expect that periods of rivalry should lead to regime change away from dyadic democracy relative to the rivals' regime type before the onset of rivalry.

As discussed above, several scholars have noted a tendency for civil liberties and political rights to be extended to previously excluded groups during wartime or rivalry; we now consider the impact of the termination of rivalry on democracy. The more peaceful international environment resulting from the end of rivalry may be conducive to the expansion of democratic rights and liberties in the former rivals. Indeed, some scholars might argue (Gates, Knutsen, and Moses 1996; Thompson 1996) that peace creates the possibility of democracy, particularly when the peaceful period follows a history of warfare.

In many cases, governments that extended additional rights or liberties during war or rivalry may attempt to reverse these changes after the conclusion of the war, only to find that liberties and rights can be difficult to take away once they have been granted. Rueschemeyer, Stephens, and Stephens (1992, 70) illustrate this point with a 1946 quote from U.S. Senator Barkley of Kentucky, who noted that he could not refuse to vote for the peacetime extension of democratic rights to all races, colors, creeds, religions, ancestries, and origins after having voted to subject men from all of these backgrounds to compulsory military service during the war. In cases in which rights and freedoms have been granted for the first time during war—or rivalry—we thus expect that many of these rights and freedoms will continue to be granted after the end of the conflict in question.

Where political rights and freedoms have not been enjoyed during wartime or rivalry, we also expect that pressures may build for their extension afterward. Most dramatically, previous research has shown that the end of war—particularly an unsuccessful or costly war—can lead to regime change in the involved states (e.g., Bueno de Mesquita, Siverson, and Woller 1992). Authoritarian regimes have been replaced with political democracy in cases ranging from the Axis powers after World War II to Argentina after the Falklands War. Our current emphasis on rivalry rather than war, though, involves a much broader effect. With the end of serious conflict, we see governments willing to relinquish powers to the citizenry that they heretofore guarded jealously to meet the demands of external threats. Similarly, popular demands may increase for more active participation in government, as opposition to the government is no longer considered traitorous and the justifications for restraints on popular rule are no longer as compelling.

Certainly the movement toward democracy by many states in Eastern Europe and elsewhere after the Cold War is suggestive of this effect. Once the political and military competition comprising the Cold War decreased to a level that was not as threatening to national security, many of the formerly authoritarian states in Eastern Europe (and, indeed, many of the formerly authoritarian republics that had made up the Soviet Union itself) began to democratize. Thus, we anticipate that the end of militarized conflict in rivalries should be followed by regime change toward democracy in one or both rival states, relative to the rivals' regime type during the militarized period of rivalry.

The causal direction of the relationship between rivalry and democracy is a potentially complex one. We acknowledge that our tests below are of the most preliminary character and do not necessarily capture the full range of this complexity. Nevertheless, we include this aspect of the rivalry approach to the democratic peace as an illustration of the kinds of questions and analyses that are suggested by that approach.

Research Design

We explore the democratic peace for *all* rivalries during the 1816–1992 period. Classifications of regime type and democracy level follow Dixon (1994), and are based on Polity III data (Jaggers and Gurr 1996). The Polity III data set includes indices of institutionalized democracy and autocracy that each range in value from 0 to 10, based on five specific polity characteristics: competitiveness and regulation of political participation, competitiveness and openness of executive recruitment, and constraints on the chief executive. For analyses requiring a dichotomous measure of democracy, we use Dixon's (1994, 22) classification of democracies as states scoring at least a 6 on the 0 to 10 Polity III index of institutionalized democracy. For analyses involving a continuous measure of democracy, we use Jaggers and Gurr's (1996) "Democ – Autoc" measure that subtracts each state's autocracy score from its democracy score. The dyadic measure is taken as the score of the *least* democratic state in the dyad, which can range from positive 10 (highly democratic, no authoritarian characteristics) to negative 10 (highly authoritarian, no democratic characteristics). This use of the minimum score in the dyad rather than the average of two states' democracy scores allows us to capture effects that depend on both sides being democratic, thereby avoiding the risk of coding a dyad as more democratic when one state in the dyad is highly democratic and the other is mildly democratic or even slightly authoritarian in nature. This "Democ – Autoc" measure has been argued to be superior to either the democracy or autocracy index alone, and has been found to be highly correlated with numerous alternative measures of democracy (Jaggers and Gurr 1996). In general, we find that our results are quite robust, with little substantive difference when using these different measures of dyadic democracy. This robustness greatly increases our confidence in the results as not deriving solely from a quirk of data operationalization.[1]

---

[1]In earlier analyses, we found similar results using the dichotomous and continuous joint-democracy indicators presented by Russett (1993), as well as the continuous democracy indicators

Empirical Results

Rivalry as the Focus of Analysis

Our first hypothesis suggested that democratic dyads should become involved in fewer rivalries than other dyads. The evidence, depicted in tables 6.1 and 6.2, supports this expectation. Table 6.1 lists the number of rivalries begun while both states were democratic, while one state was democratic, and while neither state was democratic. Additionally, this table lists the number of dyad-years in the interstate system since 1816 in which both, one, and neither members of a given dyad were democratic. These dyad-year totals are used to determine the unconditional probability of a rivalry breaking for each rivalry type during a given year (e.g., .00173 for isolated conflicts). This probability is then used to calculate the expected number of rivalries that should have been observed for each dyad type based on the number of eligible dyad-years, if dyadic democracy has no impact on the probability of rivalry.

Table 6.1 indicates that 66 rivalry relationships began while both states were democratic, which is significantly less than the 107 that should be expected based on the number of joint-democratic dyad-years in the interstate system ($Z = -3.93, p < .001$). Additionally, almost all rivalries that began while both states were democratic remained confined to low levels of rivalry, with only 11 proto-rivalries and two enduring rivalries (as noted below, however, only one is a democratic dyad throughout its lifetime) emerging from the 66 total rivalries. All three types of conflict are significantly less likely to begin between two democratic adversaries. Table 6.1 also reveals that rivalries are less likely than expected to begin between one democracy and one nondemocratic state across all three types of rivalry. All three types of rivalry relationship are significantly more likely than expected for dyads in which neither side is democratic.

Another illuminating point in table 6.1 concerns the probability of rivalry breaking out. Although the probability of any type of rivalry beginning in any type of dyad is low overall (the probabilities in the table range from .00004 to .00224), it is instructive to compare these probabilities across dyad types. Joint democratic dyads have a .00142 probability of beginning any type of rivalry in a given year, while the probability is 1.36 times greater (.00193) for mixed dyads with only one democracy, and over twice as great (.00294) for dyads containing no democracies. The probability of enduring rivalry is almost three times greater for dyads with only one democracy and four times greater for dyads with no democracies than for joint democratic dyads. Overall, there is a consistent pattern of increasing rivalry formation as one moves from democratic dyad to neither democratic. Furthermore, although the differences are apparent for all

---

employed by Dixon (1993, 1994). The observed similarity in results under different democracy indicators increases our confidence in the robustness of our findings.

TABLE 6.1: Dyadic Regime Type and Probability of Rivalry Onset

Rivalry Type	Dyad-Years[a]	Rivalries Begun	Rivalries Expected	Probability of Rivalry
Isolated conflict	509,122	880		.00173
Both democratic	46,519	53	80	.00114
One democratic	255,588	364	442	.00142
Neither democratic	207,015	463	358	.00224
$\chi^2 = 54.05, d.f. = 2, p < .001$				
Proto-rivalry	509,122	223		.00044
Both democratic	46,519	11	20	.00024
One democratic	255,588	101	112	.00040
Neither democratic	207,015	111	91	.00054
$\chi^2 = 9.95, d.f. = 2, p < .01$				
Enduring rivalry	509,122	63		.00012
Both democratic	46,519	2	6	.00004
One democratic	255,588	27	32	.00011
Neither democratic	207,015	34	26	.00016
$\chi^2 = 5.87, d.f. = 2, p < .055$				
Total	509,122	1,166		.00229
Both democratic	46,519	66	107	.00142
One democratic	255,588	492	585	.00193
Neither democratic	207,015	608	474	.00294
$\chi^2 = 58.28, d.f. = 2, p < .001$				

[a]Excludes the following dyad-years in which a rivalry of any type was ongoing: 317 in which both states were democratic, 3,041 in which one side was democratic, and 3,317 in which neither side was democratic.

categories of rivalry, the disparities become greater with the increasing severity of the rivalry (that is, the findings are most stark with respect to enduring rivalries).[2]

These results strongly support the first hypothesis, because joint democratic dyads are much less likely than other types of dyads to become involved in rivalries of any type. Pairs of democratic adversaries account for a small absolute number of all rivalry relationships—only 66 rivalries of any type, and

---

[2]We acknowledge that some of the democratic dyads in the last few decades have not had the requisite period in which to become enduring rivalries. Yet those democratic dyads have had the opportunity to have isolated and proto-rivalries and are less likely than other dyads to have those types of rivalries; this suggests that the results on enduring rivalries, which are the strongest, will not likely disappear with the passage of time. These findings are also consistent with Maoz (1997), which looks at dispute behavior among all dyads, all politically relevant dyads, and enduring rivalry dyads.

TABLE 6.2: Dyadic Regime Type During Rivalries, by Type of Rivalry

Dyadic Regime Type	Type of Rivalry			
	Isolated (%)	Proto (%)	Enduring (%)	Total
Always joint democratic	53 (85)	8 (13)	1 (2)	62
Sometimes joint democratic	4 (17)	9 (39)	10 (43)	23
Never joint democratic	823 (76)	206 (19)	52 (5)	1,081
Total	880 (75)	223 (19)	63 (5)	1,166

only two enduring rivalries—but a skeptic might suggest that this is only because the small number of joint democratic dyads in recent history offer few opportunities for rivalry. As table 6.1 reveals, when the opportunity for rivalry is considered, the few observed cases of joint-democratic rivalry are significantly fewer than might be expected if democracy has no impact on the likelihood of rivalry.

Democracy and Peace within Rivalries

It is also important to consider the democratic status of rival adversaries during the course of their rivalry. Although table 6.1 categorizes rivalries based on the democratic status of their participants at the outbreak of rivalry, the regime type of one or both rivals may change during the course of the rivalry. A rivalry that begins with one or no democratic adversaries may later see both become democratic, and a rivalry that begins between two democracies may see the end of democratic rule in one or both states. Table 6.2 thus expands on table 6.1 by considering the regime type of rival adversaries over the entire duration of their period of rivalry, classifying each rivalry as always joint democratic, never joint democratic, or mixed (including both joint democratic and nondemocratic periods).

A total of 62 rivalries remain joint democratic for their entire duration between 1816 and 1992, including only eight proto-rivalries and one enduring rivalry.[3] Most conflictual relationships between two democracies thus remain confined to relatively low conflict levels, with 85 percent of such relationships remaining limited to the level of isolated conflict and only one reaching full-fledged enduring rivalry. Twenty-three more rivalries, including four that began under conditions of joint democracy, change regime type during the duration of the rivalry, meaning that they experienced both joint democratic and

---

[3]The enduring rivalry between two democracies is the nineteenth-century rivalry between the United States and Great Britain, which involved eight low-level militarized disputes.

nondemocratic periods, including nine proto-rivalries and 10 enduring rivalries.[4] The vast majority of all rivalries, though, never experience any periods of joint democracy. Over 80 percent of the cases in each type of rivalry remain nondemocratic over their entire duration, totaling 1,081 of the 1,166 rivalries in table 6.2 (93 percent). Although the number of cases is small, it is nonetheless startling that 43 percent of the mixed cases (those that have joint democracy at some point in the rivalry, but not for the whole period) are enduring rivalries— this is at least eight times the rate for rivalries with consistent regime types for the rivals. This suggests the proposition, not fully explored here, that regime instability or change in general may prolong rivalries.

Given that rivalries are constructed with militarized dispute data, it is not surprising that we confirm for rivalries what has been found previously for wars and disputes, that democratic states are less likely to confront each other with the threat or use of military force. The rivalry approach allows us to extend this finding, however, demonstrating that not only are militarized disputes relatively rare among democracies, but they are also not generally repeated between the same states.

The second and third hypotheses focus on "regime change rivalries," or those rivalries in which the rivals become jointly democratic or move away from that status during the course of an ongoing rivalry. As table 6.2 reveals, there are 23 such regime change rivalries in our data set: four cases of isolated conflict, nine proto-rivalries, and 10 enduring rivalries. It should be noted that our empirical analyses of regime change rivalries focus on the 19 cases of proto- or enduring rivalry that change democracy status during the rivalry. Cases of isolated conflict last for such short periods of time (often only two or three years) and include only one or two militarized disputes, which does not give us a satisfactory basis for comparison across democratic and nondemocratic periods.

Our second hypothesis suggests that regime change rivalries should be less conflict-prone while both rivals are democratic than when one or both of the rivals is not democratic. Table 6.3 addresses our second hypothesis by examining the probability of militarized conflict occurring during rivalry, based on the rivals' democratic status in each year of their rivalry.[5] The results in table 6.3

---

[4]The 10 enduring rivalries that experience limited periods of joint democracy include rivalries involving the United States against Ecuador and Peru in the mid to late twentieth century, Great Britain, France, and Belgium against Germany in the early twentieth century, Israel against Syria due to a brief period of Syrian democracy according to the Polity III data, Turkey against Greece and Cyprus in the late twentieth century, Japan against South Korea, and India against Pakistan. Of these 10 regime-change enduring rivalries, only the Cyprus–Turkey case experiences enough democracy to average joint democratic status over the period of rivalry using our measure of democracy. The other nine cases remain nondemocratic on the average, reflecting protracted periods of nondemocratic rule in one or both states and only limited periods in which both states could be considered political democracies.

[5]This table includes the active militarized portion of each rivalry, or the period between the outbreak of the first dispute in the rivalry and the conclusion of the final dispute. Additionally, it

TABLE 6.3: Militarized Dispute Propensity in Regime-Change Rivalries

Dyadic Regime Type	Militarized Dispute Years (%)	Nondispute Years	Total
Proto-Rivalry			
Both democratic	18 (22)	64	82
One democratic	15 (22)	54	69
Neither democratic	6 (33)	12	18
Total	39 (23)	130	169
$\chi^2 = 1.20, p < .55$			
Enduring Rivalry			
Both democratic	29 (22)	103	132
One democratic	89 (38)	145	234
Neither democratic	4 (31)	9	13
Total	122 (32)	257	379
$\chi^2 = 9.90, p < .01$			
Total			
Both democratic	47 (22)	167	214
One democratic	104 (34)	199	303
Neither democratic	10 (33)	21	31
Total	161 (30)	387	548
$\chi^2 = 9.37, p < .01$			

generally support our expectations. Militarized conflict in regime change rivalries is generally less likely when both rivals are democratic than when at least one rival is nondemocratic. Militarized disputes break out in 22 percent of all the years in which both are democratic, compared with 34 percent of the years in which only one state is democratic and 32 percent of the years in which neither is democratic. This result is statistically significant for enduring rivalries ($\chi^2 = 9.90, p < .01$) and overall ($\chi^2 = 9.37, p < .01$), although the effect is weaker in proto-rivalries because there is virtually no difference between dyads including one or two democracies.[6]

---

includes a 10-year period after the end of the final militarized dispute in the rivalry, because a new dispute in this period would have had the effect of extending the rivalry. This approach allows us to capture a possible effect of extending the rivalry. This approach allows us to capture a possible effect of democratization on the avoidance of future conflict that would extend a rivalry, which might have been missed by stopping the analysis with the conclusion of the final dispute in each rivalry.

[6]There is no relationship between the severity of disputes and whether the rivalry is in a joint democratic or other period.

TABLE 6.4: Democracy and Conflict in Regime-Change Rivalries

Regime Type	Disputes	Years	Percent
Proto-Rivalry	43	173	0.25
Two democracies	13	69	0.19
One democracy	16	64	0.25
No democracies	6	17	0.35
Transition to dem.	7	16	0.44
Transition to auth.	1	7	0.14
Enduring Rivalry	159	379	0.42
Both democracies	16	99	0.16
One democracy	100	211	0.47
No democracies	5	13	0.38
Transition to dem.	23	33	0.70
Transition to auth.	15	23	0.65
Total	202	552	0.37
Both democracies	29	168	0.17
One democracy	116	275	0.42
No democracies	11	30	0.37
Transition to dem.	30	49	0.61
Transition to auth.	16	30	0.53

On the one hand, there does appear to be some pacifying effect on dispute occurrence when joint democracy is present. On the other hand, this effect is apparent only for enduring rivalries, with proto-rivalries showing no difference in patterns of dispute occurrence during joint democracy expectations. It is evident that rivalries have a certain kind of stability that is not easily dislodged (something postulated by the punctuated equilibrium model in the second part of this book), and even changes in the regimes of the two rivals may not be enough to change the rivalry patterns. That militarized disputes still persist in some of these rivalries suggest that the dynamics driving the rivalries may be stronger than any pacifying effects of joint democracy, a concern that we address below.

Table 6.4 compares the frequency of disputes in regime change rivalries according to the different regime configurations at the time. We also consider dispute frequency during regime transition periods (defined as the year the transition occurred and the one immediately following it) in order to investigate claims that democratizing periods are especially dangerous ones (Mansfield and Snyder 1995a, 1995b). The table reports the number of militarized disputes that occurred, the number of years included, and the mean number of disputes per year; as many as four disputes occur in several individual years in the data set.

TABLE 6.5: Democracy and Conflict in Post-Transition Periods

Rivalry Type	Disputes	Years	Percent
Transitions to nondemocratic dyad status			
Proto-Rivalry	5	45	0.11
1–5 years	1	13	0.08
6–10 years	3	13	0.23
11–15 years	1	10	0.10
> 15 years	0	9	0.00
Enduring Rivalry	62	122	0.51
1–5 years	27	39	0.69
6–10 years	14	26	0.54
11–15 years	5	17	0.29
> 15 years	16	40	0.40
Total	67	167	0.40
1–5 years	28	52	0.54
6–10 years	17	39	0.44
11–15 years	6	27	0.22
> 15 years	16	49	0.33
Transitions to democratic dyad status			
Proto-Rivalry	2	55	0.04
1–5 years	1	26	0.04
6–10 years	1	18	0.06
11–15 years	0	10	0.00
> 15 years	0	1	0.00
Enduring Rivalry	15	97	0.15
1–5 years	15	59	0.25
6–10 years	0	30	0.00
11–15 years	0	8	0.00
> 15 years	0	0	0.00
Total	17	152	0.11
1–5 years	16	85	0.19
6–10 years	1	48	0.02
11–15 years	0	18	0.00
> 15 years	0	1	0.00

There are several consistent and notable patterns. First, the years of joint democracy are those with the lowest frequency of dispute formation in rivalries. Overall, periods of joint democracy are more than twice less likely to have a dispute in a given year than when one or both of the rivals is not a democracy. Second, it is quite apparent that the transition periods are the most dangerous for rivalries. The transition to democracy period has the highest rate of dispute formation of any condition. Nevertheless, it may be the transition process itself and not necessarily the direction of the regime that is responsible for this conflict proclivity. In enduring rivalries, the transition phase is very conflict prone whether the move is toward greater democracy in the rivalry or toward more authoritarian governments.

The third hypothesis suggests that regime change rivalries should be likely to end shortly after the change to joint democracy. Consistent with earlier findings, we find strong confirmation for our proposition that rivalries are more likely to end when both rivals are democratic than when at least one of the rivals is nondemocratic. The evidence in table 6.5 shows that disputes, which perpetuate rivalries, dissipate quickly in enduring rivalries after a transition to a democratic dyad. Significantly, transition away from joint democratic status did not produce a similar effect. Although dispute frequency tails off somewhat over time, the rate of dispute formation is still high and such rivalries, especially enduring ones, continue well into the future. Further examination of the regime change rivalries in our data set indicates a general tendency for these rivalries to end while both states are democratic. Over half of the regime change rivalries (11 of 19, or 58 percent) end while both sides are democratic, including seven of nine proto-rivalries and four of 10 enduring rivalries. Of course, seven of the nine proto-rivalries and seven of the 10 enduring rivalries are considered censored because their militarized period of rivalry has ended less than a decade before the end of the militarized dispute data. Even removing these censored cases, though, both proto-rivalries (United Kingdom–Netherlands and United Kingdom–Sweden, both of which ended in 1917) ended while joint democratic, as did the United Kingdom–Germany enduring rivalry in 1921. The other two uncensored enduring rivalries are Belgium–Germany and France–Germany, both of which ended at the close of World War II without joint democratic status—but which would be transformed into joint democratic relationships shortly thereafter.[7]

---

[7] We also ran an event history analysis of joint democracy and rivalry termination. The presence of joint democracy significantly increases the likelihood of rivalry termination ($\chi^2 = 6.79$, $p < .01$); rivalry termination is three times as likely under joint democracy than under other conditions. The analysis includes only the militarized portion of the rivalry, up to the conclusion of the final MID in the rivalry.

TABLE 6.6: Democracy Levels before and during Rivalry

Time Period[a]	Mean (SD)	N
Proto-Rivalry		
Before rivalry	−5.61 (3.90)	44
1st rivalry decade	−6.00 (3.89)	44
Later in rivalry	−5.95 (3.80)	44
$F = 0.13, p < .88$		
Enduring Rivalry		
Before rivalry	−5.02 (4.01)	24
1st rivalry decade	−5.15 (4.74)	24
Later in rivalry	−4.82 (3.47)	24
$F = 0.04, p < .96$		
All Rivalries		
Before rivalry	−5.40 (3.92)	68
1st rivalry decade	−5.70 (4.19)	68
Later in rivalry	−5.55 (3.70)	68
$F = 0.10, p < .91$		

[a] Refers to the average dyadic democracy level in the 10 years before the rivalry began, in the first ten years of the rivalry, and in the remainder of the rivalry. This table includes only dyads for which complete data are available (i.e., dyads for which the Polity III data set includes democracy data for both the prerivalry period and portions of two separate decades within the rivalry), and excludes rivalries that can be considered "censored" because a new dispute toward the end of the time period studied (1978–92) would have prolonged the period of rivalry.

Rivalry and Democracy

The previous analyses used democracy as an independent variable to predict changes in rivalry behavior. In this section, we reverse the causal arrow and explore the impact of rivalry on democracy levels. Our fourth expectation suggested that the occurrence of rivalry should lead to a general decrease in democracy levels within the rivals, relative to their democracy levels before the rivalry began. Table 6.6 presents difference of means tests for democracy levels (again, the range is from −10 for complete autocracy to +10 for complete democracy) before and during the rivalry, comparing the entire duration of the rivalry with the decade before that rivalry.[8] The results reveal that dyadic democracy levels do, on average, decrease during the course of rivalries, most notably during

---

[8] It should be noted that this table excludes cases for which democracy data are not available both before and during rivalry, which generally affects rivalries that begin with the entry of one or both rivals into the interstate system. This table also excludes rivalries that are censored, in the sense that another dispute at the end of the time period studied (1816–1992) would prolong the rivalry, to ensure that such rivalries do not distort the results. Table 6.7 is subject to a similar set of exclusions with respect to data after the end of rivalry.

TABLE 6.7: Democracy Levels during and after Interstate Rivalry

Time Period[a]	Mean (SD)	N
Proto-Rivalry		
During rivalry	–4.74 (4.45)	116
1st decade after	–4.56 (5.40)	116
2nd decade after	–4.30 (5.56)	116
$F = 0.22, p < .81$		
Enduring Rivalry		
During rivalry	-4.92 (3.10)	21
1st decade after	–4.25 (4.74)	21
2nd decade after	–3.60 (5.77)	21
$F = 0.42, p < .67$		
All Rivalries		
During rivalry	-4.77 (4.26)	137
1st decade after	–4.51 (5.29)	137
2nd decade after	–4.19 (5.58)	137
$F = 0.45, p < .64$		

Note: This table includes only dyads for which complete data are available (i.e., dyads for which the Polity III data set includes democracy data for both the rivalry period and portions of two separate decades after the rivalry) and excludes rivalries that can be considered "censored" because a new dispute toward the end of the time period studied (1978–92) would have prolonged the period of rivalry.
[a] Refers to the average dyadic democracy level during the entire militarized period of rivalry, in the first 10 years after the final dispute in the rivalry, and in the next 10 years (up to the twentieth year after the rivalry or the end of period of study in 1992, whichever comes first).

the first decade of the rivalry. They do not, on average, decrease thereafter and indeed increase ever so slightly. Yet there is considerable variation across individual cases, and the overall results are not statistically significant.

The overall effect of the onset of rivalries on democracy levels is rather small and not very consistent across rivalries. It is likely that the shifts in democracy levels are attributable to other factors. It is also apparent that except for abrupt regime changes, democracy levels do not vary substantially over time. Indeed, our earlier results suggest that most rivalries' dyadic regime types remain fairly stable using this continuous indicator of democracy, which is consistent with the earlier finding that only 23 of 1,166 rivalries include both joint democratic and nondemocratic periods. Dramatic changes in regime are relatively rare, and changes in democratization are not always in the same direction among pairs of states.

There does not appear to be a clear or substantial effect on democracy levels from rivalry onset, and we turn our attention to the effects of rivalry termination on democracy. Our final hypothesis suggested that the end of rivalry should lead be followed by a general increase in democracy levels within the rival states, relative to their democracy levels during the rivalry. Table 6.7 presents difference-of-means tests for democracy levels during and after rivalry, comparing the entire duration of rivalry with the decade after the last dispute in the rivalry and the decade following thereafter. We look at the second decade after the last dispute as we are certain that the rivalry has ended by that time and to insure that states have had sufficient time to implement democratic reforms and have them take effect. The results indicate a general positive effect, with the end of rivalry leading, on average, to an increase in dyadic democracy levels.

Although there is a general trend toward greater democratization in the aftermath of a rivalry, the magnitude of the effect is relatively small and does not reach conventional standards of statistical significance. There are a number of instances of states that become democratic after the last dispute in the rivalry, particularly following the end of World War II. A case-by-case analysis clearly shows that the end of the rivalries is associated with the establishment of democratic rule in these countries (e.g., numerous rivalries involving Japan, Italy, and Germany). Nevertheless, there appears to be no strong and systematic trend toward the spread of democracy emanating from the end of militarized conflict in rivalries. Therefore, we must reject the notion that a decline in conflict necessarily leads to an increase in democratization.

There is an important caveat with respect to interpretation of these results and indeed those regarding democracy and rivalry termination. Our results have suggested that democratization leads to rivalry termination, but not necessarily the reverse. In fact, it is quite difficult to sort out the causal direction of rivalry termination and democratization. As we noted in chapter 2, there is considerable debate over pinpointing the end of rivalries, and differing definitions of rivalry termination might produce varying results (Bennett 1997b). We conceive of rivalry termination as a process that occurs over a period of time, rather than a fixed event in space and time. Similarly, democratization is a process as well, with a democratic transition coded as occurring only after some threshold has been crossed. From these vantage points, democratization and rivalry termination might very well be interactive processes, and this should be the subject of future research. It is clear, however, the intersection is relevant only when there is abrupt change in the direction of greater democratization in a rivalry. We found very little impact from incremental changes in democracy levels on rivalry behavior and vice-versa.[9]

---

[9]This will be an important issue in the punctuated equilibrium model of enduring rivalries in the second part of the book.

Conclusion

This chapter reexamined the democratic peace in a longitudinal fashion, through the lenses of the rivalry approach. We utilized the rivalry approach to achieve four new and specific purposes with respect to the democratic peace. The first was to extend the democratic peace argument to phenomena beside war—rivalries. We found that rivalries have been rare among democratic dyads; there is only one case of enduring rivalry between consistently democratic states. A second purpose was to assess the effect of regime change when such a change precipitated a democratic dyad (or ended a joint democratic period). For the 23 rivalries that include both joint democratic and nondemocratic periods, lower dispute occurrence in democratic periods is confirmed only for enduring rivalries, but importantly there appears to be a lagged effect, with dispute formation dissipating over time. The latter is consistent with the onset and deepening of democratic norms. Third, we sought to determine whether a change to joint democracy was strong enough to terminate an ongoing rivalry. Empirical results indicate strong confirmation that rivalries are more likely to end when both states become democratic.

A fourth purpose of this chapter was to use the rivalry approach to answer questions about whether the causal arrow of the democratic peace might be reversed; that is, the beginning and end of rivalries promote less and more democratization respectively. Our findings, however, provide little evidence that the relationship between democracy and conflict is recursive. The onset of rivalry does not appear to decrease democracy levels substantially, and states do not appear to move rapidly toward democracy after the termination of rivalry. Although there are some difficulties sorting out the exact endings of rivalries and the beginnings of the democratization process, the very preliminary evidence is most suggestive of dramatic shifts to democracy being associated with the end of rivalries, and not the reverse.

The democratic peace has inspired numerous studies and great debate in the academic community in recent years. Our contribution to this research is to demonstrate the utility of moving away from pure cross-sectional analyses of democracy and war to dynamic and longitudinal assessments of the relationship between joint democracy and interstate conflict. Our results generally confirm the robust effects of the democratic peace, but also caution that democracy's relationship with conflict is a threshold one and one that is not likely to be recursive.

Part II

Enduring Rivalries

CHAPTER 7

A Punctuated Equilibrium Model
of Enduring Rivalries

Our project consists of two connected parts, the first is a new way of thinking about international conflict—the rivalry approach; the second involves exploring an important class of conflict phenomena suggested by the rivalry approach—enduring rivalries. In part 1, we focused on the rivalry approach by defining the core concept of international militarized rivalry and then looking at the theoretical and methodological implications of investigating international conflict phenomena using this theoretical framework. We found that the rivalry approach had major implications for thinking about and conducting research on questions of deterrence, crisis behavior, the democratic peace, and other aspects of war and peace.

In this second part of the book, we concentrate our efforts on enduring rivalries as empirical phenomena. The empirical patterns noted in chapter 3 indicate that enduring rivalries encompass a large portion (in some cases a majority) of the most violent international conflict over the past two centuries. Thus, in some sense, understanding enduring rivalries becomes a central component of understanding international conflict in general. Furthermore, to the extent that policy relevant guidelines can be derived from analyses of international conflict, those that help ameliorate the most deleterious aspects of enduring rivalries must have the highest priority on any research agenda.

Until recently enduring rivalries as conflict phenomena have escaped study by students of international war. The first part of this book showed that the rivalry approach sheds new light on many theories of war. Now, we argue that one needs a *model of enduring rivalries*.

By replacing "war" with "enduring rivalry," we fundamentally change the research and theoretical enterprise. For the last 30 years conflict research has used war or dispute occurrence as the consensus dependent variable. With the rivalry approach, we suggest that other aspects of international and militarized conflict deserve attention. When we move to enduring rivalries as the focus, we no longer have just one dependent variable, but multiple ones. Using the life-cycle metaphor, we find that there are three major categories of dependent variables. The first involves (enduring) rivalry birth. Here the two key questions are "why do rivalries start?" and "why do some rivalries become enduring?" Symmetrically, a second class of questions inquires about enduring rivalry termination and conflict resolution: why and when do enduring rivalries end? The third, large and heterogeneous, class consists of questions about the growth, development, and evolution of enduring rivalries.

We examine aspects of those three dimensions of the enduring rivalry life-cycle. Although we present more specific hypotheses about the beginning, evolution, and termination of enduring rivalries, we do so within a general model that encompasses all three and what we call the *punctuated equilibrium model of enduring rivalries*. We use the *punctuated equilibrium* label because our model shares many characteristics with the biological theory of punctuated equilibrium. The biological theory stresses the very uneven rates of species evolution, arguing that it occurs in spurts followed by long periods of stasis and no change. Species evolve rapidly, change little, and then go extinct quickly. This, we will argue, is the dominant pattern in enduring rivalries. States rapidly lock-in to enduring rivalries, which then change little until their rapid demise.

In the second half of this book, we propose the punctuated equilibrium model of enduring rivalries and use it as a guide to analyze several aspects of enduring rivalries. In adopting this biological framework, we borrow from the models that have revolutionized the study of evolutionary biology over the past several decades, but we also profit from the insights gained by using such models to understand political phenomena, mostly notably studies of public policy formation in the United States. Our contention is not that biological systems are identical to those occasioned by enduring rivalries, but rather that the punctuated equilibrium model in biology offers a useful and heuristic analogy by which to understand the dynamics of enduring rivalries. In describing this model, we begin by briefly discussing the biological aspects of the punctuated equilibrium model—particularly those of relevance to us—and then move to discuss its application to public policymaking. With this groundwork, we then discuss its general application to enduring rivalries. We leave specific applications, hypotheses, and empirical analyses to the four substantive chapters in this part of the book.

The Punctuated Equilibrium Model and Its Biological Origins

For decades—since the 1940s—what Julian Huxley identified as "the modern synthesis" dominated the thinking of evolutionary biologists. Prior to this synthesis, a "bewildering array of evolutionary process theories existed, each touted by a different biological discipline seemingly bent upon establishing the primacy of its own phenomena and its own insights" (Eldredge 1985, 3). The modern synthesis combined Darwin's theory of natural selection with the discovery of how genes produce variation upon which natural selection can work. Perhaps most elegantly summarized by Gould (1983, 13), the synthesis emphasized "gradual, adaptive change produced by natural selection acting exclusively upon organisms [i.e., not species]." The standard theory thus saw evolution occurring everywhere, all the time, and in an incremental fashion.

It was from a group of paleontologists outside the core of evolutionary theory (often formal and mathematical) that arose the challenge to the gradualist vision of natural selection (see Eldredge 1995 for an account of the admission of paleontologists to the "high table" of evolutionary theory). The fossil record produces little evidence for the incrementalist position. That is, the literal geological record was more supportive of abrupt changes: most fossil species disappear looking much the same as when they appeared, while new species in any local area appear abruptly and fully formed. Traditionally—starting with Darwin—this was deemed the result of the rarity and poor quality of the fossil record.

In 1972, Eldredge and Gould proposed the punctuated equilibrium model, which instead of explaining away discrepancies between data and the standard theory devised a theory that matched more directly the fossil record (see Eldredge 1995 for a survey and overview). The punctuated equilibrium model portrays evolution as primarily the product of rapid speciation. The model suggests a process characterized by long periods of stasis punctuated by the sudden appearance of new, qualitatively different species. Unlike the standard model, the punctuated equilibrium model regards speciation and evolution as rare, occurring in specific and unusual circumstances.

As Gould recounts (1987, 37), scholars working in the modern synthesis only looked for gradualist evolution in choosing their cases for study. "Over and over again in my career I have bashed my head against this wall of non-reporting [of null results]. When Niles Eldredge and I proposed the theory of punctuated equilibrium in evolution, we did so to grant stasis in phylogenetic lineages the status of worth reporting—for stasis had previously been ignored as nonevidence of nonevolution, though all paleontologists knew its high frequency." With the punctuated equilibrium model in hand, biologists began to "see" long-term stasis in species as well as periods of rapid speciation.

The most novel of the rare speciation propositions was the suggestion that the birth and death of most species occur during periods of major environmental change and shock. The most famous of these is the claim that a large asteroid hit the earth about 60 million years ago, causing the extinction of 65–70 percent of all existing species (Raup 1992). The evolutionary window of opportunity that this event opened resulted in the rise of thousands of new species.

The punctuated equilibrium model also stresses that speciation comes about through geographic isolation: "a small segment of the ancestral population is isolated at the periphery of the ancestral range. Large, stable central

populations exert a strong homogenizing influence. New and favorable muta-
tions are diluted by the sheer bulk of the population through which they must be
spread. They must build slowly in frequency, but changing environments usually cancel their selective value long before they reach fixation. . . . [Still] small,
peripherally isolated groups are cut off from parental stock. They live as tiny
populations in geographic corners of the ancestral range. Selective pressures
are usually intense because peripheries mark the edge of ecological tolerance
for ancestral forms. Favorable variations spread quickly [speciation]. Small,
peripheral isolates are a laboratory of evolutionary change" (Gould 1983, 183–
84). This, however, was already part of the modern synthesis, particularly due
to the work of Mayr (1970). Today, almost three decades after it was first introduced, the punctuated equilibrium model has been accepted by a majority of
evolutionary biologists (Gould and Eldredge 1993).

For us the essential elements of the biological version of punctuated equilibrium are that species do not necessarily evolve in a linear and incremental
fashion, but experience long periods of stability and experience change in a
rapid and sometimes unpredictable fashion. Massive shocks are needed to upset that stability and provide windows of opportunity for new species to arise.
Such notions have influenced a number of studies that seek to understand how
policy agendas are formulated and alternatives selected in American policymaking.

Punctuated Equilibrium in Public Policy Studies

Just as the gradualist model has dominated biological thinking on evolution, so
too has incrementalist thought held the center stage in research on U.S. domestic policy and budgeting. Wildavsky's (1975) work has perhaps been the most
influential in establishing the incremental model. In his study of organizational
behavior, he found that incrementalism (linear change) described the behavior
of bureaucracies well.

Just as the punctuated equilibrium approach questioned traditional biological models, so has the incremental model been challenged by those that note
large shifts in the policy process (Tucker 1982). John Kingdon (1984) authored
among the first and most influential of these studies. Kingdon's research suggested that the agenda-setting component is best conceptualized as independent
streams of problems, policies, and politics awaiting periodic, albeit fleeting, opportunities for policy choice (this is largely based on the "garbage can model"
of Cohen, March, and Olsen 1972). Within this organized anarchy, problems
frequently chase solutions and vice versa. Moreover, the availability and pop-
ularity of particular solutions—not any inherent priority or urgency of public
problems—help determine which subjects come up for consideration on the
decision agenda. The likelihood of a particular condition becoming a public
problem worthy of action, and for one policy solution to arise from amid the
primeval soup of possible alternatives to address it, is increased if a coupling

or linking of the problem, policy, and political streams occurs. When this confluence occurs, government action is taken against a problem. For this to happen, policy windows occasioned by problem opportunities must open, and viable solutions must be available and then be coupled to the problem by entrepreneurs operating within policy communities. The political environment (e.g., the national mood or partisan predispositions in the U.S. Congress) also must be amenable to policy change (for applications beyond the American political context, see Zahariadis 1996).

For Kingdon, the specific policy alternatives considered viable for selection within the policy stream remain incremental. In describing the dynamics of the policy stream, he argues that alternatives become viable for consideration only after undergoing a prolonged "softening" process. As a result of softening, an alternative's workability, affordability, and legitimacy are established within the relevant policy communities. If alternatives change, they develop more through recombination than by mutation. In sum, Kingdon's overview of the agenda-setting component portrays a decidedly nonincremental ebb and flow of agenda items that appear and disappear with striking rapidity. In contrast, the set of policy alternatives available for addressing these items is portrayed as distinctly incremental, with alternatives evolving out of previous policy options or combinations thereof. "There may be no new thing under the sun at the same time that there may be dramatic change and innovation" (Kingdon 1984, 210).

Kingdon's model of the policymaking process brought the idea of rapid change to the forefront, although he did not use the label *punctuated equilibrium* and still regarded policy alternatives as arising incrementally. Other scholars were soon to challenge those ideas and rely more heavily on the punctuated equilibrium analogy. Durant and Diehl (1989) explicitly adopted the moniker of punctuated equilibrium and argued that the elements of the foreign policy process can be characterized by rapid change and "pure mutation." Thus, some foreign policies, in their view, can be understood only by reference to a punctuated equilibrium process. Consistent with this is the idea that foreign policy attitudes of leaders and elites are relatively stable over time and are disrupted only by dramatic shocks (Russett 1990).

Other analyses of policymaking began to contain language and descriptions consistent with punctuated equilibrium. As conceptualized by Yehezkel Dror (1984), policymaking as "fuzzy gambling" refers to decision contexts characterized by unknowable consequences, problematic probabilities, and disruptive discontinuities or jumps. In his words, policymaking is "an unstable casino where the rules of the game, their mixes of chance and skill, and [their] payoffs change in unpredictable ways during the game itself, where unforeseeable forms of external 'wildcards' may appear suddenly" (9) and where "it is impossible to draw conclusions on the quality of policy making from its results"

(13). In short, fuzzy gambling scenarios are notable for the uncertainty, unpredictability, and surprise associated with the decision environment itself, with specific policy alternatives, and with disparate policy outcomes.

We noted above that scholars of evolution traditionally did not look for stasis because their theories emphasized change. A parallel has occurred in the policy literature. Wildavsky (1975) himself noted that occasionally large shifts occurred in budgeting forcing him to reestimate regression lines. Nevertheless, given his incrementalist framework, he made little of this phenomenon.

Starting from a punctuated equilibrium position, Baumgartner and Jones (1993) describe the policy process as one that is characterized by rapid changes and long periods of stasis. "Rather than making moderate adaptive adjustments to an ever-changing environment, political decision making is characterized sometimes by stasis, when existing decision designs are routinely employed, and sometimes by punctuations, when a slowly growing condition suddenly bursts onto agendas of a new set of policymakers or when existing decision makers shift attention to new attributes or dimensions of the existing situation. Complex interactive political systems do not react slowly and automatically to changing perceptions or conditions; rather, it takes increasing pressure and sometimes a crisis atmosphere to dislodge established ways of thinking about policies. The result is periods of stability interspersed with occasional, unpredictable, and dramatic change" (Jones, Baumgartner, and True 1998, 2). Thus, they find that the incrementalist or gradualist story is not so much wrong as partially true. Incrementalism and stasis describe long periods of the policy process. For Baumgartner and Jones (1993), many of the punctuations that prompt policy change are exogenous. Nevertheless, they also recognize that positive feedback mechanisms endogenous to the institutions of government can prompt such dramatic changes as well. They also make reference to new institutional actors and new ways of conceiving the relevant issue or problem as sources of change.

Jones, Baumgartner, and True (1998) tested their punctuated equilibrium model by analyzing U.S. budget allocations in the post–World War II era. They report dramatic changes at three points in the 48-year period studied, with largely incremental change occurring otherwise. Importantly, the punctuated equilibrium model is compelling, even controlling for three rival explanations. Overall, they argue that stability interrupted by dramatic change is characteristic of processes throughout national government and not confined to a few programs or subsystems. They are not alone; others (Casstevens 1980; Mayhew 1991; Peters and Hogwood 1985) have found that short periods of intense policy activity leave a substantial institutional legacy.

Military budgets provide one link between the domestic literature on policy and the concerns of international relations scholars. Here, as with other budgets, if one examines (peacetime) spending, one tends to find incremental change. But a number of scholars (Russett 1970; Diehl and Goertz 1985) have noted a ratchet effect in military spending due to major wars: military spending increased dramatically during war, but rarely does spending return to the prewar levels in the aftermath of that war.

As in evolutionary biology, studies of public policymaking have shifted away from approaches that emphasize gradualist processes and incremental change to those of the punctuated equilibrium model. We now attempt to make a further extension of that model to international conflict processes.

Punctuated Equilibrium and Enduring Rivalries

As with punctuated equilibrium in biology and policy studies, the rivalry approach points out aspects of international political life that scholars "knew," but that were never acknowledged, largely because of the lack of a theoretical framework that could make sense of them and the general tendency toward linear thinking. The rivalry approach remarks that many international conflicts are linked together in an ongoing relationship. This appears particularly obvious in the case of enduring rivalries. Yet, with rare exceptions, students of war have treated these conflicts as isolated cases.

The punctuated equilibrium model in biology emphasizes the stability of most species throughout most of their lives. The punctuated equilibrium framework for rivalries does likewise. Once we shift the focus of analysis from crisis and war to militarized relationships, we can see that enduring rivalries in particular evidence a great stability. The emphasis on stability and stasis was novel in biology, and it is also not part of any standard international relations theory of war. Except for the (neo)realists, who make broad assumptions about the perpetuity of international anarchy, little in international conflict theory stresses issues of stability (though see Goertz 1994 for an extended analysis).

There are some interesting potential links between organizational theories of foreign policy and rivalries. As the result of Allison's (1971) work in the 1970s, the organizational model was an important approach to foreign policy. In the mid-1970s, however, this approach lost momentum, although it has not disappeared. For example, Rhodes (1994) found that the U.S. Navy has followed a 15-capital-ship policy since the Washington Naval Treaty of 1922. In a different framework, these issues have resurfaced recently in "cultural" approaches to international relations (Katzenstein 1996; Legro 1994; Rhodes 1994). For example, if one compares the treatment of the Red Cross by the French military in the period 1860–1920 (Hutchinson 1996) with Kier's discussion (1995) of French interwar military culture, one cannot help but notice many commonalities. Legro (1997) also discusses the organizational resistance to change in World War II.

From our point of view, however, both foreign policy organizational models in the Allison tradition and the social constructivist literature, like their incrementalist domestic politics cousins, stress stasis but do not include the rapid change component so important in the punctuated equilibrium model.

FIGURE 7.1: Punctuated Equilibrium and Incrementalist Models

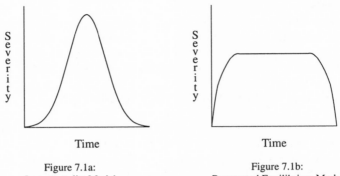

Figure 7.1a:
Incrementalist Model

Figure 7.1b:
Punctuated Equilibrium Model

The application of the punctuated equilibrium model to enduring rivalries rests on the ideas that enduring rivalries, once established, are relatively stable phenomena over time until they are dislodged by environmental shocks. Figure 7.1 illustrates the difference between the traditional view of biological evolution and the punctuated equilibrium model, and the corresponding differences between a punctuated equilibrium approach to enduring rivalries and a gradualist one. Figure 7.1a shows the gradual rise of the species/rivalry followed by a gradual decline. Figure 7.1b contrasts this with evolutionary change that is rapid at the beginning, followed by a long period of stasis, and ending with rapid death.

The first characteristic of the punctuated equilibrium model is stability. We argue that enduring rivalries exhibit consistent patterns over their lifetimes, and there is no secular trend in conflict behavior within the rivalry. Chapter 9 tests such a proposition as we examine patterns of conflict behavior that are consistent with this expectation as well as those suggested by alternative formulations. Chapter 10 looks at conflict management in enduring rivalries. A punctuated equilibrium suggests that attempts to manage conflict by exogenous forces are likely to have limited impact on the stable processes of enduring rivalries, and we empirically examine this proposition. Further expectations derived from the punctuated equilibrium model are explored in these two chapters on rivalry stability.

Although the punctuated equilibrium model predicts stasis for most of the life of a species/policy/enduring rivalry, it does expect rapid change at the beginning and end of the process. Much work in paleontology has confirmed this in the biological context, and the U.S. domestic policy literature contains similar findings. If one examines a policy at random for a short period of time, one is likely to find stasis or incremental change. It is necessary to examine the long term or focus on specific beginning or end periods to evaluate the punctuated equilibrium model. Jones, Baumgartner, and True's (1998) recent work on budgeting illustrates this: they have looked at budgeting over a much longer period than previous studies because one cannot evaluate the punctuated equilibrium model otherwise. Only when one examines budgets over the very long term does the punctuated equilibrium pattern emerge. In the case of military budgets, it is only when one compares prewar with postwar budgets that the punctuated equilibrium effect appears.

The same holds true for enduring rivalries. If one chooses isolated crises, more or less at random, or puts all disputes in one statistical hopper (a cross-sectional analysis), then one cannot evaluate the punctuated equilibrium framework. Because the punctuated equilibrium model predicts rapid change at the beginning and end of enduring rivalries, we shall focus special attention on these periods.

All this makes sense only once one is using the rivalry as the object of analysis. Within biology, one notable aspect of the punctuated equilibrium model was to refocus attention on the species level of analysis. In standard, mathematical, or genetic models of evolution, species played no real role, as evolution was changing genetic makeup. Punctuated equilibrium stressed evolution at the species level. Genes, of course, are involved but *within* the species. Not surprisingly, there have been sharp exchanges between Gould and Eldredge, on one hand and biologists like Dawkins, on the other, who see evolution taking place only at the genetic level (not surprisingly, Dawkins's best-known book is called *The Selfish Gene,* 1989).

The parallel with the rivalry approach is clear. We emphasized in the first part of this volume that new research questions and issues arise when one moves from the dispute as the object of analysis to the rivalry as the focus. Rivalry as the level of analysis corresponds, then, to the species and the individual dispute to the gene. At the core of the rivalry approach is the idea that we cannot understand key aspects of war and peace by looking only at wars and disputes (genes) taken in isolation from the rivalry relationships (species) in which they are embedded. We can find a similar situation in the study of (domestic) policy. A "policy" almost by definition implies multiple "decisions," as the policy is implemented over time. One can focus on the policy or on the individual decisions made "within" the policy. To simplify, *policy* implies multiple decisions over the long term, while *decisions* are onetime actions. Rational actor models privilege the decision, while organizational models stress the policy. Both are instrumental, but they imply quite a different view of government behavior. Not surprisingly, because enduring rivalries involve long-term conflictual relationships, we emphasize a policy model of state behavior. The punctuated equilibrium approach suggests that states make relatively long-term policy commitments and then stick with them, until some change in the environment dislodges those preferences and policy choices. We find it natural, then, to link our punctuated equilibrium model of enduring rivalries to Baumgartner and Jones's (1993) punctuated equilibrium model of domestic policy. For us, enduring rivalries are a special case, international politics, of the policymaking pattern common in domestic politics.

Another prominent characteristic of the punctuated equilibrium model, besides stasis, is the stress on environmental shocks as a key factor in the rise and decline of species. Massive environmental change—such as a large asteroid striking the earth—kills off many species and at the same time provides opportunities for new ones to evolve. The flip side of this pattern is that species are generally quite resistant to a wide range of environmental conditions and changes. We apply a similar logic to enduring rivalries. Under a wide range of system changes, enduring rivalries prove to be quite robust. This casts serious doubt on realism, neorealism, and other theories that imply that states always respond rapidly to system changes. As subsequent chapters illustrate, many rivalries survive large- and small-scale environmental changes. On the other hand, when rivalries do emerge and die off, they do so in association with massive political shocks. Similar to the biological theory, we stress system-level shocks such as world wars. Unlike the biological theory, however, we also include political shocks endogenous to the rivals, such as regime change and civil war. The commonality is that large shocks set the stage for enduring rivalries to emerge, but also provide the occasion for their termination. Chapter 10 investigates the relationship between political shocks and the birth and death of enduring rivalries.

The window-of-opportunity concept lies at the core of Kingdon's (1984) agenda-setting model. A major reason why things move rapidly in his model comes from the opening and closing of policy windows. Although policy solutions change incrementally, windows open and shut quickly. It is usually the opening of a window that changes the likelihood of agenda success from near zero to near certainty. Within the biological and enduring rivalry versions of the punctuated equilibrium model, large shocks create windows of opportunity for change. We use the same logic as Kingdon: the opening of a window is a necessary, but not sufficient, condition for the rise or fall of an enduring rivalry. Kingdon quite clearly states that without an open window the chances of agenda success are near zero: "In space shots, the window presents the opportunity for a launch. The target planets are in proper alignment, but will not stay that way for long. Thus the launch must take place when the window is open, lest the opportunity slip away. Once lost, the opportunity may recur, but in the interim, astronauts and space engineers must wait until the window reopens. Similarly, windows open in policy systems. These policy windows, the opportunities for action on given initiatives, present themselves and stay open for only short periods. If the participants cannot or do not take advantage of these opportunities, they must bide their time until the next opportunity comes along" (1995, 166). Similarly, we propose that only when a window of opportunity is opened by a political shock will enduring rivalries begin or end.

Continuing with the biological analogy, enduring rivalries, like individual species, do not exist in isolation, but rather interact in various competitive and cooperative ways. Chapter 12 introduces the concept of *rivalry linkage;* this refers to the influence that (enduring) rivalries have on each other. The dynamics of an enduring rivalry may depend, at least in part, on its connection with other rivalries. Most notably linkage with a major-major power rivalry makes the enduring rivalry more severe than would otherwise be the case.

We have seen a trend in conflict studies from the system-level studies of the 1970s to an emphasis on dyads in the 1990s. The punctuated equilibrium model suggests that characteristics of the actors/rivalry matter. Something about the rivals and their relationships makes them relatively insensitive to changes in the international environment. Yet the emphasis on political shocks and linkage means system-level factors play an important role in the life cycle of rivalries.

In chapter 4, we argued that taking rivalries as a new object of analysis means that new aspects of international war and peace become visible. Thinking about international conflict in terms of rivalries allows us to observe new facets of international relations, which then incite new theory development. The punctuated equilibrium model is our response to that empirical and theoretical challenge. In the chapters to follow, we shall frequently contrast gradualist models (e.g., Hensel 1996) of enduring rivalry with those proposed by the punctuated equilibrium framework. Our goal in this second part is thus to sketch out the broad outlines of the punctuated equilibrium model and to subject them to empirical analysis.

In the coming chapters, we focus on stasis and other patterns in enduring rivalries, and the importance of shocks to the origins and ends of rivalries. We end with an examination of the importance of the linkage between enduring rivalries as a factor in explaining how severe the enduring rivalry becomes. We consider this but an introductory survey of some of the many important facets of the phenomenon of enduring rivalries. Many others remain on the research agenda, for example the organizational decision-making model on which the punctuated equilibrium model rests. We return to this and others issues in our discussion of the future research agenda in the final chapter.

Before we begin to describe more fully and test the punctuated equilibrium model in the context of enduring rivalries, we provide a broad overview of enduring rivalries in the next chapter, extending what we did for rivalries in general in chapter 3. We also review the limited extant empirical literature on enduring rivalries as it relates to the concerns of the second part of this book and the validity of the punctuated equilibrium model.

CHAPTER 8

An Overview of Enduring Rivalries and Enduring Rivalries Research

Studying enduring rivalries narrows our focus from over one thousand rivalries of all varieties to only a small fraction of them, and an even smaller fraction of possible dyadic combinations. Nevertheless, much of the history of international war and peace over the past two centuries revolves around these pairs of states. In this chapter, we present our list of enduring rivalries and discuss some of their characteristics, extending some of the data description first presented in chapter 3. The last part of the chapter is dedicated to reviewing previous research on enduring rivalries and related subjects, with an eye to identifying any consensus in this limited body of research and assessing how that empirical evidence comports with the expectations of the punctuated equilibrium model.

General Characteristics of Enduring Rivalries

Table 8.1 presents our list of 63 enduring rivalries over the 1816–1992 period, along with the beginning and ending dates, the duration, and the number of militarized disputes for each rivalry. Among the 63 rivalries, 37 cannot be said to have ended definitely by 1992, the last date for data on militarized disputes; we refer to these as censored cases.[1] Although there is a 6-dispute minimum in order to qualify as an enduring rivalry, the mean rivalry experiences considerably more militarized disputes. Among the full set of cases, the average is 14.98 disputes, with 11.92 disputes among the noncensored cases (the total for the whole population will underestimate the true average, as some ongoing rivalries are likely to experience one or more disputes before they end). Most

---

[1]Technically there is some possibility that our early rivalries could be left-censored as well; that is, some rivalries may have actually begun before 1816, the starting date of our study. Yet an analysis of the enduring rivalry list and the earliest starting dates reveals that this is not a possibility, given our coding rules for the interconnection of disputes in the same rivalry. It is conceivable, and we have no way to verify this, that some cases identified as proto-rivalries in the early nineteenth century would qualify as enduring rivalries if it were possible to extend the time frame before 1816.

enduring rivalries also dramatically exceed the 20-year time minimum with the mean enduring rivalry lasting 37.89 years if one includes all the cases and 38.61 years if one focuses solely on those rivalries that have clearly ended.

There does not appear to be a strong secular trend toward longer rivalries over the time period, although this is difficult to ascertain given the large number of ongoing rivalries. Somewhat surprising, few enduring rivalries span large tracts of both centuries. Only three rivalries last more than eighty years. These are the dyadic rivalries among Russia/USSR, China, and Japan respectively, competitions largely over territorial expansion and hegemony in Asia. The Russia–China rivalry has its origins in the 1860s[2] and cannot be judged to have ended by 1992. This is astounding given that both countries have undergone tremendous economic changes and several dramatic regime changes (both to Communist regimes in the twentieth century). The same might be said for Japan, whose internal and foreign policy changes have been at least as dramatic. Especially notable is that these three states, at various times over the long periods in their rivalries, have been allies with one another. This illustrates that rivalries may persist even when temporary war or other alignments occur.

In contrast to the continuous rivalries between Russia, China, and Japan, there are several cases of what we have called interrupted rivalries, rivalries that abate for a period of time, only to be renewed again. The Greece–Turkey (then the Ottoman Empire) rivalry has its origins in the middle of the nineteenth century, but its militarized component ends with its last dispute in 1925. Historical animosities blossom again in 1958 and continue today, despite their common NATO membership, illustrating once again that a common external enemy will not necessarily drive allies closer together on other issues of contention. Chile and Argentina also have an interrupted rivalry, with one enduring rivalry occurring before World War I and another commencing after World War II. There are also several instances of interrupted rivalries among the major powers, including between the United Kingdom and Russia and between France and Germany respectively.

There may be a secular trend toward more intense rivalries after World War II. Whether this is a function of Cold War rivalries fought over more contentious issues or some other characteristics of the rivalry or the rivals is not clear. It may be that modern states are capable of more frequent interactions with their friends and enemies alike and that the projection of military force is also easier, thereby generating more frequent militarized interactions. Three rivalries appear especially intense, each producing more than one dispute per year on average. The United States–USSR superpower rivalry was the most intense with 1.33 disputes per year. Not far behind are Syria–Israel (1.18 disputes per year) and United States–China (1.05 disputes per year).

---

[2]The rivalry may have actually begun a century or two before this, but our study does not begin until 1816 and the rivalry does not become consistently militarized until the 1860s.

TABLE 8.1: Enduring rivalries, 1816–1992

Rivalry	Life	Disputes	Duration
USA–Cuba	1959–1990	15	31
USA–Mexico	1836–1893	17	57
USA–Ecuador	1952–1981	8	28
USA–Peru	1955–1992	6	37
USA–UK	1837–1861	8	24
USA–Spain	1850–1875	10	25
USA–USSR	1946–1986	53	40
USA–China	1949–1972	24	23
USA–N. Korea	1950–1985	18	35
Honduras–Nicaragua	1907–1929	6	22
Ecuador–Peru	1891–1955	21	64
Brazil–UK	1838–1863	6	24
Chile–Argentina	1873–1909	10	36
Chile–Argentina	1952–1984	17	32
UK–Germany	1887–1921	7	34
UK–Russia	1876–1923	17	47
UK–USSR	1939–1985	18	46
UK–Turkey	1895–1934	10	39
UK–Iraq	1958–1992	10	34
Belgium–Germany	1914–1940	8	26
France–Germany	1911–1945	9	34
France–Germany	1830–1887	12	57
France–Turkey	1897–1938	11	41
France–China	1870–1900	6	30
Spain–Morocco	1957–1980	8	23
Germany–Italy	1914–1945	7	31
Italy–Yugoslavia	1923–1956	8	33
Italy–Ethiopia	1923–1943	6	20
Italy–Turkey	1880–1924	14	44
Yugoslavia–Bulgaria	1913–1952	8	39
Greece–Bulgaria	1914–1952	9	38
Greece–Turkey	1958–1989	14	30
Greece–Turkey	1866–1925	17	59
Cyprus–Turkey	1965–1988	7	24
USSR–Norway	1956–1987	9	32
USSR–Iran	1908–1987	18	80
Russia–Turkey	1876–1921	12	45
USSR–China	1862–1986	50	124
USSR–Japan	1895–1984	43	90

Continued on next page

TABLE 8.1—*continued*

Congo Brazzaville–Zaire	1963–1987	7	23
Uganda–Kenya	1965–1989	6	24
Somalia–Ethiopia	1960–1985	16	25
Ethiopia–Sudan	1967–1988	8	21
Morocco–Algeria	1962–1984	6	22
Iran–Iraq	1953–1992	20	40
Iraq–Israel	1967–1991	6	24
Iraq–Kuwait	1961–1992	9	31
Egypt–Israel	1948–1989	36	41
Syria–Jordan	1949–1991	9	41
Syria–Israel	1948–1986	45	38
Jordan–Israel	1948–1973	13	25
Israel–Saudi Arabia	1957–1981	6	24
Saudi Arabia–N. Yemen	1962–1984	6	21
Afghanistan–Pakistan	1949–1989	11	40
China–S. Korea	1950–1987	9	37
China–Japan	1873–1958	34	85
China–India	1950–1987	22	37
N. Korea–S. Korea	1949–1992	20	43
S. Korea–Japan	1953–1982	15	29
India–Pakistan	1947–1991	40	44
Thailand–Cambodia	1953–1987	14	34
Thailand–Laos	1960–1988	13	27
Thailand–N. Vietnam	1961–1989	6	28

Rivalry in the Middle East is typically characterized as the Arab-Israeli rivalry, but this simple characterization badly misstates conflict relationships in that region. First, it ignores the five other rivalries among the largely Arab states themselves. Second, it implies that Israel's rivalries with its neighbors are largely uniform. In fact, they are quite different. Not all of Israel's disputes involve the same set of rivals (Iraq, Egypt, Syria, Jordan, Saudi Arabia). The Israeli rivalries with Syria and Egypt are far more intense than other Arab-Israeli rivalries. Furthermore, Jordan effectively opts out of the Arab alliance with Israel following the 1973 war and that particular rivalry ends. We note in passing here that it will be interesting to assess in our chapter 12 analyses how these Middle East rivalries, and others, are linked to one another.

Our enduring rivalry list results from the theoretical and operational criteria discussed in chapter 3. With a concrete set of rivalries in hand, we revisit a couple of contested issues in the conceptualization of enduring rivalry, namely power asymmetry and the notion of principal rivalries. We think both these concerns flow from a common inference that *enduring* rivalry means *severe* rivalry.

We have ourselves contributed to this notion by showing that a large percentage of wars and disputes occur within enduring rivalries. Although this is an empirical fact, our conceptualization in no way implies this. As the adjective *enduring* indicates, our list of enduring rivalries are those militarized competitions that have lasted a long time. It is absolutely crucial to separate "how long" from "how severe" a rivalry is.

Thompson's (1995) idea of principal rivalries taps, we believe, the severity dimension of (enduring) rivalries. To the extent that it does, we see no conceptual conflict, and we agree that some enduring rivalries are more important to a given state than others and are likely to be more severe. If we examine our list of enduring rivalries, we can see that major powers often have multiple enduring rivalries. Without a doubt, some mean more to the major power than others: the United States–Peru rivalry is not equivalent to the United States–USSR. Within the punctuated equilibrium framework, we see that rivalries can lock into low as well as high-level, long-term conflicts. A major part of a theory of enduring rivalries is explaining *why* some enduring rivalries are more severe than others. To answer this question, one needs *variation* in enduring rivalry severity.

A second issue raised by Vasquez (1993), initially noted in chapters 2 and 3, concerns power asymmetry and enduring rivalry. On the (realist) face of it, long-term power conflict between asymmetric dyads appears implausible. The simple, and simplistic, response would be that our list contains a fair number of such asymmetric dyads. In coarse power terms, there are 19 major-minor enduring rivalries.[3] One can push that further, since among the minor-minor dyads some notable power asymmetries exist, such as between Israel–Jordan or Spain–Morocco.

Two considerations come to mind when examining the asymmetric enduring rivalries on our list. One is that low-level conflicts often drag on. Recall that many militarized disputes do not always constitute major diplomatic incidents. If one thinks of enduring rivalries only as the most severe conflicts, then we miss a real possibility: long-term, low-level conflicts. A second fact leaps out from the list: many major-minor rivalries are linked to major-major ones. A tendency when thinking about rivalries is to ignore the linkages between them; for example, the Germany–Belgium rivalry does not develop without the Germany–United Kingdom or Germany–France rivalries. One of Vasquez's two paths to war is through conflict diffusion—our linkage concept. It appears that this is a possible path to enduring rivalry as well.

As we move to our analysis of enduring rivalries, it is important to keep in mind that when we use the term *enduring rivalry* we refer to a particular conceptualization. In particular, one should not confound the duration and severity dimensions of rivalries. We feel that a good concept and accompanying data

---

[3] We count only those that remained major-minor rivalries throughout their whole existence, as the number of major powers fluctuates over time.

set should not make controversial theoretical issues part of data collection. By remaining noncommittal, our list of enduring rivalries then permits tests of theoretical claims instead of incorporating them into coding rules.

Previous Work on (Enduring) Rivalries

In one sense, there has been an abundance of work on rivalries. Yet, in examining the scholarly literature, one does not see direct evidence of it. This is because work on rivalries has not carried the rivalry moniker and has primarily been confined to the analysis of a single prolonged competition between two or more states. Most prominent have been those concerned with the United States–Soviet Union rivalry (Bialer 1988; Nincic 1989) and the Arab-Israeli conflict (Herzog 1982). These are primarily descriptive studies that, although insightful on individual events, do not offer much in the way of a theoretical understanding of how rivalries evolve. Furthermore, they offer little in the way of generalizations that extend beyond the single case at hand. Except as excellent sources on the history of individual rivalries, we largely ignore this segment of the literature.

With the rivalry approach in mind, we can now survey the literature on enduring and other rivalries. Crucial to understanding our project and its relationship to this growing literature is the distinction between the rivalry approach and rivalries (particularly enduring ones) as an object of study. Great effort (e.g., Goertz and Diehl 1993; Thompson 1995) has gone into definitional issues (see chapter 2 for a discussion of these efforts), which is the first step in studying a phenomenon in its own right. Yet, with rare exceptions, there has been little work on explaining various aspects of the (enduring) rivalry phenomenon. Nevertheless, beyond historical works, there has been a range of research on enduring rivalries and their processes.

As it stands, the field has no general theory of enduring rivalry. Various studies address particular aspects of enduring rivalries, but none pretends to provide a global view. Above, we outlined the punctuated equilibrium model of enduring rivalries, which has implications for all stages of the rivalry life cycle. In our survey of the existing work on enduring rivalries we pay special attention to the relevance of such work for the punctuated equilibrium model.

Rivalries as a Primary Focus

More recently, the intrinsic importance of rivalries as a focus of study in their own right has been recognized. Several works address issues similar to those in this book. These include the origins, dynamics, conditions for war, and termination of rivalries. Generally, these studies have focused exclusively on enduring rivalries.

The Origins of Rivalries

Few studies deal with understanding the beginning of rivalries, exclusive of interstate conflict in general (e.g., Maoz 1982). Yet, as implied in Hensel (1996), it may not be necessary to consider the origins of rivalries (even enduring ones) as any different from the initiation of international conflict in general. Hensel argues that the behavior of the disputants in their first few militarized interactions determines whether an enduring rivalry will form or whether the competition will die out. In this way, his explanation for the origins of enduring rivalries is based on the dynamics of the rivalry process, and not on the initial conditions surrounding the first militarized confrontation between the rivals. This is largely contrary to the specifications of the punctuated equilibrium model in which rivalries lock-in early to patterns of conflict and are not much affected by factors peculiar to the first conflict interactions. In their game-theoretic analysis of four Middle East rivalries, Maoz and Mor (1996) find that the enduring rivalries exhibit acute conflict at the outset with a constant motivation to extend the conflict from the beginning. This suggests that conflicts do not "evolve" into enduring rivalries, but supports the punctuated equilibrium expectation that they exhibit severe rivalry characteristics from their origin.

Various other studies look to initial and other conditions to understand how rivalries, especially enduring ones, develop. This provides us some clues to the initial conditions that are unspecified in the punctuated equilibrium model. Levy and Ali (1998) conducted a case study of the Anglo-Dutch rivalry over the period 1609–52. They explored why a purely commercial rivalry remained peaceful for almost a half-century, but then turned into a militarized rivalry that was soon to experience three wars in relatively short succession. Initially, they point out that the Dutch and the English had diametrically opposed economic interests, which made them logical candidates to clash with one another. Reinforcing this conflict, economic liberalism determined Dutch strategies, while the British pursued a mercantilist strategy. This distinction and the structure of international trade may help explain why these two states were in dispute, but it does not necessarily account for the militarized aspects of the competition, and the authors are quick to avoid attributing too much to these factors. Brummett (1999) also cites commercial interests as the basis for the rivalry between the Ottoman Empire and Venice. We should note that a related argument has been put forward by Friedman and Lebard (1991) with respect to future relations between the United States and Japan. They contend that the Cold War held the two states together against a common external enemy (the Soviet Union) and that the absence of that threat now will lead to the two states to become serious rivals; they also argue that competition over resources will become stiff and almost inevitably involve military confrontation. Based on Levy and Ali's analysis, however, differing economic strategies or market competitions are not enough to turn a trade rivalry violent—several other factors must be at work.

One key factor is the relative power distribution between the two sides. Levy and Ali argue that British naval inferiority until the 1640s prevented them from seriously challenging the Dutch. This suggestion that power imbalance inhibits rivalry conflict is related to the contention of Vasquez (1993) and others that interactions between states of approximately equal capability will be different from other interactions and perhaps more severe. The presence of bipolarity might also make the two leading states more likely to be rivals, as might be argued in the case of the United States and the Soviet Union following World War II (Larson 1999). The logic is similar to the one here—one state cannot plausibly challenge another unless it has sufficient capabilities to make threats credible. Although approximate parity seems to be a vital condition for a militarized rivalry, two caveats are in order: one theoretical and one empirical. Theoretically, parity may not be necessary if the potential rival disadvantaged by the status quo is superior in strength. In that circumstance, preponderance by the revisionist state may be enough to start a rivalry. Empirically, it is evident that not all enduring rivalries between states take place between approximate equals. Although lists of rivals vary across the studies, a significant minority of them involve states with widely disparate capabilities. Thus, approximate parity may be important in many cases, but it is not a necessary condition for militarized rivalry.

Another key factor, noted by Vasquez (1998) in a case study of the Pacific theater of World War II, is the importance of territorial issues as a basis for enduring rivalries. Rule (1999) also notes that the competition over territory (along with ideology) was an important element in the origins of the Franco-Spanish rivalry of the late fifteenth century. Although there has been a large number of ongoing claims over territory, not all have resulted in militarized disputes or the development of long-standing rivalries. Huth (1996a) looks at the role of territorial claims since 1950 in the origins of enduring rivalries. Huth uses a modified realist model, which includes both domestic and international political factors, to explain how states become involved in enduring rivalries over territory. Importantly, he notes that the relative strength of the challenger does not have much of an effect and that states also do not frequently challenge allies or extant treaty commitments by resort to militarized action. Rather, domestic concerns, especially ethnic and linguistic ties between one's own population and those living in the disputed territory, are significantly associated with the recurrence of militarized conflict. Such findings are of special policy concern given the renewal of nationalism and ethnic conflict in the post–Cold War era.

Domestic political pressures are also important factors in other analyses of rivalry origins. Levy and Ali (1998) note that early domestic instability in England inhibited its ability to challenge the Dutch. Later domestic political pressures led that rivalry to heat up, become militarized, and go to war several times early in the militarized phase of the rivalry. Vasquez (1998) also cites domestic political pressures on Japan, which led to that state's expansionist drive in Asia and ultimately its attack on the United States. These critical findings are another nail in the realist coffin, especially the proposition that international and domestic political processes are separate (see also Wayman and Diehl 1994). Maoz and Mor (1998) importantly affirm that cooperation among rivals is quite possible, but that this does not preclude the beginning or continuation of a rivalry. Rather, the key aspect is that both sides are dissatisfied with some situation leading to the onset and expansion of the rivalry. Yet it may also be that the absence of the ability or incentive for two states to cooperate (to mutually benefit each other in any meaningful way) may be a force in promoting rivalry (see Schroeder's 1999 argument vis-à-vis the Franco-Austrian rivalry), although this alone would seem to be insufficient.

Two conference papers (Hensel and Sowers 1998; Stinnett and Diehl 1998) attempt to model the development of enduring rivalries. Each looks at the impact of structural and behavioral factors, roughly corresponding to the punctuated equilibrium and evolutionary models (Hensel 1996), respectively, on the onset of rivalry. The findings of each study reveal that both structural (e.g., power distribution) and behavioral (e.g., dispute outcomes) factors influence the development of enduring rivalries. Nevertheless, such studies do not provide tests of the two models against one another. This is similar to many studies of the democratic peace in which normative and institutional explanations are each found to have some utility in accounting for the lack of war between democratic states.

Thus, scant findings indicate that parity, territorial issues, and domestic political pressures were associated with the beginning of rivalries, with no strong mitigating effects from some early cooperation between rivals. Some questions remain about whether the origins of rivalries, even enduring ones, are any different from international conflict in general.

Our empirical analyses are not centrally concerned with the origins of rivalries in that we do not present a comprehensive model of how they come into being. Rather we limit ourselves to demonstrating (in chapter 11) that political shocks of a large magnitude are associated with the beginnings of rivalries, functioning as virtual necessary conditions. What other conditions might be necessary is left for future research, one of the many items appropriate for the concluding chapter to this book (chapter 13).

The Dynamics of Rivalries

A second set of concerns centers on rivalry dynamics, that is, the interactions between rivals following the onset of the rivalry, but prior to the termination point. As with most studies of rivalries, the dominant feature is that conflict events are not independent of each or other exogenous conflict events (this contrasts with traditional conflict analyses). Accordingly, much of the attention is focused on identifying the interconnections of conflict events. McGinnis and

Williams (1989) modeled the U.S.-Soviet rivalry over time with appropriate consideration for how past actions affected contemporary and future decisions. Even though the model was only for the superpower dyad, it appears applicable to other rivalries. More precisely, some scholars have looked at how previous interactions in the rivalry affect future behavior. Wayman and Jones (1991) consider the impact of previous disputes on subsequent disputes in a rivalry; they find that certain outcomes (e.g., capitulation) of those disputes are more likely to produce frequent future disputes or disputes that are more violent (after stalemates). Similarly, Hensel (1996) reports that decisive or compromise outcomes to disputes lessen the likelihood of future confrontations within the rivalry. There may also be some evidence of learning over the course of a rivalry. Larson (1999) argues that the United States and the Soviet Union learned conflict management and how to avoid war based on their behaviors during successive crises.

The dynamics of rivalries may not be influenced only by their own pasts, but also by their interconnections with other conflicts and rivalries. We make this point above and explicitly test for it in chapter 12. Muncaster and Zinnes (1993) create a model of an international system that is capable of tracking the evolution of rivalries, including how those rivalries influence the relations (and potential rivalries) of other states in the system. A dispute involving two states not only influences their future relations, but also impacts all other dyadic relations in the system. Also in the formal modeling tradition, McGinnis (1990) offers a model of regional rivalries that identifies optimum points for aid, arms, and alignments in those rivalries; this again provides for exogenous conflicts to influence the dynamics of rivalries.

A number of empirical studies confirm the significance of third-party conflict to the dynamics of rivalries. Ingram (1999) notes that the British-Russian rivalry was influenced by these states' relations with Asian client states. Schroeder (1999) boldly states that the Franco-Austrian rivalry was kept from being resolved by its interconnection with other ongoing European rivalries. According to Levy and Ali (1998), the end of the Dutch revolt against Spain led to the conditions that permitted Dutch economic expansion and the initiation of the rivalry with England. States sometimes have limited carrying capacities in the number of rivalries to which they can devote attention and resources. The Anglo-Dutch rivalry was also linked with the Anglo-French rivalry. England's undeclared war against France resulted in the seizure of Dutch ships that were trading with France, analogous to the contagion model noted by Siverson and Starr (1991), in which a given conflict spills over to encompass neighboring countries. The intersection of these two rivalries had the effect of escalating the competition between the Dutch and the British, who had previously managed their disputes without resort to war. Kinsella (1994a, 1994b, 1995) studied the dynamics of some rivalries in the Middle East with special attention to how the superpower rivalry influenced these minor-power rivalries.

There is a pattern of action-reaction to superpower arms transfers to that region. He finds that Soviet arms transfers exacerbated rivalry conflicts in several cases, whereas U.S. arms supplies to Israel had no strong positive or negative effects. He also notes that U.S. arms transfer policy may have actually dampened conflict in the Iran–Iraq rivalry. It is clear from Kinsella's studies that the superpower rivalry affected the dynamics of the minor power rivalries in the Middle East, although the reverse was not generally true.

Beyond the interconnection of conflicts over space and time, there is some scant evidence that certain conditions affect rivalry behavior. Hensel (1996) finds that rivalries with prominent territorial components and those that experience capability shifts among the rivals are more likely to have recurring conflict and have that conflict recur sooner. The presence of a democratic dyad also apparently has a dampening effect on conflict recurrence in the rivalry. Yet he acknowledges that the strength of these general findings varies across different phases of rivalries, citing different patterns in the early parts of rivalries versus the middle or latter phases, a contention at odds with the punctuated equilibrium model. Ingram (1999) notes a host of factors—technological, ideological, and geographical—as influences on the dynamics of the British-Russian rivalry.

In addition to the concern with the factors that affect the dynamics of rivalries, there has been some attention to the "stability" of rivalries as well as the patterns in the dynamics of rivalries. In our punctuated equilibrium conception, enduring rivalries exhibit great stability over time and their patterns are not easily disrupted. For Cioffi-Revilla (1998), stability was defined as the probability of rivalry continuation into the future. In his analysis, a hazard rate for termination was used to indicate whether rivalries had a increasing or decreasing tendency to end, with the latter signifying a stable relationship. His results indicated three phases of rivalry stability: initial stability, maturation, and termination. In the initial phase, he discovered that rivalries were very stable and therefore not prone to end in their early phases. Maoz and Mor (1998) found that the games of Deadlock and Bully were the most common in young rivalries, suggesting that the early stages of enduring rivalries are marked by hostility on both sides with few attempts (at least successful ones) at conciliation, cooperation, and conflict resolution.

The maturation or midlife period shows that rivalries become mildly unstable, with an increasing hazard rate for termination. Perhaps this indicates that many rivalries never go beyond the proto-rivalry stage and enduring rivalries are special cases that seem to run against the tide. In the termination phase, within the latter stage of rivalries, they have a strong propensity to end. There was not a great deal of variation in the stability of rivalries across various conditions, although "unbalanced" (those with capability disparities) were more unstable.

Levy and Ali (1998) point out the importance of political shocks for the stability of rivalry relationships. The Thirty Years War in Germany is cited as a shock that profoundly altered Dutch relationships with its current and potential rivals. The death of Frederick Henry also brought a lull to the Dutch-Spanish competition and set in motion events that led to increased competition with the British. In effect, an exogenous and an endogenous shock had the effect (along with some other factors) of ending one militarized rivalry and beginning another. This is consistent with our expectation that political shocks will be necessary to break established rivalry patterns.

Another focus is the patterns over time in the dynamics of enduring rivalries and the role of learning in rival behavior. We noted above our expectations about the apparent relative stability of enduring rivalries and some empirical evidence to support that notion. There are some notable patterns over time in that stability. Cioffi-Revilla (1998) reports that rivalries are less stable over time; yet some enduring rivalries buck this trend and continue for more than one generation. Some of this might be attributed to outcomes of previous disputes. To the extent that conflict produces stalemates and not conciliatory or compromise outcomes, the basis for additional and more rapidly recurring conflict is there (Hensel 1996). Another temporal pattern is the tendency for twentieth-century rivalries to be more unstable. The twentieth century has significantly more rivalries than its predecessor, owing largely to the relative ease with which states can interact with one another and the larger number of states in the international system; in effect, the "opportunity" (Most and Starr 1989) for rivalries is greater. The greater number of rivalries (of all varieties including enduring ones) may mean that states must divide their attention and resources more broadly than in the past, and it may not be surprising that some rivalries end quickly as states move on to meet other, more pressing challenges.

Of course, the declining stability of rivalries in this century might also be related, in part, to another trend uncovered by Cioffi-Revilla: bipolar systems produce more unstable rivalries than multipolar ones. The Cold War bipolar system, then, may account for the relatively greater instability than the nineteenth century, which was multipolar throughout.

Beyond trends in stability, Maoz and Mor (1998) highlight a number of patterns in the evolution of individual rivalries. A key finding is that there cannot be a fixed game assumption in trying to model the processes of enduring rivalries. The preferences and perceptions of the players shift over the course of the rivalry. Thus, iterative game analyses that use Prisoners' Dilemma or Chicken (common in deterrence analyses) to try to understand state bargaining behavior are unlikely to produce coherent results. Different game structures and preferences occur throughout the rivalry, and one must be able to understand the process of preference and structural change in order to model the interactions accurately. Nevertheless, Maoz and Mor indicate that learning (defined as a reevaluation of prior beliefs that is triggered by a discrepancy between expectations and experience) cannot really account for the game transformations that occur over the course of a rivalry. The appearance of exogenous and endogenous shocks is again associated with this transformation. Here the authors point to significant shifts in capability (consistent with Hensel 1996 noted above) and leadership change in the rival states as important factors conditioning game transformations.

Maoz and Mor do find that some adaptive learning does occur within rivalries, but their model is often incorrect in predicting the behavior of the rivals. They cite perceptual shifts about what game is thought to be in play and incomplete information about the process by scholars as possibly responsible for this discrepancy. In any case, there appears to be less learning and its subsequent impact than one might expect, although such processes are often hard to identify and assess (see Levy 1994).

Hensel (1996) has an evolutionary model of rivalries in which different kinds of rivalries—minor, proto, and enduring—are not distinct from one another at the outset. Rather, rivalries gradually evolve into more frequent and serious confrontations. Thus, Hensel reports that rivalries become more severe over time and that future conflict becomes more likely and in more rapid succession. His evolutionary model posits a rivalry process that is quite different than that of the punctuated equilibrium model; the former places more emphasis on gradual change and many shifts in rivalry patterns over time. This conforms to the notion that enduring rivalries are most dangerous in their latter phases. Vasquez (1998) also reports a pattern of rising conflict in recurrent disputes during the United States–Japan rivalry that led to World War II, although this is only a single-rivalry analysis.

Within the context of rivalries, it is not surprising that states with serious and ongoing security threats would consider augmenting their capabilities by one of the most expeditious means: military buildups. With respect to military buildups, Vasquez (1998) notes that arms races intensified the rivalries in the Pacific. Importantly, he does not indicate any deterrent effects on conflict in the rivalry stemming from those enhanced capabilities (Huth and Russett 1993).

We devote a good portion of the second half of this book to the dynamics of rivalries. Most obviously, we establish the stability of rivalries over time in the next chapter by reference to the *basic rivalry level* (BRL). We also look at exogenous influences on conflict patterns in rivalries in chapters 10, 11, and 12, considering how international mediation attempts, political shocks, and linkages to other rivalries respectively influence conflict levels in rivalries. Of course, our analysis of the democratic peace according to the rivalry approach in chapter 6 included a discussion of how regime change affected conflict patterns in extant rivalries.

War in Rivalries

Of course, most international conflict research in general has been concerned with the conditions associated with the outbreak of war. Little of the research directly on rivalries, however, has dealt with war. Those studies that use rivalries as a background condition focus on war, but they answer questions about deterrence, power transitions, and the like and their relationship to war rather than making direct theoretical or empirical contributions about rivalries and war. There are, nevertheless, a few exceptions to this pattern. Vasquez (1993, 1996) argued that geographic contiguity between rivals was the critical factor in whether a rivalry went to war or not. Geographic contiguity between rivals signifies that the conflict between them was a territorial one, and in the view of Vasquez, conflict without this strong territorial dimension will not end in war. Thompson (1999) makes a similar argument in noting that the Anglo-American rivalry did not experience war after 1812, in part, because any territory in dispute between the British and the Americans was judged not to be worth fighting over. Yet in a reexamination of the effect of territorial disputes on escalation in rivalries, Rasler and Thompson (1998a) indicate that major powers are less driven by territorial disputes. Furthermore, they find "positional disputes" must be added the equation along with contiguity to help explain when rivalries will go to war—territorial concerns alone are not sufficient.

Systemic conditions are often cited by neorealists and idealists as constraining or enhancing choices for war. Yet there are also powerful critics (Bueno de Mesquita and Lalman 1988) of the importance of systemic (as opposed to dyadic or other) factors. According to limited current research, some aspects of the international system were important for the onset of war in rivalries, but generally they were not central. The balance of power at the system level is a classic neorealist factor, but Levy and Ali (1998) note that this made little difference in the rivalry development or war between the British and the Dutch. Nevertheless, Vasquez (1998) cites another systemic variable largely ignored by realism and its variants: international rules and norms. He notes that the breakdown of the Washington Conference structure, which sought to control military competition (especially in weaponry) between the major powers after World War I, removed the rules and norms necessary to "manage" the competition between the leading Pacific states. In this way, limiting the anarchy of the international system can have a mitigating effect on rivalry competition and while perhaps international norms and rules may not be enough to prevent or end rivalries, they might assist in restraining the most severe manifestations of rivalries. A similar argument is made by Larson (1999) in her assessment of why the superpower rivalry managed to avoid war.

Other conventional factors thought to be associated with war also receive a mixed assessment from current studies. The power distribution is often a centerpiece of models of international conflict, although there is considerable disagreement among scholars whether parity or preponderance is the most dangerous condition. Geller (1998) finds no general relationship between the capability distribution and the identity of the initiator of wars in major power rivalries. Nevertheless, he points out that *unstable* capability distributions are substantively associated with the occurrence of war, although he is quick to acknowledge that they approach a necessary, but not a sufficient, condition for conflict escalation in the rivalry. Changing capability balances in major power dyads have recently been found to be significant in a number of studies (e.g., Houweling and Siccama 1991; Geller 1992; Huth, Bennett, and Gelpi 1992). Geller's findings are also consistent with dynamic models of capability change including the power transition (Kugler and Organski 1989) and hegemonic decline (Gilpin 1981) models.

Another conventional factor thought to be associated with war is alliances. Vasquez (1998) argues that the alliance structure in the Pacific did not prevent war, suggesting there was little deterrent effect. These results are largely consistent with the prevailing findings in the scholarly literature (e.g., Siverson and Sullivan 1984) that alliances have little role in the initiation of war (there has been some reevaluation of that view, see Smith 1996; Gartner and Siverson 1996). Despite this general pattern, Vasquez (1998, 217) does link alliances with the march toward war in the Pacific. He argues: "A major state's alignment with a weak state can increase the probability of war ... because weak allies led by hard-liners will not support compromises that avoid war. Therefore ... [alliances] constrain conciliatory acts." This conception of alliances and war is quite different from the traditional capability aggregation view of alliances and conflict. Instead, it suggests that we consider how alliances affect bargaining and how the alliance variable interacts with other concerns, here domestic political processes.

Domestic political processes again were found to be critical in the dynamics of enduring rivalries. Vasquez (1998) notes that domestic hard-liners pushed for war in Japan, preventing that country from making more conciliatory gestures and accepting some peace offers short of war. Levy and Ali (1998) also note strong domestic pressures in England for hard-line policies and external actions. Perhaps this is why the English adopted a hard-line bargaining strategy that prevented effective conflict management. In contrast, Thompson (1999) argues that domestic political pressures in Britain actually encouraged de-escalation and lessened the chances for war in its relations with the United States.

Another conventional factor, democratic regime type, has also been the subject of analysis vis-à-vis war in rivalries. Although subject to some controversy, international conflict research (e.g., Russett 1993) has established that stable democratic states rarely or never fight against each other in a war. Not surprisingly then, some scholars have also found some pacifying effects from democracy in rivalries. Modelski (1999) claims that the rivalry between Portugal and Venice several hundred years ago was more benign than other rivalries because of its "democratic lineage" and that democratic rivalries are more peaceful and more likely to be resolved "on their merits" rather than by military force. Thompson (1999) also cites mutual democracy as a pacifying condition in the Anglo-American rivalry. Nevertheless, Thompson and Tucker (1997) note that intense rivalries, what they refer to as principal rivalries, can occur between democratic states and indeed argue that a significant portion of pre–World War II conflict revolved around United States–United Kingdom and United Kingdom–France rivalries (although they note that direct war was avoided in each case). Furthermore, the effects of being in a rivalry were found to be more important than the effects of democracy. Monadically, democratic and other states were found to have behaved similarly within rivalries; only outside of the rivalry context were democratic states more peaceful (Rasler and Thompson 1998b).

The conditions for war in rivalries were generally not those at the systemic level according to previous research, although there was a suggestion in one case that international norms and rules might have mitigated the war in the Pacific. Unstable military balances, rather than a particular capability distribution, tended to reinforce or exacerbate the processes leading to war in rivalries. Alliances generally did not directly influence the onset of war. Nevertheless, alliances might have influenced some domestic political processes, which were found to be critical in promoting hard-line bargaining and other aggressive foreign policy actions. Territorial issues were again most often associated with conflict escalation in enduring rivalries, and joint democracy is thought to help rivals avoid war.

Not surprisingly, because we reject the causes of war framework in favor of the rivalry approach, we are not centrally concerned with the occurrence of war in this book. Instead, we have a broader concern with the *severity* of conflict, which includes war but conflict short of war as well. Thus, some analysis of rivalry dynamics in subsequent chapters may have implication for understanding war in rivalries, but our approach provides only indirect evidence for the relevant conditions.

The Termination of Rivalries

There is an extensive literature about the termination of war (e.g., Wittman 1979). Yet, this is not synonymous with the end of rivalries. Wars take place at various junctures of rivalries, at the beginning, middle, and ending phases. Thus, understanding how a particular war ends may offer few or no clues to the end of a rivalry, which may persist for years after war termination. Cioffi-Revilla (1998) argues that rivalries are unstable (and therefore more likely to "die" or end at any given point in time) the longer they persist, but this occurs only they reach midlife. Although the hazard rate for enduring rivalries may be increasing toward the end of their lives, their conflict level shows little sign of abating, and the precise time point of rivalry termination cannot largely be predicted by the hazard rate.

There are several possible answers to the puzzle of how rivalries end, something that is not well understood given the sudden and largely unexpected end to the Cold War. Our punctuated equilibrium model suggests that rivalries end suddenly, and in connection with dramatic environmental change and other, unspecified conditions. Thompson (1999) argues that rivalry termination is a "trial and error" process in which states learn more about their opponent's preferences and positions and eventually devise a solution that reconciles competing positions and protects each sides interests.

Bennett (1993, 1996) also adopts a rational choice mode in attempting to explain rivalry termination. As we suggested above, his empirical analysis finds that the occurrence of war in a rivalry does not affect the duration of that rivalry. Neither does the existence of bipolarity or the balance of power between the rivals seem to enhance the prospects for ending rivalries. Rather relatively low issue salience at the center of the rivalry contributed to shorter rivalries. Again, territorial issues were thought to be a key example of high-salience issues. As we noted above, the absence of territorial issues made rivalries less likely to start and escalate to war if they did begin; now we also see that the lack of a territorial component to the rivalry may make it end more swiftly. Bennett also notes that common external threats makes rivals less likely to continue their competition. One might assume that common external enemies engender greater feelings of amity between the rivals ("the enemy of my enemy is my friend"). Yet other rivalries reduce the resources and attention that can be directed to extant rivalries; states must make choices on which enemies to focus on and this may mean ending one rivalry in order to pursue others.

Two other approaches explore the conditions under which rivalries are terminated. Gibler (1997) demonstrates that rivalries can end with the signing of an alliance that is in effect a territorial settlement treaty. This finding is largely consistent with research discussed above that suggested a strong territorial component to the origins of enduring rivalries. Although Gibler does not investigate whether territorial disputes were important in the origins of the rivalries he considers, he does find that the rivalry ends when the territorial dispute is removed from the relationship.

There is also a plethora of studies that seek to explain the end of the Cold War (e.g., Deudney and Ikenberry 1991–92). Unfortunately, there are several problems with this literature if we are interested in insights on rivalry termination. First, much of the literature is concerned with explaining the collapse of the Soviet Union. The end of the superpower rivalry is then treated as one of many consequences of that collapse. Yet theoretically it is not clear whether there is a point being made about domestic political changes and the end of rivalries or whether the end of rivalries is somehow slightly different than the implosion of one of the rivals. Second, it is not clear (whatever the focus) that such studies can or are designed to be generalizable to rivalries other than the U.S.-Soviet one.

Despite these limitations, Lebow (1995) has attempted to use the Cold War case to develop a set of conditions he believes accounts for the thawing of U.S.-Soviet relations under Gorbachev and the winding down of rivalries in general. For accommodation to occur, he argues that the presence of the following three conditions for one of the rivals is critical: (1) a leader committed to domestic reforms, where foreign cooperation is necessary for those reforms, (2) the failure of rivalry and confrontation in the past to achieve a rival's goals and their likely failure in the future, and (3) the belief that conciliatory gestures will be reciprocated. Thus, Lebow sees the end of rivalries beginning from domestic political considerations.

Bennett (1998) attempted to synthesize many of his and other findings on enduring rivalry termination. He confirms Cioffi-Revilla's (1998) finding that enduring rivalries have a positive hazard rate, that is, an increasing tendency toward termination over time. Bennett concludes that domestic political factors and issue salience seem to be most associated with rivalry termination. He gets distinctly mixed results regarding security concerns as a driving force behind the end of rivalries. Similarly, and most important for our concerns, he also gets mixed results on the impact of political shocks on rivalry termination, an argument that we make in chapter 11. Yet his analysis of political shocks does not properly test our contention that shocks operate only as a necessary condition for rivalry termination because his analysis treats them as sufficient. Furthermore, his analysis assumes that political shocks have an immediate and single-year effect on rivalry behavior, a conception at odds with our contention that major political changes are likely to reverberate through the system over the course of several years, rather than at a fixed point. In any case, Bennett does provide some clues about the conditions for rivalry termination beyond those that we specify in chapter 11 and helps fill in some gaps not generally specified by the punctuated equilibrium model.

Recurring Conflict

A number of studies have focused on how conflict reoccurs. This is related to rivalries in that they are a form of recurring conflict that may persist over a broad time period. The part of the work on recurring conflict that concerns us is at the dyadic level of analysis (i.e., repeated conflict between the same pairs of states) rather than repeated conflict involvement at the national level (i.e., a single state "addicted to conflict"—for example, Stoll 1984) or the system level (i.e., the tendency for conflicts to cluster in time within a system). Dyadic recurring conflict most closely parallels what we signify as rivalries between the same pair of states, although usually the concern with recurring conflict has been with one-time, short-term recurrence rather than with repeated conflict over a long time period, characteristic of enduring rivalries.

The phenomenon of dyadic recurring conflict is hardly rare. Maoz (1984) reports that 76 percent of disputes are followed by another dispute between the same states. These findings are mirrored in several other studies that find a link between previous conflict and the likelihood of future conflict between the same states (Richardson 1960; Anderson and McKeown 1987). That conflicts reoccur is strongly supported empirically, but there is little understanding about why they reoccur.

A history of previous disputes between the same states is a good predictor of future conflict (Diehl, Reifschneider, and Hensel 1996), but begs the question of why that conflict is likely. The answer requires greater attention to conditions surrounding the conflict or the interactions themselves. It may be that decisive outcomes or imposed settlements in previous disputes may dampen the tendency for conflicts to reoccur, suggesting that stalemated outcomes may have the opposite effect (Maoz 1984). Hensel (1994) had similar findings, but further added that the prospects for future disputes were also influenced by shifts in military capability between the states. For example, he reports that stalemates and compromises were often followed quickly by new disputes initiated by the stronger state, which was declining in relative capabilities. Anderson and McKeown (1987) also speak of the victor in a previous dispute initiating another conflict in order to reestablish victory. Goertz and Diehl (1992b) found that recurring conflict after a territorial change was most likely when that change was formalized by a treaty and was considered very important to the losing side. Territorial changes were more stable when the losing side was relatively weak and the gaining side regarded the territory as important. Generally, United Nations intervention in a crisis has not been found to have a significant impact on whether two disputants will clash again in the near future (Diehl, Reifschneider, and Hensel 1996).

The consequences of recurring conflict appear fairly clear (and this is confirmed with respect to enduring rivalries in chapter 3). Recurring conflict between the same set of states appears to increase the chance of conflict escalation and war. Leng (1983) found that states adopted more coercive bargaining strategies in successive confrontations with same opponent, with war almost always the result after three disputes. Brecher (1984) notes similarly that protracted conflicts are more violent with a greater risk of war than nonrecurring conflict. Fearon's reanalysis (1994b) of Huth's (1988) data suggests that past confrontation lessens the probability that future deterrence attempts will be successful.

The literature on recurring conflict indicates that repeated violence between the same pairs of states is more common than might be expected and with dangerous consequences. There are some clues about what conditions recurring conflict, specifically the outcomes of previous confrontations, but the evidence is far from complete. In this study we hope to fill some of these gaps and give insights to both rivalries and, by implication, all forms of recurring conflict.

In this chapter, we have reintroduced our list of enduring rivalries, which will be the objects of study for the rest of this volume. Much of the previous work on different aspects of enduring rivalry supports the punctuated equilibrium model, but many of its expectations have not been tested directly. In the next chapter, we sketch out in more detail some of the central characteristics of the punctuated equilibrium model and begin to empirically address some of its claims.

CHAPTER 9

Stability in Enduring Rivalries

The punctuated equilibrium model in its various forms—biological, organizational and enduring rivalry—stresses that phenomena go through long periods of stasis. Formulated in the enduring rivalry context, this means that the "basic relationship" of rivals does not vary much over time.

The notion of stability in conflict relationships is generally at odds with traditional conceptions. A classic image in international security analyses is one of a competition or crisis climbing an escalation ladder and culminating in war. Herman Kahn's (1965) famous work on nuclear escalation symbolizes well that approach. Arms race models typically describe one such spiral mechanism (Jervis 1976). In the crisis literature, one often reads of crises "escalating" to war (Brecher 1993). We label the set of models that propose this type of pattern as "volcano models."[1] The imagery of these models relies frequently on the language of pressure building up to an eventual "eruption" of war. Choucri and North's (1975) lateral pressure explanation of World War I provides a good example of volcanic language. Empirically, Leng (1983) found in crisis bargaining that there was a tendency toward more coercion and escalation in recurrent disputes between the same states, with the end product of war around the time of the third dispute.

The rivalry approach moves attention away from crises, disputes, and wars to militarized relationships. Wars and disputes form a normal and expected part of an enduring rivalry. We expect rivalries to experience the "highs" of actual military conflict. The focus of the rivalry approach in general, and the punctuated equilibrium model of enduring rivalries in particular, is not on the crisis

---

[1] We use the term *volcano* as a rough analogy to the kind of process found in the conflict literature, namely one in which conflict gradually builds up to the crescendo of war. We recognize that, in practice, real volcanoes do not always follow this pattern and at times seem to erupt suddenly. Furthermore, we have conceptualized the volcano model as a onetime process, taking our cue from the causes-of-war-literature, in which one war event is considered independent of other outbreaks of war. In reality, the eruption of volcanoes at one point in time may condition the probability of future eruptions.

163

and war events but the underlying rivalry relationship, what we call the *basic rivalry level.*

The punctuated equilibrium model proposes that the basic rivalry relationship does not change significantly over the course of the rivalry. Variation will occur as periods of crisis are followed by periods of détente, but these are variations *around* an underlying and unchanging relationship. We define the "volatility" of the rivalry as the variation of conflict around the basic rivalry level. For example, the probability of war depends on *both* the severity of the basic rivalry level and the volatility of that relationship. It is possible that some severe rivalries have managed to reduce the volatility of their relationship—and hence the likelihood of war—through conflict management efforts. We focus on this consideration in the next chapter.

Traditional evolutionary theory, in contrast to the punctuated equilibrium model, emphasizes the gradual evolution of species. The enduring rivalry equivalent is a model that specifies that enduring rivalries evolve gradually from low-severity relationships to high-severity ones. In this chapter, we focus on hypotheses that stress escalatory patterns in enduring rivalries—what we call *volcano* hypotheses—in contrast to the stability predicted by the punctuated equilibrium model. Hence, we examine general patterns in the evolution of enduring rivalries. The punctuated equilibrium model predicts that there is no secular trend in enduring rivalries, merely variation around the basic rivalry level. Another pattern that supports the punctuated equilibrium hypothesis is what we call the *plateau* pattern. This consists of a rapid change from one baseline to another. Generally, increasing or convex patterns of conflict severity support the volcano hypothesis. Most of this chapter then concentrates on establishing the patterns in our 63 enduring rivalries and analyzing these patterns in terms of the volcano and punctuated equilibrium models.

The volcano and punctuated equilibrium models differ in how they picture the long-term lives of enduring rivalry. In addition, they have clear differences for the initial stages of enduring rivalries. The punctuated equilibrium model argues for rapid change and a quick lock-in of hostility patterns in the early stages of an enduring rivalry, while the volcano model proposes a gradual rise in hostility levels. Thus, a second test of the two frameworks involves examining the initial disputes of each enduring rivalry for patterns of increasing hostility, which would support the volcano model, or the relatively constant or random hostility patterns, which support the punctuated equilibrium model.

We divide our analysis of the punctuated equilibrium model into two parts. This chapter focuses on the volcano model and other escalatory patterns in enduring rivalries. The next chapter on conflict management examines deescalatory aspects of rivalry relationships. The punctuated equilibrium model contains both, but the emphasis is on the speed of each process. According to the punctuated equilibrium model, enduring rivalries are born and die quickly.

We begin our exploration of the punctuated equilibrium model of enduring rivalries by investigating some of the possible patterns, focusing especially on those that support the volcano model or the punctuated equilibrium one. The first step, however, is to specify in what domain we going to look for patterns. What does it mean to say that a rivalry is getting more severe over time? On what basis can one make such a claim? We propose that underlying each rivalry is a *basic rivalry level,* which determines the severity of disputes and wars and which can vary over time.

The Concept of a Basic Rivalry Level (BRL)

Our analysis of stability in enduring rivalries depends centrally on the concept of a basic rivalry level. Azar (1972) proposed that each pair of countries had an average level of hostile or cooperative interaction, which he termed their "normal relations range." Azar's idea of a normal relations range suggests the hypothesis that relations between states vary within certain limits. We reformulate this in terms of a basic rivalry level (BRL) around which relations fluctuate (McGinnis and Williams 1989 proposed a similar notion for the U.S.-Soviet rivalry). When we speak of patterns in the evolution of rivalries, we refer to change in this basic rivalry level. The unmeasured BRL manifests itself in the severity of disputes that arise between rivals. One obvious hypothesis is that the likelihood that a dispute will escalate to war is, in part, a function of the BRL (those with traditionally more hostile relations, that is higher BRLs, are more likely to make the jump past the threshold of war).

The punctuated equilibrium hypothesis states that the BRL does not change over the course of the rivalry. Periods of conflict and détente are "random" variations around this basic level: there is no secular trend toward more conflictual or more peaceful relations. The conflict level for successive confrontations in an enduring rivalry will be an identically distributed, random variations around the unchanging rivalry baseline. In statistical terms, the differences between dispute severity and the BRL are random variables independent of past disputes and wars and constant from one dispute to the next (i.e., the standard assumptions one makes about error terms in linear models).

The idea of a random events model is often misunderstood. For example, stars are distributed randomly in the sky, but they seem to be clustered in space (Gould 1991). Similarly, Gilovich, Vallone and Tversky (1985) have studied the "hot hand" phenomenon in basketball (the idea that players will at certain times in a game or season be more prone to making a basket) and found it to be without foundation (see Gould 1991 for an application of this model to Joe DiMaggio's 56-game hitting streak). The probability of making a basket can be explained by a model of independent events. The probability of making a shot is like to flipping a biased coin where the bias is the shooting average of the player.[2] Long strings of made (or missed shots) appear to be evidence of a pattern, but one should see such strings and clustering in a random process. For example, if one flips a fair coin four times, the probability of at least three heads or three tails is equal to that of two heads or two tails. For an unfair coin or a particularly skilled baseball player (e.g., Joe DiMaggio), one would expect the long strings to be more common (e.g., a long hitting streak) than with a fair coin or a mediocre player.

This "anti-hot-hand" model inspires our punctuated equilibrium model of rivalries. By the time a player becomes a professional, his basic ability level is fixed (at least not capable of modifiable in the short term) according to the anti-hot-hand model. One major problem is in defining a rivalry equivalent of a basketball player's shooting average. Conceptually this is the basic rivalry level of the enduring rivalry, similar to McGinnis and Williams's (1989) unmeasured rivalry dimension. The punctuated equilibrium model states that each rivalry has its own baseline that represents the bias of the coin that is flipped when a confrontation occurs. The more biased the coin, the higher the conflict level, and the more likely war will occur. For the moment, we leave as exogenous why some rivalry baselines may be higher than others. There are a variety of explanations that could be put forward; system polarity and the salience of the disputed issues are just a few possibilities. If this concept proves fruitful in the examination of rivalry trends, then an obvious item on our research agenda will be to try to understand the causes of the basic rivalry level.

In interpreting our analyses, we do not suggest that variations from the BRL (be it constant or changing) cannot be explained and are indeed "random," but rather that there is no systematic factor derived from the previous dispute (beyond that captured by the BRL). Our procedure in this is quite similar to Leng (1993), who devoted a chapter to the "structural" determinants of crisis outcomes. He found that structural factors have an important impact, but that a significant part of the variation in outcome was unexplained by structural factors. It could be accounted for by crisis bargaining. Similarly, we divide the conflict level into two parts, one determined by the BRL and the other determined by characteristics of the individual disputes. The latter part we do not attempt to explain and lump together in the miscellaneous category of "random."

The punctuated equilibrium model postulates this basic rivalry level as normally quite stable (except perhaps at the beginning and end of rivalries, or during periods of stress and shock—see chapter 11). When we speak of the evolution of a rivalry, we mean the evolution of this baseline level, not the ups and downs of crises. We conceive the periods of relative calm and the varying severities of wars and disputes as variations above and below this basic rivalry level. The idea is quite similar to our earlier work on military allocation ratios in which we calculated a "normal" level of military spending for different eras

---

[2]There is some dispute on the proposition that hot hands in an economic context are merely statistically anticipated aberrations; for example, see Brown and Sauer 1989.

based on the actual spending patterns of all major powers; states were over- or underspenders depending on their relationship to this norm (Goertz and Diehl 1986).

As Leng (1993) demonstrated, it is possible for one side to react at a significantly higher or lower level than the other during a crisis. Similarly, Hensel and Diehl (1994) have studied militarized disputes in which one side took no militarized action in response to the threat or use of force against it. Thus, it seems possible that the basic rivalry level could be different for each side. On the other hand, we emphasize that a rivalry *relationship* by definition is a dyadic one. On the personal level, a "loving" relationship is when there is love on both sides, and a happy marriage is one in which both are content. We do not deny that there may be asymmetries, but those asymmetries help *define* the relationship, which is a combination of factors on both sides of the rivalry.

Patterns of Enduring Rivalry Evolution

The punctuated equilibrium model views enduring rivalries as phenomena that establish themselves quite rapidly and then do not change much until some shock sets the stage for rivalry termination. We postulate a relatively quick lock-in for enduring rivals. Such a lock-in effect is consistent with the punctuated equilibrium hypothesis of "no change" over almost all of the rivalry. Once an enduring rivalry is under way, the particularities of the different crises, location, bargaining strategy, issue, and the like would be different, hence accounting for variations from the basic rivalry level. The more severe the basic level, ceteris paribus, the more likely a dispute is to end in war. This is the anti-hot-hand argument, as applied to enduring rivalries. The high shooting average that results in more hot hands corresponds to a high basic rivalry level that produces more wars.

Cioffi-Revilla (1998) has examined this "stability" hypothesis with a survival analysis and has found that rivalries exhibit short-term stability, some medium-term instability, and a strong tendency toward termination (an increasing hazard rate) in their latter phase. His analysis suggests another possible pattern, one with a quick lock-in effect, but with a falling rivalry level after a decade or two.

A related possibility is that a rivalry begins with some traumatic event, such as a war, and then drops immediately in its severity level and gradually withers away over time. In contrast to the previous pattern, the rivalry level is at its peak at the outset, but drops precipitously soon thereafter (rather than much later in the rivalry) and the decline is then gradual over of the rest of the rivalry. These are variations on an evolution that we call the "decreasing" pattern: there is some secular trend toward less conflictual relationships. In the next chapter we focus at length on decreasing or "de-escalatory" patterns that arise if conflict management attempts succeed in enduring rivalries.

The Volcano Model

The volcano model signifies some dynamic—usually self-reinforcing—mechanism that leads to the outbreak of war. The volcano name appropriately indicates the image of pressure building up over time until there is an explosion, the outbreak of war in most conceptualizations. There are several common themes in this metaphor. First is that conflict interactions always involve an escalatory pattern. Each successive interaction between the same states is more hostile. Second is the expectation that the process culminates in war. In effect, war is the end product, and there is little concern with what happens after that event. Third is the theme that there is a mechanism driving the process that may be endogenous or exogenous to the rivalry relationship.

The volcano model is found in a range of work on international conflict. The spiral model (Jervis 1976) is indicative of a process whereby states pursue aggressive policies, most notably arms acquisition, to protect their own security. The rivals may exhibit similar behavior as a response to those actions with the result of each side feeling less secure and more compelled to acquire further armaments or take more aggressive actions (the "security dilemma"). The expectation is that this spiral will drive competitors to ever increasing arms spending, insecurity, and hostility. The spiral will foster the conditions for war as resource scarcity, misperception, and the absence of mediating influences will exacerbate (or precipitate) the next confrontation between the enemies. Empirically, Smith (1988) reports that an exponential model of arms growth is best able to identify the outbreak of war, with that outbreak occurring roughly around the peak of the arms race spiral. Not all action-reaction models, however, are necessarily volcano-type processes. Richardsonian (1960) models allow for an equilibrium point and are rather ambiguous on the circumstances surrounding the outbreak of war (or potentially unrealistic as in the occurrence of war after complete exhaustion of resources).

The volcano process is also embedded in other studies of war. The power transition model (Organski 1958; Kugler and Organski 1989; Kugler and Lemke 1996) posits that national development drives the power capability of states and that differential rates of growth among states lead to inequities in the international system. Over time, a dissatisfied challenger will gain in strength vis-à-vis its status quo rival, and conflict will increase, with the likely result of war just after the challenger surpasses its rival. Here the mechanism driving the process is endogenous to the rivals, but exogenous to the rivalry.

Although the volcano model is common in many types of international conflict research, we are most concerned here with its application to long-standing rivalries. Most of the work on conflict escalation has been concerned with crises, which represent a more confined time frame and a narrower range of policy choice than do rivalries.[3] Leng (1993, 74) notes that one pattern in crisis escalation is a "fight," characterized by "symmetrical escalating hostility, described

---

[3] See Goertz and Diehl 1993 for a discussion of the difference between crises and rivalries.

by spiraling coercive actions," similar to what the volcano process describes. Yet this is only one of several types of escalation patterns that Leng discovers, and therefore the volcano metaphor may only have limited applicability.

In a broader temporal context, most of the work on recurring conflict between states has not focused on the severity level of successive confrontations, but only on the conditions for recurrence of conflict. Nevertheless, there is some work that suggests a volcano process over time and across crises, which is similar to the context of an enduring rivalry. Leng (1983) found that states adopted increasingly coercive bargaining strategies in successive crises with the same opponent. The result was almost always war at the time of the third confrontation. Brecher (1993) notes that crises that occur in the context of "protracted conflicts" are more prone to escalation both within the crisis itself and over time: "Actors in a protracted conflict do not see an end to their conflict and expect a recurrence of violence. Moreover, frequent resort to violence accentuates the image of violence as a protracted conflict norm . . . All this puts a premium on violent escalation in a protracted conflict crisis, including resort to war" (145–46).

There are several potential problems with the volcano model as applied to enduring rivalries. First, the approach is silent or downplays de-escalatory mechanisms that might be present in the rivalry relationship. If war does occur, it is easy to see an escalatory spiral preceding it, because by definition, earlier events are less severe and one perhaps naturally focuses on the events that lead to war (escalatory ones) as opposed to those that led in the other direction. Furthermore, not all international conflict continues to escalate until there is war; many states solve their differences without war and at a relatively low level of hostility. Leng (1993) and Axelrod (1984), in particular, have noted how reciprocal bargaining strategies can lead to more cooperative outcomes. Although enduring rivalries are more war prone than other dyads (see chapter 3), some of them nonetheless end without war.

Another problem with translating the volcano hypothesis to enduring rivalries is that war is but one potential—and potentially multiple—event in a rivalry. War may well represent the "explosion" of the rivalry, but most rivalries survive this traumatic event. Indeed, some Arab-Israeli rivalries have survived several wars. This crucial fact is ignored by volcano models, as the analysis stops at war. Within the context of an enduring rivalry, however, we must deal with competition that usually goes on after the war eruption. One possible revision of the volcano model would suggest repeated wars preceded by periods of buildup, essentially a war-cycle hypothesis embedded in a rivalry. Finally, volcano models have trouble dealing with a related problem—how can one explain wars that represent the beginning of a rivalry?

The volcano model was formulated for the study of war. For the reasons given above, it needs to be reformulated to be applied to enduring rivalries. Our reformulation involves changes in the basic rivalry level: what kind of patterns of BRL evolution are congruent with the volcano hypothesis? Hensel (1996) has taken the post hoc problem of enduring rivalries seriously and argued that countries know that they are engaged in a protracted conflict only after they have had several disputes. Loosely, they must first pass through infancy (isolated conflict) and adolescence (proto-rivalry) before becoming enduring rivals. He seems to be suggesting a general buildup of hostility and then a constant conflict level as a rivalry pattern. This contrasts with our earlier proposal of a quick lock-in of rivalry patterns after one or two disputes. More generally, there may be a gradual increase in the BRL. This buildup could continue to the very end of a rivalry, which then could be terminated by a dramatic shock. The pattern of gradually increasing severity fits with the general image of an escalatory conflict model. This pattern we term as "increasing."

One could combine the Cioffi-Revilla and Hensel ideas: a rivalry could increase to a summit and then decline until the rivalry withers away. The first half of the rivalry exhibits a typical escalatory process, while the second part shows a Graduated Reciprocation in Tension-Reduction (GRIT)-like (Osgood 1962) decreasing pattern. We call this the "convex" rivalry pattern.

A third pattern is a conflict cycle or "wavy" configuration. This shows evidence of volcano processes, but also has characteristics of the flat pattern. There may be no secular trend in the rivalry, but it goes through clearly defined periods of escalatory and de-escalatory conflict. Here we do not refer to the way this happens before and after crises, where it is the case almost by definition, but rather this pattern is manifested over a number of disputes. This wavy pattern may tend to center around the basic rivalry level, but it is a more well defined ebb-and-flow pattern than the random variations around the flat distributions of the punctuated equilibrium model. Nevertheless, wavy patterns may offer some secondary support for a modified version of the punctuated equilibrium hypothesis.

Another gray zone pattern is one in which there is a clear decline in the first part of the rivalry, followed by an escalatory pattern in the second half. This "concave" pattern does not fit well within the usual volcano metaphor because we do not expect escalatory periods to follow declining hostility levels. Of course, this must occur in the wavy pattern, but even then one expects the wavy pattern to start on the rise and not on the decline. For reasons of completeness, it is useful to include both sides of a pair: increasing-decreasing, convex-concave, and the like. It remains an empirical question if these intuitively less plausible patterns actually occur in enduring rivalries.

Figure 9.1 depicts the ideal types for six of the patterns noted previously: punctuated equilibrium/flat, increasing, decreasing, convex, concave, and wavy. In actuality, we can expect few rivalries to mirror any one pattern exactly, and our matching of a given rivalry to a particular pattern will be based on which pattern offers the best approximation of the severity level across the whole rivalry (see coding discussion in the next section).

FIGURE 9.1: Patterns of Rivalry Evolution

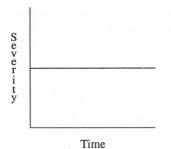

Figure 9.1a: Flat Pattern

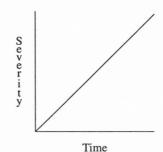

Figure 9.1b: Increasing Pattern

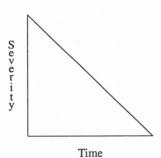

Figure 9.1c: Decreasing Pattern

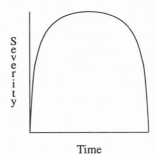

Figure 9.1d: Convex Pattern

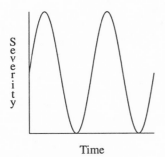

Figure 9.1e: Wavy Pattern

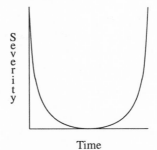

Figure 9.1f: Concave Pattern

In summary, we focus here on gradual escalatory—volcano—patterns and contrast them with the stability predicted by the punctuated equilibrium model. Two patterns clearly conform to the basic outlines of the volcano model: increasing and convex evolutions. The punctuated equilibrium postulates a flat pattern and in a modified form, a "plateau" pattern of two flat patterns in the same rivalry separated by a transition point. A third set of patterns arises from patterns generated by more de-escalatory processes represented by the concave and decreasing patterns, which pose basically different developmental models—the topic of the next chapter. The wavy process lies in the gray zone because it exhibits no secular trend, but does show several periods of rivalry buildup, as well as the pattern of decreasing conflict levels.

Research Design and Expectations

We are most interested in variations in the level of severity (corresponding to our rivalry conceptual components of military competitiveness, but this time at the dispute rather than rivalry level). One of the disadvantages of using militarized disputes as a tool of studying rivalries is that we have relatively few data points for each enduring rivalry; an enduring rivalry can have as few as six militarized disputes. Thus, in our analysis of patterns, we have few degrees of freedom with which to play. Nevertheless, we use the measure of severity first introduced in chapter 3 and described in detail in appendix B.[4]

We will look at the severity of enduring rivalries over time in order to detect patterns that are consistent with the expectations of the punctuated equilibrium and volcano models (as well as the other possible patterns). The volcano model envisions that the conflict level in the rivalry will increase over time, beginning at some low level and escalating to war or some dispute just short of war. It may be that there are several repeated patterns in the rivalry and for that contingency the volcano model predicts that the pattern of escalation will be duplicated in several cycles—escalation to high levels of conflict followed by a new set of disputes beginning at a low level, but of ascending hostility.

The punctuated equilibrium model predicts random variation in the conflict level of successive disputes around a constant baseline, because the conflict level of any given dispute is independent of the flat line. Thus, a dispute

---

[4]The duration of a dispute is also an aspect of its conflict level. The longer a dispute, the more it affects the attention and resources that a state can devote to other matters. Furthermore, longer disputes have broader and longer-lasting effects on state relationships because the accompanying times for peaceful relations are reduced and attitudes in societies adjust to the pattern of hostility between states. Duration is measured according to the number of months that the dispute lasted. Our intuitive impression is that many disputes tend to drag on, and this, combined with the difficulty of determining the termination date, leads to a wide variation in duration times. Severity and duration are thought to represent two separate dimensions of the conflict level of rivalries. The data generally support this conclusion, as the correlation between the two measures is moderate ($r = .47$). We also tested for duration patterns over time in an earlier study (Goertz and Diehl 1997) and the results are similar to those reported for conflict severity.

may be of greater, lesser, or similar severity as its predecessor. War or other severe disputes may be found at different junctures of the rivalry, and it would not be unusual to find that some rivalries begin with war or other high levels of conflict. The basic punctuated equilibrium hypothesis is, therefore, that the severity of the dispute/war in a rivalry is independent of the level of the previous dispute once we take into account the basic rivalry level.

We employ three separate tests to ascertain patterns in the evolution of enduring rivalries and thereby test the expectations of the volcano and punctuated equilibrium models, as well as identify any relationships that are not predicted by these models. First, we estimate a regression line for each rivalry in which the conflict level of each rivalry is the dependent variable and the independent variable is the number of the dispute (first, second, etc.) in the rivalry sequence. To test for nonlinear patterns (e.g., rising then falling conflict levels, as in a repeating cycle), we add polynomial terms to the equation. Because some of the rivalries have as few as six disputes, however, the small N will lead few of our results to pass statistical significance tests. In addition, we produce scatterplots of the relationships, which we then code according to the following categories: increasing, decreasing, concave, convex, flat, or wavy; we also identify "plateau" variations of the flat category. Although most of these patterns are self-evident or described above, there were several principles that guided our coding.[5] First, one observation should not change the coding decision, and therefore several observations are necessary to constitute a pattern. For example, it is possible to code a distribution as flat despite the occurrence of one dispute that was an outlier (e.g., the outbreak of a war). Second, flat patterns did not mean no variation, but rather random variation around some mean level. Third, the judgment that the conflict level is increasing or decreasing also must be based on more than one observation. Finally, wavy patterns are not those that show dramatic fluctuations from observation to observation, but are those with clear patterns or cycles across all the observations.

We are also concerned with the residuals of the regression lines rather than just the patterns. Recall that in order for the estimated coefficients to be correct, the model assumes that the residuals are identically and randomly distributed variables. Thus, another test of the BRL model is that the residuals are randomly distributed. This can be determined through statistical analysis with the Durbin-Watson test. In this analysis, correlated error terms are not merely a technical problem that needs to be corrected, but an indication that

---

[5] Given some of the results below, we might be accused of seeing (or inventing) patterns that are consistent with our punctuated equilibrium model and ignoring others. We have several responses. First, we devised the guidelines below before doing any of the actual coding. Second, during the actual coding, each of the authors independently judged the patterns and agreed on 80 percent of the patterns in this chapter and more than 90 percent of the patterns reported in the next chapter. Third, the results reported are quite similar to those from an earlier exercise (Goertz and Diehl 1998) that used a different indicator of conflict severity. As a result, we are confident of the results reported below.

the model needs substantive variables to explain the intertemporal relations. Durbin-Watson scores are calculated for each regression and then their significance level is ascertained. A large number of problematic scores would call into question not only the appropriateness of the regression model, but also the validity of the punctuated equilibrium model.

Finally, we recognize that patterns of escalation and de-escalation in enduring rivalries may not be fully apparent over the life of the rivalry, but rather confined to narrower time frames. We are particularly concerned with the "lock-in" and "fade-out" of rivalries. The punctuated equilibrium model indicates that the conflict level is quickly established in a rivalry (i.e., a quick lock-in). That same model suggests that enduring rivalries do not wither away as they move toward their termination. To test these possibilities, we examined the first three and the last three disputes in a rivalry respectively, and calculated the difference between the conflict level of the dispute in question and the mean conflict level for the rivalry as a whole. We then report how many of the "residuals" are negative. Negative residuals at the beginning of a dispute would suggest that the rivalry has a gradual buildup in the conflict level and therefore supply evidence for the lack of a rapid lock-in effect; this would be consistent with Hensel's (1996) analysis of rivalries slowly evolving into an enduring one. Negative residuals at the end of the rivalry indicate a fade-out or withering away of the rivalry. If the average number of negative residuals is approximately 1.5 (half of 3), however, then the null model expectation of random fluctuation seems appropriate. There is a quick lock-in and no fade-out, with consistent variation around the mean both at the beginning and the end, and therefore results that support the punctuated equilibrium model.

We considered other analyses, but did not find them suitable for our purposes. For example, one possibility was to consider the transition probabilities for the conflict level from time t to time $t + 1$. The punctuated equilibrium hypothesis is that the transition probabilities are the same for a given basic rivalry level, a process with no "memory." The set of transition probabilities would be greater than this average if the previous conflict level was influencing the outcome of the next dispute. The transition probabilities would vary with the different basic rivalry levels in an aggregated analysis. Thus, the punctuated equilibrium hypothesis does not stipulate that all rivalries exhibit the same dynamics, but that they may differ substantially, and we take into account this "context" (see Goertz 1994, especially on context as changing meaning) for a transition probability test. Geller (1993) has used these techniques to study power transitions in enduring rivalries. We have a continuous dependent variable (conflict level), and transition probabilities work best with clearly defined states from and to which there is a transition. But fundamentally we are interested in patterns over long periods of time, and prefer to examine them more directly via graphical and regression methods.

The punctuated equilibrium model proposes that the "structural factors" of enduring rivalry are basically constant throughout the rivalry. Fundamental—structural—changes to the rivalry should affect the baseline. In effect, our operational definition of structural change is a change in that baseline. Yet each crisis has its own specific characteristics; in statistical terms, the residuals around the regression line are the aspects of crisis bargaining that are unexplained, but not necessarily unexplainable. As in basketball, a player in some games shoots more or less than his average, and there may be good explanations for that occurrence in each instance (e.g., zone defenses, illness). These individual explanations are those of the residual.

Normally, the variance of the residuals in a regression model is of no real substantive importance. Reducing this variance is important only because this increases the accuracy (hence significance) of parameter estimates. In our situation, the size of the residuals reflects the "volatility" of the rivalry. A rivalry with a lower baseline but higher volatility may produce more wars than a rivalry with a high baseline and little variation. Whether a dispute in an enduring rivalry escalates to war is a function of *both* the BRL (mean) and the volatility (variance) of the rivalry. One possible definition of a security regime is when the baseline of a rivalry does not change, but the variance is reduced. A security regime does not try to "solve" the underlying conflict, but just to "manage" it. The Cold War seems to be a case in which the United States and the USSR developed a few rules for keeping the competition under control.

Our preference for a regression approach does not depend on any knockout arguments for its superiority. We prefer the simpler and more familiar machinery of regression models, the ease of graphical analysis, and the simple division of conflict level into dispute-specific and structural components. One major difference is that we conceive of the severity of a dispute to be a continuous variable. Event history and stochastic process models are most frequently used when there are clear, discontinuous states, such as married/single. We prefer to use a continuous, and we hope more accurate, measure of the conflict level.

One potential approach is evident in Davis, Duncan, and Siverson (1978). They examined spatial dependence by examining waiting times between dyadic wars on the system level. We are interested in dependence of severity and duration levels and not arrival (interdispute waiting) times, but the formal structure is quite similar between the two. Translating their model to our situation would involve postulating that the amount of time between disputes (as opposed to the level) is a function of the level of the previous disputes. This proposal suggests that there are different aspects of the connection of disputes over time. Our dependent variable is the conflict *level* of the dispute. Duncan and his colleagues suggest that another dependent variable could be the *timing* of the next dispute. Indeed, Hensel (1996) reports some evidence that the outcomes of previous disputes may indeed affect the timing of subsequent disputes between the same parties (see also the next chapter, where we use this as a measure of conflict

TABLE 9.1: Patterns in Enduring Rivalries

BRL Pattern	N (%) All Cases	N (%) Uncensored
Flat	47 (74.6)	18 (69.2)
Plateau-down	5 (7.9)	2 (7.7)
Plateau-up	6 (9.5)	2 (7.7)
Increasing	2 (3.2)	2 (7.7)
Plateau-up	1 (1.6)	1 (3.8)
Decreasing	5 (7.9)	2 (7.9)
Plateau-down	1 (1.6)	1 (3.8)
Convex	3 (4.8)	1 (3.8)
Concave	5 (7.9)	3 (11.5)
Wavy	1 (1.6)	0 (0.0)
Total	63 (100)	26 (100)

management success). It is possible that there are temporal connections for one but not the other, and it is possible that the conflict level and timing are completely independent of each other (i.e., the severity of a dispute is independent of how quickly it occurs after the previous one). Part of the difference is that in our case we know that the "next dispute" will occur (the post hoc character of enduring rivalry analysis), while the whole point of the Davis, Duncan, and Siverson study was to determine whether this was the case or not.

Empirical Results

General Patterns

In the first set of analyses, we explore the patterns evidenced from our regression analyses. These are summarized in table 9.1 with the full results given at the end of the chapter.

The punctuated equilibrium hypothesis suggests no secular trend in the conflict level of rivalry. Of the total, we find 74.6 percent fit the no-secular-trend pattern, with a comparable percentage for noncensored cases. Wavy cases provide more ambiguous support for the null hypothesis, but there is only one such case among the 63 rivalries. Taken together as evidence for the punctuated equilibrium model, these two categories account for just over three-quarters of the rivalry cases. This is fairly compelling evidence for the punctuated equilibrium model, even if its applicability is not universal.

Among the so-called flat cases are those that exhibit some unique patterns that we have labeled *plateau* cases. The plateau cases fit naturally within the punctuated equilibrium framework, which is why we include them in the flat category. Recall that the punctuated equilibrium model is one of abrupt change followed by stasis. This describes quite accurately the plateau pattern.

Five rivalries begin at relatively high levels of conflict and continue at that level for the first half or more of the rivalry. This is indicative of a flat pattern and a well-established BRL. Nevertheless, all five rivalries reach a transition point in which the severity of conflict drops precipitously, remaining at a lower plateau for the duration of the rivalry. This is not indicative of a gradual decline in hostility, as is characteristic of the decreasing pattern. Rather, the drop in severity is more abrupt and does not continue after the initial drop. In effect, a new, lower BRL is established in those rivalries. One may speculate about the causes for this movement to a lower plateau of rivalry severity, and these explanations include various conflict management techniques, informal agreements, and the like. One of the cases is the Israeli-Egyptian rivalry, which settles into lower conflict patterns after the Camp David Accords. That rivalry persisted after that "peace" agreement, but now at far less dangerous levels. Ben-Yehuda and Sandler (1998) report a similar shift downward in Arab-Israeli crisis severity, although they unfortunately used the term "winding down," when their data suggest a more dramatic drop from a high plateau to a low plateau. These five cases, and one case of a decreasing pattern that plateaus down to a flat BRL at the end, offer potentially interesting subjects for analysis of conflict management efforts.

There are also six rivalries that exhibit a pattern opposite to the one above: a lower BRL established in the first part of the rivalry that gives way to a significantly higher one in the second phase of the rivalry. The Iraqi rivalry with Kuwait is illustrative of this pattern, and the Persian Gulf War is only the latest manifestation of the more severe conflict between those two enemies. Together with a single case of an increasing pattern that also asymptotically increases to a plateau, these "plateau-up" cases may be subjects of an analysis that explains escalation in rivalries.

The second most frequent patterns of rivalry severity are the decreasing and concave patterns, each constituting just less than 8 percent of the rivalries. Unlike the plateau cases, the decreasing pattern exhibits a more gradual decline in rivalry severity for these cases, quite the opposite of what is predicted by the volcano model. These cases also present instances in which successful conflict management might be explored. Yet until we know what determines the BRL, we may not be able to sort out structural and exogenous influences. The concave pattern is perhaps indicative of rivalries that had the beginnings of successful conflict management, but at midlife returned to a pattern of severe confrontation. One might suspect that concave patterns were more evident among lesser-order rivalries that almost ended before they evolved into enduring ones.

We have suggested that two patterns are consistent with the general volcano model: increasing and convex. The first fits a rivalry scenario in which the rivalry is terminated by a major war and the second corresponds to a vol-cano effect followed by a GRIT-like (Osgood 1962) conflict resolution process. Only two (3.2 percent) rivalries show a strict or pure escalatory volcano pattern. The Franco-German rivalry in the twentieth century, culminating in world war, is the classic example, but we must remember that this pattern is quite excep-tional. A modified version of the volcano model might suggest a convex pattern of increasing hostility and then decreasing hostility following the apex. Never-theless only three (4.8 percent) of the rivalries (for example, Israel–Saudi Ara-bia) exhibit a convex pattern. Of our rivalries, then, less than 8 percent fit some form of the volcano model. Among the uncompleted rivalries, the percentages are only slightly higher, but still not exceeding 12 percent of the population. Even given the small Ns, few of the individual regression parameters support-ing the volcano model have estimates that are statistically significant or even in the predicted direction. Far from universally valid, this escalatory model ap-pears to fit only a small subset of our cases.

The volcano hypothesis has most frequently been applied to events just be-fore a war. Our extensions to rivalries both in terms of the lock-in hypothesis as well as trends in the basic rivalry level are natural extensions, but extensions nonetheless. We can more specifically examine the volcano hypothesis with regard to wars within enduring rivalries. Recall that Leng (1983) found esca-lating patterns in a number of repeated conflicts. A minimal definition of an es-calatory pattern would involve an increasing severity level in the two disputes before a war. Because, by definition, a war has a higher level than the preceding dispute (except in the case where that is a war as well), a minimal escalatory pat-tern requires that the dispute twice prior to the war (the "pre-prewar" dispute) have a lower level than the prewar dispute. A simple test for this is whether the difference between the two levels is positive. If we examine wars in enduring rivalries, we do indeed find a positive difference of 17, but it is not statistically different from zero ($p < .16$), owing largely to the tremendous variance across the cases.[6] Thus, even a more direct test of the volcano model in terms of con-flict level still does not provide strong support for its propositions.

Independence of Disputes

We suggested that one measure of patterns within rivalries is whether the con-flict levels were related over time. This we operationalized in terms of regres-sion line trends. If there is a connection over time, then the regression line will permit a prediction of the level of the next dispute based on the level of the last (except in the flat line case). A second test of that is whether the residuals of these trend lines are independent. The Durbin-Watson statistic tests for inde-pendence of the residuals. If there is autocorrelation, then that suggests that

---

[6]For this analysis, we were able to look only at wars in which there were two other disputes preceding it. We also relied on the Small and Singer (1982) definition of war to define a population of war dyads.

TABLE 9.2: Negative Residuals at the Beginning and End of Rivalries

	Number of Negative Residuals				
	0	1	2	3	Mean
Rivalry beginning	5	20	25	12	1.71
Rivalry ending[a]	2	14	7	3	1.42

Note: Cases that had not ended by 1992 (censored cases) are not included in this table.
[a]United States–Peru case is not included because there is no variation in severity level over the rivalry and therefore a regression line could not be estimated.

beyond the dependence found in the BRL there may be other kinds of dependence over time. Our analysis indicates that such was the case in about eight (13 percent) of the rivalries.[7] As with the basic rivalry level and volatility, such cases require special attention. It may be that a better specification of the basic rivalry level will eliminate autocorrelation problems. Again, this analysis provides support for the punctuated equilibrium model.

Mean Rivalry Levels and Volatility

Another empirical test concentrates on the residuals from the mean for the first and last three disputes in a rivalry sequence, noted in table 9.2. Within the rivalry framework, there are a variety of variations of the volcano model. First, there is the initial phase of the rivalry in which one might expect lower levels of conflict as the enduring rivalry gets under way. This we have referred to as the lock-in hypothesis. Table 9.2 shows no dramatic pattern, with a mean of 1.71. If the number of residuals were distributed randomly above and below the mean level, as is consistent with the punctuated equilibrium model, we would expect an average of 1.5 residuals to be below the mean level. The sign test (which tests whether the numbers of values above and below this level are equal) indicates no significant difference ($p < .11$). Certain patterns of the BRL, however, would lead us to expect a larger number of negative residuals. In particular, the increasing and convex trends imply negative residuals at the beginning. Indeed, the increasing and convex cases account for many of the higher negative residual rivalries.

We are working under the general assumption that there is a fair amount of variation in the BRL from rivalry to rivalry, and that this variation "explains" why disputes are likely to become wars in some rivalries and not others. The cross-sectional variation in the mean severity level (see table 9.3 at the end of this chapter) ranges from 31 (essentially serious threat level by at least one party but no fatalities) in the United States–Peru rivalry to 142 for the Israel–Jordan

[7]Because of the small sample sizes (number of disputes in each rivalry) for the regressions, we classified all Durbin-Watson scores that did not meet the significance tests at .01 and .05 in the insignificant category. These included both the so-called acceptable and ambiguous scores.

rivalry, which has been characterized by several wars. We find rivalries distributed quite evenly between these two extremes. Thus, the concept of a BRL seems as if it might provide one handle for trying to understand rivalries and war within them. This initial exploration of the concept of a BRL has the hidden agenda of trying to eventually explain why this level varies from rivalry to rivalry, as well as its evolution over time in those cases in which we see a clear pattern.

The likelihood of war is not only a function of the rivalry level, but also its volatility. Rivalries with the same mean level might have quite different variances, which would contribute to explaining why war can occur in a relatively low-level rivalry. One common empirical situation is that the variance of a random variable increases with the mean, a common form of heteroskedasticity. Substantively, we might expect to find a lot of relatively minor disputes in rivalries with a lot of wars, thus producing a large variance. In fact, there is only a weak correlation between the mean severity and the volatility of a rivalry (r = .30, $p < .02$). Indeed, one of the rivalries with the least volatility is the most severe one, between Israel and Jordan. Thus, in addition to trying to understand why mean levels are higher in some rivalries than others, we suggest a separate research agenda that consists in trying to understand why the variability of disputes is much greater in some rivalries than others. As it currently stands, there are serious problems in using the BRL level to explain war in rivalries because the BRL includes wars. Careful thought will be required to avoid making the analysis of BRLs and war nontautological, but at least conceptually the two are separate.

Conclusion

We noted at the outset that a popular image, which we labeled the volcano model, of international conflict is the escalation of hostilities over time culminating in war. In contrast we propose a punctuated equilibrium model of rivalry that emphasizes the stability of conflict relationships over time. The conflict patterns in enduring rivalries showed no strong support for the proposition that the volcano model accurately describes the evolution of enduring rivalry conflict. In terms of basic trends in enduring rivalries, we found only a small percentage (approximately 8 percent) showed increasing or convex trends over time. In contrast, we found the punctuated equilibrium patterns—no secular trend or plateau—to be the primary ones (about 75 percent of the cases) in our analysis.

Other tests gave also little evidence of a volcano effect. There appeared to be no systematic relationship between the conflict level of successive disputes and no indication of a gradual escalation of conflict even at the beginning of a rivalry. The absence of any escalatory patterns at the beginning of rivalries supports one aspect of the punctuated equilibrium model, which argued for a rapid lock-in for rivalries. Other findings also supported the punctuated equilibrium model. There was little evidence that the severity of the conflict level was related to variations in that level, and regression analyses indicated general independence of residuals across disputes.

Despite some results that indicated a constant conflict level throughout a rivalry, there were other indications of significant variation around that level. There are some enduring rivalries of a concave or convex types, and these may not have the normal variation around the basic rivalry level. Structural factors will no doubt account for some variation around the BRL level, but our analysis cannot yet indicate whether the observed patterns are merely the result of structural factors or indicative of several different relationships inconsistent with the BRL model.

The punctuated equilibrium model of rivalries seems to us to revolve around processes that *maintain* rivalries. One class of metaphors is related to momentum (Lebovic 1994). This we find an unfortunate choice of analogy because momentum in the proper sense does not necessarily imply any force maintaining the object in motion (i.e., in a vacuum, an initial push sends an object going and its momentum remains constant until acted upon by another force). We suggest that rivalries must be kept going and reproduced over time; active forces must be present to keep a rivalry alive. Lebovic speaks frequently of "predilections," which sounds close to preferences. There are reasons why leaders continue to come to power with the same predilections and why predilections do not change.

The bandwagoning or snowballing model is more generally one of positive feedback; it is this positive feedback that accelerates the process. This is most clear in arms race models, but what is less clear is that in most of these models there are negative feedback loops as well. Diffusion models (see Mahajan and Peterson 1985 for an introduction) and more generally dynamic feedback models (Richardson 1991) usually include factors that keep the process from running off into infinity. In arms race models, budget constraints act as a brake on the escalatory spiral. The convex pattern is typical of processes where the positive feedback factor is dominant at the beginning and the negative at the end.

Although not universally applicable, our results support the argument that rivalries exhibit relative stability over time in their conflict patterns. Furthermore, this stability is evident quite quickly at the outset of the rivalry and does not fade away as the end of the rivalry approaches. The stability of enduring rivalries is also evident in the analyses of the next chapter, where we examine whether international mediation attempts can modify and mitigate the conflict patterns we see here. Hence we turn now to hypotheses about conflict management and deescalation in enduring rivalries.

TABLE 9.3: Patterns in Enduring Rivalries

Rivalry	Mean(SD)	Beg.[a]	End[b]	R^2	DW	Pattern
USA–Cuba	59(42)	1	1	.17	2.24	flat*
USA–Mexico	65(51)	2	2	.10	3.34**	flat
USA–Ecuador	44(38)	2	3	.29	2.83	flat*
USA–Peru	31(00)	–	–	—	—	flat*
USA–UK	71(32)	1	1	.04	2.77	flat+
USA–Spain	37(27)	0	2	.72*	2.87	decrease+
USA–USSR	58(36)	0	2	.05	2.65	flat*
USA–China	85(51)	1	3	.16	1.72	decrease
USA–N. Korea	109(50)	0	3	.37**	2.18	decrease*
Honduras–Nicaragua	106(50)	2	1	.60	3.47**	concave
Ecuador–Peru	83(47)	1	2	.03	2.70	flat
Brazil–UK	59(44)	3	1	.84	3.15	flat++
Chile–Argentina (I)	69(36)	1	2	.53	3.60**	flat
Chile–Argentina (II)	65(39)	2	1	.43**	1.75	flat++*
UK–Germany	77(66)	2	1	.50	2.88	flat
UK–USSR	82(40)	3	1	.61*	2.65	increase++
UK–USSR	66(41)	1	2	.17	2.21	flat*
UK–Ottoman Empire	66(59)	3	1	.23	2.01	flat
UK–Iraq	62(55)	2	1	.20	1.86	wavy*
Belgium–Germany	94(64)	2	1	.91*	3.11	concave
France–Germany	100(72)	2	3	.25	3.17	increase
France–Germany	59(61)	2	1	.37	2.37	flat+
France–Turkey	63(61)	3	1	.29	2.06	flat
France–China	88(66)	3	1	.26	3.16	flat
Spain–Morocco	65(41)	2	2	.52	2.07	convex*
Germany–Italy	97(78)	1	1	.63	3.02	concave
Italy–Yugoslavia	76(55)	2	2	.29	3.21	flat
Italy–Ethiopia	78(79)	3	1	.89	3.56*	flat++
Italy–Ottoman Empire	65(64)	2	3	.44	2.81	convex
Yugoslavia–Bulgaria	105(68)	1	0	.31	3.11	flat
Greece–Bulgaria	97(58)	1	2	.74**	2.40	flat
Greece–Turkey (I)	87(62)	2	1	.13	2.96	flat
Greece–Turkey (II)	65(50)	2	1	.07	2.94	flat*
Cyprus–Turkey	75(66)	3	1	.42	3.36*	flat++*
USSR–Norway	34(21)	3	2	.12	2.79	flat*
USSR–Iran	64(43)	2	1	.08	2.72	flat*
Russia–Ottoman Empire	58(67)	1	1	.08	2.58	flat
USSR–China	81(50)	1	0	.14**	1.84	flat*

Continued on next page

TABLE 9.3—*continued*

Rivalry	Mean(SD)	Beg.[a]	End[b]	R^2	DW	Pattern
USSR–Japan	63(56)	2	1	.15**	1.34	flat+*
Congo–Zaire	68(52)	2	1	.37	3.50*	flat*
Uganda–Kenya	83(59)	3	0	.96**	3.50**	flat++*
Somalia–Ethiopia	123(39)	2	1	.13	2.68	flat*
Ethiopia–Sudan	49(32)	2	2	.19	3.27	flat*
Morocco–Algeria	103(55)	1	1	.52	3.64*	flat*
Iran–Iraq	112(47)	2	1	.42*	2.63	flat*
Iraq–Israel	81(69)	1	2	.63	2.95	flat+*
Iraq–Kuwait	101(49)	2	0	.32	2.70	flat++*
Egypt–Israel	95(55)	0	3	.23*	2.29	flat +*
Syria–Jordan	87(50)	2	3	.41	2.71	decrease*
Syria–Israel	107(45)	1	1	.06	2.62	flat*
Jordan–Israel	142(28)	1	0	.29	2.88	flat
Israel–Saudi Arabia	97(55)	2	2	.81	2.93	convex*
Saudi Arabia–Yemen	80(49)	2	1	.76	2.96	concave*
Afghanistan–Pakistan	97(46)	1	1	.05	2.53	flat*
China–South Korea	104(63)	0	3	.67*	2.40	decrease*
China–Japan	91(65)	3	2	.08	1.76	flat
China–India	74(46)	3	1	.14	2.23	flat*
N. Korea–S. Korea	125(39)	1	2	.45*	2.04	flat*
South Korea–Japan	34(15)	2	3	.67*	1.85	flat*
India–Pakistan	105(53)	1	1	.03	2.03	flat*
Thailand–Kampuchea	92(49)	3	1	.29	2.87	flat*
Thailand–Laos	87(48)	1	0	.39	1.86	concave*
Thailand–N. Vietnam	99(70)	1	2	.30	3.55*	flat*

[a]Number of positive residuals at beginning, out of three possible.

[b]Number of negative residuals at end, out of three possible.

R^2: * Significant at .05 level. ** Significant at .10 level.

DW: * Problematic at .05 level. ** Problematic at .01 level.

Pattern: *Right-censored case. +Plateau down case. ++Plateau up case

CHAPTER 10

The Conflict Management
of Enduring Rivalries

In this chapter we pursue two agenda items: (1) our continuing evaluation of the punctuated equilibrium model of enduring rivalry and (2) the use of the rivalry approach in the analysis of conflict management in enduring rivalries. Our analysis of the punctuated equilibrium model in the previous chapter focused on escalatory processes, whereas here we look at de-escalatory—conflict management—aspects of enduring rivalries. More generally, we have argued that the rivalry approach provides a natural framework for the study of conflict management. It is virtually impossible to think about medium- to long-term conflict management without some sort of rivalry in mind.

The punctuated equilibrium model does not prove optimistic in its predictions for conflict management in enduring rivalries. Just as it does not expect gradual escalatory processes, it does not predict gradual de-escalatory ones. The findings of the previous chapter indicate that long-term conflict management success is not common in enduring rivalries. Yet it is worth pursuing a closer examination of patterns in enduring rivalry from the conflict management perspective. Thus, this chapter builds and expands on the analysis begun in the previous chapter.

Several aspects of the relationship between the punctuated equilibrium model and conflict management merit further examination. First, we need to conceptualize more clearly conflict management success within the punctuated equilibrium context. We argue that long-term successful conflict management can take various forms, some of which contradict the punctuated equilibrium model, but others are consistent with that framework. For example, one key aspect of enduring rivalries is their volatility. One form of successful conflict management involves reducing volatility, hence the likelihood of war. This can occur without a change in the basic rivalry level, and therefore it is consistent with the punctuated equilibrium model.

The same applies to short-term conflict management success. At first blush, the punctuated equilibrium model would seem to imply that conflict management does not significantly affect the severity of the next dispute in the rivalry. Given the stability predicted by the punctuated equilibrium model, this seems natural. Nevertheless, we argue that the variation from the basic rivalry level depends on crisis-specific factors, among which we can include conflict management efforts. The punctuated equilibrium model clearly implies no medium-to long-term conflict management success, but is not inconsistent with short-term impacts.

Our examination of the punctuated equilibrium model in the context of conflict management parallels in many ways that of the escalatory hypotheses in the last chapter. We discuss the long-term de-escalatory hypotheses in contrast with—although sometimes consistently with—the punctuated equilibrium framework. Also, we examine the conflict management parallel to the rapid lock-in of the punctuated equilibrium model of enduring rivalry. We examine whether enduring rivalries end quickly in accordance with the punctuated equilibrium model or slowly, which corresponds to a gradual conflict termination model. By the end of this chapter, we will have subjected the punctuated equilibrium model to an evaluation from both the volcano and conflict management sides. We think this is appropriate within the rivalry approach, which focuses on rivalries in terms of both war and peace.

Our second agenda item involves illustrating the usefulness and importance of the rivalry approach to the study of conflict management in general, although with particular emphasis on enduring rivalries. Enduring rivalries are the context for much war, but also much conflict management activity. We have already used the rivalry approach to examine the democratic peace, and we now continue in this vein by looking at conflict management issues through rivalry glasses.

Broadly speaking, there are a number of ways of dealing with conflicts, ranging from noncoercive to coercive strategies (e.g., avoidance, negotiation, referral to an international organization, adjudication, mediation, and feuding). The conflict management strategy that relies on third parties to resolve a conflict is, on the face of it, particularly apposite in the context of international relations. It is after all a voluntary, consensual, ad hoc, and nonbinding method of conflict management that can work best in a system of states, each of which will only too jealously guard its autonomy and sovereignty. States abide by tacit "rules of the game" only insofar as such rules serve their national interests. In what is traditionally described as an anarchic system, conflict management by third-party peacemakers of any sort seems to offer a promising solution to the problem of conflict. Here we first discuss what it means for conflict in an enduring rivalry to be managed. We then examine just how effective the most prominent form of third-party conflict management, mediation, really is in abating or managing enduring rivalries.

Although conflict management can be successful in resolving all manner of conflicts, internal as well as external, the most difficult context for successful mediation and third-party intervention is that of an enduring rivalry. As we noted in chapter 3, enduring rivalries represent the most dangerous conflicts in the international system. Can international efforts at conflict management break the stability of rivalries and mitigate the dangerous conflict patterns contained therein? There are both theoretical and policy implications that follow from this question.

Our concern with the conflict management of enduring rivalries is also motivated by more than theoretical concerns. From a policy perspective, we are concerned that the stability of conflict patterns within rivalries suggests that states or third parties may be able to do little about mitigating or stopping these most serious conflicts. Our emphasis on political shocks, largely out of the control of the rivals or other actors, further heightens our interest in identifying factors directly manipulable by decision makers that can make a positive difference in moderating or ending enduring rivalries. For us, an obvious place to start is with international mediation attempts, the efforts of third parties to manage external conflict. The existence of an enduring rivalry inherently implies that the rivals themselves have to a substantial degree already failed to manage some aspects of their own competition.

We begin with a general discussion of what conflict management connotes in the context of enduring rivalries. This includes past conceptions as well as our own specification of different ways that conflict management might be conceived and measured with respect to enduring rivalries. We then move to an empirical analysis of a certain form of conflict management, mediation, considering its frequency, timing, and impact on enduring rivalry dynamics. There are several specific issues of concern here. We wish to explore how often mediation actually occurs in the context of enduring rivalries and understand at what phase mediation efforts are undertaken (if indeed they are made at all). Are mediation efforts only made in the most severe rivalries, or are they attempted in rivalries before they become enduring? At what stage in the rivalry is mediation attempted, and how does this fit in with the prescriptions derived from the extensive literature on timing and mediation success? Beyond a description of mediation in the context of rivalries, we wish to assess its impact on the medium-term dynamics of rivalries. Do mediation efforts make a difference? Do they help to postpone the onset of violence, lessen conflict severity, or prevent a war?

Conflict Management and Enduring Rivalries:
A Conceptual Overview

To say that governments "manage" their conflicts does not, strictly speaking, refer to conflict reduction. The more intuitive use of the term suggests that a resort to violence is the antithesis of conflict management.[1] As we use the term, conflict management refers to behavior taken by states to reduce conflict levels or to avoid certain kinds of conflict, such as war. We believe this interpretation conforms to common usage. Unfortunately, the discipline lacks a widely shared concept of what constitutes conflict management as a dependent variable. As a result we also lack systematic, comparable, and accepted indicators of conflict management. As we gain a clearer idea of the concept of successful conflict management, we should also have a clearer idea about what indicators are appropriate. Conversely, the development of indicators forces us to confront theoretical ambiguities.

Beyond the implication of reduced hostility levels, conflict management often seems to refer to *both* the efforts to control the relationship and the success of such efforts. What does it mean when someone says, "The United States and the USSR managed their conflict"? Is conflict management a dependent or independent variable? We take conflict management, as an independent variable, to be actions such as mediation, negotiation, or security regime formation that have generally been the core of the literature on conflict management and resolution. What has been much less clear in this literature is the identity of the conflict management dependent variable, what we will frequently call successful conflict management. For example, Kriesberg (1992) in his study of "conflict resolution" in the United States–USSR and Middle East enduring rivalries provided a number of tables of negotiation attempts and agreements, but nowhere did he present tables of the *effect* of these management activities. In essence, he suggested that sometimes the management efforts were effective, without giving a clear explanation of the observed changes in behavior.

In the causes-of-war literature, the use of wars, militarized interstate disputes, or crises as dependent variables is so routinized and accepted that it is no longer justified, but merely announced. The literature on deterrence success illustrates the other end of the spectrum, where a lively debate continues about the character and coding of the dependent variable. We argue that an essential first step lies in conceptualizing and developing measures of conflict management dependent variables. We can speculate ad nauseam on the impact of efforts to manage conflicts, but until we have a clear idea of what behavior is affected, we are spinning our wheels for little forward movement.

---

[1] Deterrence illustrates the ambiguity about what it means to manage a conflict. Deterrence is a hostile, military threat, and nations are encouraged to show strength militarily to increase the credibility of that threat. Such actions may not fall under what most people mean by conflict management.

Our approach starts by inquiring about the kinds of behavioral change that we would expect to see if states in fact were able to manage conflict successfully. Of course, to detect behavior that counts as successful conflict management does not mean that mediation, security regimes, and other conflict management independent variables are necessarily the explanation. Such behavior may result from exogenous factors that one would not label as foreign policy efforts to manage conflict. The end of the Cold War provides part of the explanation for the end of some Third World rivalries. A realistlike explanation of reduced conflict levels would probably start by looking for long-term changes in basic power relationships. Yet until we have a dependent variable with which to work, such speculation remains just that.

One can perhaps divide conflict management dependent variables into three kinds: (1) short-term effects, (2) medium-term effects, and (3) conflict termination. For example, détente refers to the kind of short- or medium-term phenomena that interest us. Détente is more than one successful treaty and lasts more than a few years. We sharply distinguish conflict management from conflict resolution. Conflict resolution implies a fundamental change in dyadic relationships whereby the resort to militarized actions is no longer likely (Miall 1992). We consider successful conflict management to refer to the reduction *within* an *ongoing* rivalry of conflict levels without eliminating hostility altogether.

The punctuated equilibrium model has different implications for shorter- and longer-term conflict management as well as conflict termination. In order to evaluate the punctuated equilibrium model in terms of de-escalatory or conflict management patterns, however, we need to know what conflict management—as a dependent variable—means in an enduring rivalry context. Therefore, our principal goal in this section is to develop the concept and measures of successful conflict management. Most of our analysis will address issues of theoretical description and measurement. At the same time, by embedding this analysis in a rivalry framework, we hope to shed some light on rivalry relationships and their evolution, as well as to evaluate the merits of the punctuated equilibrium model.

Conflict Management Dependent Variables: A Brief Survey

Before turning to our own proposals for conflict management dependent variables, it is useful to briefly survey the explicit or implicit dependent variables used by prominent researchers in this literature. It is important to review the common short-term dependent variables because one plausible strategy is to extend these variables to the medium-term range. Another important issue relates to whether one should include cooperative actions as part of the dependent variable or focus only on the conflictual end of the scale. In this regard, one must be clearly distinguish between the independent and dependent variables. The act of negotiation might itself be an indicator of improved conflict management, but at the same time a negotiation may be considered the independent variable explaining reduced conflict levels.

Cooperation-Conflict Scales in Events Data

Many of those who employ events data use as their dependent variable some form of "conflict minus cooperation" (Goldstein and Freeman 1990; Kegley, Richardson, and Richter 1978; Lebovic 1985). Our conception of conflict management focuses explicitly on the hostile range of relations, which we suggest is more appropriate. The basic logic behind the use of the entire spectrum of the conflict-cooperation continuum is that the results represent a history of a relationship "expressed as fluctuations over time along a scale of net cooperation" (Goldstein and Freeman 1990). When aggregating cooperative and conflictual events, however, we obscure that some of what constitutes cooperative events is precisely what we envisage being causally related to changes in the character of conflictual relationships. For instance, in the coding of the more recent version of the WEIS data (Goldstein 1992), making substantive agreements with an adversary is considered a highly cooperative event, as are other events that might result from mediated or negotiated disputes. By creating an aggregated index, one virtually eliminates the possibility of using such cooperative events as potential explanations for successful conflict management. Making all events part of the dependent variable inhibits our ability to understand the influence of cooperation on conflict more fully.

Short-Term Dependent Variables

One of the characteristics of most research into the success of efforts to manage international conflict—be it through third-party diplomatic initiatives or military and economic interventions—is that the effectiveness of the effort is largely operationalized in terms of short-term outcomes. Bercovitch (1991) has systematically coded the outcome of conflict mediation efforts using four categories that reflect the degree of success of the specific mediation effort. These categories are (1) the partial or (2) full settlement of the issues, (3) the establishment of a cease-fire, and (4) unsuccessful outcomes. Each of these focuses on the mediation attempt itself, not the overall relationship between antagonists. Others also have a short time horizon, paying particular attention to the outcome of the specific mediation effort (Kramer, Pommerenke, and Newton 1993; Curry and Pecorino 1993). This type of short-term outcome is illustrated most clearly by focusing on a specific case, for example the conflict in the former Yugoslavia. There have been numerous cease-fires and partial resolutions negotiated and signed by the warring parties, only to have the killing start again after a brief respite. Many individual management efforts were clearly successful at achieving the short-term goal of bringing a halt to the fighting, opening up transport lanes, or giving passage and safe havens to civilians. Yet despite many short-term successes in conflict management, the medium-term character of the conflict may have changed very little. The key issue here is the specificity of the dependent variable. Using a different example, the United States and the USSR negotiated an agreement after the Cuban missile crisis guaranteeing Cuban security and a commitment to a nuclear-free Cuba. This agreement can be considered successful because it has been honored by both sides (with occasional minor controversies), but the Cuban agreement did not automatically alter the longer-term U.S.-Soviet rivalry.

Taking a broader view of conflict management does little to relax the emphasis on short-term outcomes. For example, Licklider (1993) considers civil wars to have ended when the military aspects of the conflict have been terminated for at least five years. Although five years may seem like a long time by some operational criteria, it is quite conceivable—even likely—that most enduring rivalries go through multiple phases without engaging in military hostilities for periods of up to five years. By our standards, and in the logic of international rivalries, five years is still a relatively short time horizon.

Those who examine the role of military or economic interventions as a form of conflict management also generally adopt a short-term outcome framework. Regan (1996), for example, focuses on the role played by third-party military or economic interventions in controlling the violence between parties in civil disputes. By his operational criteria, a successful intervention is one that contributes to the cessation of hostilities for a period of at least six months. This short time frame is justified on the grounds that six months gives political decision makers reason to claim success, but also adequate time for diplomatic initiatives to be organized and implemented.

In studies of the effectiveness of intervention by international organizations, the predominant focus has been on short-term impact (e.g., Butterworth 1978; Haas 1986). Most prominent has been the ability of international organizations to achieve cease-fires or otherwise prevent escalation of ongoing conflicts. Even studies of peacekeeping that include broader concerns than conflict abatement, nevertheless tend to define success in terms of short-term achievements such as feeding refugees or conducting a democratic election (Druckman and Stern 1997). The only exceptions may be Diehl (1994a) and Diehl, Reifschneider, and Hensel (1996), which consider the ability of international organizations to discourage a renewal of armed conflict in the future and thereby promote true conflict resolution.

Virtually wherever one looks in the literature on conflict management, the outcome of the management efforts adopted by researchers relies predominantly on short-term consequences. Although there may be good reasons to believe that this is the time frame of importance to political decision makers, a short time horizon constrains our ability to draw logically elegant and empirically sound generalizations about the ability of states to manage conflict over the long haul. This is particularly important when we seek to understand conflict management within enduring rivalries. We suggest that this overarching consensus on a limited horizon can obscure the longer-term, and interactive, effects of conflict management initiatives.

Medium- and Long-Term Conflict Management Dependent Variables

We suggest that posing the question of medium-term conflict management in terms of the outcome variable can provide payoffs for our understanding of how enduring rivalries are managed. A key facet of conflict management consists of reductions in the overall level of hostility in the conflict. This is particularly relevant when the conflict involves long-standing rivals. In this context, conflict management efforts (i.e., independent variables) are effective if they help to reduce the long-term intensity of the rivalry. For example, a series of efforts to manage a conflict actively could result in a gradual decline in the number, intensity, and duration of militarized disputes between rivals, to a level that minimizes the short-term probability of the outbreak of a war.

A mechanism that might account for the discrepancy between the observed success rates in earlier studies (Bercovitch 1989; Bercovitch and Langely 1993; Bercovitch and Regan 1997) and the potential for conflict management efforts to achieve longer-term success can be found in the role played by mediation attempts. Earlier studies have focused on the attributes of the mediator, characteristics of the international system, or the specific conflict context as predictors of the success of the mediation effort. It is hypothesized that the context in which these efforts are undertaken affects the ability of the mediator to bring about some resolution. What we suggest, however, is that the process of bringing conflicting parties to a bargaining table can have a longer-term impact on the progression of the rivalry relationship. For example, a single mediation effort, whether successful or not, may have only a marginal effect on the overall rivalry relationship. But the strategy and density of efforts to manage the conflict may display considerable medium-term effects, even though many of the specific attempts at management have failed. The act of participating in a negotiating or mediating forum appears to convey, at minimum, an acknowledgment that trade-offs are possible, maybe even desirable. The short-term attempts at finding the appropriate mix of trade-offs may not bear fruit, but the more, and the more regularly, conflicting parties come to the table, the greater the likelihood that we would see medium-term results. This longer-term perspective can only be observed if one adopts a view of conflict management (dependent variable) commensurate with what we propose here.

Conflict Management as Declining Basic Hostility Levels

As suggested above, conflict management success can be evaluated on two dimensions. On the one hand, a particular mediation effort may result in a cease-fire, bilateral negotiations can end with a truce, or a multilateral conference may lead to a partitioning of disputed territory. In each such instance, success would be evaluated in terms of the outcome of the specific diplomatic effort. On the other hand, conflict management success can be judged in terms of reductions in the overall level of hostility in the conflict. This would be particularly relevant when the conflict involves long-standing rivals. In this sense, conflict management efforts (i.e., independent variables) would be effective if they helped to reduce the overall trend in the intensity of the rivalry. For example, a series of efforts to manage a conflict actively could result in the number, intensity, and duration of militarized disputes between rivals gradually declining to a level that minimizes the short-term probability of the outbreak of a war. In the first instance, the success of conflict management is conceived in terms of nearly dichotomous outcomes, either successful or not. In the latter view of conflict management—the one we adopt—the outcome is considered to be a continuous variable, with variation in a long-term trend being an observable indicator of the effectiveness of management efforts. Given this framing of the problem, rivalries provide a natural theoretical framework within which to explore the role and effectiveness of management efforts. By definition, enduring rivalries are hostile, militarized relationships that can play out over decades; similar to marriages, they offer many opportunities for interventions in an effort to manage the conflict.

This general conceptualization seems relatively unproblematic. The heart of the matter is how can we tell if relationships are improving in a rivalry, and therefore determine the relative effectiveness of conflict management efforts. We have used the phrase "level of hostility," but we need to be more precise and provide some explicit behavioral criteria.

Conceptually, one form of conflict management success occurs when the BRL decreases. A declining BRL indicates that, for whatever reasons, relations between rivals are improving. Candidates for successful conflict management are thus those rivalries that have periods of a declining BRL. One might suggest that including only *declining* BRL levels is too strict a criterion for successful conflict management: a flat, unchanging BRL means that the rivals "manage" to keep the rivalry from getting worse. This remark raises several concerns. First, in chapter 9, we presented a flat BRL as the dominant mode of rivalry severity over time. Implicitly, this suggests that various efforts to influence hostility levels have no long-term impact. Second, empirically, if it were common that rivalries showed increasing BRLs, then a constant BRL would appear in that context to be successful conflict management. Nevertheless, such does not appear to be the case, as increasing patterns of severity were relatively rare among enduring rivalries. Third, a flat BRL would signify successful conflict management if it occurred after a period of a steadily increasing BRL (such as the plateau case in the previous chapter). Fourth, common usage implies that conflict management means improved relations. *"Détente"* meant a change in relations. The persistent hostility of the United States and USSR throughout the 1950s does not fall under most people's definition of conflict management.

This is the first of many times in which we will argue that conflict management implies behavioral change. After all, the purpose of such management is to alter the course of the conflict. If the initial course of the rivalry is escalatory, a *change* to a flat line may be attributable to successful conflict management, but if the trend of the BRL of the rivalry appears basically flat from the start, then a continuation of that stable trend is not an example of success. One important caveat is in order. The absence of behavioral change should not necessarily be counted as a failure in conflict management. Some enduring rivalries (for example, USSR–Norway and United States–Peru) persist at very low levels of severity, and there is little that mediation and other conflict management efforts can do to ameliorate the rivalries further, short of facilitating their termination.

Enduring rivalry patterns with periods of declining basic rivalry levels constitute one important type of successful conflict management. These are the flip side of the volcano hypothesis discussed in the last chapter. Similar to escalatory patterns, such conflict management patterns would throw into doubt the punctuated equilibrium model, typified by the flat, unchanging BRL pattern. Returning to table 9.1 in the previous chapter, we note that there are several patterns that might be indicative of conflict management. Five cases involved flat distributions that shifted from a higher plateau to a lower one. This behavioral shift may be indicative of successful intervention by a third party or the rivals themselves managing their competition at lower levels. Similarly, decreasing or convex patterns of severity also are potentially identifiable as those in which conflict management occurred. Collectively, however, these constitute only 13 cases, or approximately 21 percent of all enduring rivalries.

About a quarter of all enduring rivalries contain periods of successful conflict management. We thus have the problem of whether this glass is three-quarters empty or one-quarter full. Clearly, the dominant pattern remains the flat punctuated equilibrium one. Nevertheless, conflict management is not rare. One can compare this to wars as a percentage of all militarized disputes, only about 4 percent. Also, worthy of note are the plateau cases that *both* indicate conflict management success and fit the punctuated equilibrium model. Clearly there is sufficient material to investigate what distinguishes the modal punctuated equilibrium pattern from the somewhat rare cases of conflict management success.

Conflict Management as Avoidance of Extreme Forms of Conflict

Trends in the BRL constitute but one possible form of conflict management. Most general concepts are multifaceted, and conflict management is no exception. The basic rivalry level refers to the *average* level of hostility. Some disputes are more severe, some are less so, and the BRL focuses on the center of gravity of rivalry hostility. Recall that we do not include rivalry termination in our analysis; hence the rivalry is always ongoing in this study. We examine conflict management *within* rivalries. Militarized disputes thus form a part of

TABLE 10.1: High BRL Enduring Rivalries and War Avoidance

Rivalry	BRL	Number of Wars
Jordan–Israel	142	3
N. Korea–S. Korea	125	1
Somalia–Ethiopia	123	1
Iran–Iraq	112	1
USA–North Korea	109	1
Syria–Israel	107	4
Honduras–Nicaragua	106	1
Yugoslavia–Bulgaria	105	2
India–Pakistan	105	3
China–South Korea	104	1

an expected rivalry future. In this context, conflict management can refer to the *avoidance* of the most severe conflicts in an ongoing rivalry relationship. Hence, our second conception of successful conflict management uses the occurrence or nonoccurrence of the most severe conflicts and wars in an enduring rivalry.

Conflict management defined as war avoidance does not contradict the punctuated equilibrium framework. War results from a combination of the basic rivalry level and crisis-specific factors—volatility. The punctuated equilibrium model makes clear claims about the evolution of the BRL, but says little or nothing about volatility or extreme values.

Of course, it may be the case that the enduring rivalry was not serious (i.e., a low BRL) and hence war was very unlikely: it is not difficult to avoid something that is not likely to occur anyway. Of course, for war to become probable, a low BRL must have a large volatility. Enduring rivalries without war *and* a high BRL or frequent disputes would be good places to look for successful conflict management. It is not easy to maintain a high level of conflict intensity without something going wrong in one dispute or another. If war is avoided, then management efforts may be the explanation.

A rough indication of successful conflict management in this regard can be defined by looking at the rivalries with the highest BRLs and those with the largest number of disputes. Here we again roughly define the basic rivalry level as the mean severity of all the disputes in the enduring rivalry. We list the top 10—roughly the top 15 percent—by these criteria and look for states that were successful in war avoidance. Table 10.1 gives the results for the high BRL group and table 10.2 for high dispute frequency category. It should be noted that the calculation of the mean basic rivalry levels *includes* all wars, so the existence of a high BRL without war is a particularly strong test.

TABLE 10.2: High Dispute Enduring Rivalries and War Avoidance

Rivalry	Number of Disputes	Number of Wars
US–USSR	53	0
USSR–China	50	3
Syria–Israel	45	4
USSR–Japan	43	4
India–Pakistan	40	3
Egypt–Israel	36	5
China–Japan	34	5
US–China	24	1
China–India	22	1

In general, we note that high frequency and high BRL rivalries do not avoid war. There is no high BRL rivalry that did not experience war at least once. The rivalry with the highest BRL not to experience war is between Morocco and Algeria (BRL = 103). A severity score of 100 is just the dividing line at which disputes begin to involve battlefield fatalities. If this is the average for a rivalry, it is perhaps not too surprising that things eventually get out of hand. Quite famously, the United States and USSR operated under a tacit norm to avoid direct and official contact between their armed forces. Generally rivals that operate at a very high level of hostility must make only a slight escalatory leap to war, and it is evident from our results that they are not successful all the time in controlling that escalation. Another indicator of rivalry severity is the number of disputes it generates. Again, we suspect a rivalry that generates many crises is a severe one, and war is likely to occur eventually. Among high dispute frequency enduring rivalries, only the United States–USSR rivalry managed to avoid war. More commonly, frequent dispute rivalries go to war several times, something that might be predicted just given the large number of conflictual interactions. War avoidance must be an important part of the concept of successful conflict management; if war occurs, then in an important sense conflict management efforts have failed. Not surprisingly, virtually all severe enduring rivalries failed on this count.

More nuanced than the complete absence of war in a rivalry would be trends in the incidence of severe disputes and war. For example, if there were several wars in the first half of the rivalry and none in the second half, then that would suggest that the rivals have done something to manage their rivalry. Thus, one variation on this second conflict management indicator is a decreasing trend in extreme severity values over the course of the rivalry. This mimics the analysis of the BRL using the highest dispute level reached by the rivalry instead of all dispute values.

TABLE 10.3: Patterns in Extreme Values

Pattern	Number of Cases (%)	
Flat	25	(40)
Increasing	16	(25)
Decreasing	6	(10)
Convex	2	(3)
Concave	9	(14)
Wavy	5	(8)
Total	63	(100)

We examined trends in extreme values by plotting the "moving maximum." The moving maximum is a variation on the moving average, where the maximum statistic replaces the mean. At any given time, the value equals the most severe of the previous five disputes (including the current dispute if one is under way).[2] For this moving maximum to go down requires an extended period of less severe disputes. The occasional, odd or sporadic low-level dispute does not indicate successful conflict management, but a long string of such disputes does. The moving maximum methodology, like the moving average, is a data-smoothing technique, and it eliminates much of the variation between observations. Hence clear patterns are more likely to emerge. The impact of a war is limited in the BRL analysis, to just one point, often among dozens. With the moving maximum, a war usually continues to determine the value of the maximum for the next four disputes (because wars receive very high severity values), hence accentuating high points in a rivalry. This may be appropriate because one might want to weight wars more heavily than other disputes. For example, if there is only one war in the rivalry and it occurs at the beginning, then the pattern is likely to be decreasing (e.g., China–South Korea). If the war occurs in the middle, then the pattern is likely to be convex.

Of course, trends in the extreme values are related to the BRL. If we think of the BRL as a something akin to an arithmetic mean, then it will clearly be influenced by the presence or absence of extreme values. Nevertheless, the mean does include low-severity as well as high-severity disputes, and a large number of low-severity disputes will dilute the effects of a war on the BRL.

Table 10.3 provides a summary of the different patterns we coded in the evolution of extreme disputes and wars. Contrasting this table with BRL patterns in table 9.1, we find that there are significantly more nonflat patterns; flat is still the modal pattern, but now it constitutes significantly less than 50 percent of the cases. From a conflict management standpoint, the decreasing and convex patterns (collectively about 13 percent of the sample) are interesting

---

[2]For the initial disputes in a rivalry, we coded the first two disputes as missing on the moving five-dispute maximum statistic; for the third and fourth disputes we used the maximum of all previous disputes in the rivalry.

in that rivals have managed to deescalate their hostile interactions even while continuing their competition. Notably, all three rivalries involving the Korean peninsula exhibit this pattern. Somewhat discouraging is the frequency of patterns that suggest rising hostility over the life of a rivalry, at least with respect to extreme incidents. One-quarter of the cases exhibit increasing extreme values, and another 14 percent show a concave pattern. These cases suggest that rivals are increasingly facing more severe confrontations and perhaps war as the rivalry matures. It is perhaps these cases that account for Hensel's (1996) moderately strong findings among rivalries as a whole that severity increases with the length of rivalries. Even though the most severe rivalries rarely avoid war, we see a variety of different patterns in the evolution of the most severe conflicts and wars. We often tend to think about war as the result of some process, but some of the patterns we detect start with a war. War may not as much occur *in* an enduring rivalry as be the *cause* of the enduring rivalry. Effective conflict management in these instances is as much the attempt by states to deal with the sequels of war as they are attempts to prevent the next one.

Conflict Management as Reduced Volatility of Rivalries

Related to the incidence of extreme disputes and wars as a measure of conflict management is what we have termed the "volatility" of rivalries. If the BRL is similar to a regression curve or mean, then volatility is approximately the variance around that curve. The basic idea behind the BRL is that the level of each dispute is an identically distributed, independent random variable centered on the BRL, and therefore volatility is the variance of those dispute levels around the BRL. The statistical analogy emphasizes that conceptually the BRL and volatility constitute separate—and possibly independent—facets of conflict management. In practice, they are weakly correlated ($r = .30$; statistically this means heteroskedasticity).

Normally, the variance of the residuals in a regression model is of no real substantive importance. Reducing this variance is important only because this increases the accuracy (hence significance) of parameter estimates. In our situation, the size of the residuals reflects the volatility of the rivalry. A rivalry with a lower baseline, but higher volatility, may produce more wars than a rivalry with a high baseline with little variation. Whether or not a dispute in an enduring rivalry escalates to war is a function of both the BRL (mean) and the volatility (variance) of the rivalry. One possible indicator of effective conflict management is when the baseline of a rivalry does not change, but the variance is reduced. This is epitomized by the Cold War, in which the United States and the USSR developed a few rules for keeping the competition under control, even though intense competition remained the norm. Lower volatility in a rivalry should mean greater predictability for the rivals and therefore less misperception that could lead to war.

The volatility of a rivalry is linked to the occurrence of extreme values. This connection is generally much more important than the link between extreme values and the mean. Extreme values by themselves indicate a larger variance, and therefore greater volatility. Yet the logic of the argument for the use of extreme value analysis as a way of understanding conflict management carries over to volatility. Limited volatility or decreasing trends in volatility each permit the inference that states may be doing something to keep their conflicts under control. We have already discussed the problem regarding the relevance of cooperation in the analysis of conflict management. A similar issue arises with volatility. The elimination of lower-level disputes, while keeping those at a high level, also reduces the variance. Yet we would not regard this as effective conflict management, as we are interested in the reduction of the most serious disputes between rivals, not necessarily those conflicts that have little or no chance to escalate to war. One possible solution is to define volatility as the variation above the BRL, excluding the effect of variation in low-level disputes. Just as we do not include cooperative events in our measure of the BRL, we can exclude changes in volatility that result from changes in low-level dispute activity. This parallels the extreme value argument as well; we are not really concerned with the evolution of the lowest-level conflicts, but rather the highest ones.

We measure volatility in a manner analogous to the moving maximum method outlined above. Instead of a moving maximum, however, we can calculate a "moving variance." Unlike the maximum, we need a sample mean to calculate a sample variance. This is not as easy as it might appear. One of our criteria for coding patterns is that one or two disputes should not affect the final coding decision, but by constructing the BRL using regression-like techniques, *all* observations enter the calculations. Of course, we could remove outliers, using smoothing techniques, but this means that each BRL must be individually crafted. Getting a computer to recognize patterns that seem obvious to the human eye is a nontrivial matter; one need but briefly examine the artificial intelligence literature on pattern matching to be convinced of this. The cases that we coded as flat in chapter 9 seem less problematic in this regard. In this particular case, the mean dispute level for the whole rivalry seems like a good first-cut approach. Of course, even here extreme values have an impact, but much less than they can have on a regression curve. Therefore, in this analysis we limit ourselves to the rivalries that we have coded as flat (chapter 9, appendix).[3] In addition to the cases we had to eliminate because we had no numeric estimate of the BRL (i.e., all nonflat rivalries), insufficient data eliminated a further group of rivalries, giving us only a final total of only 12 rivalries. Our method of constructing the moving variance only uses above average disputes; hence we lose

---

[3] We also did not consider so-called plateau case variations of the flat distribution. From a conflict management perspective, these are variations of the increasing and decreasing patterns and therefore not appropriate for consideration of volatility.

a substantial number of data points for each rivalry. Our final sample thus effectively includes only flat BRL rivalries with frequent disputes.

With only a limited number of cases, distinct patterns across cases are hard to discern. Nevertheless, cases of declining volatility, such as that in the United Kingdom–USSR rivalry, might be considered evidence of successful conflict management. Convex patterns suggest a midcourse adjustment in rivalry hostility and the establishment of norms or procedures for controlling the competition. The India-Pakistan rivalry is an example of this pattern. With only 12 rivalries as a sample we cannot draw any definitive conclusions, but nevertheless we note that that there were three flat, four increasing, two convex, one decreasing, and two wavy patterns. These results fit generally with those of the moving maximum analyses, a decrease in the number of flat cases with more "increasing" cases. In contrast with the theme of this chapter, it is the punctuated equilibrium and volcano patterns that dominate our analyses. In the case of volatility, we see only one decreasing and two convex patterns, which show conflict management success. As we move from the basic rivalry level to the extreme value and volatility analyses, we roughly see an increase in the proportion of escalatory patterns.

In many ways, it is unfortunate that data and methodological difficulties prevented us from carrying out an analysis of all rivalries. Conceptually, we find volatility (variance) superior to the moving maximum as a measure. Instead of using only maximum values and suppressing all other information, the moving variance gives extra weight to extreme values (because distances to the BRL are squared) but also includes information from all above-average disputes. The funnel-like effect of decreasing variance seems to capture an important aspect of what conflict management is about, particularly in ongoing rivalries. Because rivalries are ongoing and many rivalries show no change in the basic rivalry level, reducing volatility may constitute their only means of conflict management.

Summary

In summary, we have examined several forms of conflict management as a dependent variable: (1) the evolution of the basic rivalry level, (2) the evolution of extreme values and the absence of war, and (3) the evolution of volatility. In all cases, conflict management is operationalized as a *change* in the rivalry relationship in the direction of less conflict. These three facets of conflict management all invoke change, but change of different kinds. We proposed that changes in basic rivalry levels and volatility constitute relatively uncorrelated dimensions of conflict management. Students of war tend to think of conflict in terms of unidimensional scales, be it the cooperation-to-conflict of events data or the level-of-force scale used in COW data.[4] We suggest here that conflict

---

[4]The duration of a dispute seems quite independent from its severity, but duration is rarely used as a dependent variable in conflict studies.

management may be multidimensional, and that any attempt to collapse it into one dimension will be problematic, and possibly unwise. Each of these facets of conflict management is worthy of study in its own right.

Our results on medium to long-term conflict management have implications for the punctuated equilibrium model of enduring rivalry. Because this model most directly refers to the basic rivalry level, its implications for volatility and extreme conflict are less clear. We found that a significant minority of enduring rivalries had successful conflict management periods, but the dominant pattern was the flat one predicted by the punctuated equilibrium model. This parallels the results on the volcano hypothesis in the previous chapter where we found only a limited number of rivalries with escalatory phases.

Extreme conflict and volatility patterns all focus in various ways on deviations from the BRL. In one way or another they center on the most severe disputes in an enduring rivalry. Here the punctuated equilibrium model does not make clear predictions. Changes in volatility or extreme conflict patterns may both be consistent with an unchanging basic rivalry level.

Although we stress conflict management in this chapter, some of our analyses of extreme conflict within enduring rivalries support the volcano model of enduring rivalry. In our various analyses of extreme conflict patterns and volatility, we found a larger percentage of escalatory patterns than we did in our focus on the basic rivalry level. If we change the meaning of *escalatory* from the basic rivalry level to the extremes of rivalry, then we find somewhat stronger support for the volcano hypothesis than in the previous chapter.

This has ambiguous implications for the punctuated equilibrium model. On the one hand, to focus *only* on the most extreme conflicts of a rivalry certainly is biased. Yet, on the other hand, if there is a clear trend whereby the most severe disputes are getting more severe, then one can argue that the rivalry in some sense is escalating. In summary, the relationship between the basic rivalry level, volatility, and extreme conflict remains an important item for future research.

Mediation in International Rivalry

The focus of the last part of this chapter is directed toward assessing the impact or success of mediation on rivalry conflict. There are several implications and caveats associated with this focus. First, we note that we are analyzing the conflict *management* of rivalries, especially enduring ones, and not necessarily conflict *resolution*. Conflict management is a lower threshold standard to meet than conflict resolution. For mediation to be effective in our study, it must lead only to creating stability in the rivalry and facilitating circumstances that allow the rivals to avoid the most severe manifestations of militarized conflict. If mediation does indeed produce conflict resolution or termination of the rivalry, then clearly it has also managed the rivalry positively and more. Nevertheless, we save the issues of conflict resolution and termination of rivalries for the next chapter and concentrate instead on conflict management.

Consistent with the conflict management focus, we also concentrate on the medium-term impact of mediation attempts. That is, we are concerned with how mediation attempts affect the behavior of rivals in the aftermath of those efforts. Accordingly, this section is not concerned with whether mediation efforts have a cumulative effect over time in a rivalry or whether conflict patterns in rivalries are altered permanently or in the aggregate, but only with whether rivalry behavior is changed (if at all) in the approximately 5–10 years on average following third-party intervention. This is not to say that such long-term concerns are unimportant; indeed, they were the topic of the first part of this chapter. We now concentrate on the more immediate effects of mediation, which is consistent with the goals of most mediation attempts and may be easier to discern than long-term impacts, in which time and many intervening factors may make an assessment of earlier mediation efforts quite difficult.

Finally, we should clarify what we mean by the success or positive impact from mediation on rivalries. We regard mediation as having an impact if it changes the subsequent conflict behavior of the rivals. The standard for this judgment is a comparison of state behavior in segments of the rivalry with and without mediation attempts (this is the interrupted time-series design noted in chapter 5). Any beneficial impact from mediation, and this is considered along several dimensions (avoiding war, delaying conflict, lessening its severity), can be said to represent success, although clearly we are interested in the magnitude of beneficial impacts, not merely their existence.

We begin our investigation with a review of the relevant literature on mediation and relate this to enduring rivalries, recognizing that there currently is little scholarly research that addresses questions similar to those posed here.

Insights from Mediation Research

International conflicts can be managed by the parties themselves (through coercion or some form of negotiation), or more often by some exogenous actors (e.g., the UN, a regional organization, a state, etc.). Mediation is widely regarded as the most common form of exogenous intervention in international disputes (Bercovitch 1984; Butterworth 1976; Holsti 1987), and not surprisingly the focus of most extant research on conflict management. Indeed, over 70 percent of the conflict management efforts in rivalries are mediation attempts.

Although seeking a mutually agreeable solution through mediation is becoming increasingly popular in all areas of social life, there is much about its performance and effectiveness that we do not understand. Clearly, mediation cannot be effective or successful in each and every dispute (for a review, see Wall and Lynn 1993). Some disputes may be amenable to mediation; in others, the parties may have to rely on different means. There is considerable agreement among many scholars and practitioners that mediation is more suitable than law or force in dealing with international conflicts, but there is also some disagreement on what precisely constitutes international mediation. However we view it, and whether we study mediation from a historical, normative, or prescriptive perspective, mediation makes sense only if it is placed in the overall context of conflict management and its special features are recognized within this context.

Mediation is an aspect of conflict management without a universally accepted definition. Some studies (e.g., Northedge and Donelan 1971; Moore 1986) purport to describe mediators' stances or what mediators do. These are narrow definitions. Such definitions of mediation are consistent with the attempt to capture the "essence" of mediation and to draw boundaries between mediation, conciliation, facilitation, good offices, shuttle diplomacy, fact-finding, and other related activities. This seems to be a futile exercise. When entering a dispute, a mediator may change his or her stance and exhibit all, or any combination, of these behaviors. This is why we prefer to shape the analysis by adopting a definition that will remove unnecessary quibbling over the boundaries between conciliation, facilitation, good offices, and so forth, and will focus on behavior rather than on motives and intentions of actors in conflict. We define mediation as "a process of conflict management where disputants seek the assistance of, or accept an offer of help from, an individual, group, state or organization to settle their conflict or resolve their differences without resorting to physical force or invoking the authority of the law" (Bercovitch, Anagnoson, and Wille 1991, 8). This is a broad definition, but one that places mediation in the overall context of conflict management, draws attention to the basic components of mediation (namely, disputing parties, a mediator, and a specific conflict management context), and permits comparisons across levels and types of conflicts.

Does mediation actually work? Does it have any impact on international conflicts and if so, how to assess it? These issues are clearly at the heart of this section. In most contexts, it is possible to ascertain that a particular strategy works by assessing (through personal interviews with those directly involved) the degree of satisfaction the parties have had with a mediated outcome. One may also study the rate of compliance with any outcome, its speed, efficiency, or capacity for implementation. Dealing with the kind of conflicts we do, all we can do is examine how mediation attempts work by noting their impact on the parties' subsequent conflict behavior. When parties cease or limit violent interactions, or experience greater time lags between such interactions, mediation may be said to have been successful. If the parties carry on fighting with roughly the same frequency and levels of hostility, then clearly mediation has had little or no impact. The basic proposition we wish to test here is that mediation, because of its character, informality, and flexibility, is an effective conflict management approach in moderating enduring conflict.

We are mindful that assessing conflict outcomes, or the impact of mediation, is conspicuously tricky. Often there are as many evaluation criteria as there are scholars. Notwithstanding these difficulties, we are convinced that it would be valuable to examine, in a systematic fashion, the influence that mediation may have on the different types of conflict. How will the type of dispute, as our main independent, contextual variable, affect the frequency, timing, and effectiveness of mediation?

Type of Dispute

We approach our study by assuming that any mediation strategy must, first and foremost, be adaptive and contingent. Different mediators do different things in different situations, and the particular form of any mediation behavior depends on who the parties are, what the dispute is all about, and who the exogenous managers are. Intense and protracted disputes, evidenced here by enduring rivalries, may call forth different forms of mediation than disputes over relatively insignificant issues.

It seems a truism to suggest that the kind of dispute will have a significant impact on the success or failure of any mediation attempt. Kressel and Pruitt (1989) conclude that unfavorable dispute characteristics are likely to defeat even the most adroit mediators. Similarly, Ott (1972) argues that the success or failure of mediation is largely determined by the character of the dispute, with the characteristics and behavior of the mediator marginally influential at best. We intend to go beyond such statements and actually unravel some dimensions of conflict, code their presence and impact systematically, and analyze how mediators actually perform in different kinds of rivalries. We begin by reviewing the theoretical consequences of one of the defining aspects of enduring rivalries, that of intensity.

When we consider dispute intensity, we are immediately confronted with two fundamental difficulties: definition and operationalization. Although intensity is often regarded as an important dispute characteristic, what precisely does it signify? A number of scholars (e.g., Burton 1968; Young 1972; Jackson 1952) claim that intense disputes (however measured) are particularly suitable for mediation, as they usually offer a conspicuous solution, and the parties, having exhausted themselves, are ready to countenance any way out of their predicament. Others (e.g., Frei 1976; Kressel and Pruitt 1989) conclude that parties in high-intensity disputes will show a greater inclination to reject mediation efforts. Under the rubric of intensity, all sorts of diverse factors such as the severity of prior conflict, the level of hostility, levels of anger and intensity of feeling, as well as the strength of negative perceptions (most enduring rivalries would score high on each of these dimensions) are included. There is no suggestion how these can be operationalized. In their discussion of public sector mediation, Kochan and Jick argue that the intensity of a dispute will be negatively related to the effectiveness of the mediation process (1978, 213). Yet, here again, what they mean by intensity is not made explicit.

To avoid this confusion, we will use one relatively simple indicator to test the hypothesis that mediation is less likely to be offered or to succeed in intense disputes. The most accessible surrogate measure of conflict intensity, and the one relevant to our concerns, is rivalry type (isolated, proto, and enduring categories, which on average represent increasing degrees of length, severity, and conflict frequency). Enduring rivalries, on average, can be considered the most intense conflicts given their relatively long duration, higher levels and frequency of violence, and large number of wars and fatalities that occur in that context. Thus, enduring rivalries might be expected to have more mediation attempts, although the impact of individual mediation attempts may be less in this context.

Previous studies (e.g., Bercovitch and Langley 1993) have shown a very clear pattern of the inverse relationship between intensity as measured by fatalities and successful mediation. Only 39 percent of all mediation attempts in the 1945 era had *any* degree of short-term success in mediating disputes where fatality levels exceeded 10 thousand, compared to 64 percent success rate in disputes where fatality levels were lower than five hundred.

In discussing enduring conflicts, we have to be aware that the number of fatalities may give us a rather misleading picture. Some high-fatality disputes can last years or even decades, while in others a considerable number of casualties may be experienced in a relatively short time. The "age" of a dispute, as Frei (1976) notes, has to be taken into account as well as the level of fatalities. This is where the concept of enduring rivalries, with its emphasis on the long-term dynamics of a relationship, comes in so usefully.

Timing of Conflict Management and Mediation

One of the most intriguing issues in the study of mediation relates to the issue of timing of third-party initiatives. When is the best time, if such a time does exist, to initiate mediation? And how can this "right moment" be identified conceptually and defined empirically? The discussion in this section will be devoted to addressing these questions.

Scholars agree that conflict management in general, and mediation in particular, can function best if the moment of entry is just right. The importance of proper timing has been highlighted by a number of scholars, though often in a tautological fashion. Conflicts, like any other social process, go through various points or distinguishable phases. Certain mediation attempts can be successful if made at the right point or phase. Mediation timing, and its relation to the "life cycle" of a rivalry, can be posited as another independent variable.

Northedge and Donelan note that mediation attempts can be successful "when there exists a concatenation of circumstances already tending toward an improvement of the situation" (1971, 308). Zartman (1985) has suggested that the parties assessment of the dynamics of the conflict, its combination of plateaus, precipices, deadlocks, and deadlines, will produce a distinct moment of "ripeness." The assumption here is that in the waxing and waning of the complex social forces that make up an international conflict, there are moments (e.g., a change in power relations) that may affect the perceptions and attitudes of the disputants and thus the likelihood of mediation success.

When we examine the scholarly literature on mediation, we find broad agreement with Touval that "mediation should take place at a propitious moment" (1982, 8), but that is where the agreement ends. Some theorists, such as Claude (1971) and Edmead (1971), have suggested that mediation efforts should be initiated as early as possible in a dispute, certainly long before positions become fixed, attitudes harden, and an escalating cycle becomes entrenched. From an ethical perspective, this is an attractive proposition. It is better to initiate mediation early to avoid further suffering. But are the parties ready to accept and partake in mediation in earnest? Can "windows of opportunity" be detected so early in rivalries?

Others (e.g., Kriesberg and Thorson 1991) believe that conflicts have to go through some phases, as well as moves and countermoves before a serious attempt to mediate it should be made. Mediation is clearly more likely to be successful when disputants think that they can gain a better settlement through mediation than through unilateral action. This normally occurs when a conflict has gone through a few phases and crises, and a workable alternative to combat appears feasible (Zartman 1985). This juncture, usually described as a "ripe moment," occurs when (1) the parties perceive a hurting stalemate, or an impending catastrophe, or all unilateral actions are blocked, and (2) when a powerful mediator can, through the use of leverage, create a perception that mediation timing is right. Either way, there is agreement that ill-timed mediations are bound to fail, but some disagreement over the specifics of mediation timing.

Most scholars who accord considerable importance to timing (e.g., Ott 1972; Pruitt 1981; Rubin 1981; and Moore 1986) suggest that mediation will be more successful if it is initiated well into a conflict, when costs have become intolerable and both parties accept that they may lose too much by continuing their dispute. This notion also receives some empirical support in one of the few studies to actually assess the impact of timing (Bercovitch and Langley 1993). Here we wish to pursue this question further and test for mediation timing in different rivalry types. What happens if a conflict is of long-standing duration with repeated resorts to militarized conflicts? Is mediation timing different in enduring rivalries than in proto- or isolated rivalries? And what if there are a few mediation attempts, as is the case in most conflicts? Do they occur at the beginning, middle, or final phases of a militarized competition? How, in short, is mediation embedded in an enduring rivalry?

The essence of mediation timing is the creation of a right atmosphere of political willingness and dyadic impasse. Exploiting the right moment or initiating mediation at just the right time can usually only be ascertained a posteriori, but here we want to postulate that enduring conflicts will attract more mediation efforts, and that most of these efforts might take place later rather than earlier in the life cycle of an enduring rivalry. Parties in such a conflict are willing to tolerate repeated cycles of conflict, and to run greater risks than other parties. Enduring rivals are in it for the long haul. We anticipate that they will neither expect, nor welcome, early mediation.

How does the punctuated equilibrium model of enduring rivalries fit into the analysis of mediation effectiveness? In many ways, it is a continuation of the hypothesis that the more intense the conflict, the lower the success rate. The punctuated equilibrium model suggests that conflict management has little long-term impact on enduring rivalries. In this section, however, we focus principally on medium-term impacts of mediation on the next dispute in the rivalry (although not immediate changes in behavior such as a cease-fire). Short-term mediation success does not necessarily contradict the punctuated equilibrium model. Many factors influence the volatility of a given crisis, and one factor could well be mediation efforts. At the same time, the punctuated equilibrium model implies that this does not happen frequently and that in general mediation is likely to have little effect on the course of the enduring rivalry.

In summary, we might expect that mediation attempts in rivalries will be more common in the most severe rivalries (enduring ones), but perhaps not be as successful in that context given the difficulty of resolving long-standing grievances and the history of violent relations between the two sides. With very little prior research to rely upon, these expectations must be regarded as tentative, and our study is largely exploratory. With this in mind, we move to an empirical description and assessment of mediation attempts in rivalries.

Research Design

Unlike other empirical analyses, we are limited in the scope of our analyses by the character of the mediation data available to test our propositions. First, we can only look at mediation attempts in the context of rivalries since 1946. Although this is in one sense greatly limiting, international mediation efforts were considerably less frequent prior to this time period, and international organizations (frequently the principal agents of mediation attempts) are rare in the nineteenth century and only fully developed and numerous after World War II. We are also confined to rivalries that have at least one dispute with 10 or more fatalities according to Bercovitch (1993). His mediation data cover only conflict management attempts in rivalries that meet or exceed this threshold and therefore were are unable to assess the full population of rivalries, some of which have no fatalities.[5] Nevertheless, even with these restrictions, we are able to analyze 555 rivalries of all varieties over the period 1946–92: 35 are enduring rivalries, 112 are proto-rivalries, with the remaining 408 rivalries being in the isolated category.[6] As we indicated in the first part of the book, although we are interested in enduring rivalries, we use the isolated and proto varieties as control groups for comparison, and indeed they facilitate the test of several of our expectations that propose differences in mediation attempts and success across the rivalry continuum.

Wars and the severity of conflict are identified and measured as in previous chapters. To assess less dramatic impacts of conflict management, we are also interested in whether militarized disputes are less frequent or delayed in rivalries as a result of a mediation effort. Thus, we look at the mean time (measured in years) or "waiting time" from the time of one dispute to the next dispute, comparing those waiting times that include mediation to those that do not.

Beyond these basic measures of conflict level and waiting times, we "contextualize" the measures by looking at their relationship to the mean value of the rivalry. This is consistent with the notion of the basic rivalry level, that rivalries have a relatively stable pattern of conflict over their lifetimes. Thus, we can assess whether mediation attempts result in a lower than average conflict level or a longer waiting time than is typical in the rivalry. Purely cross-sectional analyses may not be able to identify this effect, especially if there is a bias toward mediation attempts occurring in more severe disputes or rivalries. Some comparisons will be made between rivalries with and without conflict management. In addition, however, we will compare the relative effectiveness of mediation efforts on disputes within the same rivalry. In this way, we can hold constant many of the idiosyncratic elements of a rivalry and understand whether mediation affects the conduct of the rivalry (by comparing the evolution following a mediation attempt with postdispute periods that have no mediations).

Identifying instances and characteristics of rivalries is only half of the equation. We now turn to international mediation efforts and their components. We use the term *mediation* to refer to the wide range of third-party activities that are acceptable to the adversaries and are designed to manage or resolve a dispute without resort to force or invoking authoritative rules (Bercovitch 1991). For an operational listing of these attempts, we turn to Bercovitch's (1993) International Conflict Management (ICM) data set that covers all international conflict management attempts in rivalries with 10 or more fatalities over the period

---

[5] There is some difference in the recording of fatality levels between the Bercovitch and the COW data sets. In those instances, we necessarily relied on the Bercovitch codings, as they were the basis for selecting cases in the identification of mediation attempts.

[6] Only rivalries beginning in 1946 and afterward are included. Rivalries that began prior to 1946 and continued after that (and hence are left-censored) are dropped from consideration.

1946–92 (summary descriptions of this data are given in Bercovitch, Anagnoson, and Wille 1991). For our purposes, we focus only on those mediation efforts in disputes between two recognized states (according to Small and Singer 1982), the population from which rivalries are drawn.

We merged the data set on rivalries with that on mediation and determined whether or not a given rivalry included any attempts at international conflict management. A mediation attempt occurs in a rivalry if it involved a third party trying to manage a conflict between the same two states that constituted the rivalry. The mediation attempt had to take place within five years of the first militarized dispute in the rivalry or 10 years after the last dispute in the rivalry. In the rivalries identified, there were 618 different instances of mediation attempts.

Beyond the presence or absence of mediation attempts, we are also interested in their timing. For the descriptive analysis of timing, we divided rivalries into three equal segments from the time of the first militarized dispute to the last dispute: early, middle, and late. We also considered whether conflict management attempts occurred in the five years prior to the first dispute or 10 years after the last dispute, thereby creating two more phases: before and after. For our analysis of the impact of mediation timing on conflict in the rivalry, the measure used was the elapsed time (measured in years) from the onset of the rivalry (defined as the beginning of the first dispute) to the dispute on which the mediation effect was supposed to exercise an impact. The immediate, short-term outcome of a mediation attempt was coded as successful if there was a partial or full settlement between the protagonists at the time, and unsuccessful in all other cases, taken from the categories in the ICM data. We expect that favorable outcomes of mediation attempts in the immediate aftermath might make conflict less severe or likely in the medium term.

The likelihood and severity of future conflict in rivalries are also influenced by factors other than the existence and timing of mediation attempts. Thus, we include two other factors that have been found to have an important impact on recurring conflict in another study (Hensel 1994): issues and previous dispute outcomes. Some conflict issues are more prone to recurring conflict, and states may be more willing to risk violence in pursuit of certain issues; this is consistent with our earlier notion that some dispute characteristics are less amenable to mediation and conflict resolution. In particular, territorial issues could be the most dangerous (Vasquez 1993; Hensel 1994). Accordingly, in looking at the possibility of future conflict, its severity, and its timing, we code whether the last dispute in the rivalry involved territorial issues or not for either rival, relying on the information reported in the Correlates of War data set on militarized disputes (Jones, Bremer, and Singer 1996). We anticipate that a territorial dispute is more likely to produce a war or serious conflict in the future and in a shorter interval of time than conflicts over other issues. We also include a control variable for whether the previous dispute ended in a compromise or not.

TABLE 10.4: Mediation Attempts in Rivalries, 1946–1992

Rivalry Type	Management (%)	N	Without (%)	N	Number of Attempts
Isolated	35	144	65	264	233
Proto	45	50	55	62	142
Enduring	66	23	34	12	243
Total	39	217	61	338	618

Note: Unit of analysis is rivalry.
$\chi^2 = 14.33$, significant at .01.

Compromise outcomes may improve relations between protagonists and make them less likely to fight in the future or limit the violence or delay its onset between them when there is a confrontation. This is consistent with the earlier discussion that noted mediation efforts must correspond to positive or ripe environments, which recent compromises between rivals might represent. Thus, we also include a dichotomous variable for compromise outcomes (yes/no) in our multivariate analyses.

Empirical Results

In the first set of analyses, presented in table 10.4, we look to the frequency of conflict management attempts in the three types of rivalries. Our concern is both with the likelihood that a given rivalry will involve conflict management and with the number of attempts in each rivalry type (as a rivalry may experience multiple conflict management attempts). Our expectation is that enduring rivalries, the most intense of conflict types, will draw a disproportionate number of conflict management efforts. In general, less than 39 percent of rivalries of all varieties experience any international conflict management. Some 66 percent of all enduring rivalries, however, involve at least one attempt. Enduring rivalries are almost twice as likely as isolated rivalries to attract external conflict management, and almost 50 percent more likely to have mediation than proto-rivalries. In some sense, this is both comforting and logical in that the international community directs its attention to the most serious problems and the ones that reappear on the international security agenda.

The attention given to enduring rivalries is also reflected in the number of mediation attempts. Although enduring rivalries constitute only about 6 percent of all rivalries in this sample, they attract almost 40 percent of all conflict management efforts; the average enduring rivalry with conflict management has over 6.9 individual conflict management attempts, whereas the typical proto-rivalry has only 1.3 on average. For any given rivalry, the expected number of mediation attempts for enduring rivalries is almost 10 times greater than for isolated rivalries. Thus, we conclude that enduring rivalries have a higher

TABLE 10.5: The Timing of Mediation in Rivalries

Rivalry Type	Before % (N)	Early % (N)	Middle % (N)	Late % (N)	After % (N)
Isolated	38 (89)	4 (10)	4 (9)	1 (11)	54 (114)
Proto	19 (27)	13 (18)	6 (8)	6 (9)	27 (80)
Enduring	1 (3)	29 (70)	30 (73)	37 (89)	3 (8)
Uncensored Cases					
Isolated	15 (16)	6 (6)	1 (1)	5 (5)	68 (79)
Proto	11 (9)	9 (7)	5 (4)	7 (6)	37 (55)
Enduring	0 (0)	55 (6)	27 (3)	0 (0)	18 (2)

Note: Unit of analysis is mediation attempt.

probability of attracting an effort at conflict management, and among those rivalries that do involve third-party conflict management, enduring rivalries will experience more numerous mediation attempts.

We noted in the theoretical section that conflict management attempts are most effective when a conflict is ripe for settlement, generally after states have locked in to their hostility patterns and have reached an impasse in the settlement of their competition (direct diplomatic and military initiatives have not resolved the dispute). Table 10.5 provides an analysis of when various mediation attempts have been launched vis-à-vis the different stages of a rivalry: before the onset, in the early phase, middle phase, latter stages, or after the final dispute. Because many of the rivalries in our sample had not ended as of 1992 (and therefore we are technically uncertain of which phase they actually are in), we include analyses for all cases as well as only for those that had ended by 1992 (uncensored cases).

It is evident that few conflict management efforts (with the exception of isolated rivalries) occur prior to the onset of the first militarized dispute in enduring rivalries. The international political (and scholarly) community is not very skilled at anticipating serious conflict and is often reluctant to take action even when the storm clouds appear. These findings illustrate that recent calls for effective early warning systems and preventive diplomacy have a basis in the empirical reality in that the international community tends not to respond to conflict prior to the first threat or actual use of force. This late effort is evident in isolated and proto-rivalries in that a majority of conflict management efforts take place following the last dispute. At this stage, there are two possible interpretations to this pattern of late intervention. On the one hand, it may be that in these cases the international community does not react until the threat of future conflict is past. In contrast, it may be that the mediations appear to be late in the

TABLE 10.6: The Impact of Mediation on the Likelihood of War—Logit

Variable	Estimate	S.E.	Significance
Intercept	4.47	0.86	0.0001
Mediation success	1.39	1.43	0.3306
Compromise	−1.96	0.89	0.0281
Territorial	−3.24	0.91	0.0004
Timing	−0.06	0.03	0.0131
Rivalry type	3.07	0.95	0.0013

Association of Predicted Probabilities and Observed Responses

Concordant = 88%   Somers' D = 0.77
Discordant = 11%   Gamma = 0.78
Tied = 2%

game because they are effective in preventing future conflict and thereby facilitate the end of the rivalry. The empirical evidence below, however, is more consistent with the first interpretation. The conflict management efforts in enduring rivalries are spread throughout the life of the rivalries, but this may be misleading in that many enduring rivalries are ongoing. From this analysis, there is the suggestion that conflict management efforts are not always timed so as to ensure maximum effectiveness; such efforts are distributed broadly over the life of rivalries (although rarely early in the life of rivalries, and commonly after conflict has subsided in brief, less intense competitions).

We now turn our attention to the impact that conflict management efforts have on the behavior of rivals in conflict. The first concern is with the ability of conflict management efforts to lessen the likelihood of war. We conducted a logit analysis (as the dependent variable is dichotomous) that considered the impact of mediation, its timing, and other control variables on the likelihood that the next dispute in the rivalry would result in war. We analyzed only those rivalries that had at least one mediation attempt, so as to compare periods with and without mediation efforts while holding most other contextual factors constant.

With respect to mediation, the results are somewhat disappointing. Initial analyses looking at the presence or absence of mediation attempts did not affect the future likelihood of war between rivals. The most coherent set of results is that given in table 10.6. There, the key mediation variable was short-term mediation success. The effect of mediation success on future war was not statistically significant, and the sign of the coefficient is actually *positive,* suggesting that such mediation had the effect of increasing the probability of future war, rather than decreasing it. The positive sign of the coefficient is probably not a function of any negative results of short-term successful mediation, but rather a

TABLE 10.7: The Impact of Mediation on Conflict Levels in Rivalries

Variable	Estimate	S.E.	Significance
Intercept	−2.10	2.07	.31
Mediation	−8.49	4.45	.06
Compromise	−8.55	7.20	.24
Territorial	15.57	3.15	.0001
Timing	−0.17	0.10	.10
Number of mediations	0.18	1.22	.88

Note: $R^2 = .03$, $F = 6.79$, $p < .0001$.

selection effect. That is, mediation attempts occur primarily in the more severe rivalries, and take place at critical times in those rivalries, when the danger of war is the greatest. Thus, mediation attempts, and even short-term successes, may correspond to violent phases of rivalries.[7]

All of the other variables predicting war propensity were significant and generally in the expected direction. Not surprisingly, rivalry context (here relative severity along the rivalry continuum) affected the propensity of future war, with enduring rivalries most likely to experience war (this mirrors the results in chapter 3). Also as expected, mediation in the latter part of the rivalry seems more conducive to settlement as subsequent escalation to war is reduced. Among the control variables, compromise outcomes and territorial issues (surprisingly) had the effect of lessening the future chances for war. Overall, however, mediation appeared to have little role in reducing the prospects for war in the short to medium term.

Beyond looking at the effect of mediation attempts on subsequent war outbreaks, a more sensitive analysis considers their impact on conflict severity, including those confrontations that do not cross the threshold of war. If conflict management cannot always inhibit war, perhaps it might lessen the severity of future conflict. In general, there was little effect from mediation on conflict levels across the three rivalry types, although the sign of the coefficient was in the postulated direction (negative, indicating lower conflict levels). There was also little difference across different rivalry types.

Table 10.7 shows the impact of conflict management on the severity of disputes following those efforts; we use regression analysis on rivalries that had at least one mediation attempt. Here we define "conflict level" not in an absolute sense, e.g., number of fatalities, but with regard to what is normal for the rivalry in question. The dependent variable is thus the difference between the conflict severity of the dispute and the average conflict level (BRL) for the

---

[7]The results were not significantly altered by considering the number of mediations (i.e., there was no additive value to multiple mediation efforts.)

TABLE 10.8: The Impact of Mediation on Dispute "Waiting Times"

Variable	Estimate	S.E.	Significance
Intercept	3.73	0.29	.0001
Mediation	6.51	0.57	.0001
Compromise	0.53	0.86	.53
Territorial	−1.60	0.40	.0001
Timing	−0.05	0.02	.001
Number of mediations	−0.54	0.15	.0002

Note: $R^2 = .17$, F = 33.17, $p < .0001$.

rivalry; hence, a negative value means that the dispute was less severe than normal for that rivalry (the logic is similar to the indicator constructed in our analysis of military allocation measures—see Goertz and Diehl 1986). That is, we explored whether mediation efforts were conducive to lower-than-average conflict levels in the next dispute in the rivalry. An intercept of zero (our results are not significantly different from zero) means the average dispute severity for a given rivalry. The effects of the various independent variables are from this rivalry-specific value (this is the contextualizing idea: success/severity is relative to what is normal for the rivalry in question). Mediation here does have a slight effect in lessening the relative severity of future conflict, as does intervention later in the rivalry. Again, the total number of mediations has little effect. There remains the suggestion that the most serious and likely severe conflict will attract a larger number of mediation attempts. In this context, more mediation attempts are likely a symptom of problems rather than a desirable circumstance. Overall, the fit of the model is poor, and mediation attempts do not have a dramatic effect in any event. When one shifts to stratified analyses according to rivalry type, the mediation variable is not significant suggesting that the significant effect in table 10.7 is largely the product of sample size rather than substantively important.

If mediation has little impact in stopping or mitigating war and other violent conflict, perhaps it might be able to delay the onset of that conflict. In a final analysis of the impact of mediation, we look at the "waiting times" (the time from the conflict management effort to the next dispute between the rivals)[8] for disputes that were preceded immediately by a conflict management attempt and those that were not. The results are reported in table 10.8. Mediation attempts do have the effect of delaying the onset of new conflict by approximately six years on average, a modest achievement. Yet territorial issues tend to prompt more frequent conflict. The later the time in the rivalry and the more mediation attempts, the quicker the onset of new conflict, again suggesting selection

---

[8]In some cases, this waiting time is actually negative, indicating that in some cases a second dispute starts up before the first one has ended.

effects rather than a causal impact. The effects of mediation were generally stronger in shorter rivalries, as enduring rivalries proved to be more resistant to the effects of all the variables. This is probably the result of firm BRLs that tend to be hard to displace once established early in the rivalries.

The largely insignificant results vis-à-vis mediation in this section are concordant with the spirit of the punctuated equilibrium model. Although we analyzed mediation in all types of rivalries, the results apply with even more force to enduring ones. The one clear-cut impact of mediation success we discovered involved the increased waiting times between disputes. Successful mediation appears to delay the onset of the next dispute, but does not affect how severe that conflict will be.

The Withering Away of Rivalries

In our final analysis of de-escalatory patterns, we look at the end period of enduring rivalries. Here we focus on the contrast between a gradual withering away of enduring rivalries versus the sudden death postulated by the punctuated equilibrium model.[9]

We have suggested in our presentation of the punctuated equilibrium model, and we confirm this in a subsequent chapter, that some sort of shock was a necessary condition for the termination of rivalry. Behind that hypothesis was the implicit belief that rivalry termination was not the result of a gradual improvement of relations, but rather a result of dramatic change. In terms of conflict termination, the decreasing trends and the convex trends both indicate gradually improving relations between rivals. If we assume that the flat, wavy, increasing, and concave patterns are evidence against an evolutionary view of rivalry termination, only about 12.6 percent of rivalries show evidence of a fade-out effect, and even fewer among the uncensored cases (approximately 11.5 percent).

Just as we examined the lock-in effect for rivalries as a whole by examining negative residuals at the beginning of rivalries, we also can examine the fade-out effect by looking for negative residuals at the end of rivalries (see table 9.2 again). There is no systemic trend toward gradual improvement in rivalry relationship. The evidence for the absence of a fade-out is perhaps stronger than in the case of lock-in (mean = 1.42 for completed rivalries and 1.45 for all rivalries). The sign test for the number of negative residuals for severity is also not significant ($p < .52$). This confirmation is perhaps not surprising given our results about trends in the BRL in which less than 13 percent of rivalries showed some kind of declining trend over the last part of the rivalry. Yet if we examine those rivalries with two or three negative residuals at the end, we discover few

---

[9]We recognize that some lingering hostility may persist between rivals, years after the end of the rivalry (e.g., Japanese feelings toward China). Nevertheless, the punctuated equilibrium model posits that the militarized component of the rivalry abruptly ends.

that are declining or convex cases. Just as we examined the volcano hypothesis before wars, we can translate the fade-out hypothesis into a "war-weariness" one after wars. Yet if we define fade-out after war as declining levels (symmetrically to the volcano hypothesis before) we find that the difference between the immediate postwar dispute and the following one is barely positive (mean $= 0.30$) and not significantly different from zero ($p < .98$).

In short, both our analysis of fade-out after wars as well as at the end of rivalries confirms the punctuated equilibrium perspective. In neither case do we see a gradual winding down of severity levels. These results parallel those for the lock-in hypothesis; there, we found no indication of any gradual increase in severity levels in the early stages of rivalry. In summary, at both ends of enduring rivalries we find no indication of gradual change; when change occurs—birth or death—it appears to happen quickly.

Conclusion

This chapter had two central topics, the investigation of conflict management within interstate rivalries in general and enduring rivalries in particular, and our ongoing evaluation of the punctuated equilibrium model of enduring rivalry.

Although this is largely an exploratory analysis of de-escalatory patterns, conflict management, and mediation in rivalries (it is one of the very first systematic and empirical studies of mediation and enduring rivalries), we did discover a number of significant patterns and were able to verify or disconfirm some of our hypotheses. It was most evident that enduring rivalries experience more mediation efforts than other conflicts. Compared to other less intense rivalries, enduring ones were up to twice as likely to involve a third party (almost two-thirds of enduring rivalries actually had at least one mediation effort), and the average number of mediation attempts was significantly greater in the enduring rivalry context. Thus, as we anticipated, the most serious forms of international conflict draw the greatest attention of third-party efforts.

Few of the other patterns of mediation in rivalries were as strong. Contrary to some prescriptions, we did not find mediation efforts to occur later in enduring rivalries. Mediations generally occurred at various stages of the rivalry process, although a significant number of mediations occur very late in isolated and proto-rivalries. Given our other results, this indicates the international community was late in dealing with the conflict, and not necessarily successful in preventing future conflict.

Consistent with this was the finding that few mediation efforts occurred in enduring rivalries prior to the onset of militarized conflict, suggesting the inadequacy of early warning capacities or the failure of political will on the part of the significant actors in the international system. Mediation did not necessarily take place in the latter stages of enduring rivalries either, although this conclusion is tentative given the large number of ongoing enduring rivalries in the study.

Overall, we found mediation attempts to have relatively little impact on the behavior of states in rivalries, but we did not test for cognitive or perceptual impact. They did not apparently influence the likelihood of subsequent war between rivals. If anything, mediation attempts were associated with a greater likelihood of war between rivals. Yet this was probably a result of the selection effect that mediation is more likely when conflict is most serious or dangerous, and mediation may be the last-ditch effort before rivals resort to war in order to resolve their disputes. This is certainly true across rivalry types, and we suspect a similar effect is present even within rivalries.

The rivalry approach allowed us to focus on the impact of mediation beyond its capacity (of lack thereof) to prevent war, considering the impact on rivalry dynamics such as conflict severity and occurrence short of war. The most notable effects of mediation were found in their relationship to dispute "waiting times" or the interval from one dispute to the next. We found that positive mediation outcomes could, in some rivalries, lead to a delay in the onset of new militarized conflict.

These tentative analyses support the punctuated equilibrium model rivalry dynamics. The basic rivalry levels appear largely unchanged by mediation efforts (except a modest effect on waiting times), at least in the short and medium term. Furthermore, the presence or absence of those efforts does not appear to have any impact on significant deviations from those levels, namely the occurrence of war. Finally, our somewhat unsystematic assessment suggests that a political shock approach, outlined in the next chapter, to the end of rivalries appears more valid than one based on incremental change or on the effects of international conflict management. Our results may also call into question some of the broad applicability claimed for conflict management and mediation research. Enduring rivalries may represent a special class of conflict in which standard methods or strategies of diplomatic intervention may be different or largely ineffective.

In terms of gradual versus rapid fade-out of enduring rivalries, we found no evidence of gradual patterns of declining severity at the end of enduring rivalries, which is exactly what the punctuated equilibrium model would predict. It may well be that with finer-grained data, such as events data, one could detect the gradual improvement of relations, but within our data limitations we can find no such effect.

We have stressed the link between an organizational, decision-making model and the punctuated equilibrium approach to rivalries. In Kingdon's (1984) influential policy model, political entrepreneurs play a key role in putting items on the agenda. International mediation can play a similar role in international relations. One of the things that Kingdon emphasizes is that these political entrepreneurs are around for a long time and experience repeated failures before they succeed—if they do at all. In statistical terms, the political entrepreneur variable is likely to be insignificant. Kingdon argues that they are important and succeed only when the time is ripe—to use the mediation literature's term.

Part of Kingdon's definition of ripeness is a favorable "political context." In the next chapter, we examine one way favorable political contexts arise, which is through political shocks of various types. We argue that political shocks form a *necessary* condition for the formation and demise of enduring rivalries, just as Kingdon argues that a favorable political context is a necessary condition for an item to make it onto the agenda. Nevertheless, other factors need to arise to constitute *sufficient* conditions for rivalry initiation and termination. The actions of international political entrepreneurs such as conflict mediators can serve to create such sufficient conditions. If Kingdon's model applies to international conflict, then it is important for mediators to hang around because it is very hard to predict when the political context will be ripe for mediation to have an impact.

TABLE 10.9: Conflict Management Patterns

Rivalry	Extreme Values	Volatility
USA–Cuba	concave	low n
USA–Mexico	convex	low n
USA–Ecuador	flat	low n
USA–Peru	flat	low n
USA–UK	flat	low n
USA–Spain	decreasing	n.a.
USA–USSR	flat	convex
USA–China	concave	n.a.
USA–North Korea	flat	n.a.
Honduras–Nicaragua	flat	n.a.
Ecuador–Peru	flat	increasing
Brazil–UK	increasing	low n
Chile–Argentina (I)	flat	low n
Chile–Argentina (II)	increasing	n.a.
UK–Germany	increasing	low n
UK–USSR	increasing	n.a.
UK–USSR	decreasing	decreasing
UK–Ottoman Empire	increasing	low n
UK–Iraq	concave	n.a.
Belgium–Germany	flat	n.a.
France–Germany	flat	n.a.
France–Prussia/Germany	increasing	n.a.
France–Ottoman Empire	flat	low n
France–China	increasing	low n
Spain–Morocco	decreasing	n.a.
Germany–Italy	flat	n.a.
Italy–Yugoslavia	flat	low n
Italy–Ethiopia	increasing	low n
Italy–Ottoman Empire	increasing	n.a.
Yugoslavia–Bulgaria	flat	low n
Greece–Bulgaria	flat	low n
Greece–Turkey (I)	increasing	increasing
Greece–Turkey (II)	concave	n.a.
Cyprus–Turkey	increasing	low n
USSR–Norway	concave	low n
USSR–Iran	flat	flat
Russia–Ottoman Empire	concave	low n
USSR–China	wavy	wavy

Continued on next page

TABLE 10.9—*continued*

Rivalry	Extreme Values	Volatility
USSR–Japan	wavy	n.a.
Congo–Zaire	increasing	low n
Uganda–Kenya	increasing	low n
Somalia–Ethiopia	flat	increasing
Ethiopia–Sudan	concave	low n
Morocco–Algeria	flat	low n
Iran–Iraq	increasing	increasing
Iraq–Israel	flat	low n
Iraq–Kuwait	increasing	low n
Egypt–Israel	wavy	n.a.
Syria–Jordan	flat	n.a.
Syria–Israel	flat	flat
Jordan–Israel	concave	low n
Israel–Saudi Arabia	flat	n.a.
Saudi Arabia–Yemen	flat	n.a.
Afghanistan–Pakistan	flat	low n
China–South Korea	decreasing	n.a.
China–Japan	wavy	wavy
China–India	convex	flat
N. Korea–S. Korea	decreasing	flat
South Korea–Japan	decreasing	n.a.
India–Pakistan	wavy	convex
Thailand–Kampuchea	flat	low n
Thailand–Laos	concave	n.a.
Thailand–N. Vietnam	increasing	low n

CHAPTER 11

Breaking the Stability of Rivalries: The Impact of Political Shocks

Over the previous two chapters we have emphasized the stability of enduring rivalries, but enduring rivalries also begin and end. The same is true of all biological species: they develop and eventually go extinct. The punctuated equilibrium model, both in biology and in its enduring rivalry version, argues that major shocks set the stage for enduring rivalries or species to arise and are also part of the explanation of their demise. If we examine the idea of stability or equilibrium, it *means* relative insensitivity to perturbation. A measure of stability, for example, in the natural sciences, is based on the size of the force needed to destroy the equilibrium. Hence, the natural flip-side of the our emphasis on stability of enduring rivalries is the proposition that large forces and shocks are required to disrupt enduring rivalry stability.

By political shock, we mean a dramatic change in the international system or its subsystems that fundamentally alters the processes, relationships, and expectations that drive nation-state interactions. For example, the end of the Cold War was a major political shock in international relations. In the 1980s, none thought the end of the Cold War would come soon, a reflection of the incremental thinking so common in international relations. The domestic political revolution in the USSR not only ended the U.S.-Soviet rivalry, but many of the conflicts in the Third World that were fueled by this rivalry as well. At the same time the end of the Cold War has also provided the setting for the rise of some new rivalries.

If enduring rivalries are the result of well-entrenched causes, then the end of a particular rivalry or the beginning of a new rivalry should be associated with some dramatic change in the environment or the actors. These shocks may be exogenous to the rivalry, such as the occurrence of a world war, or endogenous, such as the change in the administration or regime of one of the rivals following a civil war. Therefore, in assessing the effects of political shocks on enduring rivalries, we consider dramatic changes at two levels of analysis: domestic and international.

In the biological model of punctuated equilibrium, it is predominantly environmental shocks—such as massive climatic change—that cause the extinction of species. In an analogous manner, we argue that huge changes in the international political system make rivalry initiation and termination possible. For example, in line with neorealist thought, we suggest that dramatic power rearrangements in the major-power system constitute one kind of environmental shock important to the rise and decline of enduring rivalries.

Unlike the biological model, however, we also include political shocks endogenous to the rivals. By this we mean major changes in the domestic politics of one or both of the rivals. Environmental shocks influence the opportunity structure of states, whereas domestic political changes introduce new ideas, values, and foreign policy goals. Thus, although we consider both external and internal shocks as important, the role that these shocks play can differ significantly.

Looking at political shocks necessitates a move away from traditional linear thinking. Instead, the punctuated equilibrium model considers dramatic change as a key independent variable but also expects that many relationships will remain stable over time in the absence of shocks and in some cases in spite of them. In contrast to chaos theory, which examines how small changes have great effects, the punctuated equilibrium model emphasizes large changes that have large potential impact. With respect to enduring rivalries, we conceptualize their initiation and termination as occurring in a nonlinear fashion during favorable conditions created by abrupt political shocks of various sorts. Shocks make rivalry initiation and termination *possible;* that is, those shocks are necessary conditions for dramatic changes in what are normally stable relationships.

In summary, our punctuated equilibrium model proposes that massive political shock at the system or state/domestic level opens a window of opportunity for rivalries to begin and end.[1] Not all windows of opportunity are jumped through, and not all political shocks result in rivalry or its termination. Nevertheless, we shall see that few rivalries can break through closed windows.

---

[1] It might be argued that under some circumstances political shocks contribute to the maintenance of a rivalry. Yet, this is contrary to the punctuated equilibrium model, and we do not investigate that possibility, although it might deserve a place on a future research agenda. Nevertheless, it is highly unlikely that shocks are anything approaching necessary conditions for the continuation of rivalries.

Political Shocks and Enduring Rivalries

System Shocks

Much of international relations theory stresses the importance of system-level factors on state behavior. This theoretical specification ranges from neorealism (Waltz 1979) to agent-structure perspectives (Dessler 1989). The punctuated equilibrium model—similar to its biological ancestor—is very much an agent-structure framework. Unfortunately, neither the neorealist nor the agent-structure literature has produced many specific theoretical propositions that have clearly testable implications.

We can contrast the punctuated equilibrium model, which emphasizes dramatic change, with the relatively static or gradualist perspectives of neorealism or agent-structure theory. For example, Waltz borrowed heavily from natural selection models through their use in economics. He argued that states would be "socialized" through an—implicitly gradual—process by which power-maximizing realist states would prosper while other kinds of states would fail (see Cederman 1996 for a formal simulation that uses a gradual evolutionary model). By implication, these changes do not occur rapidly. The agent-structure literature is less clear, but it does not recognize radical structural change as a key factor.

The punctuated equilibrium model directly links system changes to state behavior. In the quantitative literature, it is relatively rare to find analyses that employ variables at multiple levels of analysis. The overwhelming tendency is to employ the same level of analysis for *all* variables. For example, systemic change as a predictive factor was employed in Singer, Bremer, and Stuckey 1972 using capability distribution and in Bueno de Mesquita 1978 using polarity tightness as system-level dependent variables respectively. Yet empirical studies rarely look at the effect of systemic factors at levels of analysis other than the system. The difficulty arises in specifying the mechanisms that link system characteristics (here system shocks) with lower-level processes. The punctuated equilibrium framework uses variables from at least two levels of analysis; the environmental shocks are system-level variables, which then influence state-level rivalry behavior. Unlike neorealism, which has little dynamic about it, the punctuated equilibrium model stresses the importance of change as much as the power distribution itself.

With respect to enduring rivalries, system shocks influence them in at least two ways. First, system shocks transform the environment in which international relations occur. This transformation opens up new opportunities for conflict, such as the possibility of a U.S.-Soviet rivalry in the new bipolar world after World War II. While some windows of opportunity are opened, a system shock may also change the environment such that some rivalries come to an end; France and Germany cease to be rivals (and even become allies) after 1945. Second, and related in some ways, systemic changes have a dramatic impact on some bilateral or multilateral relationships. Thus, "opportunities" occasioned by the political shocks are differentially distributed across the units of the system (Most and Starr 1989). The end of the Cold War, for example, led to a severing of many patron-client relationships between the Soviet Union and Third World countries. This has led some proxy conflicts to wither away in the absence of the military and political support previously provided by the superpowers. Thus, system shocks alter the general environment for the formation and continuation of enduring rivalries, but they also directly influence some state-level relationships that affect rivalry processes.

In this chapter, we explore three types of system-level shocks: (1) those occasioned by world wars, (2) dramatic changes in territorial sovereignty, and (3) rapid shifts in the power distribution. World wars are considered to be system-defining events. They tend to sweep away existing patterns of international interactions and encourage new patterns to emerge. Specifically, we anticipate that world wars will alter many of the sources of contention between rivals; in effect, world wars may be a culmination of several disputes and rivalries (Midlarsky 1988). Similarly, world wars may change the structure of the system, perhaps transforming a system from a bipolar to a multipolar one or influencing the tightness of that system type. In either case, some states will find themselves in opposing coalitions or in conflict over issues or concerns occasioned by the new world order. Therefore, we expect that as some enduring rivalries end with a world war, others will begin.

A second shock to the system involves dramatic alterations in the territorial sovereignty of the system. Systemic territorial change derives from many transfers of territory, which may help resolve existing rivalries or give rise to new ones. In addition, massive territorial change may give rise to the emergence of new states in the system, which not only disrupts patterns of interactions, but creates more opportunities (Most and Starr 1989) for rivalries as the number of possible rivalry dyads increases. Thus, one might expect that the dramatic increase in the number of states around 1960 might be associated with the onset of new rivalries.

Third, alterations in the prevailing power distribution among the major powers could shock the system and lead some rivalries to end while others begin. The neorealist framework will give primacy to this explanation for changes in rivalry patterns. Some major power rivalries may end because one rival will be unable to compete in the changed environment; correspondingly, the emergence of new major powers may create new opportunities for rivalries. In addition, a change in the power distribution among major powers may shift traditional allegiances, and one's former rival may now become an ally against a new threat. The balance-of-power argument assumes just such a change. Minor powers could also feel the impact of capability shifts among the major powers. Existing patron-client relationships could shift, ending some rivalries that were "subsidized" by the major powers, or facilitating the rise of other proxy conflicts. This is particularly the case if rivalries are "linked" to one another, as we demonstrate in the next chapter. The overriding assumption is that the power distribution conditions the form and structure of international relations, including enduring rivalries. Dramatic changes occurring in that distribution will influence state and dyadic behavior.

We anticipate that shocks at the system level will have an impact on all enduring rivalries. We should note that the three types of system shocks investigated here are not mutually exclusive. There is some overlap, but the collinearity of the three is far from perfect, and operationally we attempt to keep them distinct as much as possible. For example, world wars result in significant territorial change and power redistribution, but there are periods of great territorial transfer and power change independent of world wars (Goertz and Diehl 1992b).

Roughly speaking then, environmental shocks focus on opportunity factors in the birth and death of (enduring) rivalries. When Most and Starr (1989) proposed the opportunity-and-willingness framework, they were motivated by Sprout and Sprout's (1965) model of "environmental possibilism," which located opportunity at the system level. The punctuated equilibrium model focuses on three particular environmental factors: dramatic changes in power, massive systemwide wars, and dramatic changes in the configuration of territorial sovereignty.

State Shocks

The punctuated equilibrium model includes a particular view of the foreign policy process. As we have seen in the previous two chapters, it emphasizes the stability of policy in terms of an organizational model of government. The beginning and end of an enduring rivalry represent policy changes of major magnitude. Traditional realist thought attributes radical policy shifts to large changes in the international system. We agree with that formulation, but add that this view is incomplete. New policies also come with new leadership and forms of government representing new interests and ideas.

A brief survey of the literature on U.S. domestic policy indicates that major policy shifts occur with new leadership. We can recall that the Depression in the United States existed for several years before a presidential election brought in Roosevelt and his New Deal policies. Even the incrementalist policy literature supports this view. Hence, unlike many views of international relations, we find that the characters of the government and of its leaders do matter, because when they undergo radical change, so often too does foreign policy. We focus on *militarized* international rivalries, and quite clearly some systems of government (e.g., military dictatorships) and some political leaders prefer the military instruments of foreign policy. This generates and continues (enduring) rivalries. We limit our analyses to the most radical kinds of domestic political shocks, but the same logic leads to an inclusion of domestic and governmental variables as keys in understanding rivalries in general.

We have already examined one potential form of domestic political shock in our analysis of the democratic peace in chapter 6. More generally, we believe that four political shocks in domestic politics may affect potential or existing rivalries: (1) the achievement of independence, (2) the occurrence of a civil war, (3) the shift of either rival to a democracy, and (4) regime change in either rival. All of these imply a clear change in the character and personnel of the government in a rival state.

By our definition, an interstate rivalry cannot involve a state that has not achieved its independence. The emergence of a reorganized, new member of the international system can have several effects that promote the formation of rivalries. First is the mere increase in the number of interactions that stems from having another state in the area or system. Second, a new state is a shock to neighboring states who have been accustomed to a set pattern of interactions with their neighbors; most new states are former dependent territories and as such have had relatively peaceful relations with their neighbors. Third, a new state changes, almost by definition, the balance of power in the immediate area, which raises uncertainty. Fourth, newly independent states may feel a need to gain international legitimacy or status through conflict (Maoz 1989). Finally there is the threat that the new state will be the victim of other states that opposed independence and that seek to return to the status quo ante or see the new state as a weak target, capable of little resistance. Thus, we expect that when a state gains its independence it will be more likely to become involved in rivalries shortly thereafter. Along these lines, Maoz (1989) found that some newly independent states were more likely to become involved in militarized disputes.

Previous work on the connection between civil and interstate conflict has focused on the effect of the former during that period of domestic unrest. Here we hypothesize that civil war may also influence the conduct of rivalries. First, we anticipate that some ongoing rivalries will end as the state in a civil war turns its attention and resources to consolidation of power and to domestic problems. At the same time, however, the regime may seek legitimacy by initiating conflict against a foreign enemy, seeking to rally public support and distract attention from lingering domestic problems. Distraction or diversion (Levy 1989; Miller 1995) might be the response to a civil war, with the ending of ongoing enduring rivalries for some states and the beginning of conflicts for others.

The effects of civil wars may be magnified if the opposition is victorious in the war and a regime change occurs (Maoz 1989). The change in regimes can prompt different alliance configurations and ideological affinities. A regime change may also precipitate new hostilities with former allies who had been ardent supporters of the old regime. In effect, it is presumed that a regime change, not merely a leadership change, indicates a deep alteration in the preference structure of that state's foreign policy. This may lead to new disputes with states or end what may be long-standing competitions between historical enemies.

As we demonstrated in chapter 6, when a state becomes a democracy it may alter its rivalry patterns with a democratic rival, such that the rivalry is prone to end shortly thereafter. This is consistent with Bennett's (1997a) finding that rivalry termination is associated with movement toward democracy by the rivals. Thus, a fourth endogenous shock to a rivalry could be the shift of one rival to democracy just prior to the beginning or end of the rivalry. Yet the shift to democracy may also signal the beginning of a rivalry, in that such a shift may lead to a greater number of "mixed dyads," pairs of potential rivalries with one state's being democratic and the other nondemocratic. According to some recent evidence, such dyads are thought to have the greatest propensity for conflict. Explanations sometimes focus on psychological perceptions such as "in-group, out-group" models to explain this increased propensity (Herrmann and Kegley 1995). We should note, however, that we did not find such an effect among "mixed" rivalries in chapter 6.

In summary, the four state-level shocks—democracy, independence, regime change, and civil war—are expected to make states more likely to enter a rivalry, and to terminate ongoing ones (except for independence). For the time being, we do not consider the impact of state-level shocks on states outside the dyad, although we recognize that state-level shocks (e.g., a civil war) may affect the calculations and positions of other states in the area. Models of contagion (Most, Starr, and Siverson 1989) and conflict interdependence models (Muncaster and Zinnes 1993) do make such assumptions.

The Nature of the Effects of Political Shocks

We should emphasize that not every political shock will produce a new rivalry or end existing ones. There are many conditions (not all known or specified here) for the start or conclusion of a rivalry, and a political shock is only one of them. Furthermore, there are several varieties of political shock that could have an impact on the beginning and termination of rivalries. We propose that a shock opens a window of opportunity for the beginning and end of enduring rivalries. While not often realized, window-of-opportunity explanations imply necessary condition hypotheses. In the U.S. domestic politics literature, Kingdon's (1995, 166) influential use of the window-of-opportunity metaphor gets more concretely expressed in terms of necessary conditions: "In space shots, the window presents the opportunity for a launch. The target planets are in proper alignment, but will not stay that way for long. Thus the launch must take place when the window is open, lest the opportunity slip away. Once lost, the opportunity may recur, but in the interim, astronauts and space engineers must wait until the window reopens. Similarly, windows open in policy systems. These policy windows, the opportunities for action on given initiatives, present themselves and stay open for only short periods. If the participants cannot or do not take advantage of these opportunities, they must bide their time until the next opportunity comes along." Hence the possibility of policy change when a window of opportunity does not exist is almost zero: an open window is necessary but not sufficient.

Thus, we expect that some political shock is a *necessary* condition for the initiation and termination of an enduring rivalry. It is not a sufficient condition, as, for example, not all independences lead to an enduring rivalry. Overall, we expect that few rivalries will begin or end without close temporal proximity to some political shock. In other words, a political shock opens a window of opportunity for rivalry initiation and termination, but whether governments exploit this opportunity—sufficiency—depends on other factors as well.

Despite the general effects of political shocks, they do not necessarily affect different types of conflict with the same magnitude. We do anticipate, however, that there will be little difference between proto- and enduring rivalries with respect to their initiation. Political shocks will produce new conflicts that may or may not mature into enduring rivalry. There are a variety of other factors, most unconnected with political shocks, that seem to influence whether a proto-rivalry will become an enduring one. These include the dynamics and outcome of disputes in the rivalry, moderate shifts in capability between the rivals, and the rise of other, potentially supportive rivalries involving the two states in question. In contrast, political shocks should have a differential impact on the termination of proto- and enduring rivalries. Shocks should have a strong influence on both, but enduring rivalries should be more resistant to individual shocks. We have noted earlier that enduring rivalries represent a kind of stability in international affairs that is not easily subject to change. In that sense, they are more stable than proto-rivalries and better able to weather the occurrence of political shocks. Thus, we anticipate that an enduring rivalry will end with some political shock, but it may be less likely to end with one specific shock than proto-rivalries.

The Empirical Analysis of Political Shocks

Operationalizing the Political Shock Concept

In keeping with the hierarchical theory of political shocks, we propose to examine shocks at the system and state levels. Because of this hierarchy, there is some overlap, and we are sensitive to this duplication in our coding. Guiding our consideration is the desire to reflect accurately the importance of the shock without needlessly and theoretically unjustified duplication of shocks. In coding shocks, we tried to code only the first system shock in the causal sequence (e.g., a world war) and not also a consequential shock deriving from that initial shock (e.g., dramatic change in the power distribution). A related concern is the assumption that shocks are relatively rare. We could easily prove our hypotheses if we identify a large number of shocks. This is particularly crucial in that by coding too many shocks we risk having a trivial necessary condition.

By reducing the number of shocks to a minimum, we provide a more rigorous test of our expectations.[2]

At the system level, the measurement of world wars is a straightforward one. World War I (1914–18) and World War II (1939–45) are the only wars involving all the major powers, and the magnitude of those two wars (in terms of duration, intensity, and severity) is far greater than any other conflicts in the period.

The magnitude of territorial changes is measured according to the aggregate area, in square kilometers, exchanged multiplied by the number of exchanges for all territorial changes involving the major powers (Goertz and Diehl, 1992b). We determine the threshold for a territorial shock inductively, by identifying extreme values in the distribution of total territorial changes across time, in the same fashion as one identifies world wars as extreme outliers in the Small and Singer (1982) list of wars. We decided that, for a territorial shock to occur then, there must be a minimum of eight territorial exchanges totaling at least five million square kilometers. The two cases that fit these criteria are the race for colonies in the late nineteenth century (1884–94) and decolonization around 1960 (1956–62). In these cases, we code the systemic shock as affecting only European states.[3] The acquisition of colonies in the late nineteenth century was carried out almost exclusively by European states and had little effect on the Western Hemisphere (the only other region with a significant number of independent states at the time). Similarly, the decolonization process largely influenced those same European states, which saw their empires wither away. Of course, decolonization directly affected states in Africa and Asia. Yet these shocks are felt mostly at the state level and will appear as state-level shocks through independences (see below).

Shifts in the systemic power distribution are measured according to the sum of the changes in the capability shares among major powers, along the military and economic dimensions (Singer, Bremer, and Stuckey 1972). The level of shock is the sum of all changes for all countries for all indicators compared to the previous 10 years. We assume that a shock must last more than one year, representing a permanent change in international affairs. Again inductively, the average index score was approximately 100, and there were only three periods (excluding the world wars) when there was a pronounced and sustained shock, indicated by values around 400 to 600. The first such shock was the period surrounding the Italian and German unifications in the nineteenth century (1859–71). This is coded only as a system shock for Europe, given that the changes occurred on that continent and likely had less impact globally; again, it is also the case that the global system was largely Eurocentric at the time. The other

---

[2] A shock is coded for the year(s) of the actual shock plus 10 years. For example, if the beginning of a rivalry occurs within the period 1939–55, then it is said to coincide with the World War II shock.

[3] Turkey is considered part of Europe for these purposes.

two power shocks have broader global origins and impacts. The period 1890–1901 not only involves power restructuring in Europe, but is the period in which the United States and Japan join the club of major powers, with profound consequences for Asia, the Americas, and the rest of the world. The third shock occurs in 1989–92 with the breakup of the Soviet Union and has clear global implications.[4]

State independence cases are identified through consulting Goertz and Diehl's (1992b) list of territorial changes (as revised and reported in Tir et al. 1998) and selecting the subcategory of cases involving national independence. Civil war is defined according to the Small and Singer (1982) criteria and involves internal conflicts with at least one thousand battle-related fatalities.

For measures of democracy and regime, we again rely on the Polity III data (Jaggers and Gurr 1996) that we utilized in chapter 6. There are 10 dimensions of democratic and authoritarian rule. Examining a histogram of dyadic regime changes for enduring rivalries over the full period of the study, we decided to code a regime change as occurring when there was a shift on six of 10 dimensions, indicating both the large magnitude of shift and across many dimensions. For a democratic regime shift, the empirical distribution suggested a cutoff of seven and in the direction of democracy. Thus, the regime change variable is designed to capture dramatic internal political changes in either rival, whereas the democracy variable is specifically concerned with dramatic regime in one particular direction—toward democracy. In the case of overlap, we coded the democracy variable rather than a duplicate regime change shock.

A summary of all the shocks at each level of analysis during the period 1816–1992 is given below. We note that all constitute a major change in a political system, either national or system-level.

Beginning and Endpoints of Enduring Rivalries

As we noted in chapter 2, determining the beginning and end dates for rivalries poses difficult problems. The first behavioral indicator that a rivalry exists is the beginning of the first militarized dispute in the rivalry. Analogously, the last behavioral indicator for the end of the rivalry is the end of the last militarized dispute. Our position (see chapter 2 for details) is that the rivalry begins "sometime" in the 10 years before the first dispute and ends sometime in the 10 years following the last dispute in the rivalry. It is evident that it is difficult to pinpoint the exact date of rivalry termination, much as it is difficult to point with certitude that cancer has been cured. Just as rivalries may have no concrete starting or ending point, so too do political shocks occur over time. For example, we can say with some degree of validity that the USSR collapsed around 1991, but specifying a month or a day would be false and misleading.

---

[4]Note that the shocks and their geographic impact are more narrowly defined than in an earlier study, Goertz and Diehl 1995b. This was done in order to make a more accurate specification. The narrower operational definition also provides a more stringent test of our claims about the relationship between such shocks and the initiation and termination of rivalries.

TABLE 11.1: Political Shocks, 1816–1992

System Level
World Wars
World War I, 1914–1918
World War II, 1939–1945
Territorial
1884–1894
1956–1962
Power Distribution
1859–1871
1890–1901
1989–1992
State Level
National independence
Civil war
Regime change
Democratization

Furthermore, it will normally take time for the effects of the political shock to work their way through the political process.

Because we consider the rivalry to have begun sometime in the 10 years prior to the first dispute, we look for political shocks during that period. We include the first dispute in this as well since, for example, a world war might be simultaneously a shock and the first dispute in the enduring rivalry. Similarly for rivalry termination, we see if a shock occurs simultaneously with the last dispute or in the following 10 years. For example, the last dispute in the Franco-German rivalry was World War II, which is one of our system shocks; hence, we consider this case to support our hypothesis. One did not really know that the rivalry was over until the U.S. occupation of Germany was completed and the Germans regained control over their government. Given the character of political shocks and the fuzziness of beginning and end dates, we believe that our procedure provides an acceptable compromise, as it does not impose specific dates on phenomena that have none.

Empirical Results

In looking at the effects of political shocks on enduring rivalries, we consider the impact on the beginning and end of rivalries as well as how the effects vary in comparison to proto-rivalries.

TABLE 11.2: Political Shocks at the Beginning of Enduring Rivalries

	Necessity	
	No shock	Shock
	4.8%	95.2%
	(3)	(60)
Confidence interval for $\hat{p}$ =.952 (3/63) is [.87,.99]		

	Trivialness		
	No shock	Shock	Total
No initiation	167	648	815
Rivalry initiation	3	60	63
Total	170	708	878

Note: Pearson $\chi^2(1) = 9.27, p = 0.002$.
Fisher's exact test = 0.001.
One-sided Fisher's exact test = 0.001.
Ns in parentheses.

The Beginning of Enduring Rivalries

In looking at the beginning of enduring rivalries, we anticipate that they will be conditioned by a political shock sometime in the previous 10 years. Yet because there is a variety of shocks and individually they are infrequent, not all rivalries will begin with the same shock. We first look at the aggregate results to see how many enduring rivalries began following a shock of any sort; these results are given in table 11.1. Over 95 percent of enduring rivalries begin within the 10 years following any of the political shocks. The only three enduring rivalries not proximate to a political shock at their outset were those between the United States and United Kingdom, Brazil and the United Kingdom, and France and Germany in the militarized rivalry beginning in 1911. This strong finding largely confirms our argument that political shocks are virtual necessary conditions for the onset of rivalries.

We need to open a methodological parenthesis here concerning our hypothesis and the means to test it. We have proposed that a political shock opens a window of opportunity for the initiation of enduring rivalries: it provides a necessary condition for their initiation. This is similar in content and form to Kingdon's (1984) hypothesis that a favorable political context is a necessary condition for an item to make it onto the agenda.[5] The hypothesis states: given that the rivalry has begun, we will find a political shock associated with it. This

---

[5] Kingdon (1984) does not use the exact words *necessary condition,* but he frequently says that the probability of an item making it onto the agenda is very low without a window of opportunity. This in substance is a necessary condition.

means that we need examine only the beginnings of enduring rivalries. This is a key point because it appears that we are selecting on the dependent variable. In fact, we are. As Dion (1998) demonstrates, this is legitimate in the case of necessary condition hypotheses. This works here because of the statistical form of the hypothesis: *given* that rivalries begin, we find them preceded or accompanied by political shocks. In statistical terms, this means that we are looking at the independent variable given dependent variable, the reverse of the usual specification. Substantively, we view political shocks as part of the cause of rivalry initiation and termination, but given the form of our hypothesis, a necessary condition, the methodology for testing changes significantly (for details see Dion 1998; Braumoeller and Goertz 1997; and Harvey 1998).

A second key methodological point is that the null hypothesis here is that rivalry initiation is always associated with political shocks. Our hypothesis is that a political shock is a necessary condition for rivalry initiation; this is then the null hypothesis, and (in terms of table 11.1) the shock-within-ten-years column should be 1.00.[6] The appropriate statistical test is thus a *p*-test that the proportion of position cases is 1.00. As Braumoeller and Goertz (1997) demonstrate at length, however, necessary condition hypotheses are never tested correctly in this fashion (e.g., Bueno de Mesquita 1981). They also discuss the problems with using the 1.00 standard as the null hypothesis and suggest using .95 instead. They propose as a statistical test that one construct a confidence interval around the observed proportion, and if that interval includes .95, then the necessary condition or null hypothesis is accepted. We note that this test is a much tougher one to pass than the usual, and incorrect, 2×2 measures of association (e.g., Yule's Q in the case of Bueno de Mesquita).[7]

As table 11.1 indicates, we find that the political shock hypothesis is supported by the data for rivalry initiation. The observed proportions of shocks within 10 years is .952 (3/60); hence a confidence interval constructed around this certainly includes the null hypothesis value of .95. Thus, one has no reason to reject the necessary condition hypothesis. We find that political shocks do set the stage, opening a window of opportunity for the initiation of enduring rivalries.

We believe that the above results demonstrate that shocks are necessary conditions for the initiation of rivalries. Nevertheless, one criticism may be that we have coded so many shocks that the strong results are guaranteed, and therefore the necessary condition is a trivial one; a similar critique is made of Bueno de Mesquita (1981) by Majeski and Sylvan (1984). Here we need again to open a methodological parenthesis to discuss the concept of a "trivial" necessary condition. Although most have an intuitive notion of what this means, we

---

[6] Another peculiarity of necessary condition testing is that the researcher *wants* to accept the null hypothesis, contrary to the usual situation where rejection supports the substantive hypothesis.

[7] Braumoeller and Goertz (1997) require also a second test based on power considerations for necessary condition hypotheses, but this is only relevant to small-*N* (i.e., 5–10) studies. All our hypotheses pass this test.

need a concrete and statistical definition. Braumoeller and Goertz (1997) provide a conceptual analysis of trivialness and suggest a statistical measure for it. Generally, for our purposes, it revolves around seeing whether there were frequent political shocks in years in which the enduring rivalry did *not* begin and comparing that rate to the percentage of rivalries that began with shocks. The second part of table 11.1 provides this analysis. We calculated the number of years preceding the enduring rivalry when shocks did and did not occur, starting with 20 years before the beginning of the enduring rivalry.[8] A trivial necessary condition in this context would then be that political shocks were occurring most of the time prior to the rivalry, hence not surprisingly also around the beginning point. The data in the table, however, indicate that this was not the case. Although political shocks were frequent (this is due to the 10-year impact given to each shock), both chi-square and Fisher's exact tests are significant at .002 levels. Thus, the hypothesis that political shocks are a virtual necessary condition for rivalry initiation is not "trivial," at least in the statistical sense.

It might be argued that we have only looked at enduring rivalries and not all possible dyads. Yet we did analyze the effects of shocks on all types of rivalries and found results similar to those reported above. This is not surprising in that it is often other factors beside political shocks that affect whether conflict remains isolated, evolves into a proto-rivalry, or matures to an enduring one. Thus, political shocks can be said to have an impact on the beginning of conflict, although we have not yet considered all possible dyads (including those that have not experienced conflict) for a full test of the proposition.

As another way to address the trivialness question as well as to determine the relative importance of different kinds of shocks, we disaggregate the results and examine the impact of each of the shocks at the each level of analysis. We compare the rivalry formation rate in the immediate postshock period to the 10-year period immediately preceding the shock. Because individual shocks are relatively rare, there is less of a problem in overspecifying their number. Furthermore, if shocks are important as a virtual necessary condition, then the formation rate for rivalries should be higher immediately after a shock than in earlier periods.

The results in table 11.2 exhibit a consistent pattern of enduring rivalries being more likely to begin after political shocks, although the impact varies according to the type of shock. In most cases, there is a dramatically lower formation rate for rivalries in the decade before a shock. New rivalries are far more likely in 10 years after a shock, and this is consistent for all types of shocks. If shocks were merely incidental, it seems unlikely that such a pattern would emerge across all levels of analysis and shock types.

---

[8] Clearly, not all countries existed as states 20 years before the enduring rivalry started; in those cases we went back as far as possible.

TABLE 11.3: Shocks and Rivalry Initiation: Comparison Across Time

Shock	0–10 Years after shock, %	0–10 Years before shock, %
World wars	39.7	9.5
	(25)	(6)
Territory-system	52.4	9.5
	(33)	(6)
Power-system	9.5	7.9
	(6)	(5)
Independence	38.1	7.9
	(24)	(5)
Civil war	31.8	19.1
	(20)	(12)
Regime change	52.4	34.9
	(33)	(22)
Democracy	20.6	17.5
	(13)	(11)

Note: *N*s are given in parentheses.

Most notable is the effect of some shocks at the system and state levels. World wars and territorial shocks are about five times more likely to generate new rivalries than periods without such shocks. At the state level, enduring rivalries are over four times more likely to start in the period after one state achieves its independence than in the control group time periods; 24 of the rivalries begin immediately after such a shock and only five in the previous 10-year period.

The results in table 11.2 indicate that our general results are not the product of a weak or trivial necessary condition. In all cases, we see a significant difference—sometimes dramatic—in the rate of rivalry formation immediately after a shock as compared to control group periods.[9] This analysis guards against the claim that our table 11.1 results are spurious. Looking at individual shocks, which are relatively small in number, we see a consistent pattern across shock type and level of analysis, suggesting that shocks truly influence the formation of enduring rivalries. The result is not merely a function of an excess of coded shocks.

Overall, the results conform to our expectations. Almost all of the enduring rivalries begin after some kind of political shock, suggesting that such events are virtually necessary conditions for the onset of rivalries. The results also

---

[9] In an earlier study, Goertz and Diehl 1995b, we also confirmed that rivalry formation was lower in the 11 to 20-year period after the shock as the shock effect decayed and even lower in all other nonshock years, for each type of shock.

TABLE 11.4: Political Shocks and the Termination of Enduring Rivalries

	Shock	No shock
All cases	90.5%	9.5%
	(57)	(6)
Confidence interval for $\hat{p}$ = .905 (6/63) is [.80,.96]		
Uncensored cases	76.9%	23.1%
	(20)	(6)
Confidence interval for $\hat{p}$ = .769 (6/26) is [.56,.91]		
Quasi-censored cases	80.6%	19.4%
	(25)	(6)
Confidence interval for $\hat{p}$ = .769 (6/26) is [.625,.93]		

clearly indicate that rivalries begin at a much higher rate than in other periods, suggesting that shocks really do matter.

The End of Enduring Rivalries

The results for the end of enduring rivalries mirror those for the onset of those competitions, and the empirical findings are given in table 11.3. Over 90 percent of the rivalries had their last dispute in the 10-year period after a political shock. Yet these strong results may distort the magnitude of the effect. Thirty-nine of the 65 rivalries studied here had not yet ended in 1992, when the study stops. The censored cases are treated "as if" they had ended as of their last dispute. Because the censoring date of 1992 coincides with the system shock of the end of the Cold War, all the censored cases get coded as ending with a shock. Obviously, some of the censored rivalries terminate because of the end of the Cold War; just as obviously, some will continue. If we confine our analysis to those rivalries that actually ended (uncensored cases), a more conservative comparison the impact of political shocks is still evident. Almost 77 percent of the rivalries ended with a political shock, again suggesting something like a necessary condition, albeit slightly weaker than with the beginning of rivalries. Using the Braumoeller and Goertz (1997) test, we find that the confidence interval does not include .95 (although only barely so), and hence does not support the necessary condition hypothesis.

We include in table 11.3 results with what we label *quasi-censored* rivalries, those that seem likely to have ended with the collapse of the USSR. Using this set of enduring rivalries, we find that almost 81 percent ended with political shocks. As table 11.3 indicates, even in this case the confidence interval does not cover .95, though it comes closer, ending at .93.

We found six rivalries that did not end with a political shock: with the date of their last disputes they are United States–China (1972), Brazil–United

TABLE 11.5: Shocks and Rivalry Termination: Comparison Across Time

Shock	0–10 Years after shock, %	0–10 Years before shock, %
World wars	12.7	11.1
	(8)	(7)
Territory-system	6.3	4.8
	(4)	(3)
Power-system	63.5	4.8
	(40)	(3)
Civil war	4.8	0
	(3)	(0)
Regime change	42.9	46.0
	(27)	(29)
Democracy	39.7	33.3
	(25)	(21)

*Note: N*s are given in parentheses.

Kingdom (1863), United Kingdom–Germany (1921), United Kingdom–Russia (1923), Greece–Bulgaria (1952), and Jordan–Israel (1973). Of these we note that several ended in the wake of major wars, civil or international. United Kingdom–Russia and Greece-Bulgaria end following civil wars, while United Kingdom–Germany and Jordan–Israel terminate following serious international wars.[10] If we consider that four of these six "exceptions" actually support the spirit of the political shock hypothesis, we arrive at 24 of 26, or 92 percent of the uncensored cases following the political shock hypothesis and 29/31 or 94% of the quasi-censored cases favoring the hypothesis. Clearly these numbers pass the necessary condition tests described above.

Again we conducted for the end of rivalries disaggregated analyses similar to those for the beginning of rivalries. The findings in table 11.5 are weakly supportive of the importance of shocks. At the system level, there is a marginal impact from world wars and territorial shocks (the latter of which may be the consequence of rivalry termination, rather than the instigator). The most notable effects are from dramatic changes in the power distribution. In that context, rivalry termination is 13 times more likely in the 10 years after the shocks than in the decade prior to the shock. We should note, however, that this may be somewhat misleading in that the shock of the end of the Cold War is said to impact all ongoing rivalries, when in fact we can expect some of those ongoing rivalries to continue into the next century. Even excluding those cases,

---

[10]The first three rivalries technically do not fit with our expectations because they experienced one, but only one, dispute after the political shock. The last case is one in which the 1973 war does not qualify as a systemic political shock, but did have a significant impact on Middle East relations.

however, the effect is still significant, and power shocks may play an important role in ending rivalries. Endogenous shocks at the state level appear weakly related to enduring rivalry termination. In most cases the direction of the results supports the punctuated equilibrium model, but rarely in a strong fashion.

In summary, we find some support for the punctuated equilibrium model and its emphasis on political shocks as important in rivalry termination. Nevertheless, the results are not as strong or consistent as for rivalry initiation. If we take only uncensored or quasi-censored cases, the data fail to pass the necessary condition statistical test. Nevertheless, if we examine the six exceptions, four of them generally support the political shock hypothesis; recoding these would make both the uncensored and quasi-censored data pass the statistical tests. Disaggregated analyses also showed a clear, but weak, pattern of more frequent rivalry termination after political shocks than in preshock periods. We conclude that political shocks are a weak necessary condition for rivalry termination. Although they appear to play a role, much remains to be explained.

Extending the Political Shock Approach to Proto-Rivalries

We have already seen that enduring rivalries are sensitive to political shocks, but the same logic might apply to proto-rivalries, not to mention what we have called isolated rivalries. With respect to the onset of rivalries, we anticipated that shocks would be "just as necessary" for proto- as for enduring rivalries. Indeed, an empirical analysis demonstrated no great difference between enduring and proto-rivalries in their formation (almost 85 percent of proto-rivalries begin with a political shock, as compared to over 95 percent of enduring rivalries). Individual shock analysis also systematically shows proto-rivalries to be slightly less inclined to begin with a shock than enduring rivalries. Political shocks only help generate militarized disputes. Whether those disputes are repeated and evolve into an enduring rivalry is determined by other factors occurring after the political shock. In that sense, political shocks are windows-of-opportunity for both enduring and proto-rivalries.

We conceive of political shocks as "more strongly necessary" for the end of enduring rivalries than the proto variety. Because enduring rivalries represent a peculiar kind of stability in international affairs, we thought that they would be more difficult to dislodge than other phenomena, hence the increased necessity of shocks. Shocks may be essential to that process, but many enduring rivalries weather those changed circumstances. Empirical findings do not, however, fully support these expectations. Overall, proto-rivalries are about as likely to end with a political shock as enduring ones (less likely for all cases, actually more likely for uncensored ones). An analysis of individual shocks indicates a pattern that proto-rivalries are indeed at least twice as likely to end in some cases as are enduring rivalries from shocks such as territorial and civil war ones. Nevertheless, in other cases the magnitude of differences, although still in the predicted direction, is small. In the case of power shocks, however, enduring rivalries look much more vulnerable than proto-rivalries, perhaps because such power relationships play such a critical role in the most serious elements of international relations discourse.

Conclusion

The punctuated equilibrium model argues that enduring rivalries represent a peculiar kind of stability in international relations. We earlier demonstrated that such stability in international rivalries is not easily disrupted, and in this chapter hypothesized that a shock of some type was necessary to upset that continuity. In particular, we hypothesized that political shocks at the systemic and state levels would be necessary to start or end a rivalry. Our expectations have largely been confirmed. Over 95 percent of enduring rivalries began with at least one shock. Over three-quarters of the enduring rivalries that ended within the time period of study did so immediately following a political shock.

In general then, political shocks set the stage for the creation and termination of international conflict, including enduring rivalries. In that sense, they are virtual necessary conditions. Whether a conflict develops into an enduring rivalry or merely is a proto-rivalry depends a variety of factors unrelated to shocks. The same proves true for rivalry termination; after a political shock the rivalry is ripe for resolution, but other factors need to enter in to complete the set of sufficient conditions. What is clear is that shocks are vital ingredients in these processes.

Political shocks matter because they compel, sometimes at least, leaders and peoples to conclude that foreign policies need to be changed. We think this particularly true at the end of enduring rivalries; the fact that a rivalry has become enduring in some sense indicates that foreign policies have failed over a long period of time. Leng (1993) indicated how insensitive that realpolitik thought was to any kind of disconfirming evidence. The recent exchange between Vasquez (1997) and (neo)realists only confirms Leng's findings.

CHAPTER 12

Linkages between Enduring Rivalries

The previous chapter focused on one way that the international environment influences enduring rivalries: systematic shocks provide the occasion for the initiation and termination of many rivalries. Within the punctuated equilibrium framework, it is not so much the structure of the international environment that matters, but rather the change in that structure. Systemwide shocks are but one environmental factor that influence enduring rivalries. In this chapter, we investigate another key one: the linkage between a given rivalry and other enduring rivalries in the international system.

We propose that linkage to a "favorable" international rivalry environment constitutes one reason for increased stability and severity of a given enduring rivalry. Close ties between enduring rivalries reinforce rivalry stability (duration) and increase the severity of enduring rivalry. Here, we focus on rivalry severity and leave on the agenda the connection between severity and stability. Nevertheless, we note that there is a clear tendency for more severe rivalries to be longer-term ones. As we discussed in chapter 3, many wars take place in longer-enduring rivalries.

The dominant trend in recent years has been to focus on dyadic aspects of international conflict. The rivalry approach with its emphasis on dyadic relationships over time fits within that general trend, as it stresses the links between conflicts *within* dyads. Nevertheless, we cannot ignore the impact of the broader environment on these dyads. The punctuated equilibrium model, like all natural selection models, focuses on the importance of system-level factors. Similarly, we investigate the linkage *between* rivalries.

The war diffusion literature provides the most relevant theoretical and empirical guideposts to our linkage framework. The academic and practitioner literature is filled with metaphors on the expansion of conflict. Most are references to passive processes, such as contagion or diffusion, but equally common are the notions of bandwagoning, domino effects, and proliferation, which imply a more purposive connection between different conflicts. What all these metaphors have in common is an emphasis on how conflicts are interrelated to one another over space and time. Similarly, our analysis suggests that exogenous factors, here other rivalries, influence the evolution and dynamics of rivalry behavior. Certainly rivalries develop and evolve from many internal influences: regional or global ambitions, territorial and ethnic competitions, and power transitions to name a few. Yet, a focus solely on the internal components of rivalry behavior ignores that some enduring rivalries are connected with one another across space and time. That is, the dynamics of one rivalry may affect the conflict and wars that occur in the other rivalry, including increasing the severity or volatility of the BRLs. For example, the rivalry between Syria and Israel (and its propensity to escalate to war) was influenced by the course of the Israel–Egypt rivalry. Equally or more significant, some minor-power rivalries may be linked to higher-order competitions between major powers. Continuing with the same Middle East example, the superpower competition between the United States and the Soviet Union conditioned the actions of their patron states in the Arab-Israeli rivalries. The methods of these linkage influences are varied, including political pressure, arms transfers, alliance ties, and the like. Nevertheless, the evaluation of rivalry behavior may be incomplete without consideration of how that behavior is influenced by, or influences, other international conflict.

Looking at how rivalries are linked with one another has a dramatic impact on how one would construct strategies for conflict management. If the behavior of rivalries is conditioned by exogenous factors, then a conflict management strategy that concentrates only on the behavior and concerns of those two states may be misguided. The actions of third-party states may serve to either enhance or undermine efforts to regulate or resolve the competition between the rivals; perhaps not surprising then, the cooperation of third-party actors is crucial in some UN actions such as peacekeeping (Diehl 1994a), even when the primary parties are supportive of international intervention and mediation. If linkages exacerbate conflict, conflict managers may need to take steps, to the extent possible, to prevent or limit such interconnections. The success of the American-led forces in containing the conflict and defeating Iraq in the Persian Gulf War was, in part, a consequence of preventing Saddam Hussein from linking that conflict to the Arab-Israeli rivalries (which he tried to do by provoking an Israeli retaliation against Scud missile attacks). Less obvious is that linked rivalries suggest that the way to manage or resolve rivalry A could be by diplomatic initiatives directed at rivalry B or C. This type of strategy generally runs counter to most conflict management strategies, which tend to focus on severe crises between the given actors without concern for the fallout from these crises or the long-term consequences of those interventions. Thus, amelioration of tensions in some Southeast Asian rivalries did not occur until there was moderation in the hostility between the United States and its rivals China and the Soviet Union respectively.

The concept of linkages across rivalries dyads implies that conflict management involves regional and perhaps global solutions to interstate conflict problems. This may make conflict resolution more difficult, and perhaps elusive, but this view may be more realistic than narrow and short-term strategies that yield limited results. Finally, even if conflict management is problematic, at least the linking of rivalries may be an early warning indicator of worsening conflict or war. Decision makers may be able to adjust their strategies and behaviors accordingly, thereby avoiding mistakes from misperception or poor planning.

While our linkage framework shares some similarity with the war diffusion literature, notable differences exist. In the next section, we analyze how our rivalry approach differs from traditional studies of contagion and war expansion. We then discuss how rivalries can become linked and delinked with one another, and we empirically describe the patterns of those processes. Our primary analyses concern the impact that linkage has on conflict patterns in enduring rivalries.

War Diffusion or Rivalry Linkage

As we first suggested in chapter 4, the scholarly literature offers a number of different ways in which conflicts are connected to each other, what we refer to as linkage. The predominant concern has been with how conflict can spread from one area to another or from one set of countries to another. To mix metaphors, the concern is with how conflict can "spill over" or "diffuse" into neighboring areas. In contrast, we propose a model of rivalry linkage to understand how linked enduring rivalries can be mutually reinforcing.

When comparing rivalry linkage with war diffusion, one must keep in mind the fundamental difference in the focus of analysis. Here we focus on enduring rivalries, while the war diffusion literature uses individual—usually not dyadic—conflict. This has a number of key consequences. At the top of the list lies the direction of causality. The work on conflict diffusion (for a review, see Most, Starr, and Siverson 1989) generally explores how conflict involving nation A at time t influences the likelihood of conflict at time $t + 1$ involving nation B. Rivalry linkage stipulates that the severity and stability of rivalries AB and CD are influenced by their *mutual* linkage. In short, the war diffusion literature sees the causal influence running in one direction (along with time), whereas with rivalry linkage it usually runs in both directions.

The mechanisms of conflict diffusion are sometimes unspecified (e.g., Davis, Duncan, and Siverson 1978), sometimes limited to facilitating conditions such as geographic proximity; other times causal mechanisms such as alliances are studied (Siverson and Starr 1991). One of the major failings of the diffusion literature is imprecision concerning the different ways that war actually spreads. Fundamentally though, war produces a profound effect on the relationship between a warring party and one or more of its neighbors. One scenario is that a neighboring state joins the ongoing war, because of alliance ties or because its national security interests are directly affected. A neighboring state may also be drawn into a war, as the fighting does not respect national boundaries; the spread of the Vietnam War into Cambodia is an example. A neighbor may also take advantage of the preoccupation of a warring state to attack it, in effect starting a new war rather than directly joining the existing conflict. In addition, the diffusion literature envisions scenarios in which the probability of war between states C and D is influenced by an ongoing war between states A and B. The ongoing war may alter the power distribution in the region, rearrange existing alliances or relationships, or create new opportunities for conflict. Although these are all possibilities, diffusion research often makes no distinction among them and does not test for their relative propensity. In part, this may account for why the work on diffusion has consistently uncovered only weak, albeit statistically significant, relationships.

There are other studies related to the diffusion literature. Scholars who study "bandwagoning" and "balancing" behaviors (Walt 1987; Jones 1994) consider how states intervene in ongoing conflict, and this gives a more purposive explanation than the standard diffusion literature. Nevertheless, such studies cannot assess how two or more *different* conflicts affect each other, being able to account only for the *expansion* of existing war and not the creation of a new conflict. Spatial autocorrelation studies (e.g., Anselin and O'Loughlin 1992) more closely relate to our analysis of rivalry linkage. There the spread of conflict occurs simultaneously, and the analyses include explanations for the presence and strength of conflict dependence on a regional level. Nevertheless, such studies are geographically based and do not consider the nongeographical causal factors explaining how conflicts might be intertwined.

The diffusion literature and its variants do not provide a suitable framework for understanding how enduring rivalries are related to one another. More closely akin to our analyses are some models of world wars that explicitly note the intersection of conflicts as fundamental in producing a global war. Midlarsky (1988) refers to the *overlap* of conflicts, noting that such connections may be key to understanding how systemic war might spread. He cites the example of German actions against France and Russia at the outset of World War I as a result of Germany's perceived need to show unconditional support of Austro-Hungarian actions against Serbia. Vasquez (1993; see also Vasquez 1998 for an application) extends Midlarsky's analysis by focusing on more than just alliance or other linkages between different actors and conflicts. Vasquez also notes that issues can become linked across conflicts. Such issue linkage can increase the probability of world war if (1) the issues in one conflict become associated with more violence-prone territorial issues in another conflict, (2) the resolution of one crisis is inhibited by escalation in another crisis, or (3) crises linger and accumulate over time (which is critical in Midlarsky's model).

Vasquez explicitly cites the presence of a serious rivalry as a condition that might lead a war to expand to global conflict. He argues that rivals (here major powers since they are a prerequisite for a world war) can limit the conflict behavior of their allies or develop rules and norms of action among themselves so that the management of the primary major-power rivalry is not jeopardized. Whatever the explanations, both models of world wars are based on the assumption that different conflicts or rivalries are interrelated, and that such a connection is a critical component in producing world wars. What these studies lack for our purposes (which are different from those of Midlarsky and Vasquez) is an understanding of how conflicts affect each other in the absence of world wars and how minor-power conflict is linked to other minor-power conflict.

An analysis of militarized dispute behavior (including war and lower-level conflict) found that multiparty disputes tended to last longer and be more severe than dyadic disputes (Gochman and Maoz 1984). These results apply only to single integrated disputes, but the logic might be equally applicable to different disputes that implicitly are multiparty because of the linkages between different rivalries. The logic might also be extended from single disputes to rivalries as a whole. Taken together, the studies of world wars and individual disputes suggest that interconnected rivalries will have an exacerbating effect on conflict.

A few studies explicitly consider the impact of specific rivalries on one another. Empirically, Goldstein and Freeman (1990) explore the triangular relationship in the Cold War period between the United States, the Soviet Union, and China and find modest support for the effect of dyadic interactions on other conflict relationships (see also Ashley 1980). For example, the warming of relations between the United States and China in the Nixon administration was largely to shore up each state's position vis-à-vis their Soviet rival. Throughout the Cold War, there was significant discussion of proxy conflicts in the Third World, but little of this interest was translated into research on the interconnection of superpower conflict and conflict between less developed states.

Muncaster and Zinnes's (1993) framework includes provisions, through a networking system, for the relationship of states C and D to change with the disputatious behavior occurring between states A and B; much of this is based on the classic formulation, "The friend of my friend is my friend . . ." Schrodt and Mintz (1988) explore how the conditional probabilities of dyad interactions are affected by other dyadic interactions. In a limited test of some Middle East countries, they find a high degree of interdependence in the frequency of events, although they cannot specify whether such interdependence produces more conflictual or cooperative actions. They do, however, note that the actions of one dyad increase, but do not constrain, other dyadic interactions.

In summary, the punctuated equilibrium model stresses how that individual enduring rivalry has links to the larger enduring rivalry system. The stronger the linkage between the rivalry and the relevant rivalry environment, the more stable and more severe the enduring rivalry. An international system with severe and long-term enduring rivalries between major powers provides a setting that encourages both the major-power as well as minor-power enduring rivalries. In much of our earlier discussion of the punctuated equilibrium model we emphasized the organizational and domestic factors in their stability, but now we examine how linkage to other enduring rivalries can exacerbate an enduring rivalry.

Forms of Rivalry Linkage

We need to give concrete expression to the general notion of linkage. Unlike the war diffusion literature, which treats contiguity and alliances as *different and independent of one another,* we prefer to use the overarching concept of linkage, which can take various forms. Just as power can be enhanced through a variety of mechanisms (arms, conscription, alliances), so too can linkage be strengthened or weakened by various elements, some of them not under the control of decision makers. In testing the effects of linkage, we are concerned not only with the individual forms of linkage, but also with linkage as a whole.

Not all rivalries are linked to one another in space and time. We assume that enduring rivalries have varying degrees of linkage and that such linkage is confined to sharing the same temporal space (we assume the latter for simplification purposes and recognize that cross-temporal linkages are possible, although less likely). Linkage can take different forms with varying intensities, and we consider those connections that are clear and/or involve security issues as "direct" linkage. There are several ways in which rivalries can be directly linked. Most obviously is the connection of states in different rivalries through alliance ties. States that are allies have similar security concerns, and the interdependence of those security interests lead the actions of one state to have an impact on the interests of its allies. They have also made an explicit choice to connect their mutual security fates. Rivalries in which the participants are aligned on opposite sides with states in another rivalry would seem to have the tightest linkage. The rivalry between the two Koreas was therefore closely linked with the rivalries involving the United States, the Soviet Union, and China.

Not all rivalry behavior is directly linked through formal alliances. It may also be the case that ties across rivalries are strong, yet informal. Throughout the Cold War, the superpowers were heavily involved in "proxy" conflicts between other states in the world. The conduct of those proxy conflicts in Asia, Africa, and the Middle East were influenced by the political support, arms transfers, and military aid provided by the superpowers. The end of the Cold War produced fewer manifestations of superpower competition that exacerbated the lower-level rivalries, leading to some peace settlements (e.g., Cambodia, Angola).

FIGURE 12.1: Forms of Rivalry Linkage

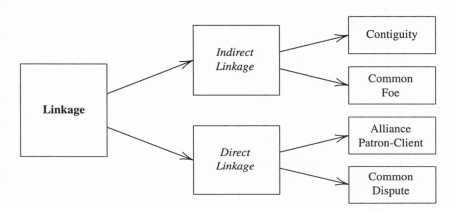

Finally, rivalries can be directly linked by the intersection of common security interests among the participants, even in the absence of an alliance. The
most notable example of this is when states have a common enemy, as is the
case with Egypt's and Jordan's rivalries with Israel. If rivalries become closely
linked in this fashion, they can begin to form what Buzan (1983) calls a "security complex." A security complex is "a group of states whose primary security
concerns link together sufficiently closely that their national securities cannot
realistically be considered apart from one another. Security complexes tend to
be durable, but they are neither permanent nor internally rigid" (1983, 106). Although security complexes are broader than rivalries, these rivalries and related
conflicts are often at the heart of the complex and define its parameters. Indeed
those who adopt security complexes as a framework for analysis are urged to
focus attention on "sets of states whose security problems are closely interconnected" (1983, 113–14). For example, in South Asia, the India–Pakistan rivalry
affects the relationship that each of those states has with its neighbors, especially China.

There are other instances in which the connection between rivalries is much
looser, and we label these linkages "indirect." To be indirectly linked, the conflict issues involving the two sets of rivals may not be intimately connected, but
nevertheless share some common concerns. It may also be the case that rivalries exist in the same geographic region and the actions of one rivalry influence
regional relations and the balance of power such that other conflicts in the area
are affected. We do not expect that the impact of rivalry linkage will be as great
for indirectly linked conflicts, and it is possible that the effects may even be the
opposite of direct linkage.

Our conception of linkage has several components that figure 12.1 illustrates. The kinds of linkage that we study do not necessarily exhaust the universe of possible forms. These four forms do, however, represent good starting points, with at least two of them (contiguity and alliances) having received extensive prior study. Because we do not consider these linkage forms as independent, we are also interested in how they interact. In particular, we suspect that they interact in a synergistic fashion.

Most forms of linkage result from the conscious actions of the rivalry participants. Linkage by contiguity is outside the immediate control of governments, but linkages by dispute, alliance, or common foe arise from actions taken by those governments. Key to understanding linkage and its effects is to understand when rivalries link and delink.

Just because rivalries are linked with one another does not necessarily mean that such linkage is constant throughout the two rivalries. Some rivalries may indeed run identical courses from start to finish. Nevertheless, because rivalries begin and end at different times, their intersection can be far from perfect. Furthermore, the basis for their linkage (i.e., alliances, common security concerns, etc.) may arise sometime toward the middle or even the end of the respective rivalries. Thus, we recognize that the linking of rivalries does not imply that such connection exists from the outset of either rivalry. Symmetrically, rivalries can be "delinked" as well as linked. The severing of the strings that tie the rivalries together or the end of one of the rivalries itself can signal that two sets of military competitions are no longer influencing one another. We suspect, however, that rivalry linkage occurs early in rivalries and remains in place until near the end of the competitions. This expectation is consistent with our punctuated equilibrium model characteristics of a quick lock-in to rivalry patterns and an absence of a fade-out effect.

Of course, enduring rivalries will be largely unrelated to some other rivalries. The diffusion literature tends not to distinguish between direct, indirect, and unlinked conflict and considers only two forms of linkage (formal alliances and contiguity); perhaps this is another reason why the diffusion effect is found to be so weak. We consider other forms of linkage (patron-client relationships, common foes, and common confrontations) in addition to those specified in the diffusion approach. Beyond different forms of rivalry linkage, we also consider it important to specify the casual direction or hierarchy in the effects that flow from that linkage, although we do not fully explore this aspect in the empirical analyses below.

Linkage and the Hierarchy of Causation

A key issue is the causal order by which some international conflicts affect other conflicts. As noted above, in diffusion models, this is achieved by temporal ordering, but we attempt to explain what in some cases are almost simultaneous effects across space. We see some rivalries as the *result* or *consequence* of others (or at least made much worse). In our view, many of the effects occur in a hierarchical fashion with major-power rivalries influencing the dynamics of minor-power rivalries. For example, the continuation of the rivalry between North Vietnam and Thailand was, in part, facilitated by the Vietnam War. This relationship may sometimes produce conflict abatement. Ameliorated relations with one opponent may be the result of an intensified enduring rivalry with another competitor. Nonhierarchically linked rivalries are ones in which the causal arrow runs strongly in both directions. The linked rivalries before World War I typify such cases. Although some may argue that occasionally, notably involving the United States and Israel, the tail wags the dog, it is not surprising to encounter "patron-client" terminology with its implicit causal arrow.

The concept of a casual hierarchy of conflict is not unknown in the international conflict literature, although it is the exception more than the rule. Although not directly tied to rivalries, "nested games" (Tsebelis 1990) deal with the interrelationship of two decisions in what appear at first glance to be separate games. In actuality, one decision is nested in—that is, part of a larger game—and an understanding of strategy requires an understanding of that interrelationship. Thus, what may appear to be a suboptimal choice at one level is actually optimal in the context of the higher-level game. Instead of "nested," we prefer the concept of "linked." Although the hierarchical character of nested games is reflected in some rivalries, in other cases the rivalries are relatively equal vis-à-vis each other. Applied to rivalries, one might conceive of some rivalries being linked in a hierarchical sense with other conflicts, such that rivalry interactions at one level may be conditioned by concerns of another rivalry. For example, a United States–Cuba rivalry may be nested in the larger U.S.-Soviet rivalry; the state of the latter may influence U.S. behavior in the former. Directly relevant to our concerns, Kinsella (1994b) finds that the arms transfers of the superpowers have some effect on the conflict occurring in minor-power rivalries in the Middle East, although the effect is neither primary nor uniform. Similarly, McGinnis (1990) posits that the security of regional rivals is influenced by arms transfers and alignments. Another rivalry, especially those involving major powers, may affect the availability and cost of those elements.

One distinction that we believe is crucial (there may be others) is the power status of the rivals. The direction of causation depends on that power status. The "power hierarchy" creates a causal one whereby "higher" level rivalries (between major powers) influence lower-level ones, but not vice versa. That is, conflict between or involving major powers is presumed to have a significant asymmetrical effect on minor-power conflict. Major powers, through the encouragement of proxy conflicts, arms transfers, military and economic aid, and a range of other policies, can affect the course of conflicts involving smaller patron states. In those cases, we assume a hierarchy of major-power rivalry or conflict "causing" minor power conflict.

FIGURE 12.2: Hierarchy of Causation

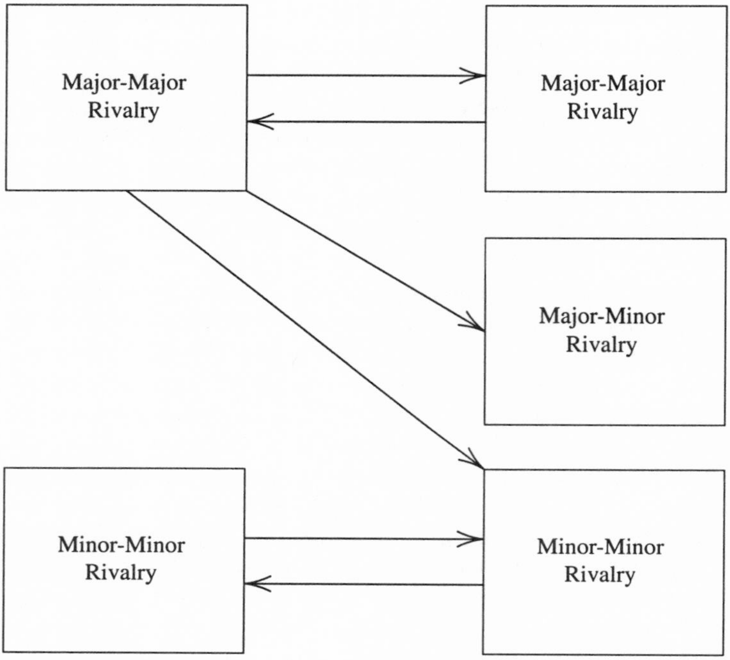

Although we study the linkages of only enduring rivalries here, one could use the same principle in establishing the direction of causality between enduring rivalries and those competitions of a lesser magnitude and duration, what we have referred to as proto-rivalries and isolated rivalries. We assume that states pay more attention to their most critical security threats and that all other conflict is, at least in part, conditioned by the dominant security concern. Thus, for example, Cold War tensions influenced U.S. policy toward both its allies and small states at their periphery, such as Vietnam and Angola. Enduring rivalries are assumed to be the most salient conflicts. They last the longest, reflect fundamental security concerns, and provide the greatest threat of war. We assume therefore that enduring rivalries will be hierarchically above lower-level international conflict. The hierarchy of causation patterns that drive our analyses are illustrated in figure 12.2. The basic principle is that when power is symmetrical, causality is symmetrical. In figure 12.2, we see two-directional causal arrows between major-power rivalries and between minor-power rivalries. In cases of power asymmetry, such as between a major-power rivalry and a minor-power one, the causal arrow goes only in one direction.

Research Design

Rivalries and conflicts are said to be directly linked if one of the following criteria is met during the lives of the two rivalries. First, rivalries are directly linked if each rival is connected to a state in the other rivalry through a formal alliance (for a list see Small and Singer 1969)[1] or an established patron-client relationship.[2] Thus, for example, the United States–Soviet Union rivalry is directly linked to the Israel–Egypt rivalry during the Cold War. Some of the recent diffusion literature (Siverson and Starr 1991) identifies alliances as one agent of the diffusion effect, but we add the possibility of patron-client relationships, which may tie states even more closely together than formal alliances. A second way of establishing direct linkage is if both rivalries share at least one of the same militarized disputes as a part of each's rivalry ("common dispute"). Continuing with the above example, the 1973 Arab-Israeli War is common to both the Israel–Egypt rivalry and the superpower rivalry. Either the presence of an alliance or a common dispute involving all rivals suggests a strong interrelationship between the two rivalries. The expectation that the rivals are influenced by the other rivalry seems reasonable.

We first define rivalries as indirectly linked when at least one rival is geographically contiguous (Gochman 1991) to at least one state in another rivalry.[3] An AB rivalry is linked to a CD one if state A or B is contiguous to state C or D. Using contiguity as a measure of indirect linkage is consistent with the diffusion literature, which relies extensively on shared borders for the spread of conflict (Most, Starr, and Siverson 1989). Enduring rivalries are indirectly linked by common foe if one of the rivals is simultaneously involved in both rivalries; for example, the rivalry AB is indirectly linked to a rivalry involving states B and C. We exclude those cases of major-minor rivalries that are linked by common foe to other major-minor rivalries. Major powers are capable of participating in several different rivalries simultaneously, sometimes in different parts of the world; the connection between these rivalries is often tenuous at best. Eliminating these instances allows us to ignore superficial linkages such as that between the France–Ottoman Empire rivalry and the France–China rivalry in the nineteenth century, which have no substantive connection and would seem to exercise no constraint on the French ability to act in either case.

---

[1] We use one of the latest versions of the Correlates of War Project list of alliances, which extends from 1816 to 1984. For the period after 1984, we assume that all alliances in existence at the outset of the period continue throughout the whole period. The exception, of course, is the Warsaw Treaty Organization (WTO), but this does not affect any of our linkages after 1984.

[2] From our own estimations, we coded the patron-client relationships, and they are listed on the web site described in Appendix A.

[3] We made one slight change in that we did not code the United States and the USSR as contiguous despite the proximity of Alaska to Siberia across the Bering Straits. In addition, we chose to ignore colonial borders as indicative of contiguity, given that such contacts between states are more peripheral and less important empirically than homeland borders (Goertz and Diehl 1992b).

Rivalries with two major powers (Small and Singer 1982) are considered hierarchically above rivalries involving at least one minor power. Because of the principle of hierarchical causality elucidated above, we consider only the effect that linkages have on the conflict behavior of rivalries involving at least one minor power. Thus, because we believe major-major power rivalries are causal agents in the linkage effect, and therefore that their conflict patterns are not altered by linkage, we drop these 12 cases from the analysis.[4] The incidence of war in rivalries is again defined by the presence of a military conflict resulting in one thousand or more battle-related fatalities (Small and Singer 1982). For our analyses, the basic rivalry level again will be considered the mean conflict level (first introduced in chapter 9) and the volatility defined as its variance over the course of the rivalry. We will be concerned with how the BRLs of linked rivalries fluctuate in conjunction with one another.

Empirical Results

Descriptive Analysis

Our first set of analyses concerns the extent to which enduring rivalries are linked and the form that those linkages take. Our expectation is that rivalries higher on the hierarchical ladder are more likely to be linked to one another. Major-power rivalries are so important to the international system that those that take place simultaneously will be likely to influence one another. The small number of major powers at any given time and the limited geographic constraints on major powers also seem conducive to rivalry linkage. We do not have preconceptions about which forms of linkage will be predominant. In table 12.1, we identify the total number of rivalries that are linked to a particular rivalry as well as the four possible forms (two types of direct and indirect connections respectively) those linkages might take.

The most stunning finding is that all but one enduring rivalry (Honduras vs. Nicaragua) is linked to at least one other rivalry at some point in their existence by alliances (including patron-client relationships), contiguity, common dispute participation, or common foe in overlapping time periods. The average enduring rivalry is connected to approximately 17 other rivalries, many times connected by multiple forms of linkage (e.g., both alliances and common foe forms). Alliances are the most frequent method of linkage; the average rivalry is linked to 14.4 other rivalries through alliances. Geographic proximity is, not surprisingly, also a prominent form of linkage, especially among the large number of rivalries in the dense area of states in Europe. Overlapping disputes are not as common as one might have expected. This illustrates that rivalries may

---

[4]Empirically, their inclusion does not dramatically affect the results reported below, and the conclusions that we draw from those analyses would not change by their inclusion.

TABLE 12.1: Number and Types of Linkage with other Enduring Rivalries

Rivalry	Begin	ERs	Cli	Foe	Ctg.	All.	Dsp.	Lks.
USA–Cuba	1959	26	9	5	0	16	1	31
USA–Mexico	1836	2	0	2	0	0	0	2
USA–Ecuador	1952	28	9	6	2	18	0	35
USA–Peru	1955	28	9	6	3	18	0	36
USA–UK	1838	4	0	3	2	2	1	8
USA–Spain	1850	5	0	2	3	4	1	10
USA–USSR	1946	38	16	10	15	26	13	80
USA–China	1949	34	12	9	13	25	7	66
USA–N. Korea	1950	34	9	6	12	27	4	58
Honduras–Nicaragua	1907	0	0	0	0	0	0	0
Ecuador–Peru	1891	9	0	2	4	9	0	15
Brazil–UK	1838	4	0	1	1	3	0	5
Chile–Argentina	1873	1	0	0	1	0	0	1
Chile–Argentina	1952	7	0	0	2	7	0	9
UK–Germany	1887	16	0	5	9	13	10	37
UK–USSR	1876	16	1	6	15	16	2	40
UK–USSR	1939	39	15	6	18	34	13	86
UK–Ottoman Empire	1895	18	0	6	12	18	10	46
UK–Iraq	1958	27	0	4	11	25	5	45
Belgium–Germany	1914	18	0	3	13	16	15	47
France–Germany	1830	9	0	1	7	8	0	16
France–Germany	1911	18	0	4	13	17	15	49
France–Turkey	1897	18	0	6	16	17	10	49
France–China	1870	11	0	4	9	4	2	19
Spain–Morocco	1957	15	0	1	1	15	0	17
Germany–Italy	1914	18	0	6	11	16	15	48
Italy–Yugoslavia	1923	22	0	4	6	21	7	38
Italy–Ethiopia	1923	16	0	3	6	16	7	32
Italy–Turkey	1880	18	0	7	13	15	10	45
Yugoslavia–Bulgaria	1913	18	0	2	9	16	11	38
Greece–Bulgaria	1914	20	0	2	7	20	10	39
Greece–Turkey	1866	16	0	5	11	11	10	37
Greece–Turkey	1958	21	0	1	14	15	1	31
Cyprus–Turkey	1965	20	0	1	13	16	1	31
USSR–Norway	1956	30	14	5	16	17	3	55
USSR–Iran	1908	41	15	8	30	32	1	86
Russia–Turkey	1876	17	0	8	17	14	10	49
USSR–China	1862	45	17	12	31	29	2	91
USSR–Japan	1895	44	15	9	27	33	10	94
Congo Brazz.–Zaire	1963	6	0	0	2	6	0	8
Uganda–Kenya	1965	6	0	0	3	6	0	9
Somalia–Ethiopia	1960	7	0	1	3	5	0	9
Ethiopia–Sudan	1967	7	0	1	5	6	0	12
Morocco–Algeria	1962	15	0	1	1	14	0	16
Iran–Iraq	1953	21	0	4	18	15	2	39
Iraq–Israel	1967	15	0	7	11	14	4	36

Continued on next page

TABLE 12.1—*continued*

Rivalry	Begin	ERs	Cli	Foe	Ctg.	All.	Dsp.	Lks.
Iraq–Kuwait	1961	15	0	3	10	13	3	29
Egypt–Israel	1948	17	0	4	7	16	6	33
Syria–Jordan	1949	14	0	2	11	9	4	26
Syria–Israel	1948	14	0	5	11	11	6	33
Jordan–Israel	1948	11	0	5	9	11	4	29
Israel–Saudi Arabia	1957	11	0	5	9	11	4	29
Saudi Arabia–N. Yemen	1962	13	0	1	11	10	0	22
Afghanistan–Pakistan	1949	24	0	1	12	23	0	36
China–S. Korea	1950	19	3	6	13	13	5	40
China–Japan	1873	31	2	7	13	27	9	58
China–India	1950	15	3	5	13	9	0	30
N. Korea–S. Korea	1949	15	0	3	12	14	3	32
S. Korea–Japan	1953	14	0	4	8	6	0	18
India–Pakistan	1947	22	0	2	8	17	0	27
Thailand–Kampuchea	1953	12	0	2	2	10	2	16
Thailand–Laos	1960	15	0	2	6	10	0	18
Thailand–N. Vietnam	1961	15	2	2	6	10	5	25

ERs: Number of linked enduring rivalries.
Cli: Number of patron-client linked enduring rivalries.
Foe: Number of enduring rivalries linked by common foe.
Ctg: Number of enduring rivalries linked by contiguity.
All: Number of enduring rivalries linked by alliance.
Dsp: Number of enduring rivalries linked by common disputes.
Lks: Total number of links.

be linked with one another by more than being part of the same military confrontations and that ignoring other interrelationships when third states are not directly involved in conflict could be misleading.

Our expectation that major powers would have the greatest frequency of linked conflict is largely confirmed. Most of the rivalries that occur after World War II are in some way connected to the superpower or other superpower-related rivalries. In this sense, treating the United States–USSR rivalry as the centerpiece of postwar relations is confirmed here. The Russian-Japanese rivalry is linked to the greatest number of rivalries (44), but this is largely a function of the long duration of that rivalry, although one could make a case that the causal direction here runs both ways. More interesting is the relatively small number of linked rivalries with Latin American rivalries, whose competitions seems to persist in relative isolation, but also from our earlier analyses at relatively lower levels of severity. If such linkage has a substantive impact on conflict behavior, this evidence is a powerful indictment of traditional analyses that look at conflict only cross-sectionally. Of course, it may be that linkage is an essential component for rivalries to become enduring and that an examination of proto-rivalries and isolated conflicts might reveal that linkages are relatively uncommon.

TABLE 12.2: The Timing of Rivalry Linkage

	Ally	Contiguity	Common Dispute	Common Foe
Mean	7.38	−2.95	8.78	10.31
S.D.	16.65	23.76	13.72	19.89

Note: Mean is the time from the onset of the rivalry to the occurrence of the first linkage.

Among the linked rivalries, we are also concerned with when two or more rivalries become tied together. It is conceivable that rivalries could become linked from the outset of each competition, somewhere in the early stages of the rivalries, at "midlife," or toward the end of the rivalries. Of course, this may vary across the two rivalries, as we cannot expect that the rivalries will begin at the same time, although this is true in some cases. It is our expectation that the linkage will occur relatively early in the period of temporal overlap between the two rivalries. The basic rivalry level assumes that there is a fairly rapid lock-in effect in the rivalry competition, as we have demonstrated in chapter 9; rivals adjust quickly to patterns of competition and thus set the tone for the rest of the rivalry. We anticipate that this is also the case with linked rivalries. If such competitions do not include ties to other conflicts toward the outset, then it is not likely that the competition will deviate substantially to incorporate new influences or patterns after the rivalry has reached maturity. The results of this analysis are given in table 12.2.

Across different types of linkage, a rivalry becomes linked to another rivalry within 11 years of its onset, depending on the linkage type, although there is considerable variation within each of the linkage types. The first time that rivalries are linked by a common foe is almost one-third of the way through their lives, again making such a connection a poor early warning indicator. Those rivalries linked by contiguity do so the quickest, even demonstrating a negative time to linkage because contiguity is a constant and the linkage between two contiguous rivalries occurs at the time of the onset of the first rivalry (which may be several years before the other rivalry begins). The average first linkage in all cases begins sometime in the early part of rivalries. After that initial linkage, of course, further ties to other rivalries also occur. This meets our expectations of an early lock-in period and demonstrates that time is tight for conflict managers who wish to avoid the expansion or interconnection of conflict.

Symmetrically, we are interested in patterns of delinkage as well as linkage. We would expect that rivalries become delinked at or around the time of their termination; that is, rivalries stay linked for most of their lifetimes. If one

TABLE 12.3: The Timing of Rivalry Delinkage

	Ally	Contiguity	Common Dispute	Common Foe
Mean	3.15	−3.23	0	6.35
S.D.	17.98	17.86	0	13.47

Note: Mean is the time from the occurrence of the first delinkage until the end of the rivalry.

rivalry ends (especially a major-power one), this may lessen the hostility and facilitate the conclusion of its linked counterpart. Table 12.3 shows when rivalries become delinked. The first incidence of delinkage usually occurs between three and six years before the last dispute in a rivalry, about what was anticipated, and perhaps signaling the beginning of the termination phase of the rivalry.[5] Again, this pattern fits with a punctuated equilibrium model in which there is no gradual fade-out of rivalry conflict behavior, but a quick and coterminous change in all rivalry processes.

The Impact of Linkages on Rivalry Conflict

Above we established that enduring rivalries are strongly linked to one another and that such linkages are present during most years of the rivalries affected. An obvious next step is to ascertain whether rivalry behavior is influenced at all by those linkages. We should note that there is some significant collinearity between different forms of linkage, such that rivalries are often simultaneously connected by more than one mechanism. Table 12.4 details the extent of that collinearity. The correlations range from .12 to .56. Thus, there is some risk that the specific parameter estimates in the regression analyses reported below will be contaminated by covariation of the predictor variables. Thus, we offer some caution to the reader in interpreting such individual standard error estimates, and we prefer to rely primarily upon the degree to which the four linkage types can collectively account for variations in conflict patterns.

We first consider whether rivalries that are linked have a higher mean severity level than those that are not. Our expectation is that linked rivalries will have a greater basic rivalry level than unlinked conflicts. Cross-sectionally, we look at all rivalries and their mean basic rivalry level under various conditions of linkage.[6] Of course, there are many other factors that influence that basic level, beside the exacerbating effects of being linked to other conflict, and thus we expect linkage to be moderately associated with higher BRLs.

---

[5] Of course, the censored data may indicate that this figure is too low.

[6] We include all censored cases in our analyses. Since these have not yet ended, we cannot know for sure their mean severity levels, but (1) we have at least 20 years of rivalry to work with and (2) we find that the BRL in most enduring rivalries is flat, hence unlikely to change from what we already have.

TABLE 12.4: Intercorrelations among Different Forms of Rivalry Linkage

	Ally	Contiguity	Common Dispute	Common Foe
Ally	1.00	.12	.55*	.16
Common foe	.12	1.00	.51*	.56*
Contiguity	.55*	.51*	1.00	.36**
Common dispute	.16	.56*	.36**	1.00

*Significant at .0001. **Significant at .01.

Related to this first expectation is our second prediction that there will be greater variation around the basic rivalry level in linked rivalries. Recall that the punctuated equilibrium model argues that the basic rivalry level is relatively stable over time. Yet the severity of crises does fluctuate, sometimes quite dramatically, around the basic rivalry level. We believe that such volatility is, at least partly, the result of exogenous influences—here the exacerbating impact of conflict from another rivalry. Although two rivals may have developed a way of managing their conflict and keeping it within bounds, that stability may be upset when they become involved on opposite sides of a larger dispute with another pair of rivals. A corollary of this expectation is that war is most likely to occur in linked rivalries, as the disputants are least able to manage their conflict and accommodate their preferences short of war.

The hypothesized exacerbating effect of rivalry linkage should be affected by the directness of the rivalry linkage. The most positive effects should stem from rivalries that are directly linked. Enduring rivalries are thought to be the centerpiece of security complexes and other interstate relations in a given region. Therefore, we expect a strong positive relationship between directly linked enduring rivalries. In other circumstances, enduring rivalries may only be indirectly connected to other rivalries. This means that enduring rivalries are a factor in state calculations, but also that other factors as well may condition the basic rivalry level more.

Table 12.5 reports our analysis of the impact of linkages on the basic rivalry level. First, more than a quarter of the variance is accounted for in this model, impressive considering that a variety of structural and some other exogenous factors, unspecified in the model here, also influence the basic rivalry level. Second, the effects are notable for direct forms of linkage (common disputes) as hypothesized above. Third, we see that the effects of individual forms of linkage may be weak, but collectively and in combination with other factors they are quite significant.

TABLE 12.5: The Impact of Rivalry Linkage on the Basic Rivalry Level

Variable	Estimate	S.E.	Significance
Intercept	67.56	6.23	.001
Ally	.49	.46	.30
Common foe	−4.03	2.82	.16
Contiguity	1.33	.77	.09
Common dispute	1.70	.81	.04

Note: Dependent variable: basic rivalry level.
Model F-value: 4.42.
Model significance: .001.
$R^2 = .27$.

The idea that rivalry conflict is more severe when it is linked through common dispute participation is consistent with findings in the traditional war literature that multilateral disputes and wars are often the most hostile and dangerous interactions. The effects of the other form of direct linkage, alliances, may be muted in the model because defense pacts and other such agreements might just as easily have a deterrent or mitigating effect on the escalation of conflict as they have an exacerbating one. Sharing a common foe actually has a negative effect on a BRL, although the negative parameter estimate is not statistically significant. This may occur because states, especially minor powers, have a limited "carrying capacity" to conduct rivalries. That they may face multiple rivals or are entangled in multiple rivalry relationships suggests that they exercise some prudence in allocating resources and attention to those rivalries. Thus, the only way they may conduct multiple rivalries at the same time is to limit the severity (and thereby the risk of war) for each of them.

The effects of linkage on the volatility of rivalries were similar to that for the BRL[7] and are reported in table 12.6. Again, around 20 percent of the variance in volatility is accounted for by rivalry linkage. Direct linkage is again significant, with sharing a common dispute increasing volatility. The inclusion of multiple actors in rivalry conflict may make that conflict unpredictable to the actors from dispute to dispute, and thus producing greater variation around the BRL. When rivalries intersect in a given dispute, there will be counter-pressures from high severity and low severity rivalries on each other, with the severity of a given dispute likely deviating from each rivalry's normal patterns. The other direct form of linkage, alliances, has the expected positive sign and is nearly statistically significant. Both the indirect linkages have negative coefficients, but do not approach statistical significance standards.

Beyond the focus mean severity and volatility in a rivalry, we are also concerned with the more traditional conflict patterns—war. Similar to the analyses

---

[7] As noted previously, although these are positively correlated, they are not dramatically so and are clearly separate conflict dimensions of a rivalry.

TABLE 12.6: The Impact of Rivalry Linkage on Volatility

Variable	Estimate	S.E.	Significance
Intercept	2,188	355	.001
Ally	43	26	.11
Common foe	−179	161	.27
Contiguity	−18	44	.68
Common dispute	120	46	.01

Note: Dependent variable: volatility of basic rivalry level.
Model *F*-value: 2.78.
Model significance: .04.
$R^2 = .19$.

with the basic rivalry level and its volatility, we ran a series of regressions seeking to predict the number of wars in a rivalry by reference to various forms of linkage; the results are also quite similar (see table 12.7).[8] The significance of the positive intercept indicates that enduring rivalries experience war even without any form of linkage, suggesting that linkage is not a necessary condition for the most severe form of conflict in a rivalry. Nevertheless, the four linkage variables account for over half of the variance in the number of rivalry wars, a far more powerful impact than was evident with respect to the BRL and volatility. Sharing disputes is again the most important form of linkage, although we repeat our earlier caveat about multicollinearity and the instability of parameter estimates. The greater volatility of some linked rivalries indicates that such deviations upward to war may be likely. Yet beyond making one's own conflict worse, war in one of the linked rivalries may trigger a similar event in the other rivalry, in many of the same ways as envisioned in the diffusion literature (e.g., joining an ongoing war); the expansion of the Austro-Hungarian war with Serbia to World War I is the classic example. Overall, rivalries are much more likely to experience war when they are linked in the same multilateral dispute, extending the findings of Vasquez (1993) and Midlarsky (1988), who pointed out the dangers of world wars emanating from linked multilateral competitions.

[8]The similarity may in part be because the basic rivalry level measure includes wars, which score the highest on the conflict level scale used to build the basic rivalry level. In addition, the regression technique assumes that it is possible to have negative values of the dependent variable (number of wars), when in fact the lower limit of our cases is zero. Nevertheless, one might interpret such possible negative values as representing greater cooperation, and the use of the technique is essentially sound. Finally, linkage by common dispute includes some wars, and therefore one might argue that we get positive correlations because the same thing is on both sides of the equation; nevertheless, common dispute linkage was not found to be significantly associated with the frequency of war.

TABLE 12.7: The Impact of Rivalry Linkage on the Frequency of War

Variable	Estimate	S.E.	Significance
Intercept	.50	.24	.04
Ally	−.01	.02	.58
Common foe	−.16	.11	.14
Contiguity	.02	.03	.35
Common dispute	.20	.03	.001

Note: Dependent variable: number of wars in the rivalry.
Model F-value: 14.94. Model significance: .001.
$R^2 = .56$.

Conclusion

We hypothesized that when enduring rivalries become interconnected with one another, the potential for serious conflict and escalation increased. In effect, rivalry linkage could be a warning signal that international competitions could worsen and war was a strong likelihood. We initially discovered that enduring rivalries are more interconnected with one another than had been previously believed; all but one enduring rivalry studied was connected with at least one other rivalry. Such linkages were also not transitory. Most commonly, rivalries tended to link up with one another relatively early in their existence and did not become delinked until late in the competition. Indeed, many linkages lasted for the full life of the rivalry. This is consistent with the expectations of the punctuated equilibrium model of rivalries.

The impact of rivalry linkage on conflict was clear, although not always as uniform as we had expected. The basic rivalry levels of linked conflict were higher than those levels of unlinked conflict. The volatility of some linked enduring rivalries was also greater, although the results were slightly weaker. The findings were largely the same for the frequency of war as they were for the basic rivalry level and volatility, although the linkage variables accounted for significantly more of the variance there (more than half).

A number of other paths for future research are suggested by the work here. That all the enduring rivalries are linked with other rivalries in some fashion leads one to question the role of linkage in the formation of enduring rivalries. Do enduring rivalries reach their mature status, in part, because they are connected to other conflict? Might rivalries die out before reaching enduring status if they were not so intimately tied to other competitions? These are empirical questions that are suggested by our findings, but not confirmed in their own right.

The uncovering of rivalry linkages also has consequences for conflict management. First, it should be evident that rivalry linkage is an early warning indicator to policymakers that conflict between these two states could be severe and that war is strongly probable. On the other hand, there may be little that decision makers can do about this interrelationship. Only alliances and patron-client linkages are directly manipulable by the rivalry participants, and the linkage is likely to take place very early in the competition (in the case of alliances and geographic proximity, the linkage preceded the onset of one of the rivalries in many cases). Consequently there may be little lead time and perhaps even less maneuvering room available to deal with the dangers of linkage. Furthermore, waiting for rivals to intersect in the same crisis is not frequent enough to be reliable and may occur too late in the process. Even if options are available, it may be hard to sever the linkage (alliances for example) once the rivalries have become intertwined. Overlapping and multiple connections between rivalries further complicate efforts at delinkage. When leaders can prevent linkages from occurring, however, as they successfully did in stopping Iraq from broadening the Persian Gulf War to include Israel, then the consequences can be beneficial.

If linkage cannot be easily prevented, the clear message nonetheless is that delinkage should be strongly pursued. The delinking of conflict was not always associated with a lessening of conflict, but more importantly was related to the termination phase of many enduring rivalries. This is illustrated by a number of different cases. The United States–USSR rivalry starts to decline in severity according to our measure in the mid-1960s, leading to détente in the 1970s (and this is consistent with most common perceptions). A common explanation gives pride of place to the conflict management lessons of the Cuban missile crisis, but we also note that at the same time the linkage between the United States–China and United States–USSR rivalries was dramatically loosening. Similarly, the Arab-Israeli conflict became less severe as individual rivalries gradually delinked from that integrated conflict. Jordan was perhaps the first to delink, not taking part in the 1973 war, but the most dramatic delinkage was when Egypt made peace with Israel. It is perhaps not surprising then that except for the 1982 Lebanese War (which arose under different circumstances) the Arab-Israeli conflict has avoided major war for almost 30 years.

Even if delinkage is not possible, conflict managers need to deal with conflicts in a multifaceted way. Because rivalries can influence the course of another competition, a strategy that focuses on only one dyad is bound to be problematic (although as the Egyptian-Israeli peace agreement illustrates, it is possible and may be a key to delinkage in some cases). Instead there must be recognition that efforts in one conflict can have spillover effects in another; this can be positive if conflict severity is reduced. It can also cause difficulties if the exacerbation of one rivalry sidetracks peace efforts in another rivalry. In the former Yugoslavia, there may be some benefits to achieving a peace agreement between two of the three main protagonists—Serbs, Muslims, and Croats. Yet a dyadic peace may be just as likely to be broken apart by continued fighting in the other, remaining dyad as a peace agreement would be to foster an agreement between those two states. This represents a delicate balance and signals the desirability of a comprehensive peace strategy, although it is recognized that this may be more difficult and time consuming.

Finally, our perspective is quite different than that of Mearsheimer (1990), who mourned the end of the Cold War as the beginning of a new era of nationalist conflict. One notable aspect of the post–Cold War era is the apparent limited number of linkages between different conflicts. The war in Bosnia is not spreading because, in part, it has no connection to other European conflicts, quite in contrast to the pre–World War I powderkeg of rivalries linked through alliances (Sabrosky 1975). Certainly, there will still be cases of interstate conflict, and some of these conflicts are more probable now that the superpower rivalry is effectively over. Yet because of the absence of linkage, there is a better chance perhaps that they will not develop into enduring rivalries with their accompanying cycles of war and severe crises. Furthermore—and largely ignored by Mearsheimer and others—the end of the Cold War and the delinkage of its patron-client rivalries has led to some notable peace settlements in many long-standing external and internal conflicts. In these ways, it may be that while some structural realists will miss the Cold War, the world may enjoy some reduction in the number and severity of enduring rivalries.

CHAPTER 13

Future Research

In conclusion, we take the occasion of this chapter, not so much to look backward and summarize the previous 12 chapters of the book, but rather to direct our attention forward to areas of future research. We have stressed that the rivalry approach has implications for data, testing, and theory. We use these three broad categories to examine the general rivalry research agenda. The second part of this volume focuses on enduring rivalries, and we therefore also survey new possibilities for enduring rivalry research broadly and the punctuated equilibrium model in particular.

Extending the Rivalry Approach

Many of the ideas for using the rivalry approach to study international conflict are inherent in chapters 4 and 5. Furthermore, the illustrations used in those chapters, drawn from a wide range of topics and theoretical concerns, might easily be translated to items for a future research agenda. We will not repeat those arguments and suggestions here. Nevertheless, there are several other directions for future research involving the rivalry approach that are not developed above. We begin with data concerns, although we recognize that such considerations are not necessarily the highest priority and should in any case be subordinate to, or driven by, specific theoretical interests.

Data

The rivalry data that we described in chapter 2 were created from existing sources, which were gathered for purposes other than our own. The COW dispute data reflect a cross-sectional approach to war with an atomistic view of individual disputes. In contrast, the rivalry approach centers on interdispute connections over the long or short term. As a result, we believe our rivalry data represent only a first stage in the development of rivalry data sets.

Thompson's (1995) research agenda on principal rivalries reflects what we would call the second generation of rivalry data collection. Instead of using cross-sectional data to construct rivalries—as we do—he starts with a rivalry

concept and is collecting data on that set of principal rivalries (some preliminary results are evident in Rasler and Thompson 1998a, 1998b). In a similar
vein, Cioffi-Revilla is using the rivalry idea in his project on ancient war, which
focuses on rivalries as well as individual wars (see Cioffi-Revilla 1996 for an
overview of the project). The rivalry idea helps him better understand changes
in conflict relations over time than does merely collecting data on individual
wars.

Bennett's work on rivalry termination (1993, 1996, 1997a, 1997b, 1998) illustrates that this focus can be a significant contribution to rivalry research. He
has taken the dispute-generated rivalries and enriched them with rivalry termination dates. In contrast, we have used only existing rivalry data and adopted
much more tentative and approximate end dates. We infer that a rivalry has
ended "sometime" in the 10 years following the end of the last dispute.[1] Bennett hence takes an intermediary position. He uses existing data on rivalries
based on dispute data and then extends them with rivalry-specific, historical
information.

This volume has used a wide cross-sectional set of rivalries, 1,166 in total. One of the costs is to have relatively little data on each rivalry. Another
data strategy is to gather much more information about a few rivalries. Maoz
and Mor (1996, 1998) have adopted this approach. Many dynamic hypotheses, in particular, require more detailed information for their testing, which only
the approach of Maoz and Mor can provide. Similarly, Leng's (1993) in-depth
analysis of crisis behavior required him to look at a sample of crises ($N = 40$),
rather than all militarized disputes between states in the period studied.

Each of these three approaches to data represents an effort to move beyond
the focus on independent disputes and wars to concentrate on rivalries. In the
long run, extant data sets will be limited in how well they can address the theoretical demands of the rivalry approach. Thus, data collections directly driven
by rivalry concerns, as illustrated above, will be essential. Although we make
a general call for data sets on rivalries, there are a number of specific data priorities embedded within that broader plea.

Rivalry termination is a key issue and has attracted significant theoretical work and some data collection, but no less important is rivalry initiation.
As of this writing we know of no efforts to pinpoint when rivalries—short or
enduring—actually start. Our own beginning dates for rivalries mimic the termination scheme in that the rivalry begins "sometime" in the 10 years prior to
the beginning of the first dispute. We (as well as other scholars who work on
rivalries) pick up the first militarized manifestations of rivalry behavior, but we
thus far lack the precision necessary to understand when the competition actually begins, short of military threats and actions. Data sets that identify more
precise beginning dates would be useful in answering some key questions about
rivalry initiation, including, for example, how commercial rivalries evolve (or

---

[1] See chapters 2 and 11 for details.

not) into militarized ones, as is discussed below. As we argued in chapter 2, however, it may be difficult (even impossible) and inappropriate to assign exact dates for rivalry initiation and termination, given that these are processes and not fixed points. Nevertheless, the data and accompanying research could benefit from greater precision than we have thus far provided.

Another data priority is developing a finer-grained picture of rivalries than can be obtained with COW dispute and other existing data. Events data provide an obvious choice (Hensel 1997). Dispute data give only a very coarse and intermittent picture of rivalries. The latter is true because we know only about what is happening in the rivalry at the time of militarized conflict, but not at other junctures. Events data provide a more precise picture of rivalry behavior in that they include both conflictual behavior short of the militarized threshold and cooperative behavior between rivals. For example, many of the hypotheses generated from the punctuated equilibrium model focus on the speed of change within an enduring rivalry. These hypotheses are better examined with finer-grained data than those provided by looking at militarized disputes alone.

Related to a concern with events data, and therefore more attention to possible cooperative actions in rivalries, is the necessity of studying conflict management and conflict termination that comes with the rivalry approach. Rivalry research began with (and remains largely so today) an overwhelming emphasis on the conflictual side of rivalries. For empirical progress, we need to have data sets that include conflict management efforts as well as militarized disputes and wars. We made a first cut at this by merging Bercovitch's (1993) mediation data with our data on rivalries. We think that this is an important first step, but problems emerge because neither Bercovitch's nor COW data were conceived, designed, or coded from a rivalry perspective. Bercovitch has recently extended the range of his data from mediation attempts to third-party interventions of all sorts. Within rivalries, we would like to know about *all* significant conflict management efforts, not just those of a particular type. The rivalry approach also focuses attention on periods beyond those that just precede and closely follow major crises and wars, which are the focal points of most analyses of conflict management. The same principle applies to deterrence research. The overwhelming emphasis has been on deterrence encounters, but we need to put deterrence in the context of compellence. With cross-sectional approaches, one can ignore alternative conflict management or compellence attempts, but once the focus is placed on rivalries we need to consider all other relevant actions.

One of the key elements of our punctuated equilibrium model is the basic rivalry level and its purported stability over time. As illustrated in chapter 9, we estimated this using the severity level of disputes in the rivalry. It would be desirable to have a continuous measure of the BRL (for an attempt at something like this, see Crescenzi and Enterline 1998), rather than one that is observable only at dispute times. This would permit a better test of the punctuated equilibrium model's expectations and help us perhaps understand better when and how normal fluctuations and dramatic changes occur. It might also allow scholars to assess whether the BRL is subject at all to decay and reinforcement processes, which may not be consistent with punctuated equilibrium formulations, but which are certainly part of many psychological and physical science models. An estimate of the BRL might also be improved by consideration of more than just the severity of conflicts. One needs to understand and relate other characteristics of the competition, including the duration of conflicts, interactions (or lack thereof) on nonrivalry issues, and acts of cooperation, to the punctuated equilibrium framework. This would provide a subtler picture of the BRL as well as test for the robustness of our findings.

In short, much remains to be done on the data front. Unfortunately, many important theories and hypotheses do not get developed if suitable data sets do not exist. We suggest that as more rivalry-specific data become available, not only will we learn more about rivalries, but that the existence of such data will incite further theory development. Data generation at the same time is driven by conceptual and theoretical development, and we believe that our rivalry approach and the extant research on rivalries have produced sufficient theoretical motivation for data collection on rivalries to develop along new lines.

Testing

In the 1980s, hypothesis-testing demands drove the creation of the enduring rivalry concept and its various operational measures. Rivalries were used to select a sample of cases, which was their sole testing function in those early studies. In chapter 5, we called this the first-generation testing use of rivalries, but we also argued that the rivalry approach provided many other means for examining hypotheses, some of which we illustrated in chapter 6 on the democratic peace.

When we speak of testing in this section, we refer to using rivalries to test nonrivalry hypotheses, such as the democratic peace, power transition, and the like. The second generation of rivalry testing maintains this focus, but exploits more fully the testing possibilities of the rivalry approach. As with second-generation data gathering, we are only now beginning to see studies that utilize the wide range of rivalry methods.

First-generation testing was characterized by the use of rivalries to select disputes and wars, which were then analyzed in cross-sectional or cross-sectional time-series fashion. Huth and Russett's (1993) work on deterrence illustrates this first-generational procedure. Second-generation rivalry testing exploits first, and above all, the temporal dimension of rivalries. It uses before-and-after comparisons *within* rivalries. Gibler (1997) demonstrates this with his analysis of territorial settlement alliance treaties. He evaluated the impact of such treaties by comparing rivalries before and after these critical events.

There are numerous potential applications of this testing approach, and several of these were discussed in the first part of the book. Here, let us highlight just two of those possibilities. First, one might gain insights into the power transition by comparing power transition periods within nontransition periods in rivalries. As the contributors to the Kugler and Lemke collection (1996) have noted, war may be evident during the times of transition. Yet by comparing the frequency of conflict during the transition periods with that in other parts of the rivalry, scholars may be able to detect whether the incidence of war during transitions is spurious. It may be the case that the rivalry experiences war at several junctures, whether or not a power transition is occurring or not. Even if power transition periods are found to be more dangerous, the longitudinal perspective of the rivalry approach may be able to uncover alternative explanations for the pattern of increased conflict and facilitate a critical test between competing explanations.

A second testing possibility concerns the alleged relationship between arms races and war. Among the most controversial findings in the international conflict literature is that arms races are associated with dispute escalation. Yet, one of the most obvious specifications of a spurious relationship involves rivalries. Arms races are more likely in the context of enduring rivalries (Goertz and Diehl 1993). And we know from chapter 3 that both war in general and the likelihood of escalation in individual disputes are greater during enduring rivalries than in other conflict contexts. One hypothesis that emerges from this premise is that arms races and violent conflict are both manifestations of the enduring rivalries and thus not directly related to each other. This proposition is consistent with Sample's (1997) discovery of a large number of "no arms race, no war" cases and with Horn's (1987) reporting that longer arms races are associated with war. Enduring rivalry disputes may be inherently more prone to escalate than those earlier in the rivalry sequence (Hensel 1996). Indeed, Sample (1997) reports that "early" disputes between a given pair of states are unlikely to escalate even in the presence of arms races.

Diehl and Crescenzi (1998) reexamined Sample's (1997) data and found that evidence for a modest, positive, and statistically significant relationship between arms races and wars is largely confined to the enduring rivalry cases. That work could be extended by comparing different segments of the rivalry in which arms races were present to those in which they were absent in order to detect differences in escalatory tendencies, much as was suggested above for power transitions. The longitudinal perspective of the rivalry approach would also permit one to uncover the occurrence of arms races as *consequences* of rivalry escalation or war rather than only as causal agents. This distinction will not be apparent in static analyses and may suggest misleading conclusions about the place of arms races in the conflict escalation process.

Another characteristic of second-generation testing will be the inclusion of analyses using the rivalry as the unit of analysis. Those who use cross-sectional time-series must examine not only how a given model works for militarized disputes, but also for rivalries. For example, it is not very likely that Huth and Russett's deterrence model works equally well for all their enduring rivalries. By analyzing the poor fit and anomalous rivalries—not disputes—theory development can be facilitated. Thus, one might suggest the use of rivalry as the unit of analysis in all standard analyses of international conflict, if only as a supplement to test the robustness of the findings using conventional approaches.

A third characteristic of second-generation testing will be the inclusion of shorter-term, nonenduring rivalries. This plays an absolutely essential role in the study of conflict management hypotheses. For example, our analysis of the democratic peace would not have gotten off the ground without our use of proto-rivalries. The same holds true for Gibler's (1997) study; if the territorial settlement treaty ends a rivalry, this may well occur before it becomes an enduring rivalry. Thus, even to the extent that scholars adopt enduring rivalries as case selection devices, they must also appropriately include proto- and sometimes isolated rivalries as well, especially when theoretical formulations do not specify ongoing conflicts of a certain duration.

In summary, the future agenda of rivalries in testing involves developing procedures and methods that take into account and exploit (1) the temporal duration of rivalries, (2) the rivalry as the focus of analysis, and (3) the whole temporal gamut of rivalries from isolated to enduring. Our analysis of the democratic peace illustrates how the rivalry approach can provide new means to examine an already widely tested hypothesis. Other than Gibler's (1997) excellent study, the population of the second generation of rivalry testing remains very small. It should be a priority on a future rivalry agenda. We believe that our study and Gibler's only scratch the surface. As researchers begin to explore and exploit the rivalry approach in testing, new and rich techniques for testing will emerge.

Theory Development: Conflict Management

We have underlined throughout this volume that the rivalry approach applies to issues of both war and peace. Nevertheless, we have focused primarily on the war side of the coin. In the second part of the book, we presented a punctuated equilibrium model of enduring rivalries, and indeed much of our research agenda below is dedicated to further testing and extensions of that model. At the top of the future research agenda—at least our own agenda—lies a concentrated focus on conflict management and conflict termination in rivalries. Hence, for us, the second generation of rivalry work revolves around the conflict management side of (enduring) rivalries.

We have already briefly mentioned that the focus on conflict management has data-gathering and testing implications. On the data front, we need systematic data on conflict management variables for rivalries. In particular, we need data on efforts at mediation, arms control treaties, and proposed but failed negotiations. All these constitute activities on the conflict management side of the ledger. In terms of testing, we need to start evaluating conflict management theories in the rivalry context. There is an extensive literature on bargaining, negotiation, and mediation, largely from the fields of social psychology and labor-industrial relations. Yet this has been largely ignored (except by practitioners) with respect to international conflict. We know little about how applicable these social and psychological theories are to international relations.

A key part of this future research lies in developing conflict management dependent variables. We argued in chapter 10 that there exists no consensus of what medium- to long-term conflict management means in terms of behavior, not to mention at the conceptual level. We believe that our various proposals, developed in chapter 10, capture many commonly held ideas. Conceptualizing and measuring conflict management dependent variables forms the foundation of the policy implications of the rivalry approach for conflict management. To evaluate a policy, in the most concrete sense of the word, one needs criteria of success and failure. For example, there is only limited consensus on what constitutes success in the context of UN peacekeeping (Druckman and Stern 1997).

With data and measures of conflict management success in hand, we can begin to evaluate hypotheses and theories of conflict management. Of particular interest, in light of our work here, is the conjunction of our hypotheses about political shocks as necessary conditions, Kingdon's (1984) work on agenda setting, and Zartman's (1985) metaphor of ripeness.

The notion of the *conjunction* of factors lies at the heart of Kingdon's model and Zartman's metaphor. More precisely, it is *only* when there is a favorable confluence of factors that something makes it onto the political agenda or a conflict ripe is for resolution. Goertz (2000) has formally modeled Kingdon's ideas using necessary conditions. He argues that Kingdon makes a necessary condition claim as well as a sufficiency one. Kingdon argues an item will make it onto the agenda (1) only if the political context is favorable, (2) only if actors see a problem that needs attention, and (3) only if some political entrepreneurs provide some solution. Each of these "only if" requirements is a necessary condition for agenda success. Kingdon then argues that when these three necessary conditions happen to coincide or occur at the same time, the item actually makes it onto the agenda. More formally, the three necessary conditions are jointly sufficient (see Goertz 2000 for details).

Joint sufficiency, or as Kingdon would say, very high probability, taps Zartman's (1985) notion of ripeness. Only when a number of key factors coincide is a conflict ripe for resolution. Although much of the scholarly literature on ripeness is post hoc or tautological, the essential point is that conflict management efforts are only effective when launched in conjunction with some other favorable conditions. One such condition cited is the presence of a "hurting stalemate" between the parties, although the scholarly literature is not very specific about what other conditions might be relevant. Jointly, these conditions and a conflict management attempt are said to be sufficient for success.

Clearly our findings about political shocks as necessary conditions for rivalry termination fit naturally with ideas such as those of Zartman and Kingdon. Similar to Kingdon, we argue that shocks are necessary, but not sufficient, for rivalry initiation and termination. Also, what we count as a political shock enters into Kingdon's substantive factors either in creating a favorable context (international shocks) or political entrepreneurs (regime change variables). Our empirical analyses indicated that, on average, mediation attempts rarely succeeded in moderating rivalry dynamics. Kingdon finds the same thing for political entrepreneurs at the domestic level. But he finds also that successes are usually big ones, and that the best way to succeed is to keep pushing ideas until a ripe moment arrives.

Kingdon's model also explains the stability of rivalries. If change occurs only during a favorable confluence of factors, this itself is unlikely to happen very often. A simple numerical example illustrates this: if there are three factors, each of which is favorable 50 percent of the time, then we have a confluence of the three only 1/8 of the time (the probability of getting three heads when flipping three fair coins.)[2]

There are close links between the ripeness metaphor and the stability emphasized by the punctuated equilibrium model of enduring rivalries. Zartman's metaphor and Kingdon's model both serve to explain why change is rare. The punctuated equilibrium policy model of Baumgartner and Jones (1993) and their empirical analyses have demonstrated the stability of most U.S. domestic policies. They have also implicitly used confluence models—to give them a name—to describe certain periods of rapid policy shift:

> One cannot understand the rise and decline of the national urban initiative without appreciating the particular confluence of factors that occurred during the 1960s. An unprecedented window of opportunity opened during that time, in which three major social trends came into juxtaposition: America's postwar prosperity; social attitudes that, for brief moment in history, turned from economics to social issues: and the high watermark of the Democratic Rooseveltian coalition, led by an activist president with an ambitious domestic agenda. (Baumgartner and Jones 1993, 144)

Thus, we see developing a theory of conflict management in rivalries as beginning with many extant ideas in various scholarly literatures and being informed by many of the findings that we report in this book. Certainly, this does not exhaust the theoretical options and issues that need attention. For example, a key conflict management issue revolves around why some rivalries become

---

[2]For the same argument applied to the infrequency of war see Most and Starr 1989.

enduring. To explain why some rivalries become healthy and long-lived implies knowing why some rivalries are resolved at the proto-rivalry stage. Conflict management issues also arise at the beginning of rivalries: why do states move from the zone of peace to a state of militarized rivalry status? Throughout the rivalry life cycle, conflict management questions arise.

With the notable exception of the democratic peace, the study of war and conflict management have evolved along separate paths. As Ross (1996, 472) says:

> A paradox worth considering is how little attention the development of the field of conflict resolution has attracted from scholars of international war and peace. To be sure there are some significant exceptions, such as recent interest in the specific phenomenon of war termination, but a central reason for the absence of a broader discussion is that the core assumptions of theories of conflict resolution make little sense to the dominant theoretical approaches in international relations.

For us, perhaps the most attractive facet of the rivalry approach remains its possibilities to synthesize and embrace issues of war and peace.

Exploring Enduring Rivalries

Many issues of data gathering, testing, and conflict management apply to enduring rivalries as a special subset of rivalries. We need not repeat ourselves here, and hence we now limit ourselves to considerations directly related to enduring rivalries.

We have proposed the punctuated equilibrium model as the principle framework for understanding enduring rivalries, including their development, initiation, and termination. Obviously, our future agenda involves an examination, extension, and refinement of the punctuated equilibrium model. Before we go too far in the direction of the punctuated equilibrium model of rivalries, we think it prudent to assess its utility more carefully, especially vis-à-vis its competitors. One direction should be to explore the controversy occasioned by the punctuated equilibrium versus evolutionary (Hensel 1996) models debate on rivalry dynamics. As we noted in chapter 8, the evolutionary approach emphasized gradual development of rivalries, with an emphasis on the interactions and outcomes of the first few militarized confrontations in the rivalry sequence. There is no quick lock-in effect postulated, and indeed the dynamics of the first few confrontations in an enduring rivalry are thought to be different (generally less severe) than later disputes.

One test to distinguish between the punctuated equilibrium and evolutionary models would be to analyze conflict patterns within the population of enduring rivalries. The hypothesis to be tested could be that conflict in early stages of enduring rivalries is less severe than in later stages. A corollary proposition is that there is no significant difference in conflict severity in enduring rivalries' early stages and comparable phases in lesser rivalries. The evolutionary model is consistent with each of these hypotheses, whereas the punctuated equilibrium model would predict the opposite: more severe conflict, on the average, early in enduring rivalries and relatively consistent severity over the life of rivalries.

Hensel's (1996) aggregate analyses could not effectively test these hypotheses since the early phases of enduring rivalries are lumped together with the early parts of lesser and more numerous rivalries; therefore, enduring rivalry patterns are likely to get lost in the aggregate. His disaggregated analyses offer some insights into these hypotheses, although few direct tests. There is no statistically significant difference in severity and hostility levels in disputes that occur within different phases of enduring rivalries, although there is a slight tendency for stalemate outcomes to become more likely as the rivalry proceeds. The corollary hypothesis is not tested directly, although a cursory glance at some of Hensel's data shows mixed support for his evolutionary model. Of particular note, it is evident that decisive outcomes are much more difficult to achieve at all phases of enduring rivalries, suggesting structural factors are responsible. More direct and precise tests of the two models would help sort out which is more accurate and whether a hybrid model might best be constructed.

The priority of other items for the research agenda depends, in part, in resolving the punctuated equilibrium versus evolutionary debate. If the punctuated equilibrium model is more accurate, greater attention might be devoted to identifying further the structural factors that account for higher BRLs and therefore the greater likelihood of war in some rivalries. A research agenda occasioned by the evolutionary model would necessarily focus more on the maturation process of rivalries and on the thus far disappointing results with respect to learning. Greater attention would need to be paid to how some rivalries apparently are able to manage their conflicts (even as they endure) without war, whereas others repeatedly escalate to war.

Even if we find that the punctuated equilibrium model is superior (as we expect and our preliminary findings here indicate), our empirical findings in this book revealed that the punctuated equilibrium did not fit all enduring rivalries well. A key general item for future research thus lies in trying to understand why some rivalries deviate from the dominant punctuated equilibrium pattern. This involved analyses both in the area of conflict escalation as well as successful conflict management patterns. We have found evidence that rivalries do differ in their evolution, but we have provided no explanation for this fact.

Beyond the general elements of a research agenda on enduring rivalries, there are series of promising avenues that relate to specific elements of the rivalry life cycle.

Origins

Beyond our work on political shocks as necessary conditions for enduring rivalry initiation, no theoretical explanation exists for the origins of enduring rivalries. Within the context of the punctuated equilibrium model, it becomes even more important to study the initial period because this is when the long-term relationship gets established. Here we need to understand the escalatory process by which relationships deteriorate and hostile policies then get established between states.

A useful place to begin may be in studying how competitive relationships become militarized. One approach could be an investigation of commercial rivalries and their propensity to become militarized. There are a number of policy and theoretical imperatives that drive this focus. Levy and Ali (1998) indicate that such rivalries are an interesting point of analysis, and we need to probe the limits of generalization possible about this phenomenon, something that is not possible in a case study of one rivalry several hundred years ago. More importantly, however, understanding commercial rivalries will be an essential part of clarifying the relationship between interdependence and conflict. There has been a trend in the academic literature toward a more skeptical view of the economic interdependence-conflict relationship between states. Early work (Keohane and Nye 1977) touted the benefits of close and symmetrical ties between states and argued that war and other serious conflict was less likely between such states. In contrast, (Barbieri 1996) found that trade interdependence is positively associated with states becoming involved in militarized disputes, even controlling for a range of other influences. Studying commercial rivalries can help us understand how some competitions become militarized as well as provide further evidence on the interdependence-conflict debate.

The study of commercial rivalries has more than a theoretical rationale behind it. Academic study is often driven by contemporary policy concerns (note that the timing of the renewed interest in the democratic peace coincides with the third wave of global democratization) as much as by abstract theoretical concerns. With the rise of the "trading state" (Rosecrance 1986) and the end of the Cold War, economic rivalries are likely to be the most common form of competition between states in the world, especially among the major powers. Rather than making the analysis of militarized conflict passé, these rivalries suggest a closer examination of how competition evolves over time and when trade, resource, and other disputes are translated into more dangerous forms of confrontation. Generally, there is precious little (an exception may be Conybeare 1987 or perhaps, to some extent, Choucri and North 1975) on this subject.

Beyond the focus on commercial rivalries, there are many other traditional approaches to understanding conflict initiation, including power distributions and the like, and these are summarized elsewhere (Maoz 1982). Nevertheless, the core theoretical and empirical work that needs to be done to develop the punctuated equilibrium model revolves around the policy processes by which governments lock into rivalries, that is, when they reach the militarized stage. Our brief discussions of foreign policy decision making have relied heavily on the domestic politics literature that supports the punctuated equilibrium model. For a period in the 1970s the organizational model of Allison (1971) received a great deal of attention in international relations, but then it rapidly faded in prominence. The general sort of organizational model we propose obviously has links with the international relations literature generated in the 1970s. Yet we think that much more can be gained by thinking in the terms of Jones, Baumgartner, and Kingdon than in those of Allison. Nevertheless, foreign policy is not domestic policy, and work is required to modify and adjust an organizational politics model so that it fits international relations.

The Allison approach and the organizational model were problematic in that the latter provided no theory of significant organizational change. While the punctuated equilibrium model argues that stability is the norm, the model must also explain why and when change takes place. If we go back to the biological origins of the punctuated equilibrium theory, it would have been ridiculous for Gould and Eldredge to argue that there was no evolution. Rather, they said that evolution occurred in fits and starts. In particular, they pinpointed periods of mass extinction, which then provided the opportunity for rapid evolution (Raup 1992). Hence we need a foreign policy decision-making model that takes into account that policies do change, sometimes dramatically.

The decision-making model that we have loosely referred to as organizational is also one that focuses on domestic politics. Policies do not change, in part, because players in government have no reason to change them. Traditionally, the source of this is thought to come from the international realm, yet we suspect that domestic factors play at least as important a role. Very few elected officials in the United States had any electoral reason to be associated with conciliatory moves to the USSR, and the same is likely true (perhaps even more so) in closed systems such as the USSR. One can apply Waltz's (1979) natural selection argument using domestic instead of international politics. The 1950s saw the elimination of many bureaucrats and elected officials favorable to reconciliation with the USSR. In Waltzian fashion, the nature of U.S. policy was influenced because some policies were successful in domestic terms, while others failed. Even the massive shock of the Vietnam War did little to affect this basic state of affairs.

The field of international conflict has one well-developed decision-making model—the rational actor one—which has many opponents, but no well-developed alternatives. The punctuated equilibrium model relies on a different view of governmental decision making. It does not assume that governments, organizations, and leaders are "irrational," but rather that the "national interest" is up for grabs, as well as the best policies for pursuing that "national interest."

If we take the case of Israel, is it in Israeli national interest to put settlers in occupied territories? Should annexation be a goal of Israeli policy? Clearly both the means and the ends are up for debate. From the punctuated equilibrium point of view, those who propose the dismantling of Jewish settlements have the cards stacked against them. Colonization has marched forward under both Labor and Likud governments. As Braybrooke and Lindbolm (1963, 93) say:

> Although there is a fundamental sense in which ends govern means, there is an equally fundamental sense in which the proximate ends of public policy are governed by means. . . . Clearly what we establish as policy objectives we derive in large part by our inspection of means.

This organizational sort of decision-making model appears to underlie the punctuated equilibrium model of enduring rivalries. We have furnished no evidence, however, that such is actually the case. If we examine the histories and analyses of some enduring rivalries, we find much to support such a view. But we need more than intuitively plausible readings of particular rivalries; rather, we require systematic analysis and confirmation.

Dynamics

Based on the findings in this study, there seem to be at least three other critical areas of research concerning the dynamics of enduring rivalries: their maintenance, variation in the basic rivalry levels across rivalries, and the volatility of conflict within rivalries (including most significantly the outbreak of war). The first concern is with the maintenance of rivalries. Cioffi-Revilla (1998) and Bennett (1998) indicate that rivalries are unstable in their later phases, suggesting that some process sets into reverse the effects of rivalry maintenance factors. Yet according to conventional definitions of enduring rivalries, they can last more than 40 years. Factors are at work that seem to mitigate the unstable tendencies of rivalries, or there may be "stress" that appears only later, allowing some rivalries to persist well into the future. A valuable line of research would be to identify the conditions that make rivalries persist and conflict to recur repeatedly in the rivalry.

The studies here and elsewhere provide some clues to the conditions for rivalry maintenance. One possibility is the kind of issues or stakes under dispute. Vasquez (1998) suggests that territorial disputes are most prone to recurring conflict, given that they relate closely to concerns about national identity and can become linked to other intangible and indivisible stakes; Huth (1996b) makes similar claims in his study of territorial disputes. Hensel (1996) confirms the importance of territorial disputes in prompting future conflict and doing so more rapidly than other issues. Nevertheless, not all territorial disputes are subject to recurrence; much depends on the way that those disputes are resolved. Thus, another consideration is to go beyond the structural aspects of the rivalry relationships and concentrate on the interactions between the rival states. In effect, the past and present dynamics of a rivalry will influence its future dynamics. Maoz and Mor (1998) indicated that only when there is some dissatisfaction among at least one of the rivals does a rivalry continue. Some game structures make this all but inevitable (e.g., Bully games will leave the losing side unhappy with the inferior payoff). Yet it also suggests that certain outcomes of disputes are more likely to prompt future conflict. Those outcomes that do not resolve issues in disputes (stalemates) may lead to a return to militarized confrontation. Vasquez (1998) refers not only to territorial issues, but unresolved ones as instigators of recurring militarized conflict. Similarly, Hensel (1996) finds compromise dispute outcomes dampen the prospects for future conflict. That particular power distributions are associated with rivalry onset (see Levy and Ali 1998; and Vasquez 1998) and stability indicates that changes in them may influence which rivalries die out and which persist. One might suggest that rivalries in which there is a widening disparity in capability between the rivals are more prone to end quickly.

Our analyses indicate that even though conflict levels in most rivalries are consistent across time, some rivalries have higher basic rivalry levels than others and some exhibit more variation (volatility) than others. Another area of fruitful research would be to understand why some rivalries are far more hostile than others. This goes beyond concerns of duration and stability noted above to those of conflict intensity. Clues to the puzzle above might be found in other traditional correlates of war. One possibility suggested by Geller (1998) is that instability in the power distribution prompts greater uncertainty and threat for the rivals. One might also return to the issues in dispute noted above as an explanation; territorial and other disputes may present higher stakes that lead rivals to adopt more coercive bargaining strategies and respond to challenges with a higher level of force. Of course, certain game structures, suggested by Maoz and Mor (1998), tend to produce more conflictual outcomes (whereas some offer greater incentives for cooperation). It may be useful to compare the game structures across different rivalries to explain the higher levels of conflict in some rivalries. A focus on the game transformation process would not only help us with rivalry dynamics, but in devising strategies to "downshift" especially dangerous rivalries (assuming that game transformation conditions are manipulable by rivals or by external intervention).

Finally, the volatility of rivalries is a prime item for an enduring rivalries research agenda, not least because we share a strong concern for the most dangerous of deviations in the rivalry relationship—war. Understanding volatility and war in enduring rivalries is partly related to understanding differences across rivalries in the basic rivalry level. Those rivalries that regularly operate at a high conflict level need less of a push to cross the war threshold than those rivalries that do not move much beyond the mere threat to use military force. Yet, beyond this there still lies the concern with what factors make a rivalry more or less hostile at various points. Unstable capability distributions may ratchet a rivalry up the escalation ladder and explain why Geller (1998) found that type of instability so important in the outbreak of war among major-power rivals. By studying linked conflict, we found that conflict levels can be influenced by the dynamics in other rivalries. For example, the superpower rivalry between the United States and the Soviet Union may have influenced the course of the rivalries between Israel and its neighbors; Kinsella (1994a, 1994b) shows that the conflict levels in some Middle East rivalries were influenced by the arms transfer policies of the superpowers. Changes in rivalry conflict levels may also be affected by other challenges or disputes that a given rival may face, beyond those in the immediate rivalry; there even may be a dampening effect on outside conflict and rivalry conflict when the attention and resources of rival states are stretched. These are provocative ideas that enduring rivalry research has barely considered.

Termination

In contrast to other parts of rivalry research, there has been comparatively more done on the termination of rivalries than other subjects. Stemming largely from the work of Bennett (1993, 1996, 1997a, 1997b, 1998), a number of interesting ideas on the conditions associated with rivalry termination, including domestic political considerations, changing security configurations, and the like, have been advanced. Yet Bennett (1998) has treated those as potentially competing propositions and attempted to test each one's relative explanatory capability against one another. Perhaps a better way, suggested by the punctuated equilibrium model, is to understand how various factors work *together* to end rivalries. If political shocks are only necessary conditions for rivalry termination, then one must look for other factors that are coterminous with political shocks in order to produce the end of rivalries. This cannot be achieved when different factors are juxtaposed against one another and tested in a fashion that assumes that they are additive, and not necessary and conjunctural. Not surprisingly, the results will be mixed (see Bennett 1998) and will miss the impact that the confluence of these different factors might have in ending rivalries. Although theorizing on rivalry termination is better developed than on origins or dynamics, current work is still trapped in the conventional linear and additive thinking that is characteristic of traditional war studies.

Rivalry termination work will also be largely informed by the progress made on conflict management and resolution, as detailed above. The ways that rivals manage the competition themselves or the impact of third-party interventions may give us insights into how states successfully end a competition. Whatever the direction of future research on rivalry termination, a key priority is that greater attention be paid to rivalries that are *not* enduring. That is, many of the clues on how long-standing competitions end are likely to be found by examining rivalries that do not mature, that die out or are resolved before they become enduring rivalries. This ties back to our concern with understanding the factors that maintain rivalries. At the same time a focus on proto- and isolated rivalries may also reveal what structural or behavioral conditions make it easier for rivalries to be resolved and thereby allow the analyst to detect the absence of those conditions or trace the movement toward those conditions in enduring rivalries.

At the outset of this book, we sought to redefine the ways that scholars look at issues of war and peace. We do not believe that the rivalry approach is the only fruitful one or that a punctuated equilibrium model can account for all rivalry behavior. We are convinced, however, that they allow us to break out of the stifling norms of traditional studies of war and peace, with the results being new data, insights, hypotheses, and ultimately theories.

Appendix A
The Rivalry Web Site

The data used for the various analyses in this book are available on the web site:

http://www.pol.uiuc.edu/faculty/diehl.html

The documentation for the web site and the data files contained therein can be found in the file "rivalry.readme." This file contains the description of the data found in the files "rivalry1.data, rivalry2.data ..." All files are in ASCII format. We encourage those interested in part of the data to download the whole site (via the option provided on the web page), which is quite small, less than one megabyte.

The purpose of the web site is to provide the data used in this book for replication or further analysis. In most cases, the basic raw data are no longer the most current. Hence this site should *not* be used as a source for data on militarized disputes, regime type, and the like.

In some instances, particularly regarding descriptive statistics, the raw data provided need further processing before our results can be obtained. But in no case does this require extensive programming beyond calculating means, finding sums, and so forth.

The web site also assumes that one is in possession of this book. The file readme.txt provides only the basic data structure and variables with links to the tables of each chapter.

We welcome questions, comments, suggestions (and praise), which can be sent to either or both authors at

p-diehl@uiuc.edu

ggoertz@u.arizona.edu

Appendix B
An Index of Dispute Severity

In this appendix, we develop a new measure of dispute severity. There are several purposes in this exercise. More immediately for our needs, such a measure of dispute severity allows us to track hostility levels in rivalries. Disputes are the main signposts along the way that help define rivalries and their continuation. In chapter 3, we use the dispute severity measure to investigate whether some kinds of rivalries are more severe than others. An indicator of dispute severity is also important in developing an operational measure of the basic rivalry level (BRL), first explicated in chapter 9. Patterns in dispute severity over time help us determine whether that basic rivalry level is consistent over time, as predicted by the punctuated equilibrium model (see chapter 7), as well as whether conflict management or escalatory patterns of behavior are evident in a given rivalry.

Although the dispute severity indicator was constructed to serve our needs in this book, we also sought to construct an indicator with broader applications. Thus, we want a measure of dispute severity that has general validity, one that can be used in many theoretical contexts. In this sense, we follow J. David Singer's philosophy that good data sets can be used for multiple purposes. Most obviously, a good indicator of dispute severity is essential for studies that seek to predict conflict. The overwhelming majority of militarized confrontations do not escalate to war, and a more precise indicator of the relative severity of those disputes or crises would allow scholars to predict and explain the most and least serious of those conflicts. The implicit assumption in extant research is that these confrontations are largely indistinguishable. Furthermore, an interval measure would permit an analysis of the bargaining behavior of states and its impact on outcomes across disputes or crises. We could then assess whether conflict management strategies resulted in lower levels of conflict between states or whether the impacts were negligible. Currently we can only assess whether states are able to avoid war, and thus we have little sense whether they can manage conflict at lower levels.

In summary, this appendix has a simple goal: develop an indicator of dispute severity. Nevertheless, doing so forces us to reexamine and question basic conceptualizations and practices. It turns out that the small act of indicator construction forces an examination of some basic principles and methodological practices. Our indicator rests on these basic ideas, to which we now turn.

Causes of War: Theory and Practice

The conceptualization of war as a dependent variable in conflict studies rests on theory, data, and methodological practice. These three are deeply intertwined and cannot be completely separated. Indeed, it is because they are so interrelated that our indicator construction project requires us to examine theory, data, and methodology. At a basic level, our proposal is to replace the war/no war distinction by a continuous measure of dispute severity that includes war. This suggests that the war/no war dichotomization misses important aspects or misrepresents key dimensions of the phenomenon of international militarized conflict.

When the COW project decided to base its dichotomous definition of war on the number of military fatalities, the tension inherent in the contrast between fatalities, which are continuous, and war, which is categorical, existed. Of course, one very early—and easy—critique was that there are cases of war that fall just below the one thousand-death cutoff, or some nonwar incidents that land above (Duvall 1976). For example, the Battle of Savarino Bay is not a war, while the Soviet-Japanese skirmishes in the late 1930s were coded as wars. Indeed, this is partly the basis for a reformulation of the war data set by Siverson and Tennefoss (1982), who adopt a lower threshold of fatalities. Even the critics, however, classified war in the same dichotomous terms. The disagreement was over the fatality threshold level or its precision and not over the dichotomous conceptualization of war.

We have no objection to referring to very serious militarized disputes as wars, but the question is the degree to which we want to formulate scientific hypotheses in those terms. To choose an analogy from physics, in common parlance we talk about hot and cold water. Yet, as scientists, we want to use temperature as our dependent variable. This has important implications for the framing of hypotheses and the interpretation of statistical methods. For example, the democratic peace is framed in terms such as "democracies do not fight wars," not in terms of a hypothesis about how severe disputes between democracies are. Rummel (1995) indicates the democratic peace is most evident with respect to violence severity, a claim that cannot be properly tested with a simple war/no war analysis. The dichotomous conceptualization then produces strained discussions of whether Finland–United Kingdom in World War II counts as a "war" between democracies (Russett 1993; Ray 1995).

If we examine methodological practice, a related set of issues arises. For example, given the dichotomous dependent variable, most studies use event history statistical methods such as probit and logit. These statistical methods provide a continuous predicted value between 0 and 1. How is this usually interpreted? The answer is virtually always in terms of the probability of war; for example, a predicted value of .70 means that the predicted probability of war is 70 percent. With our continuous indicator and concept, as well as the adoption of different statistical methods, the predicted value is the level of dispute severity. As the logic of the democratic peace applies to dispute severity as well, such a dispute severity dependent variable would allow us to determine where the threshold of severity for the democratic peace really lies. It may be that it falls significantly below all wars, a finding that is not easily discernible using the war/no war classification.

Another tension lies in the conceptualization of war as a potentially multilateral event and the practice of statistical analysis of *dyads*. For example, Vasquez (1996) has argued that there are two paths leading to war, one through dyadic rivalry and the other through multilateral contagion. As we shall see below, the practice of "dyadization" of multilateral wars proves quite problematic in most works using MID data. It turns out that many dyadic relationships within a multilateral war do not deserve the label *war*, and in fact are not coded as such in the MID data set itself. For example, the U.S. participation in the Opium War was not a war from the American point of view, but certainly was from the Chinese standpoint; correspondingly China is assigned a war code, while the United States gets the use-of-force coding.

Another hidden implication of the dichotomous war/no war coding arises from the use of event history methods. These models are all nonlinear. Thus, for example, when analyzing the impact of a given variable, one normally holds the other variables either at the extremes or at their means. If one were to have an interval level dispute dependent variable, almost certainly researchers would use linear regression. Rarely are conflict theories explicit on the linear versus nonlinear question (Gelpi 1997). Most of the time this occurs as a side effect of the methodology: linear for regression and nonlinear for event history techniques. Yet some theories are implicitly nonlinear. For example, necessary condition hypotheses (which include the democratic peace and the power transition hypotheses) imply nonlinearity, and probit and logit models do not accurately test these necessary condition theories (Braumoeller and Goertz 1997). It is certainly the case that one can test linear versus nonlinear models more easily with a continuous dependent variable. Here the dichotomous dependent variable induces through the event history methodology a nonlinear model. In principle, it should work the other way around: the theory should determine the functional form of the statistical model, not the measurement of the dependent variable. It is easily forgotten, particularly in the statistical testing literature, that "theory" means more than a particular collection of variables, that it also should include functional form.

By moving from an exclusive focus on war to dispute severity, we expand dramatically the range of phenomena we can examine, which itself is a spur to theoretical development. One of the current interests in international conflict studies is conflict management and resolution. If we want to investigate and evaluate peacekeeping and mediation success, for example, we need a much finer-grained measure of dispute severity. One of our interests (see the second part of this book) is the evolution of rivalries (see also Diehl 1998). Yet it is all but impossible to track changes in rivalry dynamics without a more nuanced look at dispute severity; by focusing only on the war/no war distinction, scholars will miss trends toward increasing or decreasing (e.g., conflict management) interactions.

The core of our severity measure goes back to the original idea of the COW project: the severity of a militarized conflict is very closely related to the number of fatalities. Because we are not concerned with "war" per se, we need not worry about a strict demarcation between wars and nonwars. Of course, many problems remain. We now turn to the theoretical and practical aspects of developing a measure of the concept of dispute severity.

Previous Efforts at Measuring Conflict Severity

There have not been extensive efforts to develop interval measures of conflict severity in the international conflict literature, largely because the concern has been with understanding the conditions for war and not with more subtle variations among conflict events. In making a distinction between severities of conflict, we begin with the war/no war distinction that dominates the literature. The Correlates of War Project (Small and Singer 1982) developed the most widely used measure, although there are also other classic formulations (Richardson 1960; Wright 1965). Generally these efforts have used the number of battle-related fatalities to distinguish wars from other conflict; for Small and Singer the threshold for war is set at one thousand deaths.

The war/no war distinction has some significant shortcomings as a basis for assessing conflict severity (see Duvall, 1976). Most obviously, the simple dichotomous classification ignores enormous variations within each of the two categories. For example, there is no distinction made between crises that involved a significant use of force and fatalities on the one hand and seizures of fishing boats on the other. Furthermore, relatively minor wars such as the Football War between Honduras and El Salvador are lumped together with major conflagrations such as World Wars I and II. In addition, the Correlates of War Project list of militarized disputes, which includes disputes that went to war as well as those that did not, has some cases in which some participants are coded as having gone to war while other participants did not reach the war level. How does one categorize a conflict when some participants get a war coding and others do not? At the aggregate level, a conflict can be categorized as a war if only one disputant reaches the appropriate level of hostility or fatalities to be coded as a war. Furthermore, a state may have exactly the same number of fatalities in two different conflicts and one can be coded as a war and the other not. This makes the use of even the simple dichotomous classification problematic.

Similar to the distinction between war and its absence are attempts to distinguish whether a conflict is a crisis or not (Wilkenfeld, Brecher, and Moser 1988). An international crisis occurs when there is "(1) distortion in the type and an increase in the intensity of disruptive interactions between two or more adversaries, with an accompanying high probability of military hostilities, or, during a war an adverse change in military balance, and (2) a challenge to the existing structure of an international system . . . posed by the higher than normal conflict interactions" (Wilkenfeld, Brecher, and Moser 1988, 3). Unlike the criteria identifying war events, the ones used to distinguish between crises and other events include some relatively intangible variables. Not only does this make it difficult to again draw a dichotomous distinction, but it is not very helpful in providing any basis for constructing an operational, interval-level measure.

The International Crisis Behavior (ICB) data set makes distinctions between the severities of different crises. The ICB data set includes data concerning several dimensions of crisis severity. Severity is assessed by (1) the number of actors involved, (2) the level of involvement by great powers, (3) the geostrategic salience of the conflict, (4) the degree of attribute difference (military economic, political, cultural) between the participants, (5) the number of crisis issues and the presence of military security issues, and (6) the extent of violence in the crisis. The data set includes an index of crisis severity that is a weighted summation of the six dimensions of severity. The weights assigned each indicator are based on the number of postulated linkages between one dimension and all the others. The overall severity scores are then transformed to a 1–10 integer scale. Although this index provides an aggregate measure of crisis severity, it is not clear that it is truly interval level and it still suffers from the shortcoming that it is constructed largely independent of the actual behavior of the crisis actors. Only the violence dimension refers to any behavioral characteristics of the crisis in defining its severity. The remaining dimensions characterize the attributes of the participants or the substance and location of the crisis. The ICB method of measuring severity appears to confound the *causes* of severity from the severity dependent variable itself. For us, the first five factors would typically be part of the explanation of crisis severity, not crisis severity itself.

Other crisis data sets (Leng and Singer 1988) do not contain a specific index of severity. Rather, there is a description of individual events or actions within the crisis (e.g., verbal threat and surrender) that may provide the basis for comparative scaling in terms of severity or hostility. Indeed, such data have been used to explore the various coercive or reciprocal bargaining strategies within crises (Leng 1993). Yet it is not clear how one would aggregate these events (more than 25 thousand events across 40 crises in the Behavioral Correlates of War—BCOW—data set) to formulate an overall severity measure.

The Correlates of War MID data set includes measures of the highest level of hostility (LOH) reached during the course of the dispute by each of the participants. The scale is an ordinal one, ranging from 1 to 5, where 1 is no military response (relevant only for the target state), 2 is threat of military force, 3 is display of military force, 4 is use of military force, and 5 is full-scale war (Gochman and Maoz 1984; Jones, Bremer, and Singer 1996). Goertz and Diehl (1998) used a multiplicative scheme using the LOH scores of each rival to indicate conflict severity. Crescenzi and Enterline (1998) go one step further in constructing a "rivalry" severity score for each dyad; their technique uses the LOH score for disputes along with a time decay function. Yet their measure may be suitable when rivalries or rivalry years are the units of analysis, but the measure cannot be easily disaggregated to the dispute level although it uses a dispute severity indicator (the level-of-hostility variable) as one input. There are several limitations to the simple LOH scale. By definition "militarized dispute" limits the consideration to events that involve at least the possibility of military force and therefore does not distinguish between hostile and coercive actions that do not involve military force. Although this scheme is a useful refinement of the basic dispute/war classification, there are still problems with using it for severity. First, the five-point scale is only ordinal, incapable of distinguishing the magnitude of difference across the categories. Second, the scale does not recognize the huge differences (in costs, duration, etc.) between simple disputes and wars; indeed, war is considered only the most severe form of dispute. Third, there is little consideration of the relative symmetry of state behavior. Traditionally, conflict studies define dispute severity as the highest level of hostility achieved by *any one state in the dispute*. This codes as equivalent cases where both sides use force (i.e., 4-4 dispute) and those where one side made no militarized response (4-1 dispute). Finally, the scale does not distinguish between different war severities, therefore offering little improvement over the simple war/no war distinction.

The most recent edition of the Correlates of War dispute data set (Jones, Bremer, and Singer 1996) contains a 22-point scale for militarized action in a dispute, given in table B.1 (for an application using this scale as well as fatality levels, see Senese 1996). Although there are some helpful distinctions between actions that fall within the same category on the original five-point scale, it is not clear that the scale is even of ordinal character, much less an interval measure. Is a show of troops inherently less severe than a show of ships or planes? Are threats to blockade (technically an act of war under classical international law) different from the threat to occupy territory or go to war? One might clearly say that a nuclear alert was more serious than a simple military alert, but is a nuclear alert less severe than a mobilization or other action? These rankings are not obvious, and certainly context-specific factors may lead to a dramatic reordering of actions on a hierarchy of severity. Most critically, according to Stuart Bremer (personal communication), COW only recorded the

TABLE B.1: MID Hostility Scale

5-Level Scale	22-Level Scale
1 = No militarized action	1 = No militarized action
2 = Threat to use force	2 = Threat to use force
	3 = Threat to blockade
	4 = Threat to occupy territory
	5 = Threat to declare war
	6 = Threat to use nuclear weapons
3 = Display of force	7 = Show of troops
	8 = Show of ships
	9 = Show of planes
	10 = Alert
	11 = Nuclear alert
	12 = Mobilization
	13 = Fortify border
	14 = Border violation
4 = Use of force	15 = Blockade
	16 = Occupation of territory
	17 = Seizure
	18 = Clash
	19 = Other use of force
	20 = Declaration of war
	21 = Use of CBR weapons
5 = War	22 = Interstate war

first act within the narrower five-point hostility scale, rather than necessarily the highest act (1–22 scale within the categories); for example, if a blockade (15) by one state occurred before an act of seizure (17), only the blockade is recorded in the MID set, as both fall under level of hostility 4. This compromises the use of the 22 point scale as an accurate representation of dispute severity.

Maoz (1982) constructed an interval measure of dispute severity from an early version of the COW dispute data set. Using a 14-category scale of actions (a middle ground between later five- and 22-point categorizations), the temporal order in which various "incidents" occurred that make up a dispute, and data on these individual incidents, he constructed a dispute-level measure of severity. In some ways, the Crescenzi and Enterline (1998) measure does for rivalries what Maoz (1982) did for disputes. In each case, individual incidents or disputes and their occurrence over time are used to construct a severity indicator.

Wang (1995) developed an interval scale of U.S. responses to foreign policy crises, using insights from the both the COW and ICB data collections. He created 11 categories of responses scaled from 0 to 1 with compliance and external violent military responses representing the end points. Theoretically, one could construct a similar scale for crisis initiators or other participants, but it is not clear that all such categories would be applicable (compliance, for example, is an inappropriate category for an initiating state), and there is still a question of how to aggregate the scores of the different crisis actors.

Beyond the Correlates of War and International Crisis Behavior Projects, others have constructed hostility scales. COPDAB (Azar 1982) and WEIS (McClelland 1976) are events data collections that classify specific actions of states on 16-point ordinal and 60-point nominal scales respectively. One benefit of these schemes is that cooperative actions as well as conflictual ones are recognized. Because they are events data compilations, there are considerably more actions than are present in the MID data set. Thus, a measure of dispute severity would require an aggregation of some or all relevant events within the appropriate time frames; in some cases, a useful time-series must be constructed from the raw data (see Goldstein 1992 for a technique to do this with WEIS data). There are also several difficulties with using events data. Most obviously, events data are available only since 1945 (and then not necessarily for all countries), making longitudinal analyses of some dyads or rivalries impossible and precluding analyses of conflicts before World War II. Second, good reasons exist to believe that COPDAB and WEIS compilations may not be reliable or valid (Howell 1983). Third, the aggregation of many different events may obscure the salience of some key ones, most likely those involving military force, and the aggregated measure may underestimate the severity of the confrontation.

Finally, some scholars have argued that disputes over certain issues are inherently more dangerous or severe than other disputes, with territory being the issue most often cited (Vasquez 1993). Thus, it might be argued that some attention be given to issue in noting the severity of a conflict. We reject this implication. The issue of a given dispute is perhaps a valid predictor of conflict or escalation, but it should not be used as an indicator of the severity of that conflict. We must not confuse causal factors associated with conflict severity, with measures of the magnitude of severity itself.

The Underlying Dispute Severity Concept

In developing an index of dispute severity, we must pay attention to the underlying concept that we are trying to measure. It seems clear that if we define *severity* as "degree of military force used," then threats are less severe than displays of military force, which in turn are less severe than uses of force. Nevertheless, *severe* has other connotations. For example, most analysts consider the Cuban missile crisis as the most severe crisis between the United States and the USSR, yet this only gets coded as 4 (15) for the United States and 4 (19) for the Soviet Union in the MID data. This crisis may have been more severe than many uses of force, which receive a higher coding in the COW level-of-hostility scheme.

It is clear that severity does not always equal "degree of military force used," at least in the intuitive sense. Here, severity appears to indicate "risk of war." This is the implicit notion of severity that arises using event history methodologies (see above). We think that trying to explain the probability of war or evaluating dispute severity in terms of the risk of war constitutes a valuable, but different, research enterprise. One practical problem with using dispute severity defined as risk of war is that there is no independent evaluation or data for this. The estimates produced by event history techniques obviously depend on the model, data, and indicators used in the given study; one can hardly use these as relatively "theory neutral" measures across a wide range of topics. Part of our goal is an indicator, similar to the COW definition of war, that is usable across a range of problems and theoretical perspectives.

It is important to understand that all scales—including those in the natural sciences—include theoretical and empirical considerations. The COW level-of-hostility scale is no exception. On the one hand, obviously theoretical notions about what constitutes increasing levels of military force are taken into consideration, but that is only part of the story behind the scale. Richard Stoll reports (personal communication) that when coding disputes, researchers at the COW project noted that the scale ordering was not only a level of force 1, but also represented a common temporal order of "escalation" (this word itself implies some sort of scale) of a crisis or war. Maoz (1982) quite explicitly used an analogous temporal ordering principle to construct his interval scale.

Thus, before moving to the details of our proposed measure, we need to ask how we conceptualize severity (we will henceforth use the term *dispute* to refer to both nonwar and war disputes, unless the context indicates otherwise). There are a number of general principles that guide our development of a measure of dispute severity.

First, we look for a unidimensional measure of dispute severity. For example, events data use a cooperation-to-conflict scale, implicitly signifying *one* dimension.

Second, we believe that severity increases with the level of military threat or force.

Third, we see dispute severity ideally as a scale that increases with the level of *actual* military force. It should be explicitly stated that we are looking for a *behavioral* measure. It is quite possible that the level of hostility at the psychological level does not correspond to the level expressed in action. Here it is important to keep in mind that we want to use the dispute severity measure most often as a dependent variable. Hostility as a psychological variable is more often used as an independent variable (i.e., as an explanation of behavior). Thus, we can contrast the actual severity level against the risk-of-war perspective on dispute severity. In well-defined situations, we can talk about "objective risk," such as in classic probability, gambling, and natural science applications, but it appears almost impossible to develop something analogous for international war.

Fourth, another important distinction is that we are trying to determine the severity level for the dispute between two countries: the unit of analysis is the dyad. The dyad is the preferred unit of analysis for dispute severity given its predominance in studies of international conflict and its flexibility in application; with respect to the latter, one can aggregate dyad scores for a multilateral dispute score, but the reverse is not true. Obviously, this dispute-level variable will be constructed with data about what each participant itself has done. Even at the simplest level, however, one has to make a decision how to combine the data from the two parties into a dispute-level measure: should one add, multiply, or take the maximum of the two disputants' scores? Thus, we have at least three different options, each of which produces quite different results. We discuss these options in the next section.

Related to the fourth concern is a preference for a measure that captures the symmetry of the conflict level achieved by both rivals, the fifth general measurement principle. Frequently, the conflict level of militarized disputes has been measured by reference to the most severe acts of military force committed by one state, ignoring that the other party may exhibit a much less hostile reaction, or indeed no response at all. Some militarized disputes involve no military reaction by the target state after the initiating state threatens or uses military force (Hensel and Diehl 1994). Thus, the severity level should be greater when military actions are met with reciprocity as opposed to less hostile reactions. This is consistent with the dyad being the unit of analysis.

Sixth, we prefer an interval measure rather than the nominal or ordinal ones that generally characterize past efforts. An interval measure permits more precise conclusions to be drawn about severity and opens up a much broader range of statistical techniques and theoretical models to use in understanding dispute severity and its correlates.

Seventh and pragmatically, we are confined to constructing an indicator for which we have the necessary data. Variables that already exist in the COW militarized interstate dispute (MID) data set (Jones, Bremer, and Singer 1996) as well as the COW war data set will form the bases of our efforts.

In short, we are looking for (1) a unidimensional measure (2) that increases (monotonically, but not necessarily linearly) the level of force, (3) that uses the actual military force used or its effects, (4) that describes the dyadic dispute as a whole, (5) that reflects the symmetry of dispute participant behavior, (6) that is interval level, and finally and pragmatically, (7) is one for which we have data. Notice that unlike the Maoz (1982) scale or the simple COW level-of-hostility scale, we do not assume that this scale represents a temporal order of events.

A Measure of Dispute Severity

If we examine the basic idea behind the Small-Singer (1982) war data set, we find that the number of battlefield fatalities effectively indicates the severity of militarized conflict. They defined war as incidents that result in one thousand or more fatalities. We extend this to the principle that the severity of a war or dispute is a function of the number of fatalities, and therefore dispute severity will be, partly, a function of the number of deaths that occur in each conflict incident. This is suitable for disputes that actually have fatalities, but the large majority of militarized disputes involve no deaths. Clearly among this larger group, some disputes are more severe than others are. Hence, we need another procedure for measuring severity in nonfatality cases. The MID data set does provide information on severity levels for nonwar cases; this is contained in the level-of-hostility variable, an ordinal variable ranging from 1, no response, to 5, war, described above.

Our first operational principle in constructing a severity measure from all disputes and wars is therefore this: if fatality levels are greater than zero, then the severity level is a function of those battle deaths. The second principle is that if the fatality level is zero, then the severity level is a function of the level-of-hostility variable for the dispute. A third principle is that disputes with fatalities are more severe than disputes without deaths. We recognize that some conflicts are very serious and nearly lead to war even though there is no loss of life and that a few conflicts inadvertently result in bloodshed and death but do not pose the same risk of war. Nevertheless, the loss of life has strong symbolic, substantive, and domestic political implications and necessarily conditions the perceptions and accompanying responses of decision makers. For these reasons, we regard fatalities as a key component of our indicator of dispute severity.

Having specified our general approach, several problems remain to be solved. We must first construct interval level measures for each part of the scale, the zero- and nonzero-fatality segments. Then we must devise a mechanism to splice them together to form one overall measure that is comparable across different disputes.

We begin with the zero-fatality portion of the scale. The first question is how to combine the data from the two level-of-hostility variables (one for each disputant) to form a dyad-level value. Three simple options exist: (1) addition, (2) multiplication, and (3) the maximum of the two. Currently, almost all users of the MID data set take the maximum option, that is, the severity of the dispute is indicated by the highest level of hostility achieved by any party to the dispute. We think option 2, multiplication, makes the most sense. This alternative appears to deal with asymmetrical cases (those in which the rivals do not reach the same level of hostility) in the best fashion. To take the extreme example, one rival can reach a level of hostility of 5 (war) while its opponent

292 An Index of Dispute Severity

only reaches the second level (threat).[1] To indicate severity by taking the maximum of the two scores means this dispute is treated the same as any other war, but we think that it is less severe because the other side exhibited a relatively weak reaction. This is especially important in large, multilateral disputes. We believe that the maximum option does not fulfill the reciprocity criterion noted above. We are especially attracted to the multiplication option because the differences in scores become larger the higher the level of hostility achieved by *both* sides. Thus, our first step is to create a new scale of dispute level severity for zero-fatalities cases by taking the product of the level-of-hostility scores for each rival.[2] This then ranges from 2 (2×1) to 16 (4×4).[3]

Figure B.1 shows the distribution of cases (remember that this is for zero-fatality disputes only). The values of 4, 9, and 16 are the symmetrical nonfatality disputes, and all other values are nonsymmetrical disputes. Clearly the symmetrical cases dominate, but there are a significant number of nonsymmetrical ones.

A second step is to convert this ordinal scale into an interval one. We adopt an inductive approach and suggest that the interval scale be a function of how frequently the different levels (2–16) occur in practice. The scale thus depends on the empirical facts, but this is true of scales such as temperature, which is defined based on the behavior of substances. We propose that the relative frequencies of each level be indicated by the cumulative distribution function in this particular case, which we give in figure B.1. We rescaled the severity variable using the cumulative distribution at any given point to define the new value. For example, the original ordinal score of 4 (2×2) now has a value of 58. Cases of reciprocated use-of-force (i.e., $4 \times 4 = 16$) get a value of 100.[4]

---

[1] There are actually cases of this sort in the data set. Indeed, they are likely to be more prevalent when there is a multilateral dispute and some participants do not partake in actual warfare while others do.

[2] We must deal with the problem of missing data. Only a very small number of hostility scores are missing for the initiating side in the dispute, but just under half are missing for the target. We suspect that much of the missing hostility data consist of cases in which the disputant made no military response. In contrast with the old dispute data, the revised MID data set has very few cases where the level of hostility equals 1 (see Hensel and Diehl 1994). That almost all the missing data involve side B would tend to confirm that. Nonetheless, there are virtually no missing data for the dispute level variable, the variable that most studies use. Implicitly this suggests that the missing data for the dispute target are considered lower than that of initiator and are probably cases of no military response. And indeed Stuart Bremer (personal communication) confirms that these are indeed no military response cases. Accordingly, we have set the missing cases to the level of 1— no response.

[3] The lowest number possible is 2, as this reflects the initiation of a militarized dispute with a threat of military force and a nonmilitarized response by the target. A score of 1 for both sides is technically impossible, as there would be no dispute to begin with: militarized disputes require at least one state to threaten, display, or use military force. Yet missing data for the initiator side leads to a small number of cases ($N = 2$) have a score of 1-1 for both sides.

[4] One will notice some values of 15, which are war (5) $\times$ display (3), and these are coded as no fatality cases; see below.

FIGURE B.1: Cumulative Distribution of Dispute Severity, Nonfatality Cases

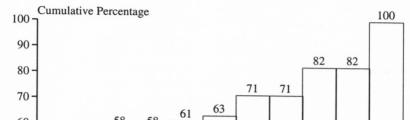

(Host. Lev. A)×(Host. Lev. B)

If we examine the results in figure B.1, we think that they have a fair amount of face validity. We note that there are relatively few cases of LOH 2 with no response (2-1 dispute), which we regard as not very severe disputes. The move from nonreciprocated verbal (2-1 disputes) threats to nonreciprocated physical ones (display of force, 3-1 disputes) is indicated by the significant jump from 6 to 23. There is another significant jump then to level 4. This level includes reciprocated threats (2-2 disputes), which we consider much more severe than the nonreciprocated ones below it. Hence, low-level, nonreciprocated disputes on our scale have low values; it when we have a reciprocal serious threat that severity increases to over 50. LOH 4 also includes uses of force that have no response (4-1 disputes). We consider that it is much better to code these at this lower level than the standard approach that treats them as equivalent to level of hostility 4-4 disputes.

If we move up to level 9—reciprocated displays of force—cases there receive a value of 71. This is a more moderate increase—about 12—from the reciprocated serious threat level of 58, which to us indicates that the movement from a serious verbal threat to a serious physical threat is smaller than the jump to reciprocated verbal threats at level 50. The scale then moves up gradually to where a display of force is matched with a use of force (level 82). Finally, there is a significant jump representing a reciprocal use of force (to 100), again emphasizing the importance of symmetry in severity.

In summary, we believe that within the limits of our data this part of the scale fits well with our theoretical considerations about severity as well as our concerns about the impact of asymmetry. It provides the kind of reasonable estimation and face validity that is similar to the use of one-hundred-point "feeling thermometers" in studies of American public opinion.

We now turn our attention to greater than zero fatality cases. Note that not all these cases are wars (and therefore some have dispute level of hostility codes of 2-16, but these are not include in figure B.1, which contains only the results for zero-fatality disputes). Both the MID data set and the COW war data set contain information about fatalities. For war cases, we used the more precise fatality numbers from the war data set. This involved matching wars from that data set to disputes in the MID data set. The MID data set categorizes them as follows: (1) 0, (2) 1–25, (3) 26–100, (4) 101–250, (5) 251–500, and (6) 501–999. If there were no precise fatality data from the war data set (i.e., cases of militarized disputes with fatalities less than one thousand, but greater than zero), we used the midpoint of these MID ranges as the fatality estimate for that disputant. The fatality level for the dyadic dispute is then the sum of the fatality levels of the two disputants.

The fatality level data in the war and dispute data sets are the total number of fatalities against all disputants. When we divide multilateral wars into dyadic cases, we need to consider whether we should take the aggregate dispute/war total for all the dyadic disputes.[5] In general we do not find this a problem, as most disputes and wars involve only two states, but it does become an issue in major multilateral wars. There, fatality levels can range from a few hundred to a few million in the same war. In fact, only the two world wars pose problems. Our solution consists of taking the minimum fatality level of the two states and multiplying that by two. This means that we consider the severity of the dispute confrontation between the two states to be best reflected by the fatalities on the smaller side. For example, we can take the extreme case of Brazil-Germany in World War II, in which Germany lost 3.5 million soldiers and Brazil only one thousand. We think that twice the Brazil fatality reflects a reasonable estimate (given our data constraints) of the severity of the confrontation between Germany and Brazil. Certainly this is much less severe than WW II conflicts between Germany and its other opponents in that conflict.[6]

---

[5]The transformation of multilateral disputes into dyads represents all possible dyad combinations from those states on the initiator side against those on the target side. Nevertheless, we eliminated some pairs in World War I, World War II, and the Gulf War. This was only done, however, when there was no temporal overlap between the war or dispute participants. That is, one state exited the dispute or war before the other state joined the conflict.

[6]For the fatality data we also need to take into account the problem of missing data. In the war data set, there were missing data for some participants in the Gulf War, namely Canada, Italy, Morocco, Syria, Bahrain, Qatar, and Oman and in some disputes (about 12 percent). As with the

FIGURE B.2: Cumulative Distribution of Dispute Severity, Fatality Cases

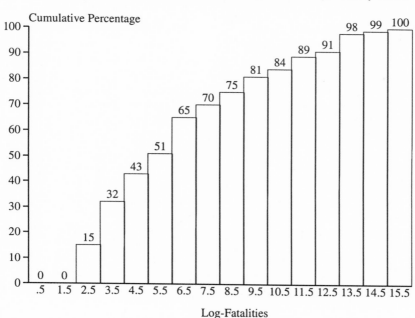

Log-Fatalities

Because the absolute number of fatalities has an extremely long tail (few wars with very large fatality levels), we take the natural log of fatality levels to mitigate the effects of those outlying values. If we look at the distribution of these log values, it has a maximum of about 15.

Our proposal to scale the nonzero-fatality cases parallels what we did for the zero-fatality cases; the interval measure is the cumulative distribution of logged fatality values, which we show in figure B.2. Again to evaluate face validity we note that the scale increases fairly rapidly with small log-fatality levels. We think this reflects that the first fatalities substantially increase the severity more than do later ones. The first one hundred fatalities are much more important than those from 1,000 to 1,100. We think that the long tail thus represents quite well the slowly increasing severity of a war once a significant fatality is reached.

The next step is to splice the nonfatality and fatality case parts of the scale together. Based on our third general principle, we put the fatality case scores right after the nonfatality ones, and therefore the overall severity measure ranges from 0 to 200, 100 coming from each part. This means, in practice, a long tail for the fatality cases, which constitute half of the scale, but only

---

level-of-hostility missing data, we set these values to zero, and thus the cases are scaled with the zero-fatality disputes.

FIGURE B.3: Cumulative Distribution of Interval Severity Scores

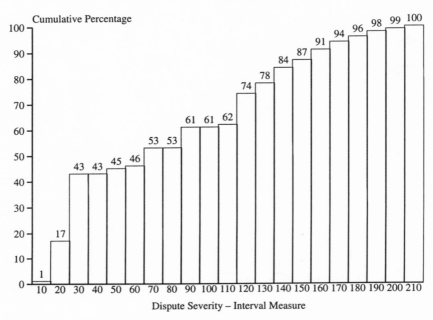

Dispute Severity – Interval Measure

about one-fourth of the cases. To make the calculation easier and to smooth things out, we fit a polynomial regression equation to these data. This permits one to calculate the interval measure based on very simple procedures. The fit of the regression line is quite good with an R^2 of over .99.[7] The equation is

$$\text{dispute severity} = 7.779 \times \text{level} - .034 \times \text{level-squared},$$

where "level" equals either the product of the level-of-hostility scores (2–16) in the nonfatality dispute dyads or the log of the sum of the fatalities plus 16. Level-squared is the square of "level." The net effect of using the formula is that a few values will fall just beyond the 200 limit, but these scores can either be scaled back to the upper limit or accepted as is; in either case, empirical analyses should not be significantly affected. In summary, the procedure for calculating the measure is relatively simple. If there are zero fatalities, then multiply the level-of-hostility variable for each rival and apply the equation. For cases with battle deaths, the fatality levels for both states are summed, then logged, then added to 16, and then the equation is applied. Figure B.3 shows the distribution of the final scores.

---

[7] We checked various other specifications with higher-order polynomials, which never produced a significantly better fit.

Overall, we sought a scale that permits us to develop and test hypotheses about the gamut of dispute severity. The scale has a clear transition point at 100, which separates fatality from nonfatality disputes. Wars in the Small and Singer sense of one thousand fatalities begin around 160 and continue to a little over 200. Because much of our interest in developing this scale focuses on nonwar disputes, we have range from zero to approximately 150–160, which we find adequate for trying to differentiate between various dispute outcomes. We find that jumps in the scale occur where we would expect them to, and that asymmetric disputes are also properly treated. The rapid increase in severity with initial fatalities followed by a long tail also fits our notions about how severity increases with number of battlefield deaths.

Our justification of the face validity of our measure follows that of the Small and Singer data set. In the final analysis the justification for the choice of one thousand fatalities was that such a cutoff produced a list that they (and others) believed were wars and excluded those that most scholars would hesitate to identify as a war. We argue similarly that our scale reflects reasonable expectations about how dispute and war severity increase with the level of force, dispute asymmetry, and number of fatalities. If our expectations and arguments about how these factors relate to dispute and war severity are valid, then we feel that our measure also can serve a useful function since the scale fits well with those general arguments. Of course, if our general theoretical arguments about level of force, dispute asymmetry, and number of fatalities and their relation to severity are flawed, then of course so is our scale.

Conclusion

It would be easy to take an interval-level measure and merely change one's statistical techniques from logit to regression without giving the issue any further thought. But using our interval-level measure (or any other one, for that matter) consists of more than doing the same old thing with a new dependent variable. Behind the war/dispute distinction lies the basic orientation that one's goal is to explain war. Within this perspective, disputes are merely the control group. The shift to a continuous variable implies that the theoretical orientation shifts as well. Now, one is trying explain *both* disputes and wars in the sense that the distinction between the two has disappeared into a general measure of conflict severity. To take the analogy from temperature scales, the standard goal is to explain why something is hot, and this is replaced by the purpose of explaining its temperature.

It would be unfortunate to reduce our argument to one about information loss resulting from the war–no war dichotomization. There are important theoretical issues at stake. To explain war in traditional studies, strictly speaking, means explaining why some disputes reach the one-thousand-fatality threshold. The severity of the war once this threshold attained is treated as irrelevant in most studies. If we take our measure instead, then one will be explaining why the war or other conflict became as severe as it did. We propose that a dispute severity measure permits us to analyze whole new sets of theoretical questions and at the same permits us to think anew about traditional procedures. War remains an important concern of conflict studies, but much conflict does not attain that level. We see the existence of a dispute severity indicator as an incitement to develop theories and to examine lower-level conflict.

References

Achen, Christopher, and Duncan Snidal. 1989. "Rational Deterrence Theory and Comparative Case Studies." *World Politics* 41:143–69.

Allison, Graham. 1971. *Essence of Decision.* Boston: Little, Brown.

Allison, Paul. 1984. *Event History Analysis: Regression for Longitudinal Event Data.* Sage University Paper Series on Quantitative Applications in the Social Sciences, series no. 07-046. Beverly Hills: Sage.

Anderson, Paul, and Timothy McKeown. 1987. "Changing Aspirations, Limited Attention, and War." *World Politics* 30:1–29.

Anselin, Luc, and John O'Loughlin. 1992. "Geography of International Conflict and Cooperation: Spatial Dependence and Regional Context in Africa." In *The New Geopolitics,* ed. Michael Ward. Philadelphia: Gordon and Breach.

Ashley, Richard K. 1980. *The Political Economy of War and Peace.* New York: Nichols.

Axelrod, Robert. 1984. *The Evolution of Cooperation.* New York: Basic Books.

Azar, Edward. 1972. "Conflict Escalation and Conflict Reduction in an International Crisis: Suez, 1956." *Journal of Conflict Resolution* 16:183–202.

———. 1982. *The Codebook of the Conflict and Peace Data Bank (COPDAB).* College Park, Md.: Center for International Development.

Azar, Edward, Paul Jureidini, and Ronald McLaurin. 1978. "Protracted Social Conflict: Theory and Practice in the Middle East." *Journal of Palestine Studies* 8:41–60.

Barbieri, Katherine. 1996. "Economic Interdependence: A Path to Peace or a Source of Conflict?" *Journal of Peace Research* 33:29–49.

Baumgartner, Frank R., and Bryan D. Jones. 1993. *Agendas and Instability in American Politics.* Chicago: University of Chicago Press.

Beck, Nathaniel, Jonathan Katz, and Richard Tucker. 1998. "Taking Time Seriously: Time Series–Cross-Sectional Analysis with a Binary Dependent Variable." *American Journal of Political Science* 42:1260–88.

Ben-Yehuda, Ben, and Shmuel Sandler. 1998. "Crisis Magnitude and Interstate Conflict: Changes in the Arab-Israel Dispute." *Journal of Peace Research* 35:83–109.

Bennett, D. Scott. 1993. "Security, Economy, and the End of Interstate Rivalry". Ph.D. diss., University of Michigan.

———. 1996. "Security, Bargaining, and the End of Interstate Rivalry." *International Studies Quarterly* 40:157–83.

———. 1997a. "Democracy, Regime Change, and Rivalry Termination." *International Interactions* 22:369–97.

———. 1997b. "Measuring Rivalry Termination." *Journal of Conflict Resolution* 41:227–54.

————. 1998. "Integrating and Testing Models of Rivalry." *American Journal of Political Science* 42:1200–1232.

Bennett, D. Scott, and Allan Stam. 1996. "The Duration of Interstate Wars." *American Political Science Review* 90:239–57.

Bercovitch, Jacob. 1984. *Social Conflicts and Third Parties*. Boulder: Westview Press.

————. 1989. "International Dispute Mediation: A Comparative Empirical Analysis." In *Mediation Research*, ed. K. Kressel and D. G. Pruitt. San Francisco: Jossey-Bass.

————. 1991. "International Mediation." *Journal of Peace Research* 28:3–6.

————. 1993. *International Conflict Management*. Data and coding manual. Christchurch, New Zealand.

Bercovitch, Jacob, J. Anagnoson, and D. Wille. 1991. "Some Conceptual Issues and Empirical Trends in the Study of Successful Mediation in International Relations." *Journal of Peace Research* 28:7–17.

Bercovitch, Jacob, and Paul F. Diehl. 1997. "Conflict Management of Enduring Rivalries: Frequency, Timing and Short-Term impact of Mediation." *International Interactions* 22:299–320.

Bercovitch, Jacob, and J. Langely. 1993. "The Nature of the Dispute and the Effectiveness of International Mediation." *Journal of Conflict Resolution* 37:670–91.

Bercovitch, Jacob, and Patrick Regan. 1997. "Managing Risks in International Relations: The Mediation of Enduring Rivalries." In *Enforcing Cooperation: Risky States and Intergovernmental Management of Conflict,* ed. Gerald Schneider and Patricia Weitsman. London: Macmillan.

Bialer, Seweryn. 1988. *The Global Rivals*. New York: Alfred A. Knopf.

Black, Jeremy. 1999. "Enduring Rivalries: Britain and France." In *The Evolution of Great Power Rivalries,* ed. William R. Thompson. Columbia: University of South Carolina Press.

Brams, Steven. 1993. *Theory of Moves*. Cambridge: Cambridge University Press.

Braumoeller, Bear, and Gary Goertz. 1997. "The Methodology of Necessary Conditions." University of Michigan. Draft manuscript.

Braybrooke, David, and Charles Lindblom. 1963. *Policy Evaluation as a Social Process*. New York: Free Press.

Brecher, Michael. 1979. "State Behavior in International Crisis: A Model." *Journal of Conflict Resolution* 23:446–80.

————. 1984. "International Crises, Protracted Conflicts." *International Interactions* 11:237–98.

————. 1993. *Crises in World Politics: Theory and Reality*. New York: Pergamon Press.

Bremer, Stuart. 1992. "Dangerous Dyads: Conditions Affecting the Likelihood of Interstate War, 1816–1965." *Journal of Conflict Resolution* 36:309-41.

————. 1993. "Democracy and Militarized Interstate Conflict, 1816–1965." *International Interactions* 18:231–50.

Brown, Michael, Sean Lynn-Jones, and Steven Miller, eds. 1996. *Debating the Democratic Peace*. Cambridge: MIT Press.

Brown, William, and Raymond Sauer. 1989. "Does the Basketball Market Believe in the Hot Hand? Comment." *American Economic Review* 79:1377–86.

Brummett, Palmira. 1999. "The Ottoman Empire, Venice, and the Question of Enduring Rivalries." In *The Evolution of Great Power Rivalries,* ed. William R. Thompson. Columbia: University of South Carolina Press.

Bueno de Mesquita, Bruce. 1978. "Systemic Polarization and the Occurrence and Duration of War." *Journal of Conflict Resolution* 22:241–67.

———. 1981. *The War Trap.* New Haven: Yale University Press.

Bueno de Mesquita, Bruce, and David Lalman. 1988. "Empirical Support for Systemic and Dyadic Explanations of International Conflict." *World Politics* 41:1–20.

———. 1992. *War and Reason.* New Haven: Yale University Press.

Bueno de Mesquita, Bruce, Randolph Siverson, and Gary Woller. 1992. "War and the Fate of Regimes." *American Political Science Review* 86:635–46.

Burton, John W. 1968. *Conflict and Communication.* London: Macmillan.

Butterworth, Robert. 1976. *Managing Interstate Conflict.* Pittsburgh: University of Pittsburgh Press.

———. 1978. *Moderation from Management: International Organizations and Peace.* Pittsburgh: University Center for International Studies.

Buzan, Barry. 1983. *People, States, and Fear.* Boulder: Lynne Rienner.

Casstevens, Thomas. 1980. "Birth and Death Processes of Governmental Bureaus in the United States." *Behavioral Science* 25:161–65.

Cederman, Lars Erik. 1996. *Emergent Actors in World Politics: How States and Nations Develop and Dissolve.* Princeton: Princeton University Press.

Chan, Steve. 1984. "Mirror, Mirror on the Wall . . . Are Freer Countries More Pacific?" *Journal of Conflict Resolution* 28:617–48.

———. 1993. "Democracy and War: Some Thoughts on Future Research Agenda." *International Interactions* 18:205–14.

Choucri, Nazli, and Robert North. 1975. *Nations in Conflict.* San Francisco: W. H. Freeman.

Cioffi-Revilla, Claudio. 1996. "Origins and Evolution of War and Politics." *International Studies Quarterly* 40:1–22.

———. 1998. "The Political Uncertainty of Interstate Rivalries: A Punctuated Equilibrium Model." In *The Dynamics of Enduring Rivalries,* ed. Paul F. Diehl. Urbana: University of Illinois Press.

Claude, Inis. 1971. *Swords into Ploughshares,* 4th ed. New York: Random House.

Cohen, Michael, James G. March, and Johan P. Olsen. 1972. "A Garbage Can Theory of Organizational Choice." *Administrative Science Quarterly* 17:1–25.

Conybeare, John. 1987. *Trade Wars.* New York: Columbia University Press.

Crescenzi, Mark J. C., and Andrew J. Enterline. 1998. "Measuring Interstate Rivalry: A Research Note." Draft manuscript.

Curry, Amy, and Paul Pecorino. 1993. "The Use of Final Offer Arbitration as a Screening Device." *Journal of Conflict Resolution* 37:655–69.

Davis, William, George Duncan, and Randolph Siverson. 1978. "The Dynamics of Warfare, 1816–1965." *American Journal of Political Science* 22:772–92.

Dawkins, R. 1989. *The Selfish Gene.* Oxford: Oxford University Press.

Dessler, David. 1989. "What's at Stake in the Agent-Structure Debate." *International Organization* 43:441–73.

Deudney, Daniel, and John Ikenberry. 1991–92. "The International Sources of Soviet Change." *International Security* 16:74–118.

Deutsch, Karl W., and J. David Singer. 1964. "Multipolar Power Systems and International Stability." *World Politics* 16:390–406.

Diehl, Paul F. 1983. "Arms Races and the Outbreak of War, 1816–1980." Ph.D. diss., University of Michigan.

———. 1985a. "Arms Races to War: Testing Some Empirical Linkages." *Sociological Quarterly* 26:331–49.

———. 1985b. "Armaments without War: An Analysis of Some Underlying Effects." *Journal of Peace Research* 22:249–59.

———. 1985c. "Contiguity and Military Escalation in Major Power Rivalries, 1816–1980." *Journal of Politics* 47:1203–11.

———. 1994a. *International Peacekeeping*. Rev. ed. Baltimore: Johns Hopkins University Press.

———. 1994b. "Substitutes or Complements? The Effects of Alliances on Military Spending in Major Power Rivalries." *International Interactions* 19:159–76.

———, ed. 1998. *The Dynamics of Enduring Rivalries*. Urbana: University of Illinois Press.

Diehl, Paul F., and Mark Crescenzi. 1998. "Reconfiguring the Arms Race–War Debate." *Journal of Peace Research* 35:111–18.

Diehl, Paul F., and Gary Goertz. 1985. "Trends in Military Allocation since 1816: What Goes Up Does Not Always Come Down." *Armed Forces and Society* 12:134–44.

Diehl, Paul F., and Jean Kingston. 1987. "Messenger or Message? Military Buildups and the Initiation of Conflict." *Journal of Politics* 49:801–13.

Diehl, Paul F., Jennifer Reifschneider, and Paul R. Hensel. 1996. "United Nations Intervention and Recurring Conflict." *International Organization* 50:683–700.

Dion, Douglas. 1998. "Evidence and Inference in the Comparative Case Study." *Comparative Politics* 30:127–46.

Dixon, William. 1993. "Democracy and the Management of International Conflict." *Journal of Conflict Resolution* 37:42–68.

———. 1994. "Democracy and the Peaceful Settlement of International Conflict." *American Political Science Review* 88:14–32.

Doyle, Michael. 1986. "Liberalism and World Politics." *American Political Science Review* 80:1151–69.

———. 1996. "Michael Doyle on the Democratic Peace—Again." In *Debating the Democratic Peace*, ed. Michael Brown, Sean Lynn-Jones, and Steven Miller. Cambridge: MIT Press.

Dror, Yehezkel. 1984. "Policy Gambling: A Preliminary Exploration." *Policy Studies Journal* 12:9–13.

Druckman, Daniel, and Paul Stern. 1997. "Evaluating Peacekeeping Missions." *Mershon International Studies Review* 41:151–65.

Durant, Robert, and Paul F. Diehl. 1989. "Agendas, Alternatives, and Public Policy: Lessons from the U.S. Foreign Policy Arena." *Journal of Public Policy* 9:179–205.

Duvall, Raymond. 1976. "An Appraisal of the Methodological and Statistical Procedures of the Correlates of War Project." In *Quantitative International Politics: An Appraisal*, ed. Francis Hoole and Dina Zinnes. New York: Praeger.

Edmead, F. 1971. *Analysis and Prediction in International Mediation*. New York: UNITAR.

Eldredge, Niles. 1985. *Time Frames: The Evolution of Punctuated Equilibria.* Princeton: Princeton University Press.

———. 1995. *Reinventing Darwin: The Great Evolutionary Debate.* New York: John Wiley and Sons.

Eldredge, Niles, and Stephen J. Gould. 1972. "Punctuated Equilibria: An Alternative to Phyletic Gradualism." In *Models in Paleobiology,* ed. T. Schopf and J. Thomas. San Francisco: Freeman, Cooper.

Elster, Jon. 1983. *Explaining Technical Change: A Case Study in the Philosophy of Science.* Cambridge: Cambridge University Press.

Enterline, Andrew. 1996. "Driving While Democratizing." *International Security* 20:183–96.

Farber, Henry S., and Joanne Gowa. 1995. "Polities and Peace." *International Security* 20:123–46.

Fearon, James. 1994a. "Domestic Political Audiences and the Escalation of International Disputes." *American Political Science Review* 88:577–92.

———. 1994b. "Signaling versus the Balance of Power and Interests: An Empirical Test of a Crisis Bargaining Model." *Journal of Conflict Resolution,* 38:236–69.

Feste, Karen. 1982. "International Enemies: A Review." Presented at the Annual Meeting of the International Studies Association, Cincinnati.

Finlay, David, Ole Holsti, and Richard Fagan. 1967. *Enemies in Politics.* Chicago: Rand-McNally.

Frei, D. 1976. "Conditions Affecting the Effectiveness of International Mediation." *Peace Science Society (International) Papers* 26:67–84.

Friedman, George, and Meredith Lebard. 1991. *The Coming War with Japan.* New York: St. Martin's Press.

Galtung, Johan. 1969. "A Structural Theory of Imperialism." *Journal of Peace Research* 5:375–95.

Gartner, Scott Sigmund, and Randolph M. Siverson. 1996. "War Expansion and War Outcome." *Journal of Conflict Resolution* 40:4–15.

Gartzke, Erik, and Michael Simon. 1999. "Hot Hand: A Critical Analysis of Enduring Rivalries." *Journal of Politics* 63:777-98.

Gates, Scott, and Gary Goertz. 1997. "Institutions and Modeling Necessary and Sufficient Conditions." Revised version. Presented at the Annual Meeting of the European Consortium for Political Research, Bern, Switzerland.

Gates, Scott, Torbjorn L. Knutsen, and Jonathon W. Moses. 1996. "Democracy and Peace: A More Skeptical View." *Journal of Peace Research* 33:1–10.

Geller, Daniel. 1992. "Power Transition and Conflict Initiation." *Conflict Management and Peace Science* 12:1–16.

———. 1993. "Power Differentials and War in Rival Dyads." *International Studies Quarterly* 37:173–94.

———. 1998. "The Stability of the Military Balance and War Among Great Power Rivals." In *The Dynamics of Enduring Rivalries,* ed. Paul F. Diehl. Urbana: University of Illinois Press.

Geller, Daniel, and J. David Singer. 1998. *Nations at War.* Cambridge: Cambridge University Press.

Gelpi, Christopher. 1997. "Crime and Punishment: The Role of Norms in Crisis Bargaining." *American Political Science Review* 9:339–60.

George, Alexander, and Richard Smoke. 1974. *Deterrence in American Foreign Policy: Theory and Practice*. New York: Columbia University Press.

———. 1989. "Deterrence and Foreign Policy." *World Politics* 41:170–82.

Gibler, Douglas. 1997. "Control the Issues, Control the Conflict: The Effects of Alliances That Settle Territorial Issues on Interstate Rivalries." *International Interactions* 22:341–68.

Gilovich, Thomas, Robert Vallone, and Amos Tversky. 1985. "The Hot Hand in Basketball: On the Misperception of Random Sequences." *Cognitive Psychology* 17:295–314.

Gilpin, Robert. 1981. *War and Change in World Politics*. Cambridge: Cambridge University Press.

Gleditsch, Nils Petter, and Havard Hegre. 1997. "Peace and Democracy: Three Levels of Analysis." *Journal of Conflict Resolution* 41:283–310.

Gochman, Charles. 1991. "Interstate Metrics: Conceptualizing, Operationalizing, and Measuring the Geographic Proximity of States since the Congress of Vienna." *International Interactions* 17:93–112.

Gochman, Charles, and Zeev Maoz. 1984. "Militarized Interstate Disputes, 1816–1976: Procedures, Patterns, and Insights." *Journal of Conflict Resolution* 28:585–616.

Goertz, Gary. 1994. *Contexts of International Politics*. Cambridge: Cambridge University Press.

———. 2000. "An Essay on International Norms." Draft manuscript.

Goertz, Gary, and Paul F. Diehl. 1986. "Measuring Military Allocations: A Comparison of Different Approaches." *Journal of Conflict Resolution* 30:553–81.

———. 1992a. "The Empirical Importance of Enduring Rivalries." *International Interactions* 18:151–63.

———. 1992b. *Territorial Changes and International Conflict*. London: Routledge.

———. 1993. "Enduring Rivalries: Theoretical Constructs and Empirical Patterns." *International Studies Quarterly* 37:147–71.

———. 1995a. "Taking 'Enduring' Out of Enduring Rivalry: The Rivalry Approach to War and Peace." *International Interactions* 21:291–308.

———. 1995b. "The Initiation and Termination of Enduring Rivalries: The Impact of Political Shocks." *American Journal of Political Science* 39:30–52.

———. 1997. "Linking Risky Dyads: An Evaluation of Relations between Enduring Rivalries." In *Enforcing Cooperation: "Risky" States and the Intergovernmental Management of Conflict*, ed. Gerald Schneider and Patricia Weitsman. London: Macmillan.

———. 1998. "The Volcano Model and Other Patterns in the Evolution of Enduring Rivalries." In *The Dynamics of Enduring Rivalries*, ed. Paul F. Diehl. Urbana: University of Illinois Press.

Goldstein, Joshua. 1992. "A Conflict-Cooperation Scale for WEIS Events Data." *Journal of Conflict Resolution* 36:369–85.

Goldstein, Joshua, and John Freeman. 1990. *Three-Way Street*. Chicago: University of Chicago Press.

———. 1991. "US-Soviet-Chinese Relations: Routine, Reciprocity, or Rational Expectations?" *American Political Science Review* 85:17–35.

Gould, Stephen Jay. 1983. *Hen's Teeth and Horse's Toes*. New York: W. W. Norton.

———. 1987. *Time's Arrow, Time's Cycle*. Cambridge: Harvard University Press.

————. 1991. *Bully for Brontosaurus: Reflections in Natural History*. New York: W. W. Norton.

Gould, Stephen Jay, and Niles Eldredge. 1993. "Punctuated Equilibrium Comes of Age." *Nature* 366:223–27.

Haas, Ernst. 1986. *The UN and Collective Management of International Conflict*. New York: UNITAR.

Harvey, Frank. 1998. "Rigor Mortis or Rigor, More Tests: Necessity, Sufficiency, and Deterrence Logic." *International Studies Quarterly* 42:675–707.

Hensel, Paul R. 1994. "One Thing Leads to Another: Recurrent Militarized Disputes in Latin America, 1816–1986." *Journal of Peace Research* 31:281–98.

————. "Political Democracy and Militarized Conflict in Enduring Interstate Rivalries." Presented at the Annual Meeting of the American Political Science Association, Chicago.

————. 1996. "The Evolution of Interstate Rivalry." Ph.D. diss., University of Illinois.

————. 1997. "What Do They Do When They Are Not Fighting? Event Data and Non-militarized Dimensions of Interstate Rivalry." Draft manuscript.

————. 1998. "Interstate Rivalry and the Study of Militarized Conflict." In *New Directions in the Study of International Conflict, Crises, and War*, ed. Frank Harvey and Ben Mor. London: Macmillan.

Hensel, Paul R., and Paul F. Diehl. 1994. "It Takes Two to Tango: Nonmilitarized Response in Interstate Disputes." *Journal of Conflict Resolution* 38:479–506.

Hensel, Paul R., and Thomas Sowers. 1998. "Territorial Claims, Major Power Competition, and the Origins of Enduring Rivalry." Presented at the joint meeting of the International Studies Association and the European Standing Group on International Relations, Vienna.

Hermann, Margaret G., and Charles Kegley Jr. 1995. "Rethinking Democracy and International Peace: Perspectives from Political Psychology." *International Studies Quarterly* 39:511–33.

Herzog, Chaim. 1982. *The Arab-Israeli Wars: War and Peace in the Middle East*. Toronto: Methuen.

Holsti, Kalevi J. 1987. *International Politics: A Framework for Analysis*, 5th ed. Englewood Cliffs, N.J.: Prentice-Hall.

————. 1991. *Peace and War: Armed Conflicts and International Order, 1648–1989*. Cambridge: Cambridge University Press.

Hopf, Ted. 1994. *Peripheral Visions: Deterrence Theory and American Foreign Policy in The Third World, 1965–1990*. Ann Arbor: University of Michigan Press.

Horn, Michael Dean. 1987. "Arms Races and the International System." Ph.D. diss., University of Rochester.

Houweling, Henk W., and Jan G. Siccama. 1991. "Power Transitions and Critical Points as Predictors of Great Power War: Toward a Synthesis." *Journal of Conflict Resolution* 35:642–58.

Howard, Michael. 1983. *The Causes of Wars*, 2d ed. Cambridge: Harvard University Press.

————. 1991. *The Lessons of History*. New Haven: Yale University Press.

Howell, Lleweyllan. 1983. "A Comparative Study of the WEIS and COPDAB Data Sets." *International Studies Quarterly* 27:149–59.

Huntington, Samuel. 1958. "Arms Races: Prerequisites and Results." *Public Policy* 18:41–46.

Hutchinson, J. 1996. *Champions of Charity: War and the Rise of the Red Cross*. Boulder: Westview Press.

Huth, Paul K. 1988. *Extended Deterrence and the Prevention of War*. New Haven: Yale University Press.

———. 1996a. "Enduring Rivalries and Territorial Disputes, 1950–1990." *Conflict Management and Peace Science* 15:7–41.

———. 1996b. *Standing Your Ground: Territorial Disputes and International Conflict*. Ann Arbor: University of Michigan Press.

Huth, Paul, D. Scott Bennett, and Christopher Gelpi. 1992. "System Uncertainty, Risk Propensity, and International Conflict among the Great Powers." *Journal of Conflict Resolution* 36:478–517.

Huth, Paul K., and Bruce Russett. 1984. "What Makes Deterrence Work? Cases from 1900–1980." *World Politics* 36:496–526.

———. 1990. "Testing Deterrence Theory: Rigor Makes a Difference." *World Politics* 42:466–501.

———. 1993. "General Deterrence between Enduring Rivals: Testing Three Competing Models." *American Political Science Review* 87:61–73.

Hybel, A. 1990. *How Leaders Reason*. Oxford: Basil Blackwell.

Ingram, Edward. 1999. "Enduring Rivalries: Britain and Russia." In *The Evolution of Great Power Rivalries,* ed. William R. Thompson. Columbia: University of South Carolina Press.

International Security. 1994. 19 (2).

Jackson, E. 1952. *Meeting of Minds: A Way to Peace through Mediation*. New York: McGraw-Hill.

Jaggers, Keith, and Ted Robert Gurr. 1996. "Tracking Democracy's Third Wave with the Polity III Data." *Journal of Peace Research* 32:469–82.

Jervis, Robert. 1976. *Perception and Misperception in International Politics*. Princeton: Princeton University Press.

———. 1979. "Deterrence Theory Revisited." *World Politics* 31:289–324.

———. 1989. "Rational Deterrence: Theory and Evidence." *World Politics* 41:183–207.

Jones, Bryan, Frank Baumgartner, and James True. 1998. "Policy Punctuations: U.S. Budget Authority, 1947–1995." *Journal of Politics* 60:1–33.

Jones, Daniel. 1989. "Enduring Rivalries, Dispute Escalation, and Interstate War." Presented at the Annual Meeting of the Peace Science Society (International), Columbus, Ohio.

———. 1994. "Balancing and Bandwagoning in Militarized Interstate Disputes." In *Reconstructing Realpolitik,* ed. Frank Wayman and Paul F. Diehl. Ann Arbor: University of Michigan Press.

Jones, Daniel, Stuart Bremer, and J. David Singer. 1996. "Militarized Interstate Disputes, 1816–1992: Rationale, Coding Rules and Empirical Patterns." *Conflict Management and Peace Science* 15:163–213.

Kacowicz, Arie. 1998. *Zones of Peace in the Third World: South America and West Africa in Comparative Perspective*. Albany: State University of New York Press.

Kahn, Herman. 1965. *On Escalation: Metaphors and Scenarios*. London: Pall Mall.

Kaplan, Herbert H. 1998. "The Early Phase of British-Russian Rivalry." In *The Evolution of Great Power Rivalries,* ed. William R. Thompson. Columbia: University of South Carolina Press.

Katzenstein, Peter, ed. 1996. *The Culture of National Security: Norms Identity and World Politics.* New York: Columbia University Press.

Kaufman, Edy. 1993. "War Occupation, and the Effects on Israeli Society." In *Democracy, Peace, and the Israeli-Palestinian Conflict,* ed. Edy Kaufman, Shukri B. Abed, and Robert L. Rothstein. Boulder: Lynne Rienner.

Kegley, Charles, Neil Richardson, and G. Richter. 1978. "Conflict at Home and Abroad: An Empirical Extension." *Journal of Politics* 40:742–52.

Kelly, David S. 1999. "The Genoese-Venetian Rivalry: Conceptual and Historical Issues." In *The Evolution of Great Power Rivalries,* ed. William R. Thompson. Columbia: University of South Carolina Press.

Kennedy, Paul. 1987. *The Rise and Fall of the Great Powers.* New York: Vintage Books.

Keohane, Robert, and Joseph Nye. 1977. *Power and Interdependence.* Boston: Little, Brown.

Kier, Elizabeth. 1995. *Imaging War.* Princeton: Princeton University Press.

Kingdon, John W. 1984. *Agendas, Alternatives, and Public Policies.* Boston: Little, Brown.

———. 1995. *Agendas, Alternatives, and Public Policies,* 2d ed. Boston: Little, Brown.

Kinsella, David. 1994a. "Conflict in Context: Arms Transfers and Third World Rivalry during the Cold War." *American Journal of Political Science* 38:557–81.

———. 1994b. "The Impact of Superpower Arms Transfers on Conflict in the Middle East." *Defence and Peace Economics* 5:19–36.

———. 1995. "Nested Rivalries: Superpower Competition, Arms Transfers, and Regional Conflict, 1950–1990." *International Interactions* 15:109–25.

Kochan, Thomas, and Todd Jick. 1978. "The Public Sector Mediation Process: A Theory and Empirical Examination." *Journal of Conflict Resolution* 22:209–40.

Kramer, Roderick, Pamela Pommerenke, and Elizabeth Newton. 1993. "The Social Context of Negotiation." *Journal of Conflict Resolution* 37:633–54.

Kressel, Kenneth, and Dean Pruitt. 1989. "Conclusion: A Research Perspective on the Mediation of Social Conflict." In *Mediation Research,* ed. Kenneth Kressel and Dean Pruitt. San Francisco: Jossey–Bass.

Kriesberg, Louis. 1992. *International Conflict Resolution: The US-USSR and Middle East Cases.* New Haven: Yale University Press.

Kriesberg, Louis, and Stuart Thorson, eds. 1991. *Timing the De-escalation of International Conflicts.* Syracuse: Syracuse University Press.

Kuenne, Robert. 1989. "Conflict Management in Mature Rivalry." *Journal of Conflict Resolution* 33:554–66.

Kugler, Jacek, and Douglas Lemke, eds. 1996. *Parity and War: Evaluations and Extensions of the War Ledger.* Ann Arbor: University of Michigan Press.

Kugler, Jacek, and A. F. K. Organski. 1989. "The Power Transition: A Retrospective and Prospective Evaluation." In *Handbook of War Studies,* ed. Manus Midlarsky. Boston: Unwin Hyman.

Larson, Deborah W. 1999. "The US-Soviet Rivalry." In *The Evolution of Great Power Rivalries,* ed. William R. Thompson. Columbia: University of South Carolina Press.

Layne, Christopher. 1994. "Kant or Cant: The Myth of the Democratic Peace." *International Security* 19:5–49.

Lebovic, James H. 1985. "Capabilities in Context: National Attributes and Foreign Policy in the Middle East." *Journal of Peace Research* 22:47–67.

———. 1994. "Before the Storm: Momentum and the Onset of the Gulf War." *International Studies Quarterly* 38:447–74.

Lebow, Richard Ned. 1981. *Between Peace and War: The Nature of International Crisis.* Baltimore: Johns Hopkins University Press.

———. 1995. "The Search for Accommodation: Gorbachev in Comparative Perspective." In *Understanding the End of the Cold War,* ed. Richard Ned Lebow and Thomas Risse. Baltimore: Johns Hopkins University Press.

Lebow, Richard Ned, and Janice Stein. 1990. "Deterrence: The Elusive Dependent Variable." *World Politics* 42:336–69.

Legro, J. 1994. "Inadvertent Escalation in World War II." *International Security* 18:108–42.

———. 1997. "Which Norm Matters?" *International Organization* 51:31–64.

Lemke, Douglas. 1995. "The Tyranny of Distance: Redefining Relevant Dyads." *International Interactions* 21:23–38.

Lemke, Douglas, and Suzanne Werner. 1996. "Power Parity, Commitment to Change, and War." *International Studies Quarterly* 40:235–60.

Leng, Russell. 1983. "When Will They Ever Learn? Coercive Bargaining in Recurrent Crises." *Journal of Conflict Resolution* 21:379–419.

———. 1993. *Interstate Crisis Behavior, 1816–1980: Realism versus Reciprocity.* Cambridge: Cambridge University Press.

Leng, Russell, and J. David Singer. 1988. "Militarized Interstate Crises." *International Studies Quarterly* 32:155–73.

Levy, Jack. 1983. *War in the Modern Great Power System, 1495–1975.* Lexington: University of Kentucky Press.

———. 1987. "Declining Power and the Preventative Motivation for War." *World Politics* 40:82–107.

———. 1988. "When Do Deterrent Threats Work?" *British Journal of Political Science* 18:485–512.

———. 1989. "The Diversionary Theory of War: A Critique." In *Handbook of War Studies,* ed. Manus Midlarsky. Boston: Unwin Hyman.

———. 1994. "Learning and Foreign Policy: Sweeping a Conceptual Minefield." *International Organization* 48:279–312.

———. 1999. "Economic Competition, Domestic Politics, and Systemic Change: The Rise and Decline of the Anglo-Dutch Rivalry, 1609–1688." In *The Evolution of Great Power Rivalries,* ed. William R. Thompson. Columbia: University of South Carolina Press.

Levy, Jack, and Salvatore Ali. 1998. "From Commercial Competition to Strategic Rivalry to War: The Evolution of the Anglo-Dutch Rivalry, 1609–1652." In *The Dynamics of Enduring Rivalries,* ed. Paul F. Diehl. Urbana: University of Illinois Press.

Licklider, Roy, ed. 1993. *Stopping the Killing: How Civil Wars End.* New York: New York University Press.

Lieberman, Eli. 1994. "The Rational Deterrence Theory Debate: Is the Dependent Variable Elusive?" *Security Studies* 3:384–427.

———. 1995. "What Makes Deterrence Work? Lessons from Egyptian-Israeli Enduring Rivalry." *Security Studies* 4:851–910.

Mahajan, V., and R. Peterson. 1985. *Models for Innovation Diffusion.* Newbury Park, CA.: Sage.

Majeski, Stephen, and David Sylvan. 1984. "Simple Choices and Complex Calculations: A Critique of *The War Trap.*" *Journal of Conflict Resolution* 28:316–40.

Mansfield, Edward, and Jack Snyder. 1995a. "Democratization and War." *Foreign Affairs* 74:79–97.

———. 1995b. "Democratization and the Danger of War." *International Security* 20:5–38.

Maoz, Zeev. 1982. *Paths to Conflict: International Dispute Initiation, 1816–1976.* Boulder: Westview Press.

———. 1984. "Peace by Empire? Conflict Outcomes and International Stability, 1816–1976." *Journal of Peace Research* 21:227–41.

———. 1989. "Joining the Club of Nations: Political Development and International Conflict, 1816–1976." *International Studies Quarterly* 33:199–231.

———. 1997. "The Controversy over the Democratic Peace: Rearguard Action or Cracks in the Wall?" *International Security* 22:162–98.

Maoz, Zeev, and Ben Mor. 1996. "Enduring Rivalries: The Early Years." *International Political Science Review* 17:141–60.

———. 1998. "Learning, Preference Change, and the Evolution of Enduring Rivalries." In *The Dynamics of Enduring Rivalries,* ed. Paul F. Diehl. Urbana: University of Illinois Press.

Maoz, Zeev, and Bruce Russett. 1992. "Alliance, Contiguity, Wealth, and Political Stability: Is the Lack of Conflict among Democracies a Statistical Artifact?" *International Interactions* 17:245–67.

Mayhew, David. 1991. *Divided We Govern.* New Haven: Yale University Press.

Mayr, E. 1970. *Populations, Species, and Evolution.* Cambridge: Harvard University Press.

———. 1982. *The Growth of Biological Thought: Diversity, Evolution, and Inheritance.* Cambridge: Harvard University Press.

McClelland, Charles. 1976. *World Event/Interaction Survey Codebook.* ICPSR 5211. Ann Arbor: Inter-University Consortium for Political and Social Research.

McGinnis, Michael. 1990. "A Rational Model of Regional Rivalry." *International Studies Quarterly* 34:111–35.

McGinnis, Michael, and John Williams. 1989. "Change and Stability in Superpower Rivalry." *American Political Science Review* 83:1101–23.

Mearsheimer, John. 1990. "Back to the Future: Instability in Europe after the Cold War." *International Security* 15:5–56.

Miall, Hugh. 1992. *The Peacemakers: Peaceful Settlement of Disputes since 1945.* New York: St. Martin's Press.

Midlarsky, Manus. 1988. *The Onset of World War.* London: Unwin Hyman.

————, ed. 1989. *Handbook of War Studies*. Boston: Unwin Hyman. Reprint, Ann Arbor: University of Michigan Press, 1993.

Miller, Benjamin. 1995. *When Opponents Cooperate: Great Power Conflict and Collaboration in World Politics*. Ann Arbor: University of Michigan Press.

Modelski, George. 1987. *Long Cycles in World Politics*. Seattle: University of Washington Press.

————. 1999. "Enduring Rivalry in the Democratic Lineage: The Venice-Portugal Case." In *The Evolution of Great Power Rivalries*, ed. William R. Thompson. Columbia: University of South Carolina Press.

Modelski, George, and William Thompson. 1988. *Seapower in Global Politics, 1494–1993*. London: Macmillan.

Moore, C. W. 1986. *The Mediation Process*. San Francisco: Jossey-Bass.

Morgan, T. Clifton. 1993. "Democracy and War: Reflections on the Literature." *International Interactions* 18:197–204.

Morgan, T. Clifton, and Sally Campbell. 1991. "Domestic Structure, Decisional Constraints, and War." *Journal of Conflict Resolution* 35:187–211.

Most, Benjamin, and Harvey Starr. 1989. *Inquiry, Logic, and International Politics*. Columbia: University of South Carolina Press.

Most, Benjamin, Harvey Starr, and Randolph Siverson. 1989. "The Logic and Study of the Diffusion of International Conflict." In *Handbook of War Studies*, ed. Manus Midlarsky. Boston: Unwin Hyman.

Muncaster, Robert, and Dina Zinnes. 1993. "The Phenomenology of Enduring Rivalries." Presented at the Workshop on Processes of Enduring Rivalries, Indiana University.

Nincic, Miroslav. 1989. *Anatomy of Hostility: The US-Soviet Rivalry in Perspective*. New York: Harcourt Brace Jovanovich.

Northedge, F., and M. Donelan. 1971. *International Disputes: The Political Aspects*. London: Europa.

Oneal, John, and Bruce Russett. 1997. "The Classical Liberals Were Right: Democracy, Interdependence, and Conflict, 1950–1985." *International Studies Quarterly* 41:267–94.

Organski, A. F. K. 1958. *World Politics*. New York: Alfred A. Knopf.

Organski, A. F. K., and Jacek Kugler. 1980. *The War Ledger*. Chicago: University of Chicago Press.

Osgood, Charles. 1962. *An Alternative to War or Surrender*. Urbana: University of Illinois Press.

Ott, M. 1972. "Mediation as a Method of Conflict Resolution: Two Cases." *International Organization* 26:595–618.

Peters, B. Guy, and Brian W. Hogwood. 1985. "In Search of the Issue-Attention Cycle." *Journal of Politics* 47:239–53.

Pinkas, Alon. 1993. "Garrison Democracy: The Impact of the 1967 Occupation of Territories on Institutional Democracy in Israel." In *Democracy, Peace, and the Israeli-Palestinian Conflict*, ed. Edy Kaufman, Shukri B. Abed, and Robert L. Rothstein. Boulder: Lynne Rienner.

Powell, Robert. 1989. "Nuclear Deterrence and the Strategy of Limited Retaliation." *American Political Science Review* 83:503–19.

Pruitt, Dean. G. 1981. *Negotiation Behavior*. New York: Academic Press.

Raknerud, Arvid, and Havard Hegre. 1997. "The Hazard of War: Reassessing the Evidence for the Democratic Peace." *Journal of Peace Research* 34:385–404.

Rasler, Karen, and William Thompson. 1998a. "Explaining Rivalry Escalation: The Contiguity Factor in the Major Power Subsystem." Draft manuscript.

———. 1998b. "Rivalries and the Democratic Peace in the Major Power Subsystem." Draft manuscript.

Raup, David. 1992. *Extinction: Bad Genes or Bad Luck?* New York: W. W. Norton.

Ray, James Lee. 1995. Democracy and International Conflict. Columbia: University of South Carolina Press.

Reed, William. 1998. "The Relevance of Politically Relevant Dyads." Presented at the Annual Meeting of the Peace Science Society (International), New Brunswick, N.J.

Regan, Patrick M. 1996. "Conditions of Successful Third-Party Intervention in Intrastate Conflicts." *Journal of Conflict Resolution* 40:336–59.

Rhodes, Edward. 1994. "Do Bureaucratic Politics Matter? Some Disconfirming Findings from the Case of the US Navy." *World Politics* 47:1–42.

Richardson, George. 1991. *Feedback Thought in Social Science and Systems Theory.* Philadelphia: University of Pennsylvania Press.

Richardson, Lewis. 1960. *Statistics of Deadly Quarrels.* Pittsburgh: Boxwood Press.

Rosecrance, Richard. 1986. *The Rise of the Trading State: Commerce and Conquest in the Modern World.* New York: Basic Books.

Ross, Marc H. 1996. Review of *Beyond Confrontation: Learning Conflict Resolution in the Post-Cold War Era. American Political Science Review* 90:471–72.

Rubin, Jeffrey. Z. 1981. "Experimental Research on Third Party Intervention in Conflict." *Psychological Bulletin* 87:379–91.

Rueschemeyer, Dietrich, Evelyne Huber Stephens, and John D. Stephens. 1992. *Capitalist Development and Democracy.* Chicago: University of Chicago Press.

Rule, John. 1999. "The Rivalry between France and Spain during the Years 1460s to 1720." In *The Evolution of Great Power Rivalries,* ed. William R. Thompson. Columbia: University of South Carolina Press.

Rummel, Rudolph. 1995. "Democracies ARE Less Warlike Than Other Regimes." *European Journal of International Relations* 1:457–79.

Russett, Bruce. 1963. "The Calculus of Deterrence." *Journal of Conflict Resolution* 7:97–109.

———. 1970. *What Price Vigilance? The Burdens of National Defense.* New Haven: Yale University Press.

———. 1990. *Controlling the Sword: The Democratic Governance of National Security.* Cambridge: Harvard University Press.

———. 1993. *Grasping the Democratic Peace.* Princeton: Princeton University Press.

———. 1995. "And Yet It Moves." *International Security* 19:164–75.

Sabrosky, Alan. 1975. "From Bosnia to Sarajevo: A Comparative Discussion of Interstate Crises." *Journal of Conflict Resolution* 19:3–24.

Sagan, Scott. 1991. "History, Analogy, and Deterrence Theory." *Journal of Interdisciplinary History* 22:79–88.

Sample, Susan G. 1997. "Arms Races and Dispute Escalation: Resolving the Debate?" *Journal of Peace Research* 34:7–22.

Schrodt, Philip, and Alex Mintz. 1988. "The Conditional Probability Analysis of International Events Data." *American Journal of Political Science* 32:217–30.

Schroeder, Paul. 1994. *The Transformation of European Politics, 1763–1848*. Oxford: Oxford University Press.

————. 1999. "The Enduring Rivalry between France and the Hapsburg Monarchy, 1715–1918." In *The Evolution of Great Power Rivalries*, ed. William R. Thompson. Columbia: University of South Carolina Press.

Senese, Paul. 1996. "Geographical Proximity and Issue Salience: Their Effects on the Escalation of Militarized Interstate Conflict." *Conflict Management and Peace Science* 15:133–62.

Singer, J. David, Stuart Bremer, and John Stuckey. 1972. "Capability Distribution, Uncertainty, and Major Power War, 1820–1965." In *Peace, War, and Numbers*, ed. Bruce Russett. Beverly Hills: Sage.

Siverson, Randolph. 1995. "Democracies and War Participation: In Defense of the Institutional Constraints Argument." *European Journal of International Relations* 1:481–89.

Siverson, Randolph, and Harvey Starr. 1991. *The Diffusion of War*. Ann Arbor: University of Michigan Press.

Siverson, Randolph, and Michael Tennefoss. 1982. "Interstate Conflicts, 1815–1965." *International Interactions* 9:147–68.

Siverson, Randolph M., and Michael Sullivan. 1984. "Alliances and War: A New Examination of an Old Problem." *Conflict Management and Peace Science* 8:1–16.

Small, Melvin, and J. David Singer. 1969. "Formal Alliances, 1816–1965: An Extension of the Basic Data." *Journal of Peace Research* 3:257–82.

————. 1976. "The War-Proneness of Democratic Regimes." *Jerusalem Journal of International Relations* 1:50–69.

————. 1982. *Resort to Arms*. Beverly Hills: Sage.

Smith, Alastair. 1996. "To Intervene or Not to Intervene: A Biased Decision." *Journal of Conflict Resolution* 40:16–40.

Smith, Teresa. C. 1980. "Arms Race Instability and War." *Journal of Conflict Resolution* 24:253–84.

————. 1988. "Risky Races?: Curvature Change and the War Risk in Arms Races." *International Interactions* 14:201–28.

Sorokin, Gerald. 1994. "Arms, Alliances, and Security Tradeoffs in Enduring Rivalries." *International Studies Quarterly* 38:421–46.

Spiro, David. 1994. "The Insignificance of Democratic Peace." *International Security* 19:50–86.

Sprout, Harold H., and Margaret Sprout. 1965. *The Ecological Perspective on Human Affairs, with Special Reference to International Politics*. Princeton: Princeton University Press.

Stinnett, Douglas, and Paul F. Diehl. 1998. "The Path(s) to Rivalry." Presented at the Annual Meeting of the American Political Science Association, Boston.

Stoll, Richard. 1984. "From Frying Pan to Fire: The Impact of Major Power War Involvement on Major Power Dispute Involvement, 1816–1975." *Conflict Management and Peace Science* 7:71–82.

Tetlock, Philip, and George W. Breslauer, eds. 1991. *Learning in US and Soviet Foreign Policy*. Boulder: Westview Press.

Therborn, Goran. 1977. "The Rise of Capital and the Rise of Democracy." *New Left Review* 103:3–41.

Thompson, William. 1988. *On Global War*. Columbia: University of South Carolina Press.

———. 1995. "Principal Rivalries." *Journal of Conflict Resolution* 39:195–223.

———. 1996. "Democracy and Peace: Putting the Cart before the Horse?" International Organization 50:141–74.

———. 1998. "An Expectancy Theory of Strategic Rivalry Deescalation: The Sino-Soviet Case." Presented at the Evolutionary Perspectives on International Relations Theory Conference, Bloomington, Ind.

———. 1999. "The Evolution of a Great Power Rivalry: The Anglo-American Case." In *The Evolution of Great Power Rivalries*, ed. William R. Thompson. Columbia: University of South Carolina Press.

Thompson, William, and Richard Tucker. 1997. "A Tale of Two Democratic Peace Critiques." *Journal of Conflict Resolution* 41:428–54.

Tilly, Charles. 1985. "War Making and State Making as Organized Crime." In *Bringing the State Back In*, ed. Peter Evans, Dietrich Rueschemeyer, and Theda Skocpol. Cambridge: Cambridge University Press.

Tir, Jaroslav, Philip Schafer, Paul F. Diehl, and Gary Goertz. 1998. "Territorial Changes, 1816–1996: Procedures and Data." *Conflict Management and Peace Science* 16:89–97.

Touval, Saadia. 1982. *The Peace Brokers: Mediations in the Arab-Israeli Conflict*. Princeton: Princeton University Press.

Tsebelis, George. 1990. *Nested Games*. Berkeley and Los Angeles: University of California Press.

Tucker, Harvey. 1982. "Incremental Budgeting: Myth or Model?" *Western Political Quarterly* 35:327–38.

Van Evera, Stephen. 1984. "The Cult of the Offensive and the Origins of World War I." *International Security* 9:58–107.

Vasquez, John. 1983. "The Tangibility of Issues and Global Conflict: A Test of Rosenau's Issue Area Typology." *Journal of Peace Research* 20:179–92.

———. 1993. *The War Puzzle*. Cambridge: Cambridge University Press.

———. 1996. "Distinguishing Rivals That Go to War from Those That Do Not: A Quantitative Comparative Case Study of the Two Paths to War." *International Studies Quarterly* 40:531–58.

———. 1997. "The Realist Paradigm and Degenerative versus Progressive Research Programs: An Appraisal of Neotraditional Research on Waltz's Balancing Proposition." *American Political Science Review* 91:899–917.

———. 1998. "The Evolution of Multiple Rivalries Prior to the Second World War in the Pacific." In *The Dynamics of Enduring Rivalries*, ed. Paul F. Diehl. Urbana: University of Illinois Press.

Wagner, Harrison. 1989. "Uncertainty, Rational Learning, and Bargaining in the Cuban Missile Crisis." In *Models of Strategic Choice in Politics*, ed. Peter Ordeshook. Ann Arbor: University of Michigan Press.

Wall, James, and Ann Lynn. 1993. "Mediation: A Current Review." *Journal of Conflict Resolution* 37:160–94.

Wallace, Michael D. 1979. "Arms Races and Escalation: Some New Evidence." *Journal of Conflict Resolution* 23:3–16.

Walt, Stephen. 1987. *The Origins of Alliances*. Ithaca: Cornell University Press.

Waltz, Kenneth. 1964. "The Stability of a Bipolar World." *Daedalus* 93:881–909.

———. 1979. *Theory of World Politics*. Reading, Mass.: Addison-Wesley.

Wang, Kevin. 1995. "Presidential Responses to Foreign Policy Crises." *Journal of Conflict Resolution* 40:68–97.

Wayman, Frank. 1982. "War and Power Transitions during Enduring Rivalries." Presented at the Institute for the Study of Conflict Theory and International Conflict, Urbana-Champaign, Ill.

———. 1996. "Power Shifts and the Onset of War." In *Parity and War,* ed. Jacek Kugler and Douglas Lemke. Ann Arbor: University of Michigan Press.

Wayman, Frank, and Paul F. Diehl, eds. 1994. *Reconstructing Realpolitik*. Ann Arbor: University of Michigan Press.

Wayman, Frank, and Daniel Jones. 1991. "Evolution of Conflict in Enduring Rivalries." Presented at the Annual Meeting of the International Studies Association, Vancouver.

Weart, Spencer. 1994. "Peace among Democracies and Oligarchic Republics." *Journal of Peace Research* 31:299–316.

Weede, Erich. 1973. "Nation-Environment Relations as Determinants of Hostilities between Nations." *Peace Science Society (International) Papers* 20:67–90.

Wildavsky, Aaron. 1975. *Budgeting: A Comparative Theory of the Budgetary Process*. Boston: Little, Brown.

Wilkenfeld, Jonathan, Michael Brecher, and Sheila Moser. 1988. *Crises in the Twentieth Century*. New York: Pergamon Press.

Wittman, Donald. 1979. "How a War Ends." *Journal of Conflict Resolution* 23:743–65.

Wright, Quincy. 1965. *A Study of War*. Chicago: University of Chicago Press.

Yamaguchi, Kazuo. 1991. *Event History Analysis*. Newbury Park, Calif.: Sage.

Young, Oran. 1972. "Intermediaries: Additional Thoughts on Third Parties." *Journal of Conflict Resolution* 16:51–65.

Zahariadis, Nikolaos. 1996. "Selling British Rail: An Idea Whose Time Has Come?" *Comparative Political Studies* 29:400–422.

Zahariadis, Nikolaos, and Christopher S. Allen. 1995. "Ideas, Networks, and Policy Streams: Privatization in Britain and Germany." *Policy Studies Review* 14:71–98.

Zartman, I. William. 1985. *Ripe for Resolution: Conflict and Intervention in Africa*. New York: Oxford University Press.

Index

Agenda-setting model, 134–35, 140, 269

Agent-structure perspective, 223

Algeria, 196

Alliances, 21, 74–77, 92, 112, 146, 157, 159, 226, 242, 244, 246, 248, 251, 266

Anglo-Dutch rivalry, 123, 149, 150, 152, 156

Anglo-German rivalry, 32, 123, 147, 232, 237

Angola, 246, 250

Arab-Israeli rivalry, 7, 32, 50, 75, 86, 93, 113, 146, 148, 169, 177, 242, 251, 261

Argentina, 114, 144

Arms race, 5, 30, 76–77, 79, 81–82, 88, 91, 94, 163, 168, 181, 267

Australia, 42

Austria-Hungary, 51, 244, 259

Balance of power, 2, 10, 156, 159, 224, 226, 247, 285

Bandwagoning, 181, 241, 244

Basic rivalry level (BRL), 11, 155, 164–70, 173–75, 177–81, 185–86, 193–201, 208, 213, 215, 252, 265–66, 276, 281

definition of, 165–67

Belgium, 91, 119, 123

Bolivia, 104

Bosnia, 27, 262

Brazil, 41, 232, 236, 294

Brazil–United Kingdom rivalry, 232, 236–37

Bulgaria, 41, 237

Cambodia, 244, 246

"Causes-of-war" approach, 1, 6, 9, 25, 73, 79, 80–81, 85–87, 91, 95, 101–2, 158, 163, 188, 282–4

definition of, 67–71

Chile, 144

Chile–Argentina rivalry, 144

China, 1, 20, 51–52, 54, 76, 82, 144, 197, 215, 236, 242, 245–47, 251, 261, 283

China–South Korea rivalry, 197

Cold War, 12–13, 20, 28, 38, 50, 70, 75, 113–14, 144, 149–50, 154, 159–60, 175, 189, 198, 221, 224, 236–37, 245–46, 250–51, 262, 273

Conflict management, 3, 11–12, 69, 73–74, 76, 96–97, 101, 138, 152, 157, 164, 167, 177, 181, 185–220, 242–43, 261, 265, 268–69, 270–72, 277, 281, 284

Conflict resolution, 3, 56, 69, 72–73, 132, 153, 178, 188–91, 201, 209, 243, 271

Cross-sectional approach, 2, 6, 8, 20, 49, 68–70, 83–88, 91, 93, 95, 100–108, 127, 179, 208, 263, 265, 267–68

in rivalry methodology, 102–4

Cuba, 41, 52, 191, 249

Cuban missile crisis, 41, 76, 79, 191, 261, 288

Cyprus, 119

Cyprus–Turkey rivalry, 119

Democratic peace, 2–3, 6–7, 9, 21, 42, 67, 73–74, 80, 83, 86, 88–89, 95–96, 102–5, 107–27, 131, 151, 155, 186, 226, 266, 268, 271, 273, 282–83